ON
UNDERSTANDING
GRAMMAR

PERSPECTIVES IN
NEUROLINGUISTICS AND PSYCHOLINGUISTICS

Harry A. Whitaker, Series Editor
DEPARTMENT OF PSYCHOLOGY
THE UNIVERSITY OF ROCHESTER
ROCHESTER, NEW YORK

HAIGANOOSH WHITAKER and HARRY A. WHITAKER (Eds.).
Studies in Neurolinguistics, Volumes 1, 2, and 3

NORMAN J. LASS (Ed.). Contemporary Issues in Experimental Phonetics

JASON W. BROWN. Mind, Brain, and Consciousness: The Neuropsychology of Cognition

SIDNEY J. SEGALOWITZ and FREDERIC A. GRUBER (Eds.). Language Development and Neurological Theory

SUSAN CURTISS. Genie: A Psycholinguistic Study of a Modern-Day "Wild Child"

JOHN MACNAMARA (Ed.). Language Learning and Thought

I. M. SCHLESINGER and LILA NAMIR (Eds.). Sign Language of the Deaf: Psychological, Linguistic, and Sociological Perspectives

WILLIAM C. RITCHIE (Ed.). Second Language Acquisition Research: Issues and Implications

PATRICIA SIPLE (Ed.). Understanding Language through Sign Language Research

MARTIN L. ALBERT and LORAINE K. OBLER. The Bilingual Brain: Neurophysiological and Neurolinguistic Aspects of Bilingualism

HAIGANOOSH WHITAKER and HARRY A. WHITAKER (Eds.). Studies in Neurolinguistics, Volume 4

TALMY GIVON. On Understanding Grammar

In preparation

CHARLES J. FILLMORE, DANIEL KEMPLER and WILLIAM S.-Y. WANG (Eds.). Individual Differences in Language Ability and Language Behavior

ON UNDERSTANDING GRAMMAR

Talmy Givón

DEPARTMENT OF LINGUISTICS
UNIVERSITY OF CALIFORNIA, LOS ANGELES
LOS ANGELES, CALIFORNIA
AND
UTE LANGUAGE PROGRAM
SOUTHERN UTE TRIBE
IGNACIO, COLORADO

ACADEMIC PRESS   New York   San Francisco   London   1979
A Subsidiary of Harcourt Brace Jovanovich, Publishers

COPYRIGHT © 1979, BY ACADEMIC PRESS, INC.
ALL RIGHTS RESERVED.
NO PART OF THIS PUBLICATION MAY BE REPRODUCED OR
TRANSMITTED IN ANY FORM OR BY ANY MEANS, ELECTRONIC
OR MECHANICAL, INCLUDING PHOTOCOPY, RECORDING, OR ANY
INFORMATION STORAGE AND RETRIEVAL SYSTEM, WITHOUT
PERMISSION IN WRITING FROM THE PUBLISHER.

ACADEMIC PRESS, INC.
111 Fifth Avenue, New York, New York 10003

United Kingdom Edition published by
ACADEMIC PRESS, INC. (LONDON) LTD.
24/28 Oval Road, London NW1 7DX

Library of Congress Cataloging in Publication Data

Givon, Talmy.
　　On understanding grammar.

　　(Perspectives in neurolinguistics and psycho‐
linguistics)
　　Bibliography: p.
　　1. Grammar, Comparative and general. I. Title.
P151.G5　　　1979　　　415　　　78-67876
ISBN 0-12-285450-0

PRINTED IN THE UNITED STATES OF AMERICA

79 80 81 82　　9 8 7 6 5 4 3 2 1

IN MEMORIAM
S.-D. Givón (1969–1976)

CONTENTS

Foreword xi

Preface xiii

1 METHODOLOGY
on the crypto-structuralist nature of transformational grammar

1.1.	Introduction	1
1.2.	The Ascent of the Formalism as Explanation	3
1.3.	The Gutting of the Data Base: Competence and Grammaticality	22
1.4.	Conclusion	43

2 GRAMMAR AND FUNCTION
toward a discourse definition of syntax

2.1.	Introduction	45
2.2.	The Discourse Presuppositions of Syntactic Constructions	50
2.3.	Discourse Markedness and Distributional Restrictions	67
2.4.	Discourse Markedness and Syntactic Complexity	74
2.5.	Syntactic Conservatism	83

2.6.	Language Acquisition	86
2.7.	Conclusion: Syntax and Communication	87

3 LOGIC VERSUS LANGUAGE
negation in language: pragmatics, function, ontology

3.1.	Introduction	91
3.2.	The Presuppositional Status of Negative Speech Acts	93
3.3.	Some Consequences of the Marked Status of Negatives	115
3.4.	The Ontological Basis of Negation	132
3.5.	Conclusion	138
	Appendix 1: Test Sheet for an Experiment on the Interpretation of English Modals	141
	Appendix 2: Total Scores for 100 Subjects of the Results of the Experiment on English Modals	142

4 SEMANTIC CASE AND PRAGMATIC FUNCTION
promotion, accessibility, and the typology of case marking

4.1.	Introduction	143
4.2.	The Case-Recoverability Problem	145
4.3.	Relativization	146
4.4.	Passivization and Promotion to Direct Object	185
4.5.	Summary	205

5 SYNTACTICIZATION
from discourse to syntax: grammar as a processing strategy

5.1.	Introduction	207
5.2.	The Diachronic Process of Syntacticization	208
5.3.	An Interim Summary	222
5.4.	Pidgins and Creoles	223
5.5.	Child versus Adult Language	226
5.6.	Informal versus Formal Speech	228
5.7.	Discussion	231

6 LANGUAGE CHANGE
where does crazy syntax come from: diachronic constraints on synchronic grammars

6.1.	Introduction	235
6.2.	Crazy Synchronic Phonology	237
6.3.	Typological Inconsistencies between Morphology and Syntax	238
6.4.	Cleft and WH-Question Revisited	246
6.5.	Pronoun Attraction and Object Relativization	249
6.6.	Some Puzzles in Swahili Relativization	252
6.7.	Mixed Typologies in Verb Phrase Syntax	253
6.8.	Frozen Syntactic Constraints	261
6.9.	Frozen Lexical Patterns	264
6.10.	Discussion	268

7 LANGUAGE AND PHYLOGENY
the SOV mystery and the evolution of discourse

7.1.	Introduction	271
7.2.	Arguments for a Neo-recapitulationist View	273
7.3.	The SOV Mystery	275
7.4.	Extrapolation Number 1: The Communicative System of Canines	277
7.5.	Pongid Communication: Brief Summary	290
7.6.	Extrapolation Number 2: Early Child Communication	290
7.7.	Presyntactic Discourse as a Phylogenetic Target	295
7.8.	A Short Summary of the Evolutionary Scenario	303
7.9.	Syntacticization as a Phylogenetic Process	304
7.10.	Vestigial Survival of Early Linguistic Modes	307
7.11.	Conclusion: The SOV Mystery Revisited	308

8 LANGUAGE AND ONTOLOGY
on construing a universe

8.1.	Introduction	311
8.2.	Space, Time, and Being	314
8.3.	Tao and the Unconstrued Universe	317

8.4.	An Unordered Binary Property: An Aborted Attempt at Individuation	318
8.5.	The First Ordered Relation: Time	319
8.6.	An Ontology of Experience in a Universe of Time	320
8.7.	The Second, Third, and Fourth Dimensions: Space	324
8.8.	Spatial Perception, Perceptual Judgment, and Calibration	324
8.9.	The Paradox of Order and Chaos	325
8.10.	Upper Bounds and Optimality	328
8.11.	The Ontology of Experience in a Spatiotemporal Universe	329
8.12.	Some Evolutionary Correlates of the Time–Space Universe	330
8.13.	Action, Agents, Intent, and Causality	334
8.14.	Experiential Criteria for Agents	336
8.15.	The Ontology of Causation and Agency	338
8.16.	The Ontological Unity of Interpersonal Behavior	344
8.17.	Closure	351

Bibliography	353
Index	367

FOREWORD

The next best thing to being mother or midwife is to be an early witness to the growth of an infant when later one is asked to foretell its promise. With Talmy Givón's *On Understanding Grammar* I have been a happy onlooker since Chapter 1, and for what my prophetic skills may be worth, I foresee it as one of the truly prized statements of our current knowledge to appear in this decade. The author has said with his usual modesty that it is a consolidation of viewpoints rather than a promulgation of discoveries. That may be. But in the process of consolidating it usually turns out that an old light in one field takes on a new brilliance in another. That is one—just one—of the virtues of this book: Well before its conception the author had made his leap away from the tunnel vision of so much of our contemporary formalism. He had explored the tunnel, and knew it from end to end; but he has since amassed a knowledge of languages that has few rivals; his familiarity with linguistic history and more than nodding acquaintance with logic, pragmatics, evolutionary theory, and philosophy bring a formidable learning to bear on a discipline whose breadth makes such learning indispensable. The book is rich in insights, even for those who have been with linguistics for a long time. And beginners can be thankful to have it as a starting point, from which so many past mistakes have been left behind.

This is a book about understanding that is done with deep understanding—of language and its place in nature and in the nature of humankind. And with understanding of how to reveal these things. It is an unpretentious book. The lessons are taught with no display, on the authority of a scholarship that is too thorough to vaunt itself and with an obvious faith in the power of plain language to describe language.

Talmy Givón shows us again that great truths are simple truths, and if it is not always a simple matter to arrive at them, that increases our debt to him.

Dwight Bolinger

PREFACE

This book is about trying to make sense out of doing linguistics and, ultimately, out of human language. Making sense is not a favorite preoccupation of linguists—the best of whom like to keep their noses close to the grindstone of fact. I respect such integrity, and hope to show that an occasional widening of our perspectives will not be detrimental to it.

It took me a while to realize that this book could have some overall coherence: It took writing the entire book to find out whether such coherence was even remotely possible. The enterprise began with Sandra Thompson suggesting that it was time to gather in one place all the divergent themes I had been pursuing over a number of years. I was a bit dubious. I knew the themes themselves had internal coherence. Discourse-pragmatics, diachronic syntax, typology, creology, the method, and ontology all had a bearing on how and why one would want to do linguistics. But it was unclear to me how they could coalesce; the field had been fragmented, there was no integrating precedent, subareas were locked in their separate boxes, language had persisted in defying facile deductive methodologies.

The coherence structure of this book resembles a circle. Language sits at the center, defiant and wide open. The various chapters straddle the rim, focusing upon the elusive center from different perspectives. The interdependencies among the various perspectives make the coherence structure of the book, and if and when we know those interdependencies more precisely, they will, it is hoped, make the coherence structure of linguistics.

Chapter 1 is about the method, about the notions of "fact," "theory," and "explanation," particularly about how these notions manifest themselves in actual practice.

Chapter 2 is a redefinition of syntax in terms of communicative function and discourse-pragmatics, and thus about the relation between the function of grammatical devices and their formal properties.

Chapter 3 is about discourse-pragmatics and how it transcends the narrow bounds of deductive logic. It is also about the function and ontology of negation in language, and how those relate to the fundamental information-theoretic principle of figure versus ground.

Chapter 4 is about the two major aspects of case systems, semantic role and pragmatic function, and how the two interact in determining the typological characteristics of grammars.

Chapter 5 returns to the relation between discourse and syntax, this time from a developmental–process point of view—diachronic, ontogenetic, phylogenetic.

Chapter 6 is about the relation between synchronic grammar and diachronic change, and how it is hopeless to try to understand one without understanding the other.

Chapter 7 is about the relationship between human language as we know it now and its phylogenetic evolution, and why it does make sense to talk about the two together.

Chapter 8 is about language and ontology, the relation between cognition and the universe, and what it all may mean.

I do not pretend to have resolved everything in this book. Language is too vast a phenomenon—to know all about it is to know all about man and the universe and thus, in principle (cf. Heisenberg and Goedel), impossible. I see language as a giant rock, we tunnel into it from various points of departure, we work mostly in the dark. What I have strived to do here is to illuminate my tunnel.

What I know about language owes much to many people. I have tried to acknowledge my many debts at the appropriate points throughout the book. There are three people that I have long considered beacons of integrity and common sense in linguistics, a field rife with fads, factionalism, and fratricide: Dwight Bolinger, for teaching that language could only be understood in the context of communication; Joseph Greenberg, for refusing to consider language without languages; and Kenneth Pike, for insisting that language was inevitably embedded in cognition, culture, and man's construction of his universe.

T.G.

ON UNDERSTANDING GRAMMAR

1

METHODOLOGY
on the crypto-structuralist nature of transformational grammar

1.1. INTRODUCTION[1]

> My view of Physics is that you make discoveries but, in a certain sense, you never really understand them. You learn how to manipulate them, but you never really understand them. "Understanding" would mean relating them to something else—to something more profound. . . .
> —I. I. Rabi, in an interview
> in *The New Yorker*,
> October 20, 1975, p. 96.

This chapter is of necessity polemic, and that is a necessity I regret and would like to apologize for. The history of American linguistics over the past 50 years is awash with acrimonious name-calling, sterile arguments, and the rhythmic rise and fall of pseudotheories and trumped-up issues whose relation to the facts of human language is tenuous at best. In the course of this sorry history, the foundations of linguistics as an aspiring empirical science have been undermined. An increasingly perverse use of key terminology such as "data," "empirical proof," "theory," and "explanation" has deprived these fundamental concepts of science of both meaning and utility in linguistics. I have been convinced for a number of years now that transformational-generative grammar on its various ideological stripes has trapped itself in a labyrinthine prison

---

[1] This chapter grew out of a lecture at the University of California, Berkeley in the fall of 1975. I am indebted to Dwight Bolinger, Erica Garcia, Derek Bickerton, Robert Kirsner, and Harry Whitaker for many helpful comments and suggestions. I also absolve them of any responsibility for the final product, and in particular for the instances in which I chose to disregard their advice.

out of which no graceful natural exit is possible, short of plowing under the entire edifice and starting afresh. I have become more and more weary of the circular, sterile, and scholastic nature of the polemics, and have come to believe that the only hope for a different linguistics lies in the actual practice of doing linguistics differently. Nevertheless, this chapter had to be written for a number of compelling reasons.

A dysfunctional paradigm in science is a conceptual trap, constraining the mind of the practitioner just as viciously as steel bars would his body. In the past few years I have witnessed repeatedly the plight of fine linguists attempting to break loose of the generative paradigm. I have watched them try and fail, and wind up not far from where they started. This chapter has been made deliberately personal in the hope of helping those who share my sobering experience with the paradigm. But in order to show where the paradigm collapses, one must first discuss it. And that is perforce polemics.

Generative grammar was born in strife and has remained under hostile sniping—from its very inception—by the rudely dethroned early generation of practitioners. Most of those could always be dismissed as outsiders who "didn't understand the issues." There is thus a certain propriety for this chapter to be written by a person like myself, who grew up within the fold and had experienced no other kind of linguistics before. Some of what I say here has been said by others, and while I tend to share Wittgenstein's sense of indifference to antecedence,[2] I would readily concede that much of the details of this chapter are not, per se, novel. The juxtaposition, I believe, is.

The kind of linguistics I will argue for can be validated only through practice, by finding out how it illuminates the vast array of facts of human language. No amount of a priori methodological arguments, however cleverly constructed, could add much to that. Still, it is useful to embed the practice in its proper methodological perspective. From my vantage point, the perspective is roughly this: For over 50 years now linguistics has been in a state of siege, in a seemingly endless crisis of its philosophy and methodology. Initially, the crisis may have been ascribed to the impact of the mechanistic views of the physical sciences on Saussure, on the one hand, and of behaviorist psychology on Bloomfield on the other. The structuralist dogma which followed has three major characteristics:

1. The a priori and arbitrary curtailment of the *data base* relevant to the investigation
2. The rise of the *formalism* as "theory"
3. The neglect or devaluation of the notion *explanation*

---

[2] "I do not wish to judge how far my efforts coincide with those of other philosophers. Indeed, what I have written here makes no claim to novelty in detail, and the reason why I give no sources is that it is a matter of indifference to me whether the thoughts that I have had have been anticipated by someone else . . . [Preface to *Tractatus Logico-Philosophicus* (1918)]."

At its onset, transformational-generative grammar brought a tide of rising hopes on all three counts. However, the cumulative experience of the past twenty years in linguistics suggests that in all fundamental ways the transformational-generative revolution has remained at the dead center of structuralist methodology.

1.2. THE ASCENT OF THE FORMALISM AS EXPLANATION

The complex interaction between *data, formal model,* and *explanation* within any scientific discipline, sits at the core of what ultimately emerges as "theory." None of the three can by itself be the theory. Nor can a viable theory be constructed if the role of any of the three is ignored or the nature of their interdependency distorted. For example, one of the most damaging practices in the history of linguistics has been the arbitrary—and a priori—delimitation of the data base, that is, the range of facts to serve as *input* for the investigation and, ultimately, as input for building the theory. There are a number of ways this can be done. First, one may adopt a formalism that is incompatible with a certain range of data, then disallow data that cannot be digested by the formalism. Alternatively, one may choose to limit one's range of the *explanatory parameters* bearing on the phenomenon under study, and then rule out various segments of potentially crucial data as "belonging to other disciplines." Both methods are equally destructive to the well-being of a science. I will deal with explanatory parameters first.

1.2.1. Explanatory Parameters of Language

It would be self-defeating to construct a theory of language, choose an appropriate formalism, and rule upon the relevant range of data, without first deciding what are the relevant parameters which bear—potentially—on the structure of language. While the following list is not likely to be exhaustive. I believe it represents the major parameters that must be considered.

1. *Propositional contents.* The structure of language and the way in which it codes messages obviously must reflect propositional contents or 'sentence-level message structure.' Whether one would want to equate this with logical structure remains to be seen, but there seems to be some level of language, most commonly associated with the *clause*,[3] that deals with the specification of the event, state or action in terms of who was the agent–subject, who was the object, and what transpired. It is thus un-

---

[3] See Chafe (1979).

likely that the structure of human language can be understood without reference to this parameter.

2. *Discourse pragmatics.* It is unlikely that the requirements of communicative structure, in terms of sequencing, theme selection, topic–comment relations, presupposition, speaker–hearer conventions, foreground–background, and so on, will not be reflected in the structure of the instrument—language—fashioned to carry on communication.

3. *The processor.* The properties and specific structure of the channels which process speech in and out of the brain—neurological, acoustic, articulatory, etc.—undoubtedly exert their influence in shaping the structure of language.

4. *Cognitive structure.* It seems unwise to rule out the general cognitive and perceptual structure of the human organism from having strong bearing on the structure of language. This is particularly true in the absence of any empirical evidence to suggest that such a priori elimination is tenable.

5. *World-view pragmatics.* Both our grammar and lexicon reflect—and are fashioned by—a constructed view of our universe. A number of important features of human language cannot be understood without reference to such world-view and the ontology which must underly it.

6. *Ontogenetic development.* It is rather unlikely that the requirements imposed by the young organism acquiring language, as well as the manner in which language is acquired by the child, should have no influence on the structure of the acquired communicative device.

7. *Diachronic change.* Since language changes constantly, and since the imprints of linguistic change are strewn, like ancient relics, across the synchronic landscape of phonology, morphology, and syntax, eliminating diachronic facts a priori—à la Saussure—from the realm of relevance to our understanding of the synchronic structure of language is both unwarranted and unwise.

8. *Phylogenetic evolution.* So far as I know, there is no shred of empirical evidence supporting Chomsky's (1968)[4] position concerning the irrelevance of evolution to our understanding of human language. It is thus conceivable that phylogeny—much like diachrony and ontogeny—has left indelible marks upon the structure of human language. At the very least, the possibility should not be dismissed a priori.

There are two ways in which the formulation of reasonable and flexible explanatory parameters is a prerequisite to an investigation. First, the selection of explanatory parameters also determine, perforce, the selection of relevant subranges of *data* to be admitted as evidence. This will be dealt with later on. Second, the selection of explanatory

---

[4] "It is quite senseless to raise the problem of explaining the evolution of human language from more primitive systems of communication that appear at lower levels of intellectual capacity . . . [p. 59]."

1.2. The Ascent of the Formalism as Explanation

parameters determines the nature and scope of *explanation* to be embarked upon. All this amounts to belaboring the obvious, and indeed it is hard to imagine a scientific discipline dealing with the study of *organisms*[5] attempting to construct an "explanatory theory" of its subject matter in which all reference to its natural explanatory parameters has been disallowed. Imagine an anatomist describing the structure of the human body without reference to the functions of various organs. But this is precisely what happened in transformational-generative linguistics: By fiat, a priori, and with no visible empirical justification, an attempt has been made to describe the structure of human language, both syntax and phonology, without reference to natural explanatory parameters. Not only describe, but in some mysterious sense also "explain." And hence the story of the formalism—The Model—masquerading as both theory and explanation.

1.2.2. The Use and Abuse of Formal Models

Formal modeling of the phenomena under investigation is an old and useful tool in science. In essence, a formal model is **nothing but** a restatement of the facts at a tighter level of generalization. Such a restatement has obvious, common-sensical advantages over a mere list of the facts:

1. Maximum clarity
2. Maximum economy
3. Maximum generality
4. Maximum exposure of correlations between "separate" facts

In constructing a formal model of the data, one strives for maximum *isomorphism* between the model and the data. In doing so, one is further constrained by the twin-edged golden rules of Leibnitz and Occam[6]:

1. The formal model should make *powerful enough* claims so as to accommodate all the data (*principium rationis sufficientis*).
2. The formal model should not make *too powerful* claims which are unwarranted by the data (*Occam's razor*).

With all these "bread-and-butter" stipulations in mind, formal modeling of raw data is of an enormous value to the investigator, helping to clarify the importance, degree of completeness and interrelatedness of the facts. It is thus an indispensible *methodological preliminary* to the real task at hand, explanation. There is one thing, however, that a formal model can

---

[5] When a discipline studies relatively simple inanimate phonemena (cf. physics or inorganic chemistry), the notion of *function* and hence of functional explanation is moot. But a nonfunctional study of a biological organism is nonsensical.

[6] Occam's and Leibnitz's principles are usually applied to explanation, but they are just as applicable to formal model building, which is a methodological preliminary to explanation.

never do: It cannot *explain* a single thing. Nor can it explain itself. Either of these two will amount to a *tautology*. Therefore a formal model *by itself* could not be "a theory" of a complex, organismic behavior, since in the realm of complex organisms a theory without explanation is not a theory. Being only a formal summary of the raw facts, a formal model cannot "make empirical claims," since this would again amount to a tautology. Nor could a formal model "predict a certain range of facts": It stands in relation to facts the same way a *rule* (type, superset) stands to individual *instances* (tokens, subsets). It is useful so long as it is a generalization, that is, a summary of *all* the facts. But precisely when it is a complete summary, the sense in which the generalization "predicts" the fact approaches tautology.

The history of transformational-generative linguistics boils down to nothing but a blatant attempt to represent the formalism as "theory," to assert that it "predicts a range of facts," that "it makes empirical claims," and that it somehow "explains." In this respect transformational linguists have gone one-up over their immediate structuralist predecessors. The latter were openly indifferent to explanation and considered the explanatory parameters of language to fall within the scope of other disciplines. They thus contented themselves with collecting the facts and categorizing them to varying degrees of formality.[7] Chomsky's early formulation (1957) makes no reference to explanation of any kind, it is rather Bloomfieldian in ignoring the natural explanatory parameters of language, and rather Harrisian in motivating the formalism purely on the grounds of simplicity–economy.[8]

How did the myth of the "explanatory power" of the formalism

[7] This may be illustrated by quoting Leonard Bloomfield: "thus he [de Saussure] exemplifies in his own person and perhaps unintentionally what he proved intentionally and in due form: That Psychology (and Phonetics) do not matter at all and are, in principle, irrelevant to the study of language . . . [1924, p. 318]." "In order to give a scientifically accurate definition of the meaning of every form of the language, one should have a scientifically accurate knowledge of everything in the speaker's world. . . . In practice, we define the meaning of a linguistic form, whenever we can, in terms of some other science . . . [1933, pp. 139–140]." "In the division of scientific labor, the linguist deals only with the speech signal . . . he is not competent to deal with the problems of physiology and psychology . . . [1933, p. 32]." The pioneering transformational work of Harris (1957) did not attempt to justify the formal model in terms of explanation. Rather, the formalism was justified in terms of economy–simplicity, i.e., cooccurrence restrictions, etc.

[8] "Despite the undeniable interest and importance of semantic and statistical studies of language [here "statistical" refers to distributional studies of text—TG], they appear to have no direct relevance to the problem of determining or characterizing the set of grammatical utterances. I think that we are forced to conclude that grammar is autonomous and independent of meaning . . . [1957, p. 17]." "The general principle is this: If we have a transformation that simplifies the grammar and leads from sentences to sentences in a large number of cases, . . . then we attempt to assign constituent structure to sentences in such a way that this transformation always leads to grammatical sentences, thus simplifying the grammar even further . . . [1957, p. 83]." "we should like the syntactic framework of the language to support semantic description, and we shall naturally rate more highly a theory of formal structures that leads to grammars that meet this requirement. . . . It is important to recognize that by introducing such considerations . . . into the metatheory that deals with grammar and semantics, . . . we have not altered the purely formal character of the theory of grammatical structure itself . . . [1957, p. 102]."

1.2. The Ascent of the Formalism as Explanation

arise? In 1962[9] Chomsky introduced for the first time his three levels of adequacy (later amplified in Chomsky, 1965). The first level, that of *observational* adequacy, is essentially a straw-man in linguistics, the "list grammar." The second, *descriptive* adequacy, obtains when the grammar "gives a correct account of the linguistic intuition of the native speaker . . . [1964, p. 63]." The "intuition" part of the formulation has remained somewhat opaque to this day. It nevertheless involves, so far as one can ascertain, the common-sensical advance from a mere list of the facts to a model with *maximal generalization,* presumably via the principle of economy–simplicity. A descriptively adequate grammar is thus expected to "specify the observed data (in particular) in terms of significant generalizations that express the underlying regularities in the language . . . [1964, p. 63]." It is *explanatory* adequacy that has remained most puzzling: "A third and still higher level of success is achieved when the associated linguistic theory [i.e., the theory in whose framework a particular grammar is written—TG] provides a general basis for selecting a grammar that achieves the second level of success over other grammars consistent with the relevant observed data [i.e., grammars with only "observational adequacy"—TG] that do not achieve this level of success . . . [1964, p. 63]." A number of questions are left wide open following this third formulation:

1. Is explanatory adequacy a property of the grammar or the theory? The text of Chomsky (1964) remains ambiguous on this issue.
2. What is the exact nature of the general basis that the associated linguistic theory must provide in order to judge between competing grammars which cover the data equally well?
3. Since the associated linguistic theory must provide that general basis in order to judge between grammars that achieve *descriptive* adequacy and those which achieve only *observational* adequacy, should one conclude that the general basis involves the degree of *generality* of the description, and thus ultimately the *formalism-internal* measure of simplicity–economy?[10]
4. Does the general basis provided by the theory involve the explanatory parameters of language, and thus go outside the formalism?

To the extent that a linguistic theory makes no reference to the natural explanatory parameters of language, it remains perforce a higher level of formalism. Explanations emanating from such a "theory" re-

---

[9] The published version I refer to here is Chomsky (1964).

[10] In a later formulation, Chomsky (1965), the impression is left that the explanatory adequacy is achieved by the *theory* (not the grammar), and that this is done when the theory can judge on some general basis between grammars that achieved—all of them—an equal measure of descriptive adequacy. That certainly rules out the criterion of generality–economy–simplicity, at least at the lower level. But no reference is then made to any other general principles, such as explanatory parameters.

main, perforce, formalism-internal, and are in principle, then, not explanations at all but rather *tautologies*.[11] In the words of I. I. Rabi, no explanation is possible without reference to "something else" (i.e., something **outside** the system), to "something more profound."

On further reading in Chomsky (1964), where case studies are used to illustrate the three levels of adequacy, it becomes clear that the general basis via which explanatory adequacy can be established is nothing but the formalism-internal principle of simplicity–economy. Thus, in discussing the general principles by which phonological sequences in English such as /blik/ and /brik/ are allowed while /bnik/ is dissallowed, Chomsky writes,

> The level of explanatory adequacy would be attained by a linguistic theory that provides a principled reason for incorporating this generalization into the grammar of English, and for excluding the (factually correct) "rule" that in the context #b——ik# a liquid is necessarily /r/. Thus the theory must provide a general evaluation measure (*simplicity* measure) which would show how the former [i.e., a generalization about consonant clusters in English—TG] but not the latter rule gives a more highly valued grammar . . . [1964, p. 64; emphasis added].

No reference to universals of phonetics, the relevant explanatory parameter, is found here.

From this point onward, mainstream transformational-generative linguistics proceeded under the threefold methodological delusion that:

1. The formalism is a theory.
2. A theory that makes no reference to the natural explanatory parameters of language is somehow endowed with explanatory powers.
3. The formalism-internal simplicity measure, a purely formal entity with no relation to the explanatory parameters of language, is somehow the source of explanatory adequacy of either grammars or the theory.

The epitome of such methodological delusion is the so-called hypothesis of "autonomous syntax," where even the rather timid attempts by the generative semanticists to introduce semantic considerations into the theory of grammar (i.e., to make the mainstream practitioners sensitive to this most obvious and most "syntaxlike" explanatory parameter of language), were vigorously rejected on formal, a priori grounds. In the following section I will offer a number of case studies purporting to illustrate the kind of circular, sterile argumentation that

---

[11] Wittgenstein's observation about the propositions of logic (and any other purely deductive formal system) must be invoked at this point: "The propositions of logic are tautologies (6.1). Therefore the propositions of logic say nothing (6.11) [1918, p. 121]."

1.2. The Ascent of the Formalism as Explanation

arose out of such utter methodological collapse in transformational-generative linguistics.

1.2.3. Some Pseudoexplanations in Linguistics

Pseudoexplanations in linguistics bring to one's mind the concept of "survival of the fittest." At first glance it looks both meaningful and reasonable. But upon further consideration it melts into tautology, since "fittest" can only be defined by "survive." As a theoretical construct, then, survival of the fittest makes no empirical claims, nor does it explain the facts. It merely relabels one phenomenon (survival) by another name (fittest). Other classics of behavioral science, such as "analogy," "stimulus–response" or "the control of IQ by a hereditary G-factor," are all of the same *nihil* explanatory value, substituting nomenclature for explanation. In this section I will illustrate how this practice has been flourishing in linguistics under the direct impact of Chomsky's concept of explanation.

1.2.3.1. THE SEMANTIC IMPORT OF TRANSFORMATIONS

The semantic corollaries of so-called "syntactic transformations" has haunted transformational-generative linguistics from birth. In a sense, one may legitimately assert that Harris' criterion for "transformational relation" between sentences was primarily semantic. This is so because cooccurrence restrictions, in spite of their forbidding formal flavor, are first and foremost a semantic phenomenon in sentences of human language. To the extent, then, that Chomsky's first model (1957) was essentially that of Harris (1957), it was already, perforce, a semantically sensitive grammar (or "semantically motivated," in factual *heuristic* terms). It was clear quite early, however, that there was a buzzing fly in the formal ointment: Transformations seemed to divide themselves into two distinct classes, those which didn't change meaning (embedding transformations) and those which did (negation, questions, imperative). The first impetus toward "handling" this problem was supplied by Fillmore (1963) who commented on the peculiar status of embedding transformations vis-à-vis all others. Next the argument for removing all semantic operations out of the T-rule component (negation, questions, imperative, passive, etc.) and transplanting them into the P-rule component was forcefully pursued by Katz and Postal (1964), then essentially adopted in Chomsky's revised model (1965). So far as one is able to ascertain, not a single empirical issue was involved in this first cycle of remodeling. Nor was any insight offered into explaining the facts of language. What was gained primarily was a measure of formal consistency of the model, whereby transformations all, uniformly, "didn't change meaning."

Matters rested there, with "semantically motivated deep structure," but not for long, since next the lexicon reared its ugly head. In his revised model, Chomsky (1965) had already planted the seeds of the next remodeling upheaval by suggesting two alternative formalisms for 'handling' the lexicon. One was the "complex symbol" format, in which semantic structure was generated by the Base Rules, and the other the "delta-node" format, in which semantics was to be tacked onto the syntax by other, yet-to-be-specified, rules.

From this seemingly innocent hedge there burst forth the celebrated doctrinal schism between generative semantics (ex-Complex-Symbol) and interpretative semantics (ex-Delta-Node), whose chief bone of contention seemed to be whether the rules that "map syntactic structure into semantic structure" (or vice versa) are to be labeled as T-rules mapping semantics onto syntax, or Interpretation-rules mapping syntax onto semantics. The fact that the proposed T-rules and I-rules were completely isomorphic, and the fact that the very same range of data was cited by both warring parties in support of their pet formalism, never seemed to dampen the combatants' passions. Nor were they disturbed by the fact that the entire exercise was performed in an empirical and explanatory vacuum. Whether transformations do or do not change meaning has remained to this day an entirely vacuous issue. They do not if you "generate" semantic structure in the "base." They do if you generate semantic structure via I-rules. The "issue" boiled down to choice of formalism, and since the two formalisms were essentially isomorphic, to nomenclature.

1.2.3.2. THE POWER-OF-THE-MODEL DEBATE

The Texas Conference on the Goals of Linguistic Theory in 1969[12] was the setting for a curious confrontation between Postal (representing generative semantics) and Chomsky (representing interpretative semantics) concerning the "power" of The Model. In a total empirical vacuum, the two common-sensical exhortations of *principium rationis sufficientis* and *Occam's razor* were pitted against each other. Postal, in a paper titled "The Best Theory," contended that GS is preferable because it has only one formal device—Transformations—mapping between meaning and syntax, as against two devices (T-rules and I-rules) in IS. In essence, he was invoking Occam's Razor. Chomsky, in a paper improbably titled "Some empirical issues in linguistics," argued that IS was preferable since it made stronger and more specific claims and was thus easier to falsify by contrary data. In essense, he was arguing from *principium rationis sufficientis*. The fact that both considerations are essential to any methodology (see Section 1.2.2) never impinged upon the discussion.

[12] Selected papers from the proceedings were published in Peters (1972).

1.2. The Ascent of the Formalism as Explanation

Nor were the two combatants bothered by the obvious isomorphism of their models, nor by the fact that no empirical issues were involved.

1.2.3.3. RULE ORDERING AS EXPLANATION

It is only fitting to cite some of my own early work as an illustration of how one can invoke the formalism as explanation. In Givón (1969, 1972a) I observed that in languages where predicates show pronominal (gender–number) agreement with subjects, conjunction reduction for constructions with conjoined subjects represented a formal problem. The singular agreement on the predicates of conjoined sentences must thus be "repaired" into plural agreement following conjunction reduction, and gender conflicts must also be resolved if the two subjects are of different genders. To illustrate this, consider the following data from Bamba, a Bantu language:

(1)   *umu-ana a-a-liile*
                PREF-child *he*-past-eat
                'The child ate'

(2)   *im-bwa i-a-liile*
                PREF-dog *it*-past-eat
                'The dog ate'

(3)   *umu-ana na im-bwa ba-a-liile*
                PREF-child and PREF-dog *they*-past-eat
                'The child and the dog ate'

In reviewing these facts, I went on to observe that obviously the two transformations—Conjunction Reduction and Agreement—must be strictly ordered with CR preceding AG. The fact that this rule-order formalism, much like the alternative post-transformational agreement-repair rules, was nothing but a formal recasting of the facts, never crossed my mind at that time. I was fully convinced that somehow I was both "making an empirical claim" and "explaining the facts."

In the same vein, I went on to observe that, obviously, subject deletion rules in languages that use verb agreement as an anaphoric device must be ordered **after** the rule of verb agreement. This pertained to data such as (again from Bemba):

(4)   *umu-ana a-a-liile*
                PREF-child *he*-past-eat
                'The child ate'

(5)   *a-a-liile*
                he-past-eat
                'He ate'

As Grover Hudson (1972) later pointed out, to begin with, there was no formal need for a statement of extrinsic ordering of the rules, since one could easily build the output of the agreement rule into the input definition ("structural conditions") of the deletion rule and have the two rules thus "intrinsically" ordered. But further, he pointed out that a general *explanatory* principle of communication was at the bottom of these phenomena, that of *avoiding irrecoverable deletion,* and that the very same principle explained similar phenomena in both phonology and semantax. Thus for example, in French and Navajo nasal consonants are deleted only if the preceding vowel assimilated the nasal feature. In other words, copying of the nasal feature—and thus its preservation—is a precondition to nasal consonant deletion. Similarly, languages with viable subject agreement on the verb ("copying") tend to allow more "zero anaphora" of the subject ("deletion"), as compared to languages without subject agreement.

1.2.3.4. THE SECOND LEXICON AS EXPLANATION

It has been known for a long time that, whatever the terminology, inflectional morphology was sensitive to the grammar. These "grammatical morphemes" normally involve the following categories: plural markers, pronouns and agreement markers, determiners–articles–deictics, tense–aspect–modals, nominal classifiers, and case-role markers. This portion of the morphology quite often involves extra-sentential considerations in the grammar, often processes of embedding which condense two sentences into one (see Chapter 5) or constraints which range over the discourse rather than the atomic sentence–clause. Translated into the generative jargon, one may say that inflectional morphology is "sensitive to transformations." That is, one must *repair* inflectional morphemes following the operations of many transformations, if one had inserted them into the sentence pretransformationally (Chomsky, 1965).

Addressing themselves to this problem, Gruber (1967a) and Givón (1969, 1972a) suggested that "what is really involved" is the "fact" that inflectional morphology constitutes a **second**, posttransformational, lexicon. And the second lexicon is inserted posttransformationally, and this greatly "simplifies" the grammar. The difference between the formalism of second-lexicon and that of posttransformational repair rules is a mere notational matter, involving no empirical considerations, although at the time neither Gruber nor myself were bothered by this. Another matter that did not bother us was the fact that a real explanatory issue was altogether lost in the shuffle of modeling and remodeling. This issue involves the observation, *diachronic* in nature, that the rise of inflectional morphology is always associated with *the condensation of discourse into syntax,* that is, with the rise of complex, embedded, multi-argument clauses out of concatenated, simple, loosely bound clauses

1.2. The Ascent of the Formalism as Explanation

with (largely) one argument per verb (see Chapter 5). The posttransformational, extrasentential scope and dependency of inflectional morphology is thus a natural manifestation of its growth and function as the signalling device associated with complex clauses and the interface between syntax and discourse.

1.2.3.5. ORDERED RULES AND THE REREGULARIZATION OF PHONOLOGICAL IRREGULARITY

The effect of successive diachronic changes on the synchronic sound system of any language is profound: They create a colossal mess of irregular distributions, partial overlaps of phonemes and complex morphophonemics.[13] It is only natural that the resulting situation requires a more complex synchronic analysis. At a certain point in the history of generative phonology, it became fashionable to suggest that the morphophonemic irregularity resulting from successive diachronic changes is "not really irregularity," but rather a "deeper underlying regularity" reflected in multiple layers of ordered "synchronic" rules. The epitome of this trend may be seen in Chomsky and Halle (1968), where the entire history of English phonology was transferred, en masse, into the synchronic phonology of Modern English, with incredibly complex ordering constraints, a thousand-years worth of ordered rules, and a set of underlying forms without a shred of surface attestation in the phonetic output of speakers. The fact that much of the analysis represented a reshuffling in the filing system—this time from diachronic to synchronic description—gave no pause to the authors. Nor were they bothered by the absence of psycholinguistic evidence in support of abstract "deep underlying segments" with no surface realization in the output, or in support of the speaker's knowledge of chains of rules which convert one unrealized abstract form into another. Somehow, mysteriously, the analysis was claimed to be explanatory and it gave rise in due course to scores of similar analyses in which the processing difficulties encountered by speakers when facing the surface chaos arising from the impact of diachronic change were neatly explained away as "deeper" underlying regularities.[14]

1.2.3.6. TAXONOMY AS EXPLANATION

The class of adjectives is a notorious swing-category in languages. To begin with, there are languages with no adjectives, and where our lexical adjectives formally belong to the category VERB and behave like other stative verbs (Krio, Topotha). Then there are languages with a rather small adjectival lexicon, involving primarily inherent–permanent

---

[13] See Hyman (1973).
[14] In my own intellectual cupboard there rests a skeleton harkening back to that era (Givón, 1970c), where I endeavored to show how the complex morphophonemics of the Bemba verb suffixes can be "explained" by extrinsic rule ordering.

properties (size, extension, shape, color, taste, texture). Most Bantu languages fall into this category, as many others do, and indeed Dixon (1970) has noted that the more inherent–permanent properties are the most likely to lexicalize as adjectives, and that more temporary-state properties (*angry, hot, sad, disturbed,* etc.) have a higher chance of lexicalizing as verbs. Finally, there are languages (Walbiri, see Hale, 1978) where many of our adjectival concepts lexicalize as nouns, but it is primarily the more inherent–permanent properties which do so, while temporary states lexicalize as (stative) verbs. To summarize briefly, a universal phenomenon seems to exist whereby the lexical categories VERB, ADJECTIVE, and NOUN occupy different areas of a *continuum,* and the scalar property of that continuum seems to be *time-stability.* At one pole—active verbs—one finds the depiction of *rapid change* in the state of the universe. Further down the scale one finds *temporary states,* which may lexicalize as either verbs or adjectives. Further down yet, one finds *inherent–permanent properties* that may lexicalize as adjectives more often, and some would even lexicalize as nouns (*youth, adult, oldster, baby*). Finally, at the other extreme of the scale one finds entities with the *highest time-stability,* those which do not change their identity over time (or change it rather slowly), and those tend—universally—to lexicalize as nouns.[15]

Given the facts summarized above, it is, of course, no accident that the lexical class ADJECTIVE has remained problematic, exhibiting even within the same language some "more noun-like" properties and some "more verb-like" ones. Further, since time-stability is a matter of degree, within the same language some adjectives—the ones depicting more temporary states—behave more like verbs, while others—depicting more inherent–permanent properties—behave more like nouns. Within the history of transformational-generative linguistics, this state of affairs precipitated a certain tug of war, whereby adjectives were proclaimed to be verbs one day (Ross and Lakoff, 1967) and nouns the next (Ross, 1969; Heny, 1972). Since adjectives exhibit both nominal and verbal properties, the discussion always hinged upon which properties were "more criterial" (difference of **kind**) and which were "less criterial" (difference of **degree**). It gave pause to no one that in **all** taxonomies the issue of difference in kind versus difference of degree is a matter of *definition* and is thus, in principle, not an empirical issue. And again, lost in the shuffle was the real explanation to the erratic behavior of adjectives cross-linguistically.

1.2.3.7. NOMENCLATURE AS EXPLANATION

One prevalent practice popularized by transformational-generative linguistics is that of "explaining" via nomenclature. It involves the

[15] For further discussion see Chapter 8, as well as Chapter 6.

1.2. The Ascent of the Formalism as Explanation

pointing out that some phenomenon in language is "really XYZ" and therefore its behavior can be understood because "that's the way all XYZs behave." There are two separate facets to this practice. First, if "XYZ" is a *class* of phenomena, then indeed what is involved here is the process of *generalization,* which is quite a respectable methodological preliminary in any investigation (see Section 1.2.2). But by virtue of pointing out that the phenomenon under study is really an *instance* of the larger class "XYZ" one has not explained the behavior of the phenomenon, but only *related* it to the behavior of other members of the class. Now, if this is followed by explanation of the behavior of the entire class "XYZ," then indeed a reasonable methodological progression has been followed. Quite often, however, transformational–generative linguistics "explained" the behavior of "XYZ"—either the individual or the class—by positing an *abstract principle* which may be translated as "all XYZs behave in a certain way." The tautological nature of such a procedure is transparent.

An instance of this practice may be seen in the attempt (Vennemann, 1973b; Bartsch and Vennemann, 1972) to explain syntactic wordorder in language by reference to the "natural serialization principle" involving the order of *operators* versus *operands*. Briefly, the head of constructions–phrases was rechristened as *operand,* with the modifier–satellite–complement as *operator*. Next, the correlation between OV and MODIFIER–NOUN syntax on the one hand and VO and HEAD–MODIFIER syntax on the other, was explained as follows, "The natural serialization principle comprises the natural constituent structure principle but says that, furthermore, the operator–operand relationship tends to be expressed by unidirectional serialization: [operator [operand]] tends to be serialized either as [the order—TG] [operator [operand]] throughout, or as [[operand] operator] throughout . . . [Vennemann, 1973b, p. 41]." When de-jargonized, this quote "explains" Greenberg's observation about the correlation between HEAD–SATELLITE syntax in NPs and VPs by stating that "the correlation exists because languages like to be consistent, that is they like to exhibit the correlation."[16]

1.2.3.8. FORMALISM AS EXPLANATION$_i$: THE $\bar{X}$ CONVENTION

The $\bar{X}$ convention was introduced by Chomsky (1973b) as a formal summary of facts that seem to indicate parallel syntactic behavior be-

---

[16] In addition, the assumption that the verb:object relation is the same—either semantically or formally—as the relation noun:modifier, both being thus instances of the class of relationships operand:operator (respectively), remains to be justified. A similar assumption is buried in Chomsky's *X̄ convention,* see Section 1.2.3.8.

tween sentences, VPs, NPs, and ADJ-Ps. It purported, initially, to "account for" parallelisms of the following type:

(6) S: *He captured the city*   (AGENT–VERB–PATIENT)
    NP: *His capture of the city*   (AGENT/GENITIVE–VERB/HEAD–PATIENT/GENITIVE)

(7) VP: *(He) knew how to write*   (VERB–COMPLEMENT)
    NP: *(His) knowledge how to write* (NOUN–COMPLEMENT)

(8) VP: *(He) writes cleverly*   (VERB–ADVERB)
    NP: *(His) clever writing*   (ADJECTIVE–NOUN)

The bulk of the "evidence" supporting the $\bar{X}$ convention (i.e., the bulk of instances falling in the class labeled by this name) has always come from *nominalizations,* so that one may well argue that the convention is merely a relabeling of the fact that if one nominalizes a sentence or a verb phrase, systematic correspondences will be found between the members of the S or VP and the members of the NP derived from them via nominalization. Somehow, however, the $\bar{X}$ convention soon began to acquire, mutatis mutandis, the mystical "explanatory power," and it somehow was supposed that it was not only a summary and labeling of a range of facts, but also an explanation of those very facts. A typical example of this may be found in the works of Lightfoot (1975, 1976a) in the area of diachronic syntax, where one finds, "Incidentally, the facts of the preceding 5 centuries, particularly the parallel changes and common rules applying both to S, AP, and NP domains, fit comfortably into the $\bar{X}$ analysis of the lexicalist hypothesis and thereby provide support for that hypothesis . . . [1975, p. 207]." The factual core of the observation involves the seeming parallel changes towards VO syntax in the VP and N–MOD syntax in the NP of English. Whether these facts are "of the same kind" as those discussed above [cf. (6), (7), (8)] and thus are legitimate instances of the class "$\bar{X}$" is, perforce, not an empirical issue, since *by definition* any parallelisms between the linguistic behavior of NPs and VPs can be claimed to be instances of this class. By invoking the $\bar{X}$ "analysis," however,[17] nothing has been explained, and in fact the exercise closely parallels Vennemann's invocation of the operator-

---

[17] The sense in which a formal summary—or labeling—of the facts can acquire the status of "hypothesis" is of course mystifying by itself. Hypotheses, so far as I can tell, can be made either about "what the facts are likely to be" or about "what is a likely cause–explanation of the facts." But the sense in which a genus–type–name can constitute a hypothesis about the species–token–named remains opaque to me.

1.2. The Ascent of the Formalism as Explanation

operand "principle" in order to explain what are essentially the very same facts of word order.

1.2.3.9. FORMALISM AS EXPLANATION$_{ii}$: THE COMPLEX NP CONSTRAINT

While a formalism per se can neither make empirical claims nor serve as explanation, it nevertheless can be the natural catalyst for explanation. As an example of this consider Ross's (1967) Complex NP Constraint. Initially the CNPC was a formal label for the fact that in many languages deep-reaching relativization (as well as WH-questions and clefting) out of too-deeply-embedded clauses is forbidden. Thus, an English construction such as (9) is an illustration of the difficulties arising by "breaking" the constraint:

(9) *The man that I saw the dog that bit*

One could of course figure out, eventually, a reasonable interpretation of (9) and render it in a less syntacticized manner as:

(10) *The man, a dog bit him, and I saw that dog*

Ross's CNPC was soon heralded as a *formal universal* of human language, and it became fashionable to "explain" the data which was summarized by the CNPC label thusly:

(11) *English cannot have NPs such as (9) because it obeys the CNPC*

Later on, Edward Keenan (1972a) observed that there are, in fact, languages which do not abide by the CNPC, and that the set of languages that allow such laxity have one typological characteristic in common: They all "strand" *resumptive* (anaphoric) *pronouns* inside the relative clause, normally in the characteristic position of the deleted coreferential argument and with its case-function markings. As an example, consider the dialect of (nonstandard) American English in which such a device is found:

(12) *The man that I saw the dog that bit **him***

At this point explanation became possible, and in Givón (1973a, 1975a) I suggested that it would be fruitful to look at the entire phenomenon in terms of perceptual strategies of speech analysis. That is, sentences including NPs such as (9) are difficult to process because the grammatical–functional relations of subject and object in the deeply embedded clause are hard to reconstruct, given the deletion, the lack of morphological indication, and the fact that there was a large gap between the head noun *the man* (object of *bit*) and the verb of which it is the object. Thus languages which "strand" an anaphoric pronoun at the original position of the "deleted" coreferential argument in the embedded clause, provide a simpler procedure for recovering the underlying grammatical–functional relations. In other words, the rather opaque surface structure of English, an SVO language, in (13), becomes more transparent in the dialect that tolerates the resumptive pronoun, as in (14).

(13)   . . . dog that bit

(14)   . . . dog that bit **him**

The proponents of the CNPC as a *formal* universal, however, looked for explanation in a different direction, and what they came up with is roughly this:[18]

(15) *Relativization where pronouns are involved is not really a chopping rule, but rather a copying rule. Therefore, all those languages with resumptive pronouns which seem to break the CNPC don't really break it at all, since the CNPC applies only to chopping rules but not to copying rules.*

The utter circularity of such an "explanation" requires no further comment. It made important typological differences between languages look trivial, differences which led to disparities in expressive power (Edward Keenan, 1972), and relegated those differences to the status of "involving different rules," that is, a formalism-internal matter.

1.2.3.10. FORMALISM AS EXPLANATION$_{iii}$: EMONDS'S CONSTRAINTS

The discussion in Emonds (1970) is another example of how the formalism could be useful as a methodological prelude to explanation, provided it is not taken to be itself the explanation. To summarize briefly, Emonds (1970) observed[19] that many "stylistic" transformations, such as topic-shifting, clefting, dative-shift, presentative movement,[20] etc., are restricted to main clauses mostly, and occur only under severe restrictions in embedded clauses. Without exception, the transformations involved here are topic–comment (foreground–background) related, and Emonds's findings may be recast as follows:

(16) *Languages perform topic–comment pragmatic operations primarily in their main clauses.*[21]

---

[18] The original argument was raised by Ross (1967) in reference to left-dislocation, but was also extended to relativization with resumptive pronouns.

[19] The insights are likely to have been much older.

[20] See discussion in Gary (1974).

[21] More precisely the reference should read "main, declarative, active, affirmative clauses." For further discussion see Chapter 2.

1.2. The Ascent of the Formalism as Explanation

So far as Emonds was concerned, what was at issue was a *formal* property of grammars, that is, the fact that two formal types of T-rules existed, "structure preserving T-rules" which apply both in main and subordinate clauses, and "root transformations" which applied only in main (root) clauses.

Things rested there until Hooper and Thompson (1973) pointed out that all the exceptions to Emonds's generalization, that is, cases where root transformations applied in nonmain clauses, could be explained by the following *pragmatic* principle:

(17) Emonds's constraint (16) may be broken in **asserted** nonmain clauses, but not in **presupposed** ones.

This opened the way to viewing the entire question in the context of functional explanation, as was suggested in Givón (1973a, 1974a):[22]

(18) *The main-declarative-active-affirmative clause is the site where the bulk of new information (assertion) in discourse is introduced. Nonmain clauses, on the other hand, contain largely background (presupposed) information. It would thus be counter-functional to perform topic–comment operations in clauses which are themselves largely background (presupposed) material. Thus, only with respect of the material that is **not** presupposed to be known to the hearer, that is, main clause material, does it make sense to perform foreground–background distinctions (further refining the information in terms of **degree** of foregrounding). Further, main clauses are in a sense*[23] *"less complex" for the purpose of speech processing. One would expect them then to "better tolerate" further syntactic complications arising from root transformations, in terms of scrambled word-order, etc.*

1.2.3.11. MORE CONCEPTUAL TRAPS: RELATIONAL GRAMMAR AS EXPLANATION

One of the most discouraging aspects of the recent history of linguistics is the way honest attempts to break the stranglehold of the generative paradigm always seem to bog down, eventually, in the very same methodological mire from which they purported to extricate themselves. The story of generative semantics in the late 1960s and early 1970s is by now ancient history. "Functionalism," grounded most firmly in phonol-

---

[22] See further discussion in Chapter 2. More recently Green (1976) pursued the argument further, claiming the existence of some residual "syntactic" control over the appearance of "main-clause phenomena" in subordinate clauses. In reply, Bolinger (1977) showed that upon more careful examination of the pragmatic context, those "syntactic" phenomena turn out to hinge upon the discourse-pragmatic context.

[23] See discussion in Chapter 2.

ogy, did not fare much better. And the recent ascent of Relational Grammar is a case in point. The initial impetus for Relational Grammar[24] was factually sound, grounded in the observation that grammatical rules (transformations) are not governed by purely *syntactic* configurations of NPs as the transformational-generative orthodoxy would have it, but rather are governed by *functional* notions such as subject, object, etc. No sooner was this valid observation made, however, than a new edifice of formalisms sprang out, all of them fancy renditions of the facts, all of them potentially "explanatory,"[25] and all oblivious to the natural explanatory parameters of language. As an illustration, let me cite the so-called *relational annihilation law* as it applies to the passive transformation. As given in Kimenyi (1976, p. 9), the RAL reads as follows:

(19) When an NP_i assumes the grammatical relation borne by another NP_j (and $NP_i + NP_j$), then NP_j itself ceases to bear any grammatical relation whatsoever. Such NPs are called **chomeurs**.[26]

Within the context of RG, arguments which "bear grammatical relation to the verb" are "terms," and only terms can govern (participate in the definition of) rules of grammar. When de-jargonized, (19) recasts the facts such as the following observation about passive sentences:

(20) *If you passivize a sentence, then the agent—erstwhile bearing the grammatical relation* **subject**—*becomes less accessible to transformational rules, thus "inactive." In particular, it cannot be repromoted via passivization (to subject), or via dative-shifting (to direct object).*

These facts are interpreted within the Accessibility Hierarchy (Keenan and Comrie, 1972, 1977[27]), where direct objects are easier to "promote" to subject than indirect objects, other "oblique" cases are even more problematic, and the "demoted" agent-of-passive is altogether inaccessible. In other words, *once you've demoted the agent via passivization, you cannot promote it back.*

Aside from the exercise in nomenclature, the formal jargon of Relational Grammar also serves to obscure a number of real facts and real explanations concerning the nature of passive sentences in human language. Those may be summarized as follows:[28]

[24] The initial spark was supplied by Perlmutter and Postal (1974), not yet in print. Explicit published formulations include Johnson (1974) and Kimenyi (1976), among many others.

[25] Perlmutter (in personal communication) disavows any explanatory claims for relational grammar, asserting that it is merely a *formal model* for the facts of language. If so, RG must relinquish the claim to the status of "theory."

[26] French colloquial for "unemployed."

[27] See discussion in Chapter 4.

[28] For more details as well as text counts from English, see Chapter 2. For further typological details, see Chapter 4.

1.2. The Ascent of the Formalism as Explanation

1. To the extent that passivization has any universal validity, it involves—at the very least—the removal of the agent from the topic position. Most often, by various means and commonly by default, another argument is then promoted to the most topical position.
2. In most languages, this operation normally involves the obligatory deletion of the agent, often without other changes.
3. Even in languages such as English, which are supposed to have an overtly expressed agent-of-passive, in terms of text-count most passive sentences are *agentless*.
4. In a number of languages with overtly-expressed agent-of-passive (including English), sentences with the agent-of-passive present are interpreted to mean that the agent is *the focus of new information*. In other words, it occupies the very opposite function of topic/subject.[29]
5. Dative-shift is also a rule involving topic–comment relations, where the argument shifted closer to the verb (i.e., "occupying the direct-object position") is *more topical*.[30]
6. What function in language could a procedure serve by which an agent is first demoted from topicality then re-promoted via passivization or dative-shifting? The entire point of passivization is to demote the agent when it is *not* the main sentential topic.
7. Other reasons, involving the typology of case-marking systems, also contribute to the seeming "inaccessibility" of agents-of-passive to further transformational manipulation.[31]

Once again, a formalism masquerading as a theory has only succeeded in deflecting the linguist from seeking explanations and, ultimately, from constructing a theory.

1.2.4. Innateness as Explanation

As Chomsky (1975) correctly observes, "Every theory of learning that is even worth considering incorporates an innateness hypothesis . . . [p. 13]." Thus the traditional argument between empiricist and rationalist has never really raged about *whether* something in the mind was innate, but only about **what** was innate. While Chomsky tends to exaggerate the supposed chaotic and noninteractive nature of language acquisition, his contention that only a restricted subset of all mathematically possible grammars compatible with the data are actually attested in human languages, is factually correct. Also reasonable is the inference

---

[29] KinyaRwanda is a case in point: Kimenyi (1976) goes as far as to suggest that sentences with overt agent-of-passive have an agent-*cleft* meaning, i.e., translating: *The ball was kicked by John* → *It was John who kicked the ball*.
[30] See discussion in Chapter 4, as well as in Shir (1979) and Morolong and Hyman (1977).
[31] See Chapter 4.

that a highly specific innate learning capacity must be postulated in order to account for the active, analytic way in which children learn a first language, as well as for the many substantive universals underlying the seeming diversity of human languages. Whether this innate learning capacity is specific to language **alone**—as distinct from cognition and perception—is to this day a wide-open empirical question. Certainly, a more careful analysis of the early stages of first language acquisition (see Chapter 5) suggests that children do not first acquire "syntax" in Chomsky's sense, but rather a *communicative system* of a much more rudimentary sort; and only later they modify it, gradually, into "syntax." All these are, however, empirical issues that can be settled through a more responsible approach to data gathering and evaluation.

From a methodological point of view, what is truly bizarre is the curious implication in Chomsky's discussion of innateness that somehow the mere fact that a rich, specific, universal language-learning capacity is wired into the human brain prenatally somehow explains something—anything—about the specific substantive universals of human linguistic structure. We are again faced here with a curious sense of explanation which boils down to tautology. Suppose a biologist were to advance the following "explanation":

(21)   *The human digestive system is built the way it is because its structure is wired into our genetic code, it is innate.*

Has he explained anything? Indeed he has not, since without reference to *function* and *evolution*[32] no explanation of the structural properties of an organism is possible. Similarly, no explanation of the specifics of the human linguistic structure is furnished by observing that "Some intellectual achievements, such as language learning, fall strictly within biologically determined cognitive capacity . . . [Chomsky, 1975, p. 27]."[33] Are any cognitive capacities **not** biologically determined? Is more being said than "we are the way we are because that's the way we (genetically) are?"

1.3. THE GUTTING OF THE DATA BASE: COMPETENCE AND GRAMMATICALITY

In the preceding section I endeavored to show how the supposed rationalist edifice of transformational-generative grammar turns out to be another structuralist detour, in which the formalism is elevated to the

---

[32] In language as well as in other subsystems of the organism, some structural properties can only be understood in reference to the phylogenetic evolution of the organism, see Chapters 6 and 7.

[33] It is not clear whether Chomsky himself has ever considered innateness as an explanation to the specific *substantive* properties of human language. But other linguists may have, see the otherwise empirically responsible discussion in Bickerton (1975, 1977).

status of "theory" and "explanation." What is left then is empiricism with a vengeance, where strong claims are made about theory and explanation which then boil down to tautology. Empiricists have traditionally prided themselves on sticking close to the data, and in fact a certain measure of empirical responsibility has always been their stock in trade. However, the pseudotheoretical baggage which transformational-generative linguistics carried into structuralism was coupled with another—equally ominous—development: the gutting, beyond recognition, of the concept of *relevant data* in linguistics.

One aspect of this development has already been mentioned above, namely that by selecting valid explanatory parameters one also selects, at the same breath, the relevant areas of data. Thus, by dissociating itself from the consideration of communicative function, speech processing, cognitive–perceptual structure, diachronic, ontogenetic and phylogenetic evolution, and world-view pragmatics and ontology, transformational linguistics had already restricted itself to the narrow band of language-internal data covered by the Bloomfieldians. A more damaging development, however, was the rise of the distinction *performance* versus *competence,* the postulation of *grammaticality*—and the elevation of all three terms to the status of theoretical significance.

1.3.1. Performance, Competence, and Controlled Experiments in Science

At the common-sensical methodological level, Chomsky's introduction of the distinction between linguistic performance and linguistic competence was both useful and necessary. The proper context for this distinction is the concept of *controlled experiment* in science. In any scientific discipline dealing with a multitude of complex variables which interact with each other, the first steps in investigating the complex phenomenology involve a great measure of *abstraction* and *simplification.* Let us consider an illustrative example from biochemistry.

Suppose I am to study the enzymatic mechanism by which the living cell converts a certain substance A into another substance B. If I first attempt to study the process *in vivo*, that is, within the context of the whole living cell or the entire organism, my life as a scientist becomes enormously complicated. Other enzymes in the living cell may interact with the one I wish to study, the concentration of both A and B within the cell must be determined, as well as the concentration of countless other chemicals bearing on the process, the temperature, gas pressure, and many other relevant factors. Given such complexity, I am at loss as to what to measure and what my measurements mean. Now, being a practical-minded scientist, I then resort to the practice of controlled experiment: I fractionate the living tissue and isolate the enzyme in question; I control the temperature, nutrient concentration, gas pressure, etc.; I keep all variables constant *except two*—and I then vary one of those under rigidly controlled circumstances and measure the effect on the behavior of the other variable. I proceed with this method until I have performed simple controlled experiments with as many of the variables as I could conceive of or isolate. Then I proceed to increase the complexity of my experiments by adding more variables into the system, having determined their interactive properties in isolation. I thus slowly combine more and more variables until my experiments begin to approximate *in vitro* (i.e., in the test tube) the system as it might be *in vivo*. Ultimately, if my methodology works out, I proceed to more complex experiments yet, studying the system *in vivo* with less and less abstraction and simplification. Somewhere near this point, I begin to construct a more realistic account of the phenomenon under investigation. The abstraction I indulged in at the beginning was a *methodological convenience*. I never proposed to construct "a theory of the organism *in vitro*," since that would not guarantee convergences with the behavior of the organism *in vivo*. Had I persisted in my abstraction to the bitter end, had I claimed that the organism *in vitro* was the ultimate object of my investigation, that it had some *theoretical* significance, my colleagues would have, in all probability, laughed me out of the lab.

The abstraction and simplification involved in choosing to *first* investigate data of linguistic competence, should have the same commonsensical motivation as the controlled experiment in other sciences. The number of variables involved in language behavior is so large, and their potential interactions so complex, that one could not crack open the phenomenology of language without a certain—often an extreme—degree of abstraction. The most obvious variables to eliminate from the linguistic test tube at the beginning would be those that are in some sense less central to the explanation of normal language structure and language function: pathological impediments, brain damage, stuttering, extreme emotional states, individual memory-capacity and computation variation, sex-related pitch differences, etc. At the very beginning, the relevant communicative context for utterances is considered over much smaller domains, that is, word, morpheme, clause, and sentence rather than paragraph or discourse. Many facts of grammar may be identified under such a methodology *in a preliminary fashion*, such as lexical items, morphology, "basic word order," the case-function system, etc.[34] But the entire procedure is motivated by methodological convenience, pure and simple. Once the linguist has established the more rudimen-

[34] Most often, the "basic" word-order discovered during the "competence" or "sentence grammar" phase of the investigation, tends to be illusory, an artifact of the isolation of clauses away from their discourse context. Only in relatively few languages, English possibly one, does the type of rigid word-order obtain via the elicitation of isolated sentences correspond to the most frequent—or "least marked"—word-order obtained in natural discourse.

1.3. The Gutting of the Data Base

tary facts, then if he is a scientist worth his salt, he would turn to enlarging his data base toward a more natural, realistic range. He would study *actual* speech *in context*; he would investigate diachronic change, enlarge the domain of explanation. He would conduct psycholinguistic experiments as an intermediate data-gathering methodology, somewhere between the total artificiality of elicited "competence" data and the extreme complexity of unelicited natural speech in an uncontrolled communicative setting.

What the linguist should never attempt to do is take the *methodological* convenience of competence and elevate it to the rank of prime *theoretical* significance. As a scientist, he has neither license nor coherent reason to assume a priori that the model of his competence data is either independent of the model of "language behavior in natural communicative setting," or that such a model could even be constructed in a coherent way. Finally, the linguist as a scientist should not persist in maintaining the abstraction and simplification of competence as a restriction on the range of data to be gathered, beyond the preliminary stages of the investigation. Such a persistence would gut the phenomenon itself, that is, the facts of the use of language as a communicative device. It would be the equivalent of the biochemist confining his investigation ad infinitum to simple *in vitro* experiments and throwing out of the test tube the most relevant variables via extraction and purification.

All this is precisely what happened to transformational-generative linguistics as a result of the elevation of Chomsky's distinction between performance and competence to the status of theoretically significant prime. To wit:

1. Artificial-sounding sentences, in isolation of communicative function and communicative context, became the stock-in-trade of linguistic evidence, to be analyzed, dissected and "explained."
2. On the basis of such "data," an independent level of grammatical organization—autonomous syntax—was postulated, with its so-called "properties" studied in great depth, whose imputed existence bore little or no relation to natural language facts.
3. All data which did not fit the resultant formal model were dismissed as "arising from performance factors," "acceptable–interpretable but ungrammatical,"[35] "not in the particular idiolect I am investigating," or otherwise ignored.

---

[35] Thus Otero (1975) writes of common Spanish sentences which he considers "ungrammatical": "if we had a complete, optimal grammar of Spanish (the only way to a definition of grammaticality in Spanish), those utterances will no doubt turn out to be a sort of fabrication of the grammar user, completely outside the range of sentences generated (directly or derivatively) by his internalized grammar . . . [p. 17]." The sentences in question, plural forms of the "impersonal passive" (*se-alquilan apartamentos* 'Apartments are being rented (here)', as against the "grammatically correct" *se-alquila apartamentos*), have been attested in the output of Spanish speakers, side by side with the "grammatically correct" variants, for over four hundred years! See similar discussion in Otero (1974).

4. The whole range of data on *language variation*—within the individual and across a community—was trivialized as a matter of dialect, idiolect, or performance lapses. The implications of extant variation for both sychronic "grammar" and diachronic change were completely ignored.
5. A concept of "grammaticality" as an *abstract* entity, divorced from communication, interpretability, acceptability, attestability, etc., was posited, and persistent data which tended to threaten the viability of this concept were relegated to the realm of "performance," "variation," "caprice," "false analogy," etc.[36]

In this fashion, after first trivializing the notions of theory and explanation, transformational-generative linguistics proceeded to trivialize the notion of data beyond recognition. What followed was an orgy of empirical irresponsibility, with one formal model chasing another in rapid succession, with data-free arguments that hinged upon purely formal notions of "economy" and "simplicity," and with linguistics as a whole becoming a sad caricature of late medieval scholasticism.

1.3.2. Grammar versus the Speaker

In this section I propose to survey a range of language facts that may be viewed from two different perspectives: In each case, one may either view a grammatical phenomenon as belonging to the realm of competence in one language and performance–text frequency in another; or one may view the phenomenon in both languages in the context of "communicative function," as being essentially *of the same kind*. The obvious inference to be drawn from the presentation is as follows: If indeed the phenomenon is of the same kind in both languages, then the distinction between competence and performance—or grammar and speaker's behavior—is (at least for these particular cases) untenable, counterproductive, and nonexplanatory.

1.3.2.1. DEFINITENESS OF SUBJECTS

In many of the world's languages, probably in most, the subject of declarative clauses cannot be referential–indefinite. In other words, the subject position in the sentence is one in which *new information* cannot be introduced. In order to violate this *categorial* constraint, the speaker must resort to a special, *marked* sentence type, the *existential–*

---

[36] Again from Otero (1975): "a speaker with a mind which has a far greater scope than its internalized system of grammatical rules . . . , is tampering with his grammar in one way or another in such cases. A Linguist who is free from the 'leave your language alone' syndrome of our behavioristic yesteryear ought to be able to recognize a human shortcoming for what it is . . . [p. 16]." The "leave your language alone" syndrome of our yesteryear is nothing but the dogged insistence of the earlier structuralists—the Bloomfieldians—that the data must be actually attested in a natural corpus.

1.3. The Gutting of the Data Base

presentative construction.[37] Languages of this type are, for example, Swahili, Bemba, Rwanda (Bantu), Chinese, Sherpa (Sino-Tibetan), Bikol (Austronesian), Ute (Uto-Aztecan), Krio (Creole), all Creoles, and many others.

In a relatively small number of the world's languages, most of them languages with a long tradition of literacy,[38] referential–indefinite nouns may appear as subjects of nonpresentative sentences, though the presentative–existential construction may exist in those languages. Thus, in English all the following types are grammatical sentences:

(22) a. *There's a man in the yard who's asking for you*
                                                                           (existential)
    b. *A man in the yard is asking for you* (REF–INDEF subject)
    c. *The man in the yard is asking for you*   (DEF subject)

Sentence (22b) is the "within the competence" of speakers of English, as are its equivalents within the competence of speakers of Hebrew, Spanish, Arabic, Japanese, etc.

Consider now the situation in Krio,[39] an English-based Creole from Sierra Leone, where one finds the following distribution:

(23) a. *ge wan man na di yad we de-ask fɔ yu*
       have one man in the yard REL PROG-ask for you
       'There's a man in the yard who is asking for you'

    b. **wan man na di yad de-ask fɔ yu*
       one man in the yard PROG-ask for you

    c. *di man na di yad de-ask fɔ yu*
       the man in the yard PROG-ask for you
       'The man in the yard is asking for you'

Sentence (23b), with a referential–indefinite subject in a nonexistential construction, is "outside the competence" of the speaker of Krio, as are its equivalents in Swahili, Bemba, Rwanda, Bikol, Sherpa, Chinese, etc. outside the competence of the speakers of those languages.

When one investigates the text frequency of sentences like (22b) in English, however, one finds them at an extremely low frequency: About 10% of the subjects of main-declarative-affirmative-active sentences

---

[37] For a discussion of existential–presentatives cross-linguistically, see Hetzron (1971). For discussion in a different context, see Chapter 2.

[38] The fact that these languages (European languages, Hebrew, Arabic, Japanese) have a long literacy tradition may or may not be significant. See some discussion in Chapter 5, on the possible connection between literacy and syntacticization. In terms of the degree of syntacticization, sentence (22a) above is *less* syntecticized, since the message is spread over two verbal clauses, while in (22b) the same message (roughly) is spread over a more compact, embedded clause.

[39] I am indebted to Sori Yilla (personal communication) for all the Krio data.

(nonpresentative) are indefinite, as against 90% definite.[40] Now, this is presumably not a fact about the "competence" of English speakers, but only about their actual "language behavior." But are we dealing with two different kinds of facts in English and Krio? Hardly. What we are dealing with is apparently the very same *communicative tendency*—to reserve the subject position in the sentence for the *topic*, the old-information argument, the "continuity marker." In some languages (Krio, etc.) this communicative tendency is expressed at the *categorial* level of 100%. In other languages (English, etc.) the very same communicative tendency is expressed "only" at the *noncategorial* level of 90%. And a transformational-generative linguist will then be forced to count this fact as competence in Krio and performance in English. But what is the communicative difference between a rule of 90% fidelity and one of 100% fidelity. In psychological terms, next to nothing.[41] In communication, a system with 90% categorial fidelity is a highly efficient system. Are we then dealing with performance in English and competence in Krio? Rather, it seems to me, the distinction between performance and competence or grammar and behavior tends to collapse under the impact of these data.

1.3.2.2. REFERENTIAL–INDEFINITE OBJECTS UNDER NEGATION

In many languages, such as Hungarian (Fino-Ugric), Sherpa, Chinese (Sino-Tibetan), Bikol (Austronesian), Bemba, Dzamba, Luganda, Rwanda (Bantu), Turkish (Altaic), Krio (Creole), and many others, referential–indefinite objects may not appear in negative sentences, whose objects may only be either referential–definite or nonreferential. Thus consider the following data from Krio:

(24)   a.   *a no   rid di buk*   (REF-DEF object)
                I NEG read *the* book
                'I didn't read the book'

         b.   *a no   rid buk*   (NONREF object)
                I NEG read book
                'I didn't read any book'

         c.   **a no   rid wan buk*   (*REF-INDEF object)
                I NEG read *one* book

         d.   *ge wan buk we-ting* a no   rid (existential subject
                have one book *REL*   I NEG read plus REL)
                'There's a book that I didn't read'

[40] See text counts in Chapter 2.

[41] Even below 90%, speakers would tend to perceive a noncategorial distribution as categorial, i.e., 100%. For further discussion, see Chapter 5, as well as Givón (1977a).

1.3. The Gutting of the Data Base

On superficial investigation, English is of the same type as Krio, since the equivalent of (24c) normally receives only a nonreferential interpretation of the object:

(25)   *I didn't read a book*
     a. *I didn't read any book*
     b. *?There's a book that I didn't read*

Thus, it seems that both Krio and English would resort to introducing a referential–indefinite object in an *affirmative* sentence [as in the existential (24d) or (25b)]. However, unlike Krio, in English it is actually possible to force-out a grammatical sentence of the type (24c). Thus consider:

(26)   a. *What happened to Mary?*
       b. *Oh, she didn't read a **book** that was assigned, and as a result she flunked her exams.*

The sentence of the type (26b), outside the competence of Krio speakers, thus seems to be—after all—within the competence of speakers of English. However, when one counts English texts, the frequency of sentences of this type *approaches zero*.[42] But nevertheless once again, the transformational-generative linguist will have to conclude that the restriction on the appearance of referential–indefinite objects under the scope of negation is expressed at the competence level for speakers of Krio, Bemba, Luganda, Rwanda, Dzamba, Chinese, Sherpa, Bikol, Hungarian, Turkish, etc., but in English (as well as a small number of other European languages with a long literary tradition[43]) the restriction is "only" on expressed at the level of performance or linguistic behavior. Is then the fact that speakers of both Krio and English would tend **not** to introduce new referential arguments in negative sentences but rather in affirmative ones two *separate* facts—one of competence in Krio and performance in English? Hardly. Rather, negative sentences in human language are **not** used primarily to *express* new information, but rather to *contradict* misguided statements by the interlocutor (see extensive discussion in Chapter 3, following). Therefore referential-indefinite nouns, that is, **new** arguments introduced into the discourse for the first time, are not likely to be introduced in negative sentences. The restriction is thus a *communicative* rule, and the difference between Krio and English

---

[42] See text counts and further discussion in Chapter 3.

[43] It may again be significant or not significant that languages in which the like of (26b) is permitted are largely European languages with a long tradition of literacy. Such a construction is certainly more *condensed* ("syntacticized") than the equivalent, looser variant in which the referential indefinite object is introduced either as the object of a preceding affirmative sentence or as subject of a preceding existential construction, i.e., *They required everybody to read **one particular book**, but Mary didn't read it*, . . . or *There was **a book** that everybody was supposed to read, but Mary didn't read it*, ...

at the level of speaker's behavior approaches zero. Once again, the distinction between performance and competence melts away under the glare of real facts and real explanation.

1.3.2.3. AGENTLESS PASSIVES

In a great many languages, probably the majority of the world's languages, passivization (i.e., the promotion of a nonagent to the main sentence-topic position) **requires** the deletion of the underlying agent.[44] Thus, consider the following data from Ute:

(27)   a.   *mamáci   taʔwóci   tḯḯu-ʔástiʔi*
             woman-SUBJ man-OBJ well-want-PROG
             'The woman likes the man'

        b.   *taʔwóci   tḯḯu-ʔásti-ta*
             man-OBJ well-want-*PASS*
             ['Someone likes the man']
             ['The man is liked']

Thus, in (27b), the only passive-type sentence in Ute, the agent must be obligatorily deleted, and so Ute is one language (among many) in which the agentless passive is a fact of "competence."

In English and a number of other languages, on the other hand, agented passives can be certainly produced. In fact, for the past 22 years, the passivization that has been discussed in the transformational-generative literature has been **only** the one *with the agent present*. Further, such passivization type constituted one of the most compelling arguments in support of the various—often warring—versions of the transformational-generative model.[45] However, if one counts actual texts of English, one discovers the following situation:[46]

1. Roughly 90% of passive sentences are *agentless*.
2. Of the 10% with overtly expressed agents, the majority are *indefinite* and **all** are expressing the agent as the *focus of new information*.

The agentless passive is thus a categorial (100%) fact of Ute "competence," but only a 90% fact of English "performance." But are those two separate facts? Hardly. Rather, we are again dealing here with *communicative* devices, and those devices may have *partially overlapping*

---

[44] See discussion of the typology of "passive" in Chapter 4.

[45] In Harris (1957) the passive transform is one of the original set which motivated the analysis. The same is true in Chomsky (1957). In Lakoff (1971) the supposed agented passives of English play a star role in the two actual empirical "proofs" cited in support of generative semantics (both turn out to hinge on a simplicity criterion rather than on fact). The transformational–generative literature is liberally strewn with the dead bodies of various "analyses" of this passive type.

[46] For text counts and further discussion, see Chapter 2.

functions cross-linguistically. Thus, in Ute "passive" sentences can be only used to code situations in which the agent is either *unknown* or *immaterial*. In English, 90% of the use of passives is of this type, while a residual 10% or so involves situations of almost the opposite nature—not only is the agent material and known, but it is the *focus* of the new information. And once again, the distinction between performance and competence would have obscured both fact and explanation.

1.3.3. Grammar, Communication, and Noncategorial Rules

The specter of noncategorial phenomena in human language has haunted transformational-generative linguistics from the start. It is indeed *anathema* to its very essence, that is, the notions of grammar, grammaticality, and competence. As suggested above, only by abstraction, simplification and the extreme *sanitization* of the data base could such notions be raised to the status of theoretical primes. Thus the sanitization of the data base involved, perforce, ignoring noncategorial phenomena in language, or relegating them to the status of variation or performance. When live discourse data are taken into account, however, it becomes obvious that noncategorial phenomena are the **rule** rather than the exception in human language. Before proceeding to illustrate this, let me first set up a general perspective for the discussion.

If language is an instrument of communication, then it is bizarre to try and understand its structure without reference to communicative setting and communicative function. Therefore, grammatical constraints, rules of syntax, stylistic transformations, and the like are not there "because they are prewired into the genetic code of the organism." Nor are they there for no reason at all. Rather, they are there to serve highly specific communicative functions. Now, since the communicative purpose of different grammatical rules is not the same, the consequences of the decision to abide by them or "break" them are also not the same. Indeed, one may ultimately be able to rank rules of grammar by the degree of their *communicative importance*, with the latter being defined as follows:

(28) *A communicative "rule" is higher on the scale of communicative importance if dispensing with its use ("breaking the rule") will result in a greater loss of* **communicative efficiency**.

The choice of "communicative efficiency" rather than "breakdown in communication" is motivated by the suspicion that we are dealing here with a *graded* phenomenon that can be *quantified* as follows:

(29) *The longer time it takes to transmit the same amount of message, or the larger the amount of repetition and redundancy*

required in the transmission, the lower is the communicative efficiency.

Thus, delivery time is, in principle, a parameter that can be quantified in natural speech.

The human communicator is not a deterministic user of an autonomous, subconscious grammar as Chomsky would have us believe. Rather, he makes *communicative choices*.[47] He uses rules of grammar for a communicative effect. He may choose to break the rule for an effect, such as poetics, metaphor, or semantic extension. He may choose to break the rule under the pressure of conflicting communicative requirements which take precedence (i.e., whose breaking will result in **greater** loss of communicative efficiency). He may also **choose** to forego the use of a more efficient strategy in favor of a less efficient one and *take the penalty* in terms of decreasing efficiency of communication, decreasing clarity, increased indeterminancy, etc. In situations where time is **not** an issue, the penalty is largely illusory. In other circumstances the speaker may **judge** that the hearer's knowledge of the background and context, the transparency of the pragmatics of the interaction, or the relative ease of inferring more information from either the context or the overtly given message, will counterbalance the breaking of a rule and help pick up the communicative slack. The loss is then largely illusory. Under other circumstances the speaker is in conflict between choosing a more efficient as against a more creative strategy, and by choosing the latter elects to pay a reasonable penalty.[48] Finally, the "grammar" may consist of alternative strategies–rules for performing the same or reasonably similar functions, enough so that the *choice* of one over the other would result in relatively small communicative consequences.

Given all this, one may, in principle, rank rules of grammar as follows with respect to "degree of categoriality":

(30)   *Communicative strategies whose removal will result in the greatest (and uncompensated) loss of communicative efficiency, will tend to appear in languages as **categorial** (100%) rules. On the other hand, strategies-rules whose violation will impair communicative efficiency to a lesser degree, may appear more frequently at the less-than-100%, and will thus often require **text-frequency** studies before they can be detected.*

While (30) above is only a suggestion, to be fleshed out by further research, it is in principle an empirically verifiable hypothesis. In fact,

---

[47] For a penetrating discussion of this, see García (1975a, 1979).
[48] Creativity is, by definition, breaking the norm and sacrificing speed for effect. At the other end, clichés have zero surprise value but maximal processing efficiency.

even at this early stage of our knowledge, one may make a number of predictions based on such a hypothesis:
1. Rules which involve the coding of the functions of arguments, including word-order, case-marking, and grammatical agreement, will be broken very infrequently and will tend to be perceived by the speakers as *categorial* rules of grammar.
2. Similarly, the intonational differentiation between presupposed versus asserted information *within* the simple clause will not be frequently broken (in languages which make use of intonation for this purpose).
3. In languages where topic–comment relations *within* the simple clause are coded via morphology or word-order, those rules will tend to be categorial.
4. On the other hand, stylistic transformations involved in coding topic–comment relations over the domain of *larger* discourse, that is, where contextual information is available more readily, will tend to be broken more often and be manifest in the speaker's behavior at a less-than-categorial level.

The epitome of indispensibility is also the **most arbitrary** and **most local** aspect of language: the choice of lexical items. The rules of the lexicon, that is, the sound:meaning correlation, is the most arbitrary element of language. And the *scope of the context* for choosing nouns, verbs, adjectives, and adverbs is most commonly the simple verbal clause. The wrong lexical choice has thus the highest chance of resulting in disrupted communication.

The facts surveyed in Section 1.3.2 illustrate the beginning of the problem of noncategorial phenomena in language. In the following space I will attempt to show how noncategorial phenomena in language tend to involve communicative *judgment* and communicative *choice*.

1.3.3.1. VIOLATIONS OF THE COMPLEX NP CONSTRAINT

In Section 1.2.3.9 I outlined the following situation: In languages which use resumptive–anaphoric pronouns in relativization, it is possible to "break" the CNPC with relatively low communicative cost. Now, suppose a speaker of American English was raised in the Ozarks, where the spoken dialect of nonstandard English makes use of resumptive pronouns in *complex* relativization (but not in simple, shallow-embedded environments). His *simple* relative clauses will look like those of Standard American English, as in:

(31)   *I saw the dog that bit the man*

In more complex contexts, our speaker would relativize **with** resumptive pronouns, and will thus diverge from the standard dialect, as in:

(32)   *I know the man that I saw the dog that bit **him***

The speaker is thus varying his strategies: First, he doesn't use the resumptive pronoun where the low complexity does not warrant its use, but only in more complex environments where he *judges* the communicative penalty to have been unacceptable if the pronoun were not used. Second, he *chooses* to break the CNPC when he has a "grammatical" strategy (the use of resumptive pronouns) that reduces the complexity and thus the communicative penalty. While one may still argue that the speaker is obeying his rules of grammar like a deterministic automaton, it is still of interest that he obeys the rules "in the *right* communicative direction," that is, "as if he *chose* to facilitate rather than obstruct communication."

Now, suppose our speaker went to school, then to college, and on to graduate school in, say, Boston, whereby his native Ozark dialect was supplanted by Standard American English. Now when he wants to express the message in (32), he has a wider range of choices. He could choose to abide by his newly acquired "grammar" of Standard American English and produce the simplified, desyntacticized equivalent of (32):

(33)   *I saw the dog that bit the man, and I know the man*

In some sense (Edward Keenan, 1972a, 1972b), (33) misses some of the pragmatic flavor (foreground–background) of (32), but the semantic content is reasonably close. But our speaker could also choose to revert back to his native Ozark dialect and reproduce (32). Now, the transformational-generative linguist would argue that the choice the speaker has involves merely *dialect switch*, that is, a sociolinguistically motivated decision whether to use one formal "grammar" or another. But it is still of interest that while "making choices between formal grammars," the speaker also seems to "make the correct choice between *complexes* of communicative strategies": Complex relativization goes *with* resumptive pronouns, simplified syntax goes *without* them. To the transformational-generative linguist such a correlation must be coincidental.

Let us contrast the behavior of the American–Ozark speaker with that of a speaker of modern Hebrew, a language in which resumptive pronouns are used as the most common relativization strategy in noncomplex environments (see Givón, 1973a, 1975a). However, the use of this strategy is not categorial for all case arguments. For example, in direct-object relativization, the resumptive pronoun is optional (and **infrequent**) in simple environments, but obligatory in complex environments:

(34)   ze   ha-ish   she-raíti   otó   etmól   (simple, with pronoun)
         this the-man that-I-saw *him* yesterday
         'This is the man that I saw yesterday'

1.3. The Gutting of the Data Base

(35) ze ha-ísh she-raíti etmól   (simple, without pronoun)
      this the-man that-I-saw yesterday
      'This is the man that I saw yesterday'

(36) ze ha-ish she-raiti et ha-kélev she-nasháx *otó*
      this the-man that-I-saw ACC the-dog that-bit him
                                          (complex, with pronoun)
      'This is the man that I saw the dog that bit him'
                                          (tr. into Ozark English)

(37) *ze ha-ísh she-raiti et ha-kélev she-nasháx
      this the-man that-I-saw ACC the-dog that-bit
                                          (*complex, no pronoun)

In describing the behavior of the Hebrew speaker (who is monodialectal), one may claim that he simply "abides by the rules of his dialect," one of which gives him the option of using or dropping the pronoun in simple environments. But, in fact, the use of the pronouns in such environment is **infrequent**, so that at the level of actual language behavior, the Hebrew speaker seems to behave just like the Ozark speaker. Furthermore, his behavior in complex environments also matches the correlation found in the Ozark speakers: With pronouns he **can** produce the complex structure (36), without them he cannot, although he could produce the equivalent of the simplified (33), that is,

(38) raiti et ha-kélev she-nasháx et ha-ísh, ve-ani makír et
      I-saw ACC the-dog that-he-bit ACC the-man and-I know ACC
         ha-ísh
         the-man
      'I saw the dog that bit the man, and I know the man'

They thus seem to be making the same communicative *choices* under the same circumstances for the same purpose, although, of course, one could insist that they are merely "abiding by the rules of grammar available in their dialects."

Another feature of Hebrew relativization is that in general when relativizing on prepositional object cases, the resumptive pronoun is obligatory even in simple environments:

(39) a. ze ha-ísh she-natáti lo   et ha-séfer
         this the-man that-I-gave to-him ACC the-book
         'This is the man to whom I gave the book'

      b. *ze ha-ish she-natáti et ha-séfer
         this the-man that-I-gave ACC the-book

Under one condition, however, this rule may be broken. If the prepositional case of the *head* noun is identical to that of the deleted coreferential argument within the relative clause, the use of the resumptive pronoun becomes optional:

(40)   *hu yasháv al ha-kisé   she-yashávti (aláv)*
       he sat   on the-chair that-I-sat   (on-it)
       'He sat on the chair on which I sat'

(41)   *hu lakáx et   ha-kisé   she-yashávti aláv*
       he took ACC   the-chair that-I-sat   on-it
       'He took the chair on which I sat'

(42)   **hu lakáx et   ha-kisé   she-yashávti*
       he took ACC   the-chair that-I-sat

One could again argue that the speaker merely "abides by his rules-of-grammar," which allow him an option in one context but not in another. But again, his rules-of-grammar seem to go by the *right* communicative choice: When the case-function of the deleted coreferential noun is recoverable from that of the head noun via identity, the resumptive pronoun—which "carries" the case marking—may be dropped, otherwise it may not.

The optional choice of pronoun in sentences such as (40) depends on other communicative considerations, related to the pragmatics of verb–object combinations. Thus, contrast (40) with (43):

(43)   a. *hu yasháv al ha-kisé   she-axálti aláv*
          he sat   on the-chair that-I-ate on-it
          'He sat on the chair on which I ate'

       b. *hu-yasháv al ha-kisé   she-axálti*
          he-sat   on the-chair that-I-ate
          {'He sat on the chair that I ate'
          {*He sat on the chair on which I ate'}

Thus, although sentence (43b) without the pronoun is acceptable, it is not acceptable under the same interpretation as (43a), since the sense of direct-object relativization ('I ate the chair') impinges upon the correct interpretation if the pronoun is not retained. Thus, in order to preserve the intended meaning, the speaker must *choose* not to exercise the option "available in his grammar" [namely (40)] and obligatorily retains the resumptive pronoun.

Finally, Kuno (1972, 1976) has observed that even in Standard English the CNPC may be broken under certain *pragmatic* conditions that boil down to the following considerations: If the speaker *judges* that the hearer has enough information, from the overt context, the pragmatics of the settings or whatever source, to help him reconstruct the underlying case-function relations of the argument *vis-à-vis* the verb, he finds it "more felicitous" to break the CNPC. But such communicative choice or judgment by the speaker is *in principle* noncategorial. It depends upon

1.3. The Gutting of the Data Base

compound *probabilities* the speaker assigns to the many variables which determine whether his message is likely to be misinterpreted by the hearer. Therefore, the CNPC is not a "matter of grammar," to be followed by the speaker as a deterministic automaton. Rather, it is used judiciously and intelligently (though not necessarily perfectly) by speakers who aim to communicate.

1.3.3.2. THE RELATIVE ORDER OF NOMINAL ARGUMENTS IN OLD ENGLISH

Through meticulous text analysis, García (1979) has shown that the relative order of the nominative versus nonnominative (or "secondary nominative") arguments in Anglo-Saxon texts is controlled only by discourse-pragmatic factors, and that in general an argument would tend to occupy the *earlier* syntactic position under the following circumstances:

1. If it is *more familiar* to the hearer
2. If the speaker wishes to *draw special attention* to it

In principle, both considerations involve a certain *probabilistic judgment* on the part of the speaker. The hearer's familiarity with an argument must be *assessed,* and while the preceding linguistic–overt context plays a role in such assessment, other considerations are also involved, such as *judging* the hearer's general familiarity with the subject matter as well as his ability to making other relevant inferences. In the same vein, the need to draw the hearer's attention to an argument depends on the speaker's *assessment* about where the hearer's attention is likely to be at any given moment, and this again is a matter of complex probabilistic judgment. These judgments that the speaker must make are *in principle* noncategorial, but they determine a "grammatical" rule such as the choice of word order. It seems, then, that once you have allowed the ghost into the machine (or the software into the hardware, the user into the grammar),[49] you cannot deny it the freedom of communicative choice, lest it would become indistinguishable from the machine.

1.3.3.3. PREVERBAL SUBJECTS IN SPANISH

Based on extensive oral text studies, Silva-Corvalán (1977) has shown that in Spanish the choice of SV syntax (as against V-first syntax) is controlled by discourse-pragmatic considerations that may be summarized as follows:

1. When the subject-topic's identity is very unambiguous, that is,
   a. There is no possibility for gender–number confusion.

---

[49] In discussing the relation between cognition and the "hardware" of neural structure, Chomsky (1975) uses the analogy of "The Ghost in the Machine," the title of Koestler's (1967) provocative monograph.

b. There are few nominal antecedents which could potentially be confused as coreferential with the subject.
c. There is no sudden, unexpected shift in the discourse topic.
d. There is no potential confusion of the topic due to the pragmatics of specific noun–verb combinations.

then V-first syntax predominates, with the subject either appearing postverbally, though most commonly appearing only as subject-agreement on the verb.

2. When one or more of conditions (a) through (d) above do not hold, S–V syntax is used, with either prenominal independent pronouns or definite full nouns.

The speaker, it seems, has to assess how difficult it is likely to be for the hearer to assign the correct reference–identification of the subject. And this is again, in principle, a complex, probabilistic, noncategorial judgment.

Similar data concerning the distribution of VS versus SV word order in Biblical Hebrew may be seen in Givón (1977a). In addition, Bolinger (1979) has noted a similar gradation of "degree of difficulty of assigning reference" in English discourse between the use of anaphoric pronouns (relatively easy identification) as against full definite nouns (relatively difficult identification). And Li and Thompson (1978) have demonstrated a similar gradation in Chinese discourse, in comparing the distribution of zero-anaphora, marked pronouns, and full definite nouns. Duranti and Keenan (1979) report a similar gradation—verb agreement > marked pronouns > full nouns > topic-shifted nouns—in Italian discourse.[50] We are thus dealing with a pervasive, universal phenomenon, and the speaker's judgment that is involved in making the choice among available "grammatical" devices is, in principle, noncategorial.

1.3.3.4. FROM TOPIC TO SUBJECT

In Chapter 5 (but see also Givón, 1976a), I discuss the historical process by which subject topic-shift ("left-dislocation") constructions eventually change into "neutral" subject constructions with grammatical agreement. The process may be summarized schematically as follows:

(44)   Topic-shift (marked)   Subject (unmarked)
        John, he left   ⟶   *John he-left*
        TOP PRO V   SUBJ AGR-V

Such a diachronic development is exceedingly common in natural language,[51] so much so that one is entitled to ask what it is that induces speakers to reinterpret the more-marked topic-shift construction into the

---

[50] For further discussion see Chapter 2.
[51] See cross-language survey in Givón (1976a). In Tok Pisin, a Pidgin language of the New Guinea Highlands, this process is reported to have occurred three successive times in the past 100 years (Sankoff, 1976).

1.3. The Gutting of the Data Base

less-marked subject construction. As discussed in Chapter 2, (but see also Duranti and Keenan, 1979), topic-shift constructions are used when the assignment of coreferential identity is judged to be *more difficult*, as compared with the use of the simple subject construction. Our question may be thus rephrased as follows:

(45) *Why should speakers increase the text-frequency of a certain "more marked" device, used when the speaker judges that the hearer will find it **harder to identify the topic**, to the point where all speakers will begin to interpret the use of such a device as being the 'unmarked case', that is, coding the situation where the topic is **easier to identify**?"*

The answer seems to be that speakers make communicative choices which are *not ideal*, but rather are a matter of judgment. And here speakers seem to choose the *overkill* strategy, that is, "when in doubt, double your effort." The high frequency of such a choice results in "demarking" a "marked" pattern, thus the diachronic change summarized in (44).

Now, the demarking of marked constructions is one of the major aspects of diachronic syntactic change, ranging over a great variety of construction types.[52] The inescapable conclusion is therefore that the speakers' judgment—in this case their choice to *overuse* a grammatical device for extra communicative insurance—is once again the live, non-deterministic ghost in the machine.

1.3.3.5. REFERENCE AND DEFINITENESS IN HEBREW

In Modern Hebrew, as well as in many other languages,[53] the numeral *one* is used to mark *referential* indefinite nouns. Thus consider:[54]

(46) a. hu kaná   séfer-*xad* etmól   (REF-INDEF)
         he bought book-*one* yesterday
         'He bought a book yesterday'

    b. hu lo   káná   (af) séfer   (NONREF)
         he NEG bought (any) book
         'He didn't buy a/any book'

    c. ha-ishá   ha-zót hi morá   (NONREF)
         the-woman the-this she teacher
         'This woman is a teacher'

    d. ha-isha   ha-zot hi morá-*xat*   she-hikarti   (REF-
         the-woman the-this she teacher-*one* that-I-met   INDEF)
         'This woman is a certain teacher that I met . . .'

---

[52] This is most common in word-order change, where rather than the order AB changing to BA, the markedness valuation of both coexisting word-orders AB and BA changes. For further discussion, see Givón (1977a) and Ard (1975).

[53] See Givón (1977b). This marking system can be found in all Creoles, in Turkish, Old French, Sherpa, Mandarin (partial), and many others.

[54] For more details see Givón (1975b).

There are cases when the noun is *logically* referential, that is, when it is clear that there must exist a *specific* individual in order for the sentence in which it is an object-of-the-verb to be true, but nevertheless the speaker of Hebrew will not use the numeral *one* which otherwise obligatorily marks referential-indefinite nouns. Thus, consider the discourse context in (47) and the three possible endings (47a,b,c):

(47) axaré she-gamárti   la-avód, yarádti   la-xanút
after   that-I-finished to-work I-went-down to-the-store
ve-kaníti   séfer . . .
and-I-bought book
'After I finished working, I went down to the store and I bought a book . . .

  a. . . . ve-áz   haláxti habáyta.
       and-then I-went home
      . . . and then I went home'. (end of story)

  b. *. . . she-xavér-xad   shel-í himlíts   aláv.
      that-friend-one of-me recommended on-it
     . . . that a friend recommended to me.
     Ve-áz   haláxti habáyta ve-karáti otó, ve- . . .
     and-then I-went home   and-I-read it, and- . . .
     and then I went home and I read it, and . . .'

  c. * . . . u-mihárti   habáyta ve-karáti otó, ve-zé   séfer
    . . . and-I-hurried home and-I-read it and-this book
       metsuyán, beemét.
       excellent   really
    . . . and I hurried home and read it, and it's really a terrific book'. (end of story)

From a strictly logical point of view, the book discussed in (47) is referential and has unique referential identity, since it was asserted to have been bought. It is, however, not marked by *one*. And the consequence of this is that the only compatible ending is (47a), where the *specific identity* of the book is *irrelevant* to the communication. On the other hand, the endings (47b) and (47c) make it clear that the specific identity of the book is indeed relevant, and they are thus infelicitous in the context where *book* was not marked by *one*. What is at issue, then, is the speaker's judgment as to whether the specific identity of the book was or was not *a central, relevant portion of the communication*. That is, whether *book* is raised as a *topic for further discussion* as against immediate *decay* within the overall message.

1.3. The Gutting of the Data Base

On the other hand, if *book* is modified by *one*, as in (48) below, the exact opposite acceptability of the endings obtains, whereby (47a) becomes ungrammatical–infelicitous while (47b) and (47c) become acceptable endings:

(48) axaré she-gamárti   la-avód, yerádti   la-xanút
      after that-I-finished to-work I-went-down to-the-store
      ve-kaníti   séfer-xad . . .
      and-I-bought book-*one*
      'After I finished working, I went down to the store and I bought a book, . . .'

Now, one could claim that the notion "central–relevant portion of the communication" is formalizable and therefore the speaker "obeys a categorial rule-of-grammar" rather than "makes communicative choices." But one could proceed to show that the criteria for "centrality to the message" can become more and more subtle, to the point where the notion of "rule" becomes moot. For example, if one used *paper* rather than *book* in (47), there would be a marked tendency not to accept *one paper* in (48), because *under normal circumstances* one always reads the same paper on the way home, and further the information gleaned out of the daily papers is normally predictable, nonunique and often trivial. Therefore, obviously the actual identity of the paper could not be important or central to the communication—even if **what** one read in the papers would be central and in fact become the topic of the next portion of discourse. But this observation, and the "grammatical" choice of not using *one* to modify *paper*, is grounded in the assumption of *what is normative* for both the speaker and the hearer. Now suppose the hearer knows that the speaker never reads the papers, let alone the same paper every day. This increases the *probability* that the selection of a *particular* paper was in fact of some importance in this case, and thus increases the acceptability of referring to that paper as *one paper* in Hebrew. It is easy to see, then, that one could go on and on in constructing finer and finer pragmatic factors bearing on the choice of *one*, and that *in principle* they depend on the *probabilistic judgment* of "norm" and are therefore not a matter of categorial rule of grammar.

1.3.4. Language Out of Context, Language without Languages

One could go on documenting the kind of empirical irresponsibility that has flourished in linguistics under the direct impact of transformational-generative grammar. The only reason why it seemed possible to so many of the practitioners that a formal model of competence and rules-of-grammar was within reach is because the study of dreamed-up artificial sentences outside their discourse context and detached from communicative function made it appear that the task at hand was manageable and finite. The trivialization of "theory" thus made it possible to trivialize the data as well. Indeed, only the most *sanitized* data could appear compatible with THE MODEL.

Within such a hermetic paradigm, the discussion of "language universals" went on as a matter of course without any serious attempt to ascertain the facts of languages other than the standard Euro-centric fare, mostly English.[55] And when the weight of bewildering cross-language diversity threatened to overpower the practitioner, he could always resort to tried-and-true abstraction, where languages are claimed to be "underlyingly" similar but "transformationally" diverse. As an illustration of the early transformational approach to substantive universals, consider the following quotation:

> Obviously the claim that languages are highly similar in their deep structures, if true, has important implications for the contrastive analysis of grammatical systems. For it means, in effect, that the contrastive analyst could concentrate most of his attention upon the transformational rules of the languages he is comparing, investigating the ways in which these rules operate to change similar deep structures into possibly different surface structures ... [Schachter, 1967].

One of the consequences of this abstract approach to "deep universals" which do not manifest in actual attested utterances, has been a rash of papers on the typology of "underlying word-order." In such a vein, Bach (1970) could claim that Amharic—one of the most rigid SOV languages on record—was really, "underlyingly" a VSO language, among other things because of the historically frozen VSO order of the pronominal elements around the verb. Similarly, McCawley (1970) could claim that English—one of the very few relatively-rigid SVO languages on record—was really, "underlyingly," a VSO language. Similarly, German was at various times claimed to be "underlyingly" an SOV language, with the SVO—V-second syntax of the main clause transformationally derived, or alternatively a V-second–SVO language underlyingly, with the SOV, historically frozen order in subordinate clauses transformationally derived. In this fashion, syntactic typology, rather than being a matter of fact, became a matter of economy, simplicity, and various ingenious "proofs." Thus Ross (1970) could claim that the transformational rule of *gapping* is determined not by surface word-order but by underlying word-order, thus "showing" that the rule of gapping is typologically consistent in its application. Sanders and Thai (1972), could then contribute "corrections" to Ross's generalization whereby an even more abstract typology could be achieved.

Altogether lost in the shuffle were Greenberg's (1966) original ob-

---

[55] The apocryphal tradition attributes to Paul Postal the remark that "a language universal must be attested in at least one language, if possible."

servations of the implicational hierarchies obtaining in the typology of word-order and morphotactics. Such observations are anathema to any categorial approach to grammar, where less-than-100% universals, that is, "tendencies," "probabilities," and statistical correlations are considered tainted evidence. The whole field of study of the interdependencies between language universals was thus ruled out of the investigation.

Just as damaging to the empirical well-being of linguistics was the cavalier treatment accorded the data base of diachronic change. As will be shown in Chapters 5 and 6, the synchronic structure of language bears the indelible marks of old as well as ongoing diachronic change. Many language universals are *mediated* primarily via constraints governing possible change, rather than constraints on synchronic states per se. But, in principle, data of language change are messy, interdependent, and noncategorial, where the generalizations are often statistical–probabilistic in nature. They are thus incompatible with the sanitized, abstract data base supporting the postulates of "competence."[56] Given the rejection of this rich but confusing data base, it is far from accidental that the few diachronic studies of syntax undertaken within this constricted framework turned to the investigation of "change in underlying representation," an invisible postulate that is an artifact of the simplicity criteria of the formalism itself. In this vein, Lightfoot could proceed to ridicule his illustrious predecessors by observing that:

> Thus the neogrammarians were unable to do anything with syntactic change because of a failure to apprehend the logical status of an abstract, formal grammar, to distinguish a level of representation distinct from surface structures, which would enable them to relate sentences and/or structures. In other words, they had no (generative) theory of syntax. Things appear to be different today: diachronic syntacticians have a notion of a grammar and can view syntactic change as *change(s) in an abstract system* . . . [1976b, p. 2; emphasis added].

Under such an analysis, irregularity due to an ongoing complex set of changes can be claimed to be "distance between the *abstract* and *surface* syntactic representation." While the subsequent move towards reregularizing the surface—the simplificatory phase—may be viewed as "change in the underlying representation" which "brings it back to closer reflection of surface structure." Once again, abstract nomenclature reigns over both fact and explanation.

1.4. CONCLUSION

Traditionally, empiricists have been noted for their love affair with the data and meticulousness in obtaining it, while remaining indifferent

---

[56] Here Saussure's rejection of the relevance of diachronic evidence to understanding the synchronic structure of language was adopted, a priori, by transformational–generative linguistics.

to theory and explanation. On the other hand, rationalists have been known for their bold and complex theoretical constructs and explanations, often remaining naive or downright sloppy in their approach to the gathering of data. Thus Skinner's concept of "stimulus–response" is just as *theoretically vacuous* as is Descartes's description of animals as automata *empirically irresponsible*. The curious thing about transformational-generative grammar is that it somehow succeeded in combining the worst methodological features of the two traditional schools of Western epistemology: The theoretical vacuity of empiricism and the empirical irresponsibility of rationalism. Such a synthesis is, to my mind, unprecedented in the annals of science. If one agrees with Chomsky's view of the central role that the study of language must play in elucidating the nature of human cognition and human behavior—indeed in constructing a Theory of Man—then one must reject transformational-generative grammar as a pseudotheory and useless methodology, and then start afresh.

2 GRAMMAR AND FUNCTION
toward a discourse definition of syntax

2.1. INTRODUCTION[1]

Of the insights introduced into the study of syntax by Harris (1957) and Chomsky (1957), none stands out more brightly than the notion of *transformational relation,* that is, the view of the syntactic structure of most sentence types as a *variant* or *function* of the structure of some more *basic* ("kernel") type. While the initial insight has undergone over the years a great number of formal modifications, it has remained an implicit core ingredient—under various more or less transparent guises—of most contemporary approaches to the study of syntax. Another insight, just as fundamental but often tacitly assumed rather than explicitly discussed, has always accompanied the notion of transformational relation. It involves the privileged status of one sentence type— the *main, declarative, affirmative, active* clause—as the "basic," "neutral" pattern, in reference to which all other syntactic types may be described. Since this insight has seldom, if ever, been challenged, and since in one guise or another it has been shared for millennia by philologists, philosophers, and grammarians, it is perhaps in order to inquire into the reasons behind its immense durability.

The few explicit arguments that have been used in the past—mostly the more recent past—to justify the privileged status of the main, declarative, affirmative, active clause-type in syntax, have been without exception of a formal, system-internal nature. They may be divided into the following, hopefully exhaustive, types:

---

[1] I am indebted to Paul Schachter, Ed Keenan, Robert Hetzron, Dwight Bolinger, and Harry Whitaker for suggestions and comments on earlier versions of this chapter.

1. *The Completeness argument.* Given a rather theory-neutral[2] goal for a syntactic description, the one of attempting to account for the *inventory of meaningful elements* in a language and their *distributions,* one may observe that the greatest distributional *freedom* and *variety* of meaningful elements occurs in the main, declarative, affirmative active clause-type. This is true of the distribution of both lexical items and syntactic constructions. On the other hand, the distribution of meaningful elements—both lexical items and syntactic constructions—in all other sentence–clause types is always more constrained.[3] The core of the completeness argument runs like this: Given the preliminary, formalism-neutral goal articulated above, it would be futile to assign to any other syntactic type except the main, declarative, affirmative, active clause the status of *point of reference* in syntactic description. Such a practice would inevitably result in a great number of meaningful elements—both lexical items and construction types—not being accounted for.

2. *The Dependency argument.*[4] Formally, the Dependency argument involves the assertion that given the syntactic variants B,C,D and the neutral pattern A, one can show that the structure of B,C,D is a *function of* the structure of A, but not vice versa. Such an argument per se is fallacious, and for reasons that are easy to discern. If indeed it is true that $B = F^b (A)$, $C = F^c (A)$, and $D = F^d (A)$, and if the functions F^b, F^c, and F^d are fully formalized, then it is mathematically possible to define—in principle with the same degree of ease—the structure of A as a *counter-function* of either of the three above, that is, $1/F^b$, $1/F^c$, or $1/F^d$, respectively.[5] Nevertheless, the argument of Dependency is not altogether lost and may be recast as follows: If F^b, F^c and F^d turn out to be *simpler* functions than their corresponding counter-functions $1/F^b$, $1/F^c$, and $1/F^d$ (respectively), then A will indeed be selected as the neutral point of reference. In other words, to the extent that the Dependency argument has any utility, it is not independent of questions of *complexity* or *economy.*

3. *The Economy argument.* Underlying the Economy argument, in all scientific inquiry, is the tacit assumption that *in the absence of any empirical grounds* for choosing between two alternative formalisms

[2] In principle, no goal is *theory*-neutral, so that *formalism*-neutral is perhaps a more realistic term. This particular goal, in the framework of the approach I am pursuing here, is only a preliminary—though necessary—step in the investigation.

[3] As I will show later on, the converse generalization is also true, namely that the freedom of distribution of the main, declarative, affirmative, active clause within the grammar (i.e., as embedded in other clause types) as well as in text is also greater. All these distributional facts can be explained by reference to the function of the various clause-types in communication, that is, in discourse.

[4] For this argument as well as for further discussion I am indebted to Ed Keenan (personal communication).

[5] Translated into the current linguistic parlance, "if you can write a formal transformation from A to B, you ought to be able to write one from B to A."

2.1. Introduction

(models) which describe the data *in an equally exhaustive fashion*, the mathematically less complex model is to be prefered. The reader will quickly recognize this argument as representing one half of the common-sensical golden rule of *rationis sufficientis* (see Section 1.2.2.). It is thus an obviously valid argument, provided one does not promote it to the status of theoretical prime.[6]

4. *The Marked Structure argument.* The Marked Structure argument, which has particular relevance to linguistics, is in essence a combined reflection of the preceding Dependency (2) and Economy (3) arguments. While suffering from a great number of potential counter examples, it nevertheless possesses a considerable, indeed seductive, intuitive appeal, in so far as the syntactic and morphological structure of a language is concerned. The argument may be formally constructed as follows: In judging two variant syntactic patterns[7] A and B as to their relative "basicness," if one discovers that all the components of A are also found in B but in addition another element, C, is also a component of B but not of A, and thus one considers C as the element which *marks* B as being distinct from A, then one is justified in considering A the basic, neutral, unmarked type and B the marked type. While the intuitive appeal of this argument to any student of natural languages is rather transparent, one must point out a number of grave pitfalls associated with it.[8] To begin with note that if the Completeness argument (1) and the Marked Structure argument (4) are taken in their purely formal sense, they yield *mutually contradictory* results. That is, argument (1) predicts that, potentially, there may appear more *meaningful elements* in the neutral sentence type than in variant types. On the other hand, argument (4) predicts that some *grammatical markers* will **not** appear in the neutral sentence type but only in variant types. What is at issue, I believe, is the need for a principled criterion (or set of criteria) by which one could differentiate "meaningful elements"—whose distribution is wider in the neutral sentence types—from "grammatical markers," whose distribution is wider in the variant types. The discerning reader should have by now detected a familiar theme, namely the traditional distinction between *lexical items* and *grammatical* (or *inflectional*) *morphology*.[9] In a sense, recognizing this makes the difficulty a bit more

---

[6] With this noted, one must also observe that it is very natural in any science to forget that the caveat "in the absence of any empirical grounds" also enjoins the practitioner to go and look for *substantive* reasons for preferring one formal model over another, that is, for more *data*. As I have suggested in Chapter 1, this natural tendency is evident in present-day linguistics.

[7] That is, in the prevailing terminology, two transformationally related types.

[8] It is reasonably clear that these pitfalls are not likely to go away through any amount of formal argumentation. As lamentable as such a state of affairs may be, it nevertheless leaves the door open for an eventual resolution on more substantive grounds. But the least one could do at this point is make the difficulties explicit.

[9] For the moment I forego considering the fact that the Completeness argument (1) involves not only lexical items but also construction types, see further below.

tolerable, since by a great number of criteria—most of those of a *substantive* nature and referring to a variety of areas and properties of language (morphology, word-level phonology, suprasegmentals, syntax, semantics, functional-pragmatics, diachronic development)—it is indeed possible to specify the difference between lexical and grammatical morphemes.[10] The difficulty is thus resolvable to quite an extent, provided one is willing to extend the discussion beyond the purely formal level.

An apparent difficulty still remaining is the fact that the Completeness argument (1) also mentions the freedom of distribution of *construction types*, that is, the embedding of one sentence type within another. This again turns out to be only an apparent difficulty. This is so because in judging the complexity of any sentence type per se, one may eliminate from consideration the instances—all of them *optional* in the normal sense used in the transformational literature—in which another sentence is embedded within the sentence type under discussion. In other words, only components which are obligatory and *necessary* to the structure of a marked or unmarked variant will be considered as criterial for the purpose of applying the Marked Structure argument.[11]

A more serious problem with the Marked Structure argument is the fact that out of the three types of clues used in syntax, *morphemes*, *intonation* and *word-order*, only the first one could be clearly subjected to the rigid criteria of the Marked Structure argument. It is a little harder to justify "complexity of intonation," although with the help of other, more substantive criteria it could presumably be done. And if two construction types differ from each other solely in word-order, it is hard to see by what purely formal arguments the order AB can be shown to be less marked than BA.

All this is not to say that arguments (1)–(4) are not useful. They do indeed possess a considerable *heuristic* merit as far as they go. However, since they are purely formal and system-internal, they contribute nothing to explaining *why* the syntax of human language is the way it is. Within an approach whereby the formalization of linguistic facts is only a *prelude* to explanation, one must seek more *substantive* criteria for supporting the privileged status of the main, declarative, affirmative, active clause in syntax. Such criteria, I hope to show, will in turn yield an explanation of seemingly "formal" properties of syntax, an explanation that will make reference to the use of language in human communication. The criteria I intend to demonstrate shortly involve the notion of *discourse presupposition*, that is, the *degree of presupposed background*

---

[10] More formal differentiation between the two is also conceivable, see some discussion in Givón (1972a, Chapter 2).

[11] In a more substantive vein, one may add that sentences are not used to mark the function of other sentences (or of smaller subparts of sentences), while grammatical morphemes are. Sentences are used to structure ("convey," "communicate") meaningful elements.

2.1. Introduction

upon which a sentence is used. With respect to such a criterion, I hope to demonstrate that—with one exception[12]—the main, declarative, affirmative, active sentence has the **lowest** presuppositional complexity in discourse, as compared to all other types. In a number of instances, the degree of presuppositional complexity boils down to a special case: How difficult a task the speaker thinks that the hearer will have in assigning unique reference to an argument ("participant," "noun phrase") in discourse.

Once all syntactic variants are graded as to their degree of presuppositionality, I will show that a number of formal properties of these variants correlate to their degree of presuppositionality:

1. More presuppositional variants exhibit greater *syntactic complexity*[13] vis-à-vis the neutral pattern (the Marked Structure argument (4), above).
2. More presuppositional variants exhibit greater *distributional restrictions* than the neutral pattern (the Completeness argument (1), above).
3. More presuppositional variants are *grammaticalized later* by children, so that at the very least their *syntax* is acquired later[14] than that of less presuppositional variants.
4. All other things being equal, more presuppositional variants often tend to exhibit greater *syntactic conservatism*, most commonly in the area of word-order change.

With respect to all these properties, I will attempt to sketch out why one should expect them to correlate to the discourse-presuppositionality of syntactic construction. While doing so, I will point out why syntax *cannot* be explained or understood without reference to its use in communication. The formal or "structural" properties of syntax will be thus shown, to quite a degree,[15] to emanate from the properties of human discourse. Finally, I will also illustrate that at least in a number of well-defined cases, a *statistical* property of texts must also play a part in explaining formal properties of syntax:

---

[12] The exception involves existential–presentative constructions and will be discussed in detail further below.

[13] Even given the discussion of the preceding Marked Structure argument, there is going to remain a certain measure of *relativity* in defining the more "complex" variants. That is, in some instances they may be more complex relative to the neutral routine used in processing the "normal," more frequent sentence type (see further discussion in Chapter 4).

[14] As I shall argue further below (but see also Chapter 5), the acquisition of the relevant *pragmatics* or communicative function is a much earlier process, and only later on the child "syntacticizes" his communicative system, condensing discourse-pragmatics into the tight, "structural" patterns of syntax.

[15] As will be shown in Chapter 5, a certain "residue" of syntax is likely to remain, but even that residue can be explained by reference to some features of the human communicative system.

5. The neutral, less presuppositional main, active, declarative, affirmative clause-type is also the *most frequent* in discourse.[16]

I will show that this observation is absolutely crucial for our understanding of the use of language in communication, and that Chomsky's a priori rejection of the relevance of statistical considerations to the study of syntax is unwarranted.[17]

2.2. THE DISCOURSE PRESUPPOSITIONS OF SYNTACTIC CONSTRUCTIONS

Without citing the relevant arguments, the treatment of presupposition here is informal and does not follow Keenan's distinction between "logical" and "pragmatic" presupposition (1971), but rather follows Karttunen (1974) in assuming that **all** presuppositional phenomena in natural language are *pragmatic*, that is, defined in terms of assumptions the speaker makes about what the hearer is likely to accept without challenge.[18] One may thus distinguish between the (presuppositional) *background* for an utterance and the *assertion* the speaker is making.[19] The phenomenon of presuppositionality ("backgroundness," "topicality") in natural language is much more complex than in logic. Thus, for example, I will consider various instances which come under the logical label of *definite description*, such as definitization, pronominalization and topic shifting, as presuppositional, though, per se, they do not involve the speaker's assumptions about the hearer's *belief* in the truth–falsity of propositions. Rather, they involve the assumptions the speaker makes about the hearer's *ability* to uniquely identify ("establish unique reference for") a reference–argument.

The syntactic variants to be discussed here fall into a number of categories:

---

[16] Obvious exceptions here would be specialized discourse types, such as law codiciles, exhortative poetry, or prayer. But it is a reasonable assumption that human language did not evolve with these discourse types playing the more central role in communication.

[17] "Despite the undeniable interest and importance of semantic and statistical studies of language, they appear to have no relevance to the problem of determining and characterizing the set of grammatical utterances . . . [Chomsky, 1957, p. 17]." Such an exclusion is only possible if the goals of the inquiry are defined in the most narrow, explanation-free fashion.

[18] Thus, what Edward Keenan (1971) refers to as "logical" presuppositions may only be a specialized, restricted case of "pragmatic" presupposition (cf. Karttunen, 1974).

[19] "Assertion" is obviously relevant to declarative sentences. Furthermore, it is easy to show that the background for a linguistic utterance cannot be finitely specified, since it includes all the background knowledge in the mind of the hearer. It is obvious, however, that speakers do distinguish, in a rough heuristic fashion, between the features of the presuppositional background that are "more relevant" for a particular utterance in a given context, and those that are "more *remotely* in the background."

2.2. The Discourse Presuppositions of Syntactic Constructions

1. *Strictly presuppositional constructions.* Relative Clauses, Cleft, Pseudo-Cleft, and WH-questions. These need not be discussed here since their presuppositional nature has been discussed extensively in the literature.[20]
2. *Embedded clause.* These are to be contrasted with the neutral main clause.
3. *Other speech acts:* Imperative, Interrogative and Negative.[21] The first two are to be contrasted with the neutral declarative, and the latter with the neutral affirmative.
4. *Constructions involving degree of definiteness–topicality of arguments:* Definite-Accusative, Topic-Shift, Passive, Anaphoric-Pronouns, Existential-Presentatives. These will be contrasted with the neutral active pattern whose subject is definite and accusative object indefinite.

2.2.1. Definiteness and the Least-Marked Pattern

Following Keenan (1976a) I will assume here that the subject of the neutral sentence type is *definite* rather than indefinite. This clearly puts a more presuppositional construction rather than a less presuppositional one in the privileged position of reference-point for syntax. I will return to the motivation for such a choice further below, when discussing the status of existential-presentative constructions. At this point I would simply like to illustrate that the decision—as well as Keenan's discussion (1976a)—are well motivated by the *statistical* properties of human discourse. That is, in human language *in context* the subject is *overwhelmingly* definite, and the data in Table 2.1 illustrate this fact.

As I will later argue,[22] both the statistical distribution in any single language and cross-language evidence cited in Keenan (1976a) and Givón (1976a) strongly support the decision to select neutral-pattern sentences with *definite* subjects as the reference point or "unmarked" type in syntax. The situation is much more problematic, however, when considering the definiteness status of accusative–direct objects.[23] As can be seen in Table 2.1, direct objects are roughly 50% indefinite and 50% definite in texts, so that a decision based on text frequency is, per se, not possible. Notice, however, that the 50% indefinites are the *bulk* of

---

[20] For an extensive discussion, see Takizala (1972) and Schachter (1973).

[21] In Chapter 3, I will show that there are grounds for considering the *negative*-declarative sentence as a different speech act, as compared to its corresponding affirmative. But since negatives cross-classify with other speech acts (while the others—declarative, imperative, interrogative—seldom cross-classify among themselves), we are obviously dealing with a "more subtle" special case.

[22] But see also, Section 1.3.2.1.

[23] Indirect and/or locative objects, the only other major object type involved commonly in the subcategorization of verbs, will not be discussed at this point. The average definiteness for these object types in text is roughly 95% for datives and 80% for locatives.

TABLE 2.1
Definite Subjects and Objects in Declarative-Affirmative-Active Clauses

Discourse type[a]	Subject				Direct object			
	Definite		Indefinite		Definite		Indefinite	
	N	Percentage	N	Percentage	N	Percentage	N	Percentage
Nonfiction	43	87	6	13	24	48	25	52
Fiction	160	90	17	10	123	64	68	36
News	36	80	9	20	15	33	30	67
Sports	63	98	1	2	31	48	33	52
Total	302	91	33	9	193	56	156	44

[a] The counts were made in the following texts: Nonfiction—Chomsky (1973, pp. 3–12), Fiction—L'Amour (1965, pp. 1–25), News—*The Los Angeles Times*, front page, 9-1-74, Sports—*The Los Angeles Times*, front page of sports section, 9-1-74. All are narrative texts, and I concur with Longacre (1979) and Hinds (1979) in considering narrative as the most basic discourse type. A law codicile, for example, will have a much higher ratio of indefinite subjects.

indefinite nouns in the text, that is, out of the total of 189 indefinite nouns in subject and direct object positions in the texts counted, 156 or 82% are found in the direct-object position. The accusative or direct-object position is thus the major avenue *for introducting new referential arguments*[24] into discourse, at least in English. Whether this is an argument for choosing sentences with *indefinite* accusative objects over those with definite ones as the neutral pattern in syntax remains an open question. The number of languages in which the syntactic pattern of clauses with definite accusatives is different from that of clauses with indefinite accusative is not large, but several typological possibilities exist, and in all of those one must resolve this dilemma if one assumes that one pattern but not the other is "more basic." In terms of degree of presuppositionality, however, sentences with indefinite accusatives are obviously *less marked* than those with definite accusatives, at least with respect to the degree to which the identity of the referents is presupposed by the speaker to be known to the hearer.[25] (In Table 2.2 I show that the degree of definiteness of the direct object has no effect on the degree of definiteness of the subject.) Finally, Table 2.3 illustrates the fact that dative–benefactive objects are, if anything, even higher in

[24] Of the other object types, datives and locatives are of high definiteness in texts, instrumentals were not counted and manner adverbials are nonreferential.

[25] Here the general criteria remain a problem nonetheless. In Givón (1975c) I suggested that there is evidence that in general (in terms of text frequency), human languages employ a communicative strategy whereby there is only *one bit of new information per proposition* in discourse (defined, tentatively, in terms of lexical word). This observation does not necessarily obviate the thrust of the argument above, since that "one bit" may include the entire VP, only the V-complement, or only the subject (as in cleft-focus). Here I merely like to point out that there is no automatic correlation between "definite" and "old information."

TABLE 2.2
Correlation between the Definiteness of Direct Objects and Subjects

	Indefinite object				Definite object			
	Definite subject		Indefinite subject		Definite subject		Indefinite subject	
Discourse type	N	Percentage	N	Percentage	N	Percentage	N	Percentage
Fiction[a]	32	100	—	—	73	100	—	—
News[b]	24	86	4	14	20	95	1	5
Total	56	94	4	6	93	98	1	2

[a] The fiction text counted is Blatty (1971, pp. 3–16).
[b] The news counted is from three combined stories in *The Los Angeles Times* (Section VII, December 5, 1974).

definiteness in English texts than subjects, and that locative objects, though overwhelmingly nonhuman, are also rather high in definiteness.[26]

2.2.2. Embedded Clauses

One type of embedded clause—namely, the relative clause—need not be discussed here at all, since its presuppositionality has been discussed extensively (see footnote 20). The reader may refer back to the discussion in Section 1.2.3.10, where Emonds's constraints are treated. The literature, in particular Hooper and Thompson (1973) and Bolinger (1979), makes it rather clear that in general main clause phenomena appear in embedded clauses when those embedded clauses are either part or the major part of the assertion. Conversely, when embedded clauses are presupposed rather than asserted, they do *not* exhibit main-clause phenomena. Thus, rather than contradicting the contention that main clauses are, in general, the locus of the asserted material ("are less presuppositional") and should be considered the reference point in syntax, the existence of nonpresuppositional embedded clauses actually *confirms* the general rule. This is so because in terms of their behavioral–syntactic properties, asserted nonmain clauses turn out to behave like main clauses.

---

[26] The high definiteness ratio of dative–benefactives is predictable from the fact that they are overwhelmingly human, that humans tend to make humans the topic of their conversation, and that topics are definite (see general discussion in Givón, 1976a, and instructive text-counts from Russian in Greenberg, 1974). The high definiteness ratio of locatives is at first surprising, since they are overwhelmingly nonhuman (see Greenberg, 1974). However, they are often introduced in discourse *relationally*. That is, once the general locale (*house*) or ownership has been established, sublocales (**the kitchen, the livingroom**) are automatically definitized via uniqueness. For text counts and discussion, see Linde (1974) and Linde and Labov (1975).

TABLE 2.3
Degree of Definiteness of Dative and Locative Objects

	Locative objects				Dative objects			
	Definite		Indefinite		Definite		Indefinite	
Text[a]	N	Percentage	N	Percentage	N	Percentage	N	Percentage
WE	102	85	19	15	76	98	1	2
HA	97	83	20	17	36	95	2	5

[a] The texts counted are Wells (1975, pp. 1–29) and Haycox (1975, pp. 5–11).

2.2.3. Nondeclarative Speech Acts

In this section I will outline the argument why nondeclarative speech acts should be viewed as more presuppositional than the declarative. Of the construction-types to be discussed, WH-questions need not be mentioned, since their presuppositional status has already been established (see footnote 20). The status of negatives will be summarized only briefly here, since it is the topic of the entire Chapter 2, where the evidence is discussed in great detail.

Imperatives and questions are *manipulative* speech acts, as compared to declaratives which are not. That is, while the declarative presupposes the *passive* agreement of the hearer to listen, manipulative speech acts must also involve the speaker's assessment of his/her *right to manipulate,* with all the social-scale factors that are involved. Further, the speaker must also assess (or "have presuppositions about") the *likelihood of the hearer's compliance,* or the *likelihood that the hearer may act on his own accord* and thus need not be manipulated. Furthermore, it is easy to show that the presuppositions the speaker makes about the *state of the world* prior to the manipulation are more extensive than those he makes prior to uttering a felicitous declarative sentence. All these claims may be found in a more formal version in Gordon and Lakoff (1971)[27] under the label of *conversational postulates.* Without resorting to the same degree of formality as Gordon and Lakoff (1971), let me briefly illustrate these claims with three speech acts based upon the same "underlying" proposition.

(1) a. *Joe went home.* (DECL)
 b. *Go home (, Joe)!* (IMP)
 c. *Did Joe go home?* (yes–no Q)

All three speech acts share the presuppositions associated with the lexical items involved (*go, home*) as well as with the proper name *Joe.* It

[27] The *focus* of the argument there is, of course, not the same.

2.2. The Discourse Presuppositions of Syntactic Constructions

is conventional to say that in declarative speech acts the speaker presupposes (a) that he himself knows the truth and is telling it sincerely; (b) that the hearer needs to be informed; and (c) that the hearer is willing to listen and, presumably, learn. Condition (a) may be equivalent to a *sincerity* condition and reformulated as: "the speaker is *sincere* in performing his speech act," But that condition is *equally* true for imperatives and questions. Next, condition (b) may be shown to be present—if somewhat trivially—in imperatives and questions as well. That is, since both are speech acts, they are used to inform the hearer—who presumably could not know it otherwise—that the speaker is "ordering" or "questioning" him. In the same sense condition (c) must also be present in the two manipulative speech acts. While it is true that the *communicative role* of these three conditions is *more peripheral* in manipulations than in declaratives, that is, they are not as central to the *intent* of the speech act,[28] one may nevertheless observe that all speech acts—being *speech* acts—subsume the conversational postulates of the declarative.[29] With this in mind, one can see how the conversational postulates associated with imperatives and questions are incremental upon those associated with the declarative. Thus, informally, the utterer of (1b) above presupposes that:

(2)   a.   Joe is not home at the time of ordering.
          b.   Joe is capable of going home, that is, he is not incapacitated, he has *control* over his actions.
          c.   The speaker is entitled (by some social-gradient criteria) to order Joe to go home.
          d.   Joe is somewhat reluctant and may not go home without prodding.

Similarly, the speaker presupposes while uttering (1c) that:

(3)   a.   He himself does not know *for sure* whether Joe is or isn't home.
          b.   The hearer does know the answer.
          c.   The hearer was not about to volunteer the information on his own, but
          d.   The hearer is nonetheless not altogether antagonistic toward giving the answer, if asked.

---

[28] They are obviously more central in declaratives, where what the speaker has to tell the hearer is the very core of the transaction.

[29] In transformational terms, one may say that manipulative speech acts are "embedded under a declarative."

e. The social gradient is such that the speaker does not feel entitled to exert stronger manipulative pressure upon the hearer, but

f. On the other hand the social gradient is such that the speaker is entitled to make at least a polite demand upon the hearer.

While these characterizations are informal, I believe they support the main point, namely that a much more complex speech-act-related presuppositions ("postulates") are involved when manipulative speech acts are performed.

In addition, Bolinger (1975) has shown that yes–no questions are not entirely neutral with respect to presupposing the truth of either the affirmative or negative proposition that is the core of the query. Rather, the speaker is already *somewhat biased* toward either the affirmative or the negative. That "bias," I believe, may be legitimately characterized as a "background-to-discourse presupposition."[30] To sum up, then, it is reasonably clear that imperatives and questions are presuppositionally more complex, more marked than the declarative.

One may begin by observing that in narrative, manipulative speech acts are outnumbered by a very wide margin by declarative sentences. I will return to discussing the significance of such an observation[31] in Chapter 7, in the context of discussing the phylogenetic development of human discourse. If this is indeed the case, then it would obviously be counterproductive to designate the much rarer types as the point of reference for syntax; that is, if one is serious about imputing some *psychological* validity to such a point of reference.

2.2.4. Topicality and Topic Recoverability

In this subsection I will discuss a more subtle variant of presuppositional markedness, involving presuppositions the speaker holds about

---

[30] Philosophers and logicians may shudder at any attempt to characterize the speaker's commitment to the truth of a proposition as "semi-presupposition." But there is much evidence to suggest that the notion of presupposition relevant to human language is not always a categorial matter of the choice between true and false. Quite often it is a matter of *degree* of commitment to believe, most likely a *probabilistic* integer assigned to propositions. This actually follows from the pragmatic definition of presupposition in terms of the speaker's beliefs (Karttunen, 1974), fortified with the common-sensical observation that humans may have more than two points on their scale of belief. Their commitment may be thus quantified over a *continuum*. For some language-specific evidence for such a continuum, see Givón and Kimenyi (1974).

[31] I am again assuming that narrative texts are more basic in human discourse. Special types of texts may have totally different ratios of manipulative versus declarative speech acts. Thus traffic signs and law codiciles may have a high proportion of imperatives, while exams may have a high proportion of interrogatives. Furthermore, it may well be that the communicative behavior of very young children—before and at the very start of the one-word stage—has a higher ratio of manipulatives over declaratives, and here ontogenesis may also reflect phylogenesis (see Chapter 7).

2.2. The Discourse Presuppositions of Syntactic Constructions

the hearer's ability to identify the reference of arguments. The subject is complex and requires joint or parallel discussion of a number of processes which usually are not discussed under the same heading.

1. Definitization and anaphoric pronouns
2. Topic Shifting
3. Passivization

In addition, the complexity is enhanced by the fact that at least two separate communicative functions are involved here.

i. For arguments that have already appeared in the relevant context: The *degree of difficulty* of assigning their correct reference upon *reintroduction* into discourse
ii. The general difference between a "known" argument ("definite") and an argument introduced for the first time ("indefinite")

Both functions can be shown to have a bearing on the overall "discourse presuppositionality" of a clause type, albeit in a different fashion. With respect to (i) above, one may say that a syntactic device will be considered *more marked* ("more presuppositional") in terms of its discourse presuppositions if it is used in situations where the speaker assumes that the hearer will have *more difficulty* in identifying the referent. With respect to (ii) above, one may say that an indefinite argument will be considered *less marked* in discourse than a definite argument. One might as well note here that it is possible to argue that the two types of discourse-markedness (i) and (ii) above are not independent of each other. This may be so since indefinites, introduced for the first time into discourse, require no assumption at all about the hearer's ability to identify their reference—there's **no** previous reference. In this sense, they are therefore the *easiest* or *least marked* in terms of criterion (i) as well. With all this in mind, let us look at the constructions to be investigated.

1.2.4.1. PASSIVE SENTENCES

In general, the function of passive sentences in language is to code sentences in the context in which *the non-agent is more topical*. This automatically means that the agent is *less topical* in a passive sentence, and the fact that it gets *removed* ("demoted") from the subject slot—the one which usually coincides with the topic—is an obvious means of achieving this end. A detailed discussion of the typological facts which support this view may be found in Chapter 4. One general characteristic of passive sentences in text–discourse[32] is that they are much *less frequent* than active sentences. This fact may be seen in Table 2.4. The explanation of this fact ought to be rather straightforward: Humans tend to talk more about *humans–agents* than about nonhumans–patients.[33] And since the subject slot is also the *topic* slot, it is more likely in human language to find agents in the topic position.

As can be seen from the text counts above, the average frequency of passive sentences in English texts is between 4% (for a less educated register) up to 18% for a highly intellectual text.[34]

Next, as mentioned in Section 1.3.2.3, the overwhelming majority of passive sentences in English texts are *agentless*. In other words, the degree of topicality of the agent argument appears to be so low that it is normally not mentioned at all.[35] This can be seen in the text counts presented in Table 2.5, in which two stylistically dissimilar fiction texts have been counted. The same fact is also corroborated by further counts in another fiction text, given later in Table 2.7.

Somewhat trivially, by measuring the *definiteness ratio per sentence*, one can already suggest that passive sentences are *more marked* in terms of their discourse presuppositionality in text. The argument goes like this: On the average active sentences have 100% definite subjects and 50% definite objects.[36] The average frequency of a definite argument in a *transitive-active* sentence is then around 75%. Now, since on the average only 18% of passive sentences have agents, even if all those agents were indefinite,[37] then given that the subjects of passive sentences are just as topical–definite as those of active sentences (i.e., around 100%—see text counts in Table 2.6), then the following reckoning must hold: In 82% of passive sentences, only the subject argument exists and it is 100% definite. In addition, the other 18% also have an agent which is 100% indefinite, and a subject that is 100% definite. In *agented* passive sentences the average *definiteness ratio* of an argument

---

[32] All the texts counted here are in English. It is expected that in a language in the midst of drifting toward an *ergative* system via the reanalysis of passive to active–ergative, the frequency of "passives" in discourse would be much higher. Such languages are, for example, Samoan, Tagalog, and Maori at their present stage (see discussion in Chung, 1977; text counts for Samoan in Chung, 1976). For such languages, however, a valid argument exists that their "passives" are not really passive any more. The distributional facts will then merely reflect this.

[33] For the high statistical correlation between the nominative case and "human," versus the accusative case and "nonhuman," see Greenberg (1974), and for a general discussion Givón (1976a).

[34] The frequency of passives is probably even lower in informal, unplanned speech, where alternative devices promoting nonagents to topicality, such as left-dislocation, impersonal constructions, etc., is much higher. For some discussion of this, see Elinor Keenan (1977).

[35] As mentioned in Chapter 1, this type of text-count is categorial in most languages that have a construction whose function is roughly equivalent to that of the English passive. For a typology of passives, see Chapter 4.

[36] Only accusative ("direct") objects are figured here. As discussed in Chapter 4, many languages restrict promotion to topic via passivization to direct objects.

[37] As will be shown further below, overtly expressed agents-of-passive are overwhelmingly indefinite.

2.2. The Discourse Presuppositions of Syntactic Constructions

TABLE 2.4
The Frequency of Active and Passive Sentences in Main-Declarative-Affirmative Clauses

Discourse Type	Actives		Passives	
	N	Percentage	N	Percentage
Nonfiction	49	82	11	18
Fiction[a]	177	91	18	9
News	45	92	4	8
Sports	64	96	3	4

[a] The two fiction texts counted are L'Amour (1965, pp. 1–25) and Orwell (1945, pp. 5–14).

is 50%. However, the relative *weighting* by the higher frequency of the agentless passive (82% versus 18%) produces a corrected overall definiteness ratio for all arguments of 82 : 9, or roughly 90%, as compared to 75% for active-transitive sentences. Trivially, at least, passive sentences are shown to have a higher discourse presuppositionality.

There is, however, a more substantive argument to suggest that indeed passive sentences are more marked in terms of the presuppositional complexity of their discourse context than active sentences. The argument is again based on the study of text distribution of both agented and agentless passives. The data are given in Table 2.7. When one probes into the nature of agentless passives, which are the bulk of passives in text, one finds the following three categories in terms of whether and to what degree the identity of the 'underlying' agent is predictable. First, one finds instances where the underlying agent is *recoverable directly* from the preceding—and sometimes following—discourse. In all these cases the agent is obviously a *referential* (rather than generic) argument. Thus consider:

(4) *Agent recoverable from preceding discourse*

"since *he* didn't want to throw up, he forced himself to eat lightly. Anubis resented *being fed small portions*. . . . [Trout, 1974, p. 22]."

TABLE 2.5
Agentless and Agented Passives in Main-Declarative-Affirmative Clauses

Text[a]	Agentless		Agented		Total	
	N	Percentage	N	Percentage	N	Percentage
LL	15	84	3	16	18	100
GO	58	79	15	21	73	100

[a] The two fiction texts counted are L'Amour (1965, pp. 1–25) and Orwell (1945, pp. 4–15).

TABLE 2.6
The Definiteness of Subjects of Passive Sentences

Text[a]	Definite		Indefinite		Total	
	N	Percentage	N	Percentage	N	Percentage
KT	78	93	6	7	86	100

[a] Trout (1974, pp. 7–47).

The subject (*he*), after eating, feeds his dog Anubis. Thus the identity of the agent in the underlined passive in (4) above is directly recoverable from the preceding immediate discourse context, given one additional piece of *general*, real-world (and culture-bound!) *pragmatic information*: That owners are the ones which *normally* feed their own dog. The presence of this added piece of information is of great importance, as we shall see further below. The identity of the underlying agent of the passive may also be recovered—though not as frequently in discourse—from the *following* discourse context. Thus consider:

(5)   *Agent recoverable from following discourse*

"and there was no telling what might have happened if *he had not been interrupted. The dog* had been whimpering and whining for some time . . . [Trout, 1974, pp. 39–40]."

Here the agent of "interrupt" is "the dog," mentioned in the sentence directly following the passive expression.

The second general category of agentless passives is one in which the identity of the *exact* agent is not necessarily recoverable to the point where unique reference can be established. Rather, based on *general*

TABLE 2.7.
Agentless and Agented Passives in Text[a]

Agentless			Agented		
Category	N	Percentage	Category	N	Percentage
Discourse context	24	31	Definite	3	25
Pragmatic knowledge	36	46	Indefinite	9	75
			Total	12	100
Lexical passive	19	23			
Total	79	100			
Total agentless:	79 = 87%				
Total agented:	12 = 13%				
Grand total:	91 = 100%				

[a] Text count is from Trout (1974, pp. 7–47).

2.2. The Discourse Presuppositions of Syntactic Constructions 61

pragmatic information, the *type* of agent that is most likely to have been involved can be established. Thus the information is not available in the direct discourse context, that is, in the presuppositions which the participants (writer, reader) may establish about the actual *referential* arguments participating in the narrative, but rather via a more general body of background pragmatic presuppositions which form the huge submerged body of the contextual iceberg upon which the thin top of *overt* discourse-transaction is perched. Thus consider:

(6)   "When *the first ship* equipped with the drive, The Golden Goose, had been revved up to top speed . . . [Trout, 1974, p. 38]."

There is no overt indication in the text preceding or following the passive in (6) who revved up the ship. But from general pragmatic knowledge one would surmise that *an engineer, a mechanic, an operator* or some such habitually-generically established agent must have been responsible. Thus saying that the agent is *predictable from general knowledge* is equivalent to saying that (*a*) it need not be mentioned; and (*b*) its actual referentially unique identity is *not important* in the particular communication.

Before proceeding to the third category, notice that, in principle, the distinction between the first and second categories above cannot be established as a matter of *kind*, but only of *degree*. In other words, these two categories may be *on a cline*. Example (4) above already supports such a claim, since it is *a mixed case*, where part of the information about the agent is available from the discourse context, but an important—probably an indispensible—part must still be gleaned from general pragmatic knowledge. As an added illustration, consider the following.

(7)   "As *everybody* knew, dogs were psychic. They saw things which men used to call ghosts. Now, *it was known that these were actually fifth-dimensional objects* . . . [Trout, 1974, p. 40]."

On the one hand, the nonreferential agent "everybody" is established in the immediately preceding discourse. On the other hand, it is really not necessary for interpreting correctly the underlying agent of the passive in (7) above. This is so because even without an overt mention, the reader would have had no trouble assigning the nonreferential "everybody," "they," or "we-all" to the passive in (7). Finally, observe the following:

(8)   "He went into the Hwang Ho, closed the port, and seated himself before the control panel in the bridge. *The stellar maps were stored* . . . [Trout, 1974, p. 37]."

The passage directly preceding this quotation established the identity of the early Chinese masters of the Hwang Ho. But is their identity as the agents of the passive in (8) recoverable from that early passage, or from the general pragmatic knowledge about what functions the master of a ship performs aboard? The answer, it seems to me, can go either way. Furthermore, by definition, *immediate context* is a matter of *degree*, that is, of *relative distance* from the relevant locus. The *obviousness* and *generality* of pragmatic knowledge, to boot, is also *a matter of degree*. Therefore, perforce, the interaction between these two sources of redundancy in discourse must be *on a cline*, and the two types cannot be categorically separated from each other. This does not necessarily obviate the text counts in Table 2.7, but only suggests that at the borderlines between categories the decision is not always easy.

The third category of agentless passives, one with much fewer tokens in the counted text, is that of *lexical passives*. Here again, a categorial distinction between this type and the second one ("agent recoverable from general pragmatic knowledge") is in principle impossible. Thus consider:

(9) "it began barking loudly and racing around. Simon tried to ignore him. Then *he became annoyed* . . . [Trout, 1974, p. 40]."

The passive verb-form in (9) may be classified as "lexical," but in the given context (*a*) the identity of the agent is obviously recoverable (the barking dog) and (*b*) it is not very clear that the dog was "the agent" of annoying Simon. Rather, it was *the reason*. Rather than directly doing something to the patient (Simon), the dog merely formed part—a crucial part—of the background situation which prompted Simon to become annoyed. Now, since reasons which people *consider* sufficiently vexing to prompt their anger are obviously a matter of *pragmatic gradation*, the sense in which the dog was the agent in (9) becomes cloudy. Thus, consider as alternative to (9):

(10) ". . . The situation was hopeless, and *Simon became annoyed* . . ."

While one could identify "hopeless situation" as the reason prompting Simon's annoyance, by no stretch of the imagination could "situation" be considered an agent. More "pure" cases of lexical passives are of course available in the text. Thus consider.

(11) "Simon almost screamed with joy. They had made it; *they weren't doomed to ride forever* . . . [Trout, 1974, p. 44]."

(12) "His intestines *were floating* up through his body and after a while *they were coiled* around his head . . . [Trout, 1974, p. 43]."

2.2. The Discourse Presuppositions of Syntactic Constructions

Of course, in (11) one could still suggest a faint echo of agent–reason for "doomed," that is, that power which was playing a cosmic joke on the wanderers, but the sense in which this is still necessary or even intended by the author becomes rather nebulous. And in (12) it is hard to distinguish between the passive "were coiled" and the adjectival-stative "were floating." There is no way in which the idea of agent is even remotely relevant.

Given the distributions in Table 2.7, one is now in the position to consider the next—this time more substantive—argument for the higher discourse markedness of passives as against active. Notice that 87% of all passives in the text counted for Table 2.7 are agentless, and of those 31% are of the type where the agent is *recoverable from the immediate discourse context*. It is reasonable to consider those 31% as a sub-type of *anaphora*, that is, a situation where the identity of the agent-argument is *known to the hearer–reader*. That, automatically, renders those agents "somewhat" *definite* or *presupposed*. Next consider the 46% of agents recoverable from general pragmatic knowledge. It is reasonable to assume that most of them are *nonreferential*, but that does not render them indefinite in the sense of "being mentioned for the first time in discourse." In fact, since they are a *background knowledge* of a general pragmatic sort, in that sense they are also part of the *presuppositional background* to the utterance. Thus, even without considering lexical passives, one can see that the bulk of passive sentences in English, namely, close to 80% of them, indeed *involve a presupposed agent*. Since the subjects of passive sentences are just as definite in text as those of active sentences, the average definiteness ratio per argument in passive sentences is again shown to be around 90%, as against 75% for active sentences.

Last, we must discuss the fact that when an overt agent appears in passive sentences in text, it is close to 90% of the time indefinite, that is, *new information*. As an example consider:

(13)   "He was beaten to death a minute later *by an enraged wino* . . . [Trout, 1974, p. 13]."

Further, even when the overt agent of passive is *definite*, it is clear that it constitutes part of the *new information* imparted by the sentence. Thus consider:

(14)   "Or had some planet whose business was being ruined *by Earth* triggered off this flood [Trout, 1974, p. 24]?"

(15)   "It had been built by the *Titanic & Icarus Spaceship Company, Inc.*, which didn't inspire confidence . . . [Trout, 1974, p. 35]."

In both (14) and (15), just as much as in (13) above, the overtly mentioned agent-of-passive is part of the new information. There is no way in which it can be recovered from the adjacent discourse context. As to recoverability via general pragmatic knowledge, this is obviously not intended in the communication contained in the passives in (13), (14), and (15), since the agents are *referential* and cannot be recovered from general knowledge. The inescapable conclusion is that in English, just as much as in KinyaRwanda (Kimenyi, 1976), the full, agented passive is used mostly when *the agent is (at least part of the) new information.*[38] This makes it clear now why (16b) below can be used as an answer to (16a):

(16)   a. **Who killed Lincoln?**
        He was killed **by John Wilkes Booth**

To sum up, then, not only was it shown above that passive sentences are *more marked* in terms of their discourse presuppositions, but also that one cannot hope to understand the passive construction without studying its functional distribution in discourse.

Perhaps as a postscript to the above discussion of passives, one should note the implications of the diachronic change from passive to *ergative* for our viewing the passive as a more-marked sentence type. As Chung (1976b,1977) has noted, the reinterpretation of passive sentences as ergative-active (with the *Instrumental-oblique* case of the agent-of-passive being reinterpreted as *Ergative* agent) coincides with a marked increase in the text-frequency of "passive" sentences, to the point where they become the main conduit for imparting new information in discourse. Hopper (1979) has also commented on this seemingly endemic tendency in the Malayo-Polynesian group. The fact that the increase in text frequency of the passive sentence type seems to be a prerequisite for its reinterpretation as type, strongly supports the claim that it is the *active* sentence that is the unmarked, main conduit of information in discourse. In other words, humans indeed tend to talk more about human-agents and thus put them in topic–subject position.

An added support for this may be seen in the following facts about ergative-type languages. Anderson (1976) has noted that most ergative languages are "surface" or "morphological" ergative-type only. That is, while the case-marking morphology groups active-agent as against nonagent, systematic grammatical behavior—in terms of Keenan's (1976a) subject–topic properties—consistently groups the ergative-agent and the subject of intransitive sentences in the same category, something like a "cryptonominative." As Comrie (1977) notes, at the beginning of the drift to ergative pattern (say, via reanalysis of the passive), ergative

---

[38] Kimenyi (1976) actually glosses all agented passives as cleft sentences, that is, *Mary was kissed by John* → *It was John who kissed Mary.* Whether this is completely justified or not, it underscores the sense that the agent is new information in Rwanda passive sentences.

2.2. The Discourse Presuppositions of Syntactic Constructions

languages are "deeper" (i.e., not only morphological), but most commonly they later on gravitate toward "surface" ergativity, that is, with only the case marking maintaining an ergative pattern but the behavioral properties conforming to a nominative system. In other words, the language gravitates back toward *reuniting the agent with the topic,* which I have suggested is the most "normal" situation in human discourse.[39]

2.2.4.2. TOPIC-SHIFT CONSTRUCTIONS, DEFINITES, AND ANAPHORIC PRONOUNS

In terms of degree of definiteness, there is no difference between a normal definite subject and a topic-shifted ("left-dislocated") subject. Thus the subjects in (17a, b) above and the topic in (17c) are all equally definite—that is, assumed to be known to the hearer:

(17)   a.   *My friend will arrive tomorrow*   (DEF)
        b.   *He will arrive tomorrow*   (PRO)
        c.   *My friend, he will arrive tomorrow*   (TOPIC-SHIFT)

There is, however, much evidence to suggest that in terms of the *degree of difficulty* the speaker assumes that the hearer will experience *in trying to identify the referent,* topic-shift constructions are more marked (see discussion in Keenan and Schieffelin, 1977, Givón, 1977b). Furthermore, in Givón (1977a) I have shown, for Biblical Hebrew text, that the three devices in (17) above may be ranked on a cline according to the *degree of obviousness* of the referent, so that in *equi-topic* chains only the anaphoric pronoun (or "subject agreement," its function equivalent) is used. When the topic is less obvious the definite full-NP subject is used, while when the subject is switched unexpectedly (or "contrastively," which is a subcase of "unexpectedly"), a topic-shift construction is used. Similar observation were made in many other languages.[40]

In terms of the first criterion for discourse markedness, then, topic-shift constructions are obviously more marked. It is easy to show that they are also more marked with respect to the criterion of definiteness. As can be seen from Table 2.1, referential direct-object arguments in discourse have roughly 50% probability of being indefinite. But topic-shifted referential direct-objects are 100% definite. Thus:

---

[39] The exception to this diachronic realignment are languages such as Dyirbal and Eskimo (see Dixon, 1972b; Comrie, 1977), where a special process—the "anti-passive"—is used to reunite the agent with the topic–absolutive case which exhibits all of the subject–topic behavioral properties. Since continuous discourse in Dyirbal is largely conjoined, and since in conjoined clauses the anti-passive rule applies *obligatorily,* it then follows that even in "deep-ergative" languages such as Dyirbal, at the actual level of linguistic behavior—discourse—the agent most commonly occupies the subject–topic position.

[40] Colloquial Spanish (Silva-Corvalán, 1977), English (Bolinger, 1979), Chinese (Li and Thompson, 1978), Japanese (Hinds, 1978, 1979), and Italian (Duranti and Keenan, 1979).

(18) a. *I saw a man yesterday*   (REF-INDEF)
      b. *I saw the man yesterday*   (REF-DEF)
      c. *The man, I saw him yesterday* (REF-DEF)
      d. **a man, I saw him yesterday*   (*REF-INDEF)

Thus, the overall definiteness ratio per argument[41] is obviously higher in topic-shifted constructions than in the neutral, nonshifted pattern, and the former are therefore shown by our second criterion to be more marked in terms of their discourse presuppositionality.[42]

2.2.4.3. THE LOWEST LEVEL OF DISCOURSE PRESUPPOSITIONALITY: INDEFINITE SUBJECTS

As pointed out by Edward Keenan (1976a) the subject in most languages is almost always definite. As shown in Section 1.3.2, this restriction may be categorial in some (probably most) languages, or manifest at the text-frequency level, as in English. But it is the **same** restriction nonetheless. What this tells us about human discourse is that it is **not** monopropositional. Rather, in human language live discourse tends to be *multipropositional*, with the subject-topic argument serving as the *continuity point*, the *leitmotif*, the common thread about which humans make assertions in multipropositional chains. There is nothing logically necessary about this type of discourse. And in fact, there are grounds for believing (see discussion in Chapter 7) that it is simply an evolved characteristic of the human information-processing and knowledge-transmission system, and that other mammals have an information-processing strategy that is much more *monopropositional*.

Now, in terms of discourse presuppositionality, it is quite transparent that existential–presentative constructions, that is, those special types which on the average represent only 10% or less of the main-clause subjects in English text, are the *least marked* of all sentence types. They are uttered in contexts where the speaker does not presuppose anything about the hearer's familiarity with the referent, since he is then introducing it into discourse *for the first time*. Trivially, too, no great difficulty of identifying the referent is involved here, since the hearer does not expect to be familiar with the new, indefinite argument. Thus, given both of our criteria of discourse presuppositionality of arguments,

---

[41] We are only dealing here with referential (nongeneric) arguments.

[42] This conclusion is certainly true for the register of educated English as well as for written text, where the frequency of topic-shift (left dislocation) constructions approaches zero (Elinor Keenan, 1977; but see some discussion in Chapter 5). The frequency of left-dislocation in unplanned discourse, child language, and Pidgins–Creoles is much higher, to the point where one may be tempted to consider it the neutral pattern.

indefinite-subject constructions are at the very bottom of the markedness scale. Nevertheless, nobody has seriously proposed these constructions as the neutral reference point for syntactic description. Furthermore, their *formal* properties, such as restricted distribution and higher complexity of structure (see Section 2.3.3.3) are similar to those one finds in presuppositionally more-marked constructions. The reason for the discrepancy is obvious: It would be futile, from the point of view of *psychological validity,* to choose as a point of reference for syntax a construction type that is rather *rare* in discourse and that is not used as the *main conduit* of information processing in language behavior. One must concede, therefore, that the criteria for markedness in syntax cannot remain divorced from the facts of statistics and functional distribution of the various clause types in live discourse. And while the criterion of presuppositional complexity goes a long way toward motivating the concept of syntactic markedness, it does not, by itself, go all the way.

As a final note one should notice, however, that at least in a trivial way the first criterion for discourse markedness of arguments, the one involving the *degree of difficulty* the hearer is assumed to experience in identifying the referent, may still turn out to justify the consideration of indefinite-subject constructions as "more marked." The argument goes roughly like this: The communicative principle which underlies the first criterion is the one which states that "the more unexpected a piece of information is, the more difficult it is to process." Since the *background expectation* in human discourse, at least in terms of frequency, are that *the topic will be maintained for a while* rather than switched abruptly, indefinite-subject constructions may be therefore likened—only by our first criterion—to topic-switch constructions, that is, clause-types used in the context in which the argument is *less expected.* In that sense, in discourse-medial positions, one is entitled to view these clauses as more marked.[43]

2.3. DISCOURSE MARKEDNESS AND DISTRIBUTIONAL RESTRICTIONS

In this section I will show how the first prediction about the formal properties of more presuppositional constructions is borne out, namely that they exhibit more stringent distributional restrictions, both in terms of their own embedding in other environments as well as in terms of the tighter restrictions they impose upon the embedding of elements and/or constructions within them.

---

[43] In discourse-initial positions, these constructions are obviously the least marked, and that's precisely where their frequency is highest. This once again underscores the fact that markedness is independent of neither discourse type nor discourse context.

2.3.1. Embedded Clauses and Strictly Presuppositional Constructions

For the purpose of the discussion in this section, one can combine the two categories. As noted by Emonds (1970) embedded constructions, including relative clauses, WH-questions, cleft and pseudo-cleft constructions, impose tight restriction in a systematic fashion on the type of syntactic devices ("transformations") that can be embedded in them. This subject has been already discussed in Section 1.2.3.8. What has also been discussed there is the fact that, as observed by Hooper and Thompson (1973), these restrictions are relaxed in non-main clauses that are *asserted* rather than presupposed. In other words, the more presuppositional clause types show more stringent distributional restrictions, while the asserted clauses approximate the behavior of the main clause—which normally contains the bulk of the assertion in sentences. The fact that all the syntactic processes discussed by Emonds (1970) turn out to involve the pragmatics of topic-focus relations is highly significant and will be discussed further below in the context of understanding these restrictions. But quite apart from explanation, the restrictions themselves are real.

Trivially at least, the distribution of embedded constructions is obviously limited to the few characteristic positions in which they can appear. More seriously, strictly presuppositional constructions such as relative clauses, clefts, pseudo-clefts, and WH-questions are rather limited in the environments into which they can be embedded. For example, infinitival complements of modal verbs ("want") or manipulative verbs ("order") do not tolerate them. They are harder to embed in sentential complements of cognition verbs ("know," "think"), and as Ross (1967) has shown, embedding them within themselves causes grave problems of complexity and incomprehensibility (see Section 1.2.3.7). It is thus clear that our generalization holds with respect to both types.

2.3.2. Other Speech Acts

It is a well-known fact that imperatives and questions are hard to distribute except at the main-clause position, and that even when embedded in some environments that admit them, they lose their illocutionary force as speech acts. In fact, at least in a trivial fashion, one may say that the imperative and interrogative speech act *can only be embedded under the declarative* (i.e., *Where is Joe?* = *I am asking you: "Where is Joe?"*). Just as indicative of the restrictions imposed on these nondeclarative speech acts is the fact that in the few cases where they can be embedded in verb complements, an otherwise presuppositional clause becomes nonpresuppositional. Thus consider:

2.3. *Discourse Markedness and Distributional Restrictions* 69

(19)   a.   *Joe didn't know that Mary left him* (= presupposed that Mary did leave him)

         b.   *Joe didn't know if Mary left him (or not)* (≠ presupposed that Mary left him)

While it is obvious that the nonpresuppositional character of (19b) is due to the nonpresuppositional nature of the yes–no question or if-clause, it is nevertheless true that the normally presuppositional verb *know* loses its presuppositionality when another speech act is embedded under it. In the same vein, direct-quote complements which are non-presupposed (i.e., they are illocutionary) cannot be embedded normally after a more presuppositional verb such as *know*, but only after the nonpresuppositional *say, think*:

(20)   a.   *Joe said: "Where's Mary?"*
                b.   *Joe thought: "Where's Mary?"*
                c.   **Joe knew: "Where's Mary?"*
                d.   *Joe said: "Leave me alone"*
                e.   *Joe thought: "Leave me alone"*
                f.   **Joe knew: "Leave me alone"*

Finally, while other speech acts can be embedded under *know*, which then loses its presuppositionality as in (19b) above, under "truly" factive verbs such as *regret*, which never lose their presuppositionality, the same embedding would be more difficult.[44]

(21)   **Joe didn't regret if Mary left him*

Thus, not only are other speech acts more restricted in distribution, but they can distribute more freely in less-presuppositional environments, a fact that again underscores the generalizations discussed in the preceding section.

Negative sentences, as is documented in great detail in Chapter 3, also exhibit extensive distributional restrictions as compared with their corresponding affirmatives. They thus abide by the same generalization outlined above.

---

[44] Bolinger (personal communication) has cautioned that example (21) will be acceptable if the verb modality is changed from PAST to IRREALIST, that is, *Joe wouldn't regret (it) if Mary left him*. But *regret* still contrasts with the "less-factive" *know* in that with the latter a similar sentence is acceptable even in the PAST modality, namely, *Joe didn't know if Mary left him*. This underscores the fact that it is the scope of the wider modality under which an expression is embedded—be that modality the verb itself or the wider-scope tense–aspect–mode—which determines the felicity of these expressions. For a general discussion, see Givón (1973b).

2.3.3. Constructions Involving Degree of Definiteness–Topicality

2.3.3.1. PASSIVE

It is not uncommon to find the tense–aspect–modal elements in a language showing a more restricted distribution in passive than in active sentences. Since quite often the passive sentence is considered a "stative," "noncontrol" form of the verb,[45] most commonly progressive aspects may not appear in passive sentences.[46] Furthermore, passive sentences of the "stative" type are restricted in their distribution in many modal environments. It is hard to embed them in complements of manipulative verbs (*order, force*):

(21)   a.   *I told John to find Mary*
           b.   **I told Mary to be found by John*[47]
           c.   *I made John find Mary*
           d.   **I made Mary be found by John*

They are restricted in complements of many modality verbs, as in (22):

(22)   a.   *John was able to reach Mary right away*
           b.   **Mary was able to be reached by John right away*

Their behavior under epistemic and root modalities is also more restricted than that of corresponding actives. Thus:

(23)   a.   *John had to reach Mary right away or else . . .*
               i. *Had to in his own judgment*   ("root" modal)
               ii. *Had to in the speaker's judgment*   ("epistemic" modal)
           b.   *?Mary had to be reached by John right away or else . . .*
               i. *?Had to in her/John's judgment*   (?"root" modal)
               ii. *Had to in the speaker's judgment*   ("epistemic" modal)

In terms of assignment of motivation (and thus "control"), these passives are again restricted. Thus:

---

[45] See discussion in Givón (1975d).

[46] Comrie (1978) has noted that there is a seemingly universal correlation between the past-perfect tense–aspect and passive–ergative constructions, as against the correlation between the active–progressive tense–aspect and active–verbal constructions. In many languages, the passive pattern is a stative–resultative derivation from the active, and as other stative verbs is incompatible with the progressive aspect.

[47] Bolinger (personal communication) points out that a sentence such as *I ordered the work to be done by Mary* is an apparent counterexample to this restriction. However, in fact Mary could not be the dative–object of *order* in this case, since she has no control as the agent-of-passive, and the sentence makes sense only as *I ordered someone else to make sure that Mary does the work*. The restriction is thus semantic–pragmatic in nature, and not merely syntactic. For further discussion see Givón (1975d).

2.3. Discourse Markedness and Distributional Restrictions 71

(24)   a. *John killed Mary accidentally*
               b. *Mary was killed by John accidentally*
               c. *John killed Mary deliberately*
               d. *Mary was killed by John deliberately*
                    i. *It was John's deliberate action*
                    ii. **It was Mary's deliberate action*

All of the above restrictions correlate to the lack of "control" on the part of the nonagent subject of passives (see Givón, 1975d). Probably the same motivation bars reflexivization of passives, a property that is agent-controlled:[48]

(25)   a. *John killed himself*
               b. **John was killed by himself*

Next, in languages where the agent-deletion type of passivization is used,[49] passive sentences obligatorily appear without the agent. This is obviously a severe distributional restriction which would bar this sentence type from being considered as point-of-reference for syntax. As an example, consider the following data from Ute:

(26)   a. *ta?wáci mamáci puníkyaay-kya*
                  man   woman-OBJ see past
                  'The man saw the woman'
               b. *mamáci   puníkyaa-ta-x̂a*
                  woman-OBJ see-*PASS*-past
                  {'The woman was seen (by someone)'}
                  {'Someone saw the woman'}

To sum up, then, passive sentences, regardless of their typology, show a more restricted distribution in the grammar (let alone in text) than the corresponding actives.

2.3.3.2. LEFT-DISLOCATION (TOPIC-SHIFTING)

This construction, as in (17c) and (18c) above, is one of the root transformations discussed by Emonds (1970), and its restricted distribution (asserted clauses only, Hooper and Thompson, 1973) is well documented and will not be further discussed here. It is interesting to

---

[48] Keenan (1976a) considers reflexivization to be a reference-related ("topic-related") property. But if that were strictly true, a sentence such as (25b) ought to be grammatical. The fact that **Himself was killed by John* is ungrammatical, suggests that in English the control of reflexivization must reside in the *topic–agent*, rather than either the agent or topic by itself. However, in Philippine languages (Schachter, 1976, 1977), reflexivization is controlled by the agent regardless of its topic status, so that the "equivalent" of **Himself was killed by John* is acceptable. In other words, reflexivization is controlled by the agent in both active and "passive" sentences.

[49] See the typology of passives, Chapter 4.

note that the presuppositionally less-marked anaphoric pronoun and definite NP do not exhibit the same restrictions. That is:

(27) a. *I know that **he** came* (PRO)
　　 b. *I know that **the man** came* (DEF)
　　 c. **I know that **the man**, **he** came* (*TOPIC SHIFT)

While this differential behavior may be attributed to *syntactic* complexity (i.e., the effect of movement rules as disruptive of speech-analysis strategies), it is nevertheless another case where the more presuppositional variant exhibits stronger distributional restrictions.

2.3.3.3. INDEFINITE SUBJECT CONSTRUCTIONS

In most languages the subject of the neutral sentence type cannot be referential-indefinite, but only definite or generic. In languages in which this is indeed a categorial constraint, a special sentence type exists via which new referential arguments can be introduced into the discourse in the *subject* position.[50] This construction type is the existential—presentative, and it has a number of universal, cross-language-shared characteristics:[51]

1. It distributes most frequently at discourse-initial position, thus indicating that it is used in discourse contexts in which the least shared background of common knowledge is presupposed by the speaker.
2. In all subject-first languages which have this device, the characteristic word-order of existential-presentatives is V-first. It thus violates the more universal tendency (Keenan, 1976a; Givón, 1976b) of the subject-topic appearing first in the sentence.
3. Many of the subject properties discussed by Keenan (1976a) are suppressed in existential-presentative sentences.
4. The kind of verb that may appear in these constructions is highly restricted, normally to *be, exist, stand–sit–lie down, live, appear,* often *remain, be left* and sometimes verbs of entrance into the scene such as *come* or *enter* (see further details in Givón, 1976b).[52]

---

[50] Introducing them as direct-objects is probably the main avenue in most languages, as suggested by the 50% indefiniteness figure even in languages, such as English, which have a viable existential presentative construction.

[51] For more details, see Hetzron (1971).

[52] Dwight Bolinger (personal communication) has pointed out that the restriction, at the discourse level, is inherently a pragmatic restriction whereby the most likely verb to be used in presentative constructions is the verb *most typically* a characteristic–stereotype action–state associated with a particular noun. Thus *be, exist, stand–sit–lie down, live, appear, remain–stay* and *come–enter* are the verbs most stereotypical of the entrance of *humans* into the discourse domain, via being there, remaining there, or entering. But consider other nouns, as in *On top of the pole there waved a flag, On a distant hilltop there burned a fire, From the distance there rang a bell.* In other words, the common presentative verbs are common because they can introduce the most common discourse topic, humans. And *be–exist–remain* can introduce **any** type of participant.

5. Quite often the agreement on the verb—or a "dummy subject" in languages that have no agreement—is of the *locative* type.

As an example consider the existential construction in Rwanda, an SVO Bantu language,[53] as well as the corresponding English construction:

(28) a. *buceeye umugabo yaa-ẑe*   (DEF-SUBJ)
next-day man   *he*-past-come
'The next day the man came'

b. *buceeye haa-ẑe   umugabo*   (EXISTENTIAL)
next-day *LOC*-past-come   man
'The next day there came a man'

The severe distributional restrictions on existential–presentative constructions are easy to document. While they distribute in the looser sentential complements of cognition and utterance verbs (*know, think, say*), they cannot appear in complements of modality (*want*) and manipulation (*order*) verbs with infinitival verb complements. Their distribution in relative clauses is severely restricted:

(29) a. *And near the bar stood a woman . . .*
b. **The woman that near the bar stood . . .*

Further, only a restricted, small group of verbs may appear in existential constructions in most languages,[54] so that it would be self-defeating to consider them the neutral point-of-reference in syntax. Since those verbs are by-and-large intransitive, passivization cannot exist in existential constructions. Topic-shifting is also, by definition, ruled out of the existential construction, since it is limited to definite or generic constituents:

(30) a. *As to this man, he stood near the bar*   (DEF)

b. **As to a man, near the bar there stood he/one*
(REF-INDEF)

c. *As to patrons, near the bar stood six of them*
(GENERIC)

As Gary (1974) has shown, a variant of existential constructions exists in English in which the subject is definite but constitutes a *surprise* information. Thus:

(31) *We stepped into the room **and there, in front of our eyes, stood Joe***

This variant is one of those considered by Emonds (1970) as a root transformation, confined mostly to main clauses. Finally, existentials

---
[53] See Kimenyi (1976).
[54] See condition (4) above and footnote 60, as well as Givón (1976d) and Hetzron (1971) for further discussion.

cannot appear in imperatives, and their interaction with negation is highly restricted. All the restrictions enumerated above are motivated by pragmatic, communicative considerations that have to do with the special function performed by existential-presentatives. But be the motivation as it may, the distribution of this construction in the grammar is highly restricted, as is the distribution of lexical items and grammatical construction within it.

2.4. DISCOURSE MARKEDNESS AND SYNTACTIC COMPLEXITY

As was suggested in Section 2.1, the formal criterion of *marked structure* is not free of controversy and cannot be applied across the board without qualifications. The easiest cases are obviously those involving grammatical morphology, where one could contrast the neutral pattern with a more-marked variant that has an *extra morpheme* which serves to mark its function and thus differentiate it from the neutral pattern. Thus, for example, existential constructions in English have the marker *there*, and in KinyaRwanda [see (28)] they have an "irregular" agreement pattern with some abstract locative rather than the grammatical "subject."[55] However, one must note that the very same construction in Mandarin Chinese[56] involves only word-order inversion (SV with definite subjects as against VS with indefinite subjects) without any added morphology. And there are no universal, principled, independent grounds by which one order can be judged more complex than the other. This does not necessarily destroy the usefulness of the concept "syntactic complexity" as distinct from semantic, propositional or presuppositional complexity. It merely points out to the possibility that syntactic complexity may be—at least in some cases—viewed *relative* to the neutral pattern. In other words:

> A construction will be considered syntactically more complex if it departs from the routine speech-processing strategy established by the norm, that is, the neutral pattern.

It is clear that if this formulation is adopted, then the role of *frequency in discourse* is not altogether irrelevant in determining what will be the *psychologically-relevant* norm, that is, the ground-zero level of expectation in speech processing, as against what will be considered a "break" with the norm. While linguists may have a hard time reconciling them-

---

[55] I have argued previously (Givón, 1976a) that grammatical agreement is really a *topic* property rather than a subject property, so that the universal tendency to suppress the subject agreement in existential constructions is a reflection of the low topicality of the indefinite subject.

[56] For details see Li and Thompson (1975) and discussion in Givón (1977b).

2.4. Discourse Markedness and Syntactic Complexity

selves to this possibility, I think psychologists would welcome it for rather obvious reasons. In general, it would be disastrous to have an independent measure of syntactic complexity that takes no account of processing complexity. And since the relationship between *background expectations* ("normal, high-frequency routines," "the most routinized strategies") and the *foreground break of expectations* is a central component of speech processing, information processing and the psychology of perception and cognition, one could not build a useful theory of syntactic complexity without reference to this principle.

Some constructions are "obviously" more complex even without grammatical morphology. All embedded constructions are of this type. In general, one may posit that the *length* of a construction is expected to correlate with complexity (though not automatically). Thus, embedding of one proposition into another obviously increases the average length of the overall construction. The *number of verbs per proposition* is also a rough measure of complexity, since in general a proposition is "grouped" around a verb. The number of arguments per verb is a sure indication of complexity, since at least at the *semantic* level, the more arguments of different case-function are in a sentence, the more "atomic" propositions are involved in the semantic makeup of that sentence.

The relation between *assertional* complexity and *presuppositional* complexity is also a wide open issue. It is clear that both contribute to the overall complexity of a construction, and that their contribution is probably reflected at both the formal "syntactic" level as well at the psychologically relevant level of processing. But two *weighting* possibilities remain wide open:

1. That the condensation of assertional material into a proposition does not have the same effect on psychological complexity as the condensation of presupposed material.
2. That the presupposed material may be hierarchized according to its "closeness" to the speech situation, that is, whether it is overtly mentioned in the close or remote preceding discourse, whether it is inferred from general pragmatic knowledge, and points in between.[57]

Finally, there is the consideration of *syntactic condensation* of the presuppositions involved in discourse and their "grammaticalization" into tight syntactic constructions without intonational breaks. As is argued in Chapter 5, the language of early childhood is characterized by "loose" constructions with pauses, while the more "syntacticized" mode is acquired later. For example, a child is more likely to use a looser *topic*

---

[57] For some discussion of the scalar nature of these phenomena, see Section 2.2.3.4.1.

construction where the adult would use the tighter, grammaticalized *subject* construction. Thus:

(32) a. *Joe, he is sick*   (topic)
      b. *Joe is sick*   (subject)

Is the complexity of (32a) and (32b) the same, since they are often used in the very same context? Or is the fact that the child assumes that it is harder to identify the topic and thus—as a general *background* phenomenon—operates linguistically at a more marked level?[58] And is a measure of *time of delivery* to be taken into account here? Since (32a) is obviously delivered slower than (33b), is there some kind of 'average complexity per time unit' that is stable overall in human communication? Further, as is discussed by Elinor Keenan (1977), children quite often *spread their discourse to other participants* in the interaction, so that while they do not utter the entire sequence,[59] they certainly keep track over the overall propositional and presuppositional contents of the utterance. Is the degree of complexity they are able to tolerate going to be weighted in such cases (an obviously desirable goal), and if so how?

I have raised all the considerations above to show that the subject of syntactic complexity, if one aims to make it relevant to language behavior and thus empirically founded, is extremely thorny and a great number of open questions are still begging not only for their answer but also for a principled, noncircular methodology. It seems to me that at this point one could at the very least abide by the *relative* criterion developed earlier (31) and hierarchize the sentence-types under discussion according to the likelihood—by cross-language typological evidence among other things—that they show a departure from the norm in terms of syntactic order. While the degree of typological variation is in some instances rather large, on the whole it seems to me that the same hierarchic scale established for presuppositionality manifests itself in terms of *syntactic distance* from the neutral pattern. The presuppositionality scale may be summarized as:[60]

(33)   *Least marked:*   Definite accusative
                             Anaphoric pronouns
                             Topic-shift
                             Passive[61]
                             Negative

---

[58] Compare the discussion earlier.

[59] For example, one participant may utter the topic and another supply the assertion. Or one may utter the presuppositional portion of a WH-question and the other the WH-pronoun.

[60] Existentials were not plotted on this scale since, for reasons discussed above, they are the lowest on the presuppositional scale but quite high on the scale of deviation from the syntactic norm.

[61] Passives from different typologies are not likely to scale at the same point, and the same is true for other construction types. The correlation sought here is obviously rough, though I believe it exists.

2.4. Discourse Markedness and Syntactic Complexity

                                  Yes–no Q
                                  Relative-clause
                                  Pseudo-cleft
                                  Cleft
        Most marked: WH-Q

In the following subsections I will attempt to indicate the types of syntactic distance that are more characteristic of these various constructions as well as some of the typological cross-language variability to be expected.

2.4.1. Embedded Clauses

Infinitival verb complements lack the subject constituent and can thus be considered *truncated,* as compared to main clauses. One may also consider the subordinating morphemes as well as the infinitival or subjunctive morphology as some type of "modification" establishing "distance" from main-clause syntax. Next, consider the well-documented phenomenon in German, where the subordinate-clause syntax is SOV while main clause syntax is V-second (in standard literary German) or SVO (in the colloquial language). Such a phenomenon always turns out to be the result of diachronic change, where the main clause syntax is consistently more innovative. We shall return to discuss this subject in Section 2.5, but regardless of the source, the case is clearly an instance of great syntactic distance between main and subordinate clause. A similar though not as complete case, with innovative SV syntax in main clause and conservative VS syntax in many (though not all) subordinate clauses can be seen in Biblical Hebrew (Givón, 1977a). A more restricted case may be seen in Kru, a Niger-Congo language, where in infinitival complements and a number of related modal embedded environments, SOV syntax has survived whereas in all other clause types SVO, the more innovative word-order, is the rule (Givón, 1975e).

2.4.2. Presuppositional Clauses

2.4.2.1. RELATIVE CLAUSES

What was said above with regard to embedded clauses applies, in the case of German and Hebrew, also to relative clauses. The diachronic processes of word-order change responsible for this are motivated by discourse-pragmatic considerations and will be briefly summarized in Section 2.5.

The typology of relative clauses across the world's languages can be found in Chapter 4. To the extent that the clause is embedded, which is true for most major types, than it is missing one argument compared to the main clause. Pronominal elements may or may not be added as extra clues to help the *recoverability* problem arising from such truncation. Quite often a subordinating element also marks the clause as different from the neutral type.

2.4.2.2. PSEUDO-CLEFT

Since these constructions involve a normal-looking relative clause, what was said about relative clauses above applies equally to this type.

2.4.2.3. CLEFT

In many languages contrastive focusing may be achieved without any major syntactic disruption of the neutral pattern. This possibility is certainly one alternative in English:

(34)   *John killed **Bill**, not Harry*

A function similar to that of intonation in English may be achieved by a focus morpheme, as in Sherpa:

(35)   *tii   mi-ti-ki   cenyi caax-suŋ*   (NEUTRAL)
       DEF man-DEF-ERG cup   break-ASP
       'The man broke the cup'

(36)   *tii   mi-ti-ki   kyé   cenyi caax-suŋ*   (SUBJ-FOCUS)
       DEF man-DEF-ERG FOC   cup   break-ASP
       'It's the *mán* who broke the cup'

(37)   *tii   mi-ti-ki   tii   cenyi kyé   caax-suŋ* (OBJ-
       DEF man-DEF-ERG DEF   cup   FOC   break-ASP   FOCUS)
       'It's the *cúp* that the man broke'

To the extent that a language has the cleft pattern, however, it is clearly a strong disruption of the neutral syntax, both in terms of the left-movement of the constituent in focus, in terms of the focus-marking morpheme (*it's* in English), as well as in the presence of relative-clause morphology and syntactic pattern, which thus introduces the additional syntactic complexity associated with those clauses.[62] This highly presuppositional construction is thus at the very top of the syntactic complexity (or "syntactic distance from the norm") scale.

2.4.2.4. WH-QUESTIONS

WH-questions, while being a different speech act than cleft-sentences, nevertheless share much of the *presuppositional* structure of the latter. Schematically one may compare them as follows:

---

[62] For the relation between cleft sentences and relativization, see Takizala (1972) and Schachter (1973).

(38) a. Shared Presupposition: *Someone killed Joe*
      b. Cleft (Declarative): *It was Mary (who killed Joe).*
      c. WH (Interrogative): *Who was it (that killed Joe)?*

In addition, there is a strong possibility (see discussion in Chapters 5 and 6) that both the *developmental* (ontogenetic) and *diachronic* development of these two constructions follows the very same process. That is, given the strong contextual presuppositionality of the sentence excepting the constituent in focus, the first stage of development involves the focus constituent alone. Then the presupposed sentence—in the form of a nonrestrictive relative clause—is added on as an *afterthought,* for added "communicative insurance." In the final stage the construction simply grammaticalizes ("syntacticizes"). Thus, schematically:

(39) a. (i) *It was **Máry**!*
          (ii) ***Whó** (was it)?*
      b. (i) *It was **Máry**, (you know), (the one) who killed Joe.*
          (ii) ***Whó** was it, (you know), (the one) who killed Joe?*
      c. (i) *It was **Máry** who killed Joe.*
          (ii) ***Whó** killed Joe?*

The similarity of these two processes is supported by a considerable body of cross-language evidence.[63] Thus, in many languages WH-questions exhibit the same complexity—relative to the neutral pattern—as do cleft sentences. In addition, they also represent an added modification upon the neutral pattern, since in WH-questions one of the arguments of the verb is deleted and replaced by an interrogative pronoun. And that pronoun normally classifies the WH-type according to the case of the argument being in interrogative focus.

One must note that, much like focus–declarative constructions, WH-questions may have two other patterns, corresponding to the pseudo-cleft construction and stress-focus (34). Thus, schematically a language may exhibit:

(40) a. **Whom did Mary kill?**   (CLEFT)
      b. *The one whom Mary killed was **who**?* (PSEUDO-CLEFT)
      c. *Mary killed **who**?*   (STRESS-FOCUS)

For further illustration and cross-language materials, see Takizala (1972) and Sadock and Zwicky (1977).

---

[63] See Takizala (1972) and Schachter (1973).

Finally, as noted by Sadock and Zwicky (1977) among many others, the more presuppositional WH-questions are much more likely to exhibit syntactic complexity, in terms of deviation from the neutral pattern, than are the less presuppositional yes-no questions. This certainly conforms to the prediction in (33) above.

2.4.3. Other Speech Acts

2.4.3.1. IMPERATIVES

The two most common features of imperatives, in terms of syntactic distance from the norm, is the lack of overt subject, and the reduced verb morphology. Occasionally other deviations may be also recorded. For example, in Kru, where the imperative is synchronically a member of a large class of modal environments that are historically the result of embedding under a manipulative verb, SOV syntax has survived in imperatives just like it has survived in all those embedded modal environments, while the neutral pattern is the more innovative SVO.[64]

2.4.3.2. INTERROGATIVES

WH-questions have already been discussed above. Yes-no questions are much less likely to deviate from the norm, and in most languages they differ from the corresponding declarative sentence only in *intonation*. In other languages a generalized interrogative "introduction" morpheme is also used, on top of the characteristic intonation. The type of word-order inversion found in English (SV in the normal pattern versus VS in the yes-no pattern) is relatively rare, and may be shown to be the result of diachronic change—doubtlessly motivated by pragmatic considerations.[65]

2.4.3.3. NEGATIVES

A full discussion of the syntax, semantics, and pragmatics of negation can be found in Chapter 3. The presence of *negative markers* is obviously the most common difference between negative sentences and the neutral pattern, though *intonation* or *tonological* differences are also extremely common. Kru is again one of the few clear instances of word-order differences between the negative and affirmative pattern. Biblical Hebrew represents a similar—though not categorial—difference, where the SV word order tends to be more frequent in negative sentences, while the more conservative VS order is more frequent in corresponding affirmatives (Givón, 1977a; as well as Section 2.5).

---

[64] For further detail see Givón (1975e).
[65] As I have shown (Givón, 1977a), the syntactic conservatism of non-main clauses is most commonly motivated by discourse-pragmatic factors, see summary in Section 2.5.

2.4.4. Constructions Involving Degrees of Topicality

2.4.4.1. PRONOMINAL OBJECTS

In a number of languages (Romance, Bantu, Iroquois) an older SOV order is reflected in bound pronouns while the more innovative SVO is found with nominal objects. In both Amharic and Akkadian the opposite case is recorded, where an older VSO word-order is frozen into the verb-bound pronominal paradigm, while the nominal syntax had changed to SOV. As will be suggested in Chapter 6, these discrepancies between the neutral nominal syntax and pronominal syntax are due to diachronic change, including pronoun *cliticization*. Since such processes are extremely common (as is pronoun cliticization), syntactic deviance of pronominal word-order from nomimal word order should be, in principle, quite common.

Finally, the replacement of a full NP by a short pronoun is by itself a deviation from the syntactic norm. This is even more true when the language uses a *zero–gap* instead of an overt pronoun.

2.4.4.2. DEFINITE OBJECTS

While syntactic differences between definite and indefinite object constructions are uncommon, some cases do exist. One such example is Mandarin Chinese (Li and Thompson, 1975), where SOV order is (partially) seen with definite objects, and SVO with indefinite ones. A partially similar case may be seen in Ute, where a subcategory of indefinites—nonreferential objects—are incorporated into the verb at a preverbal position, thus reflecting the more conservative OV syntax. Referential objects—definite as well as indefinite—appear with an increasing text frequency postverbally, that is, the more innovative VO syntax.[66] In both Mandarin and Ute, the differences are the result of diachronic change in word order, although of radically different types.

Next, in a number of Bantu languages topic-shifting is the most common device for definitizing direct objects, especially in negative sentences.[67] Thus, consider the following example from KinyaRwanda:

(41)   a. *ya-bonye umugabo*
          he-saw   man
          'He saw *a* man'

      b. *umugabo ya-mu-bonye*
          man   he-him-saw
          {'He saw *the* man'   }
          {'*The* man, he saw him'}

---

[66] Object incorporation into the verb is common cross-linguistically, see Mardirussian (1975).
[67] See discussion in Givón (1976a, 1977b).

c. *nhi-ya-bonye umugabo*
   NEG-he-saw   man
   'He didn't see *a/any* man'
d. *umugabo nhi-ya-mu-bonye*
   man   NEG-he-him-saw
   'He didn't see *the* man'

Finally, note that since *dative shifting* involves degree-of-topicality differences between direct and indirect objects (see discussion in Chapter 4; as well as Shir, 1979), it is not uncommon to find that the ACC–DAT order is "more compatible" with a *definite* accusative, while the DAT–ACC order is "more compatible" with an *indefinite* accusative. While this is less of a "major" word-order parameter, it is nevertheless a significant case where the definiteness of the object yields variant word-orders.

2.4.4.3. TOPIC-SHIFT CONSTRUCTIONS

The left-dislocation—plus common intonation break—associated with this construction certainly mark it as deviating from the neutral pattern. Anaphoric pronouns in the second portion of the construction (in languages which do not use zero pronouns) is added marking. In addition, in Semitic, Romance, and some Bantu languages, topic-shifting of objects also results in a variant VS word order in the rest of the clause, as against the neutral (and more innovative) pattern of SV.[68]

One must note, however, that in some languages, particularly strict V-first languages,[69] quite often the function of topic-shifting is achieved without any word-order change (i.e., no left-dislocation), but rather via the promotional morphology involved in passivization and definitization.[70] In such languages, obviously, the *syntactic* distance of such a construction from the neutral norm is negligible.

2.4.4.4. PASSIVE

An extensive typology of the passivization devices found across languages of the world may be found in Chapter 4. Obviously, each type involves different ways of deviating from the active norm. In terms of syntax, these deviations may be categorized as follows:

1. *Reversal of agent-patient relative order:* This is found in the Indo-European type as well as in the left-dislocation passive type.
2. *Agent deletion:* Many subtypes involve this obvious departure from the neutral norm.

---

[68] For more discussion see Chapter 4, as well as Givón (1977a). Related Bantu data may be found in Bokamba (1976).

[69] See discussion in Edward Keenan (1977).

[70] See discussion in Chapter 4, as well as Givón (1977b).

3. *The use of an auxiliary verb:* The English passive with *be, get,* or *have* is one example of this. The diachronic use of the verb *submit* in Mandarin (Li and Thompson, 1973) is also of this type. Quite often such an auxiliary verb becomes cliticized—most often into the main passive verb (Givón, 1971).

In addition, passive sentences quite often contain a number of morphological markers, such as verb-deriving affixes, agreement morphology, case marking, by which they differ from the neutral pattern.

2.4.4.5. EXISTENTIAL-PRESENTATIVES

The characteristic, syntactically deviant patterns of existential constructions have already been discussed in Section 2.3.3.3.

2.5. SYNTACTIC CONSERVATISM

When I wrote the first version of this chapter, I was convinced that somehow, by general principle, constructions that are more complex in terms of their discourse presuppositions and syntactic structure also tend to exhibit syntactic conservatism. There is a lot of evidence for this in many *specific* instances, but there are also grounds for believing that as a *general* principle this observation is neither factually correct nor very explanatory. In this section I will sketch out briefly the kind of facts and considerations that are involved.

2.5.1. Word-Order Change

There is a wealth of evidence suggesting that the major mechanism for word-order change involves the "downward" *reevaluation* of more marked pragmatic word orders involved in various topic–focus operations,[71] so that eventually they are re-interpreted as the neutral pattern. The more-marked pragmatic variants turn out to be overwhelmingly what Emonds (1970) calls root transformations, which are limited primarily to main clauses, or to more assertional clauses (Hooper and Thompson, 1973). Therefore, since the mechanisms primarily responsible for word-order innovation are in operation mostly in main–assertional clauses, obviously the syntax of these clauses is going to reflect the more innovative word-order, while the word-order of subordinate clauses is going to be more conservative.

While the general outline given above is factual, there are a number of exceptions that must be considered. In Givón (1977a) I have shown

---

[71] For the change from SOV to SVO via "afterthought-topic" ("right-dislocation"), see Hyman (1975). For the change from SOV to V-second, see Stockwell (1977). For the change from V-second to SVO, see Vennemann (1973a). For the change from VSO to SVO, see Givón (1977a).

that the more conservative VS word-order in Biblical Hebrew survives longer in clauses—such as relative clauses, focus sentences, WH-questions, object topicalization, etc.—in which the topicality of the object is enhanced relative to the downgraded topicality of the subject. While it is true that all these constructions are also more presuppositional than the neutral pattern, in principle it is also true that if the topicality of the object is not involved, then in Biblical Hebrew a more presupposed construction will tend to be more progressive diachronically, that is, exhibit more SV syntax. This is best exemplified in the case of *negatives,* whose syntax changes from VS to SV much earlier than that of the corresponding affirmatives. The general principle involved here is roughly this:

(42)   *All other things being equal, if a sentence type is more presuppositional, then the subject of that sentence tends to be more presupposed ("more topical").*

Now, since it is the enhanced topicality of the subject which turns out to drive the VS-to-SV word-order change (see Vennemann, 1973a; Givón, 1977a), then in this particular case the general pragmatic factors which precipitated the word-order change actually argue for the negative being syntactically *less* conservative than the "neutral" affirmative.

The conclusions to be drawn from this example are rather clear: While a "structural" principle may seem like a tempting candidate for controlling the overall phenomenon of syntactic conservatism, it is not that principle per se that is involved, but rather more detailed, highly specific and above all more *explanatory* discourse-pragmatic considerations.

There is one more aspect of the syntactic conservatism of **some** embedded clauses which should be mentioned here. It has to do with the frozen, quasi-lexicalized nature of some of them, in particular infinitival verb complements (of *want-* and *order-*type verbs). In a number of languages these complement clauses are bona fide nominalizations, and that tends to *freeze* their syntactic pattern while the "looser," sentential pattern of main clauses has proceeded via diachronic change. One example of such a type are VP compounds in English, where the older OV order has survived as frozen:

(43)   *street cleaner, garbage disposal, man-hunt, head-busting,* etc.

An interesting example in the same vein involves the way in which the old OV word-order has survived in the frozen, formulaic structure of cleft-predicate phrases in Yoruba, while in the main-clause predicate it has gone on to VO:[72]

[72] For the data I am indebted to Carl Lavelle (personal communication).

(44) a. ọmọ nâ wà ní   ibí
          child the be LOC here
          'The child is here'

      ọmọ na ni ó kpa adíe
      child the BE he kill chicken
      'It's the child who killed the chicken'

In (44a) the old locative copula *ni* appears before the predicate, that is, in a VO pattern. In (44b), however, it appears following the nominal focus predicate, that is, in the more archaic OV pattern.[73]

2.5.2. Morphological Innovation

The innovation of grammatical morphology is not, I believe, constrained by considerations of discourse markedness. Rather, it rises for specific needs at specific sites. For example, negative morphology obviously rises only in negative sentences. Relative-clause morphology only in relative clauses, verb-subordinating morphology only in verb complements etc. However, there are some "freezing" phenomena that may have to do with the nounlike rigidity of nominalized or frozen clauses and that, quite often, marks them as a "graveyard" area for older morphology. An interesting case involves WH-questions and cleft constructions in Bantu,[74] where the older Bantu copula *ni* seems to survive as a relic long after it had disappeared from the neutral sentential pattern. Since, in general, embedded clauses—relative, V-complements, ADV-clauses—are of a nominalized pattern in many languages, the chances of both syntactic and morphological conservatism in these frozen, quasi-lexicalized constructions is obviously high.

2.5.3. Semantic Elaboration

To the extent that semantic elaboration and expressive innovation carries more communicative weight in the clause type that contains the bulk of new information in discourse, one would indeed expect more presuppositional-marked sentence types to exhibit less innovation and thus be "more conservative." The bulk of the concrete evidence in support of such an assumption involves negative sentences as against their corresponding affirmatives, and will be presented in Chapter 3. Tense–aspect restrictions in embedded clauses, including total reduction in nonfinite and nominalized verb paradigms, are quite common cross-linguistically. For example, in Bemba, a Bantu language with sentential relative clauses and sentential adverbial clauses, of the 24 inde-

---

[73] For details see Givón (1974b).
[74] See Givón (1974b).

pendent tense–aspect markers, 7 are systematically barred from negative, relative clause, WH-question, cleft, adverb clause and pseudo-cleft constructions.[75] If this phenomenon is indeed general, it certainly strengthens the validity of the completeness argument given in Section 2.1.

2.6. LANGUAGE ACQUISITION

Ideally, it would be nice to be able to state that constructions that are more marked in terms of their discourse presuppositions are more difficult for children to acquire, or are acquired later. Unfortunately, many works on this subject structure their data gathering and data analysis in a way that precludes a noncircular, unequivocal acceptance or rejection of such a hypothesis. This is due to the fact that the acquisition of "structure" was studied without the acquisition of "function" and in isolation from the communicative and interactive environment in which child language development takes place. For example, Klima and Belugi (1973) show that the acquisition of the complex, syntactically marked pattern of negation in English is relatively late and is preceded by the aquisition of negative structures that are much more "simple." There is no evidence, however, to show when the *speech act* of negation is acquired and whether the *conceptual* complexity of negatives vis-à-vis affirmatives is an independent factor rather than tagging along with syntactic complexity.

That often the acquisition of a certain function outpaces the syntacticization of that function (i.e., the acquisition of the "structure") is slowly becoming clearer, as less restricted and more discourse and context oriented evidence is becoming more available. Thus Limber (1973) has suggested that *as a function,* WH-questions are acquired before relative clauses. While the latter are presuppositionally less complex, the former are acquired first as a *syntactically noncomplex* pattern, that is, as single WH-pronouns. Furthermore, at the time the WH-pronoun pattern is acquired, most of the NPs used by the child in discourse are still referentially unique—that is, pronouns, demonstratives, and proper names—so that there is no functional need for relative clauses, whose main function is to establish definite description.

Further, there is strong evidence (Limber, 1973; Ervin-Tripp, 1970) that in the acquisition of the WH-question pattern, the first stage involved *discourse sharing across participants,* so that the underlying presupposed sentence appears in the preceding discourse as a *declarative* sentence, then the child merely contributes the WH word, schematically:

---

[75] For details see Givón (1972a).

(45)   ADULT: *Daddy gone to work.*
         CHILD: *Why?*
         ADULT: *Peter coming to dinner.*
         CHILD: *Who?*

In fact, there is growing evidence[76] that this "spreading across participants" is one of the earliest modes of communication, whereby portions of the interaction which later on appear in the formal adult grammar as condensed inside the same construction, are shared by the participants *across* the discourse. More typically, one participant will establish the *topic–presupposition* and the other will then supply the *focus–assertion*. There is also evidence[77] that adults structure their communicative interaction with children deliberately in this manner as a teaching procedure.

More recent studies (Bates, 1976; Sconlon, 1976; Elinor Keenan 1974a, 1974b, 1975a, 1975b, 1977; Keenan and Schieffelin, 1976, 1977; Greenfield and Smith, 1976) all seem to suggest that children first acquire a communicative system with relatively simple structure, where the various parts of "propositions" are not tightly assembled together in syntactic "sentences" or "constructions." Rather, they are strung along the discourse, often across various "turns" of participants, with pauses and repetition and very little "syntactic" structure. The latter is acquired only later, via the process of "grammaticalization" (see discussion in Chapter 5). If these versions of the child language scenario are inherently correct, as I think they are, then perhaps the correlation between complexity and order of acquisition may be yet established on more solid empirical and conceptual grounds.

2.7. CONCLUSION: SYNTAX AND COMMUNICATION

If one establishes that the neutral sentence type—the main-declarative-affirmative-active clause—is indeed the type used in discourse for transmitting *the bulk* of new information, then the facts surveyed above may be understood as a set of complex dependencies whose explanation is largely rooted in this *functional* characterization of the neutral type. These dependencies may be summarized as follows:

1. *Discourse markedness*. Obviously the sentence type with the bulk of the new information–assertion will be *least presuppositional*. But one must consider that presuppositional complexity is only one dimension in the overall phenomenon of discourse markedness. Another dimension is

---

[76] See summary in Elinor Keenan (1977) as well as further discussion in Chapter 5.
[77] See Ervin-Tripp (1970).

that of *difficulty in identifying the referent*. When the speaker presupposes *more* difficulty on the part of the hearer, the construction type he uses in such a context should be considered more-marked. However, the case of indefinite-subject sentences (existential-presentative) drives home the fact that discourse markedness is in essence not an *absolute* notion but rather a *relative* one. In this particular instance, existential sentences are more-marked, that is, *communicatively more jarring* or surprising, because the norm ("background") in human communication is *multipropositional* discourse, where *topic-continuity* is the rule and *topic-switch* the exception. Ultimately, I think one may define discourse markedness as "the degree to which a discourse phenomenon constitutes a *surprise*, a break from the communicative norm." And since the norm may shift during discourse, the degree of communicative surprise is obviously relative to the norm *at any given moment*. On the background of total ignorance, new information is a break in the norm. On the background of presupposed knowledge, new information is a surprise. On the background of presupposed topic (multipropositional, equi-topic discourse), indefinite subjects break the norm. But at discourse initial, where no topic has been established, indefinite subject **is** the norm. That communicative surprise should correlate directly with *communicative difficulty* is, of course, quite expected, given the principle of *inertia* and its manifestation in communication, that is, the interplay between foreground and background.[78]

2. *Text frequency.* If human discourse involves, primarily,[79] the exchange of new information, then obviously the clause type which carries the bulk of the new information should also be expected to be the most frequent in discourse.

3. *Distributional restrictions.* In terms of the freer distribution of meaning-bearing elements, obviously the clause type which carries the bulk of new information is precisely the one where maximal elaboration is to be expected. The same is also true with the freer distribution of communicative devices that elaborate on topic–focus relations. On the other hand, the communicative loss emanating from less elaboration and less specification in presupposed clauses is more easily offset by the fact that they represent background information already accessible to the hearer. Finally, for the neutral clause type to have the widest text distribution, would also require that it had the fewest restrictions on its embedding in various grammatical environments.

4. *Syntactic complexity.* It is reasonable to assume that clauses

---

[78] Briefly, what does not move over the background is perceived as part of the background, but a move—change, break in routine—is perceived as foreground, surprise, or information. In terms of probability, a phenomenon with over 50% probability is a background, while one with under 50% probability is foreground. For further elaboration see Section 3.4.

[79] For a detailed discussion of this assumption and a contrast with animal communication, see Chapter 7.

which are more presuppositional and therefore not a critical part of the new information will also tolerate more syntactic—and thus probably more *perceptual*—complexity. It is nevertheless likely that at least in part the relevant notion of complexity is *relative,* as compared to the more frequent neutral norm. Thus psychologically relevant complexity may be, at least in part, a function of the background expectations established by the neutral norm. The seeming paradox involved here in terms of communication theory is this: In terms of *perception*, a phenomenon is easier to perceive if it is a *break* of the norm. That makes it perceptually more *salient*. On the other hand, in terms of *analysis* and *comprehension,* a less expected event—and a more rare one—is harder to analyze and process, given that better *routines* ("automatic processing strategies") are established for the more frequent event. The paradox is of course illusory: The perceptually more salient coding given to the more marked phenomenon simply serves to alert the hearer that what is coming now is a more complex, less expected, more-marked case, for which the normal processing strategies will not do, and special, exceptional strategies must therefore be activated.

5. *Syntactic dynamism:* To the extent that syntactic innovation arises from reinterpretation of marked, topic–focus variants as the neutral pattern, it is expected that the clause-type which exhibits the greatest freedom of distribution of such variants—the main-declarative-affirmative-active clause—will be syntactically less conservative. Furthermore, it is also expected that the neutral clause-type which carries the bulk of the new information will exhibit more semantic innovation and elaboration.

6. *Language acquisition:* Children acquiring their first language are obviously under *communicative stress* in two different ways:

1. They share very little of the general presuppositional background that is the prerequisite for communication.[80]
2. They have not yet learned the communicative code, conventions, processing strategies, etc.

Under such circumstances one expects, at least initially, a simplified communicative system. This system should involve the following characteristics: (a) slow rate of delivery, as measured in "bits per second;"[81] (b) a correlated high rate of repetition; (c) a correlated less condensed, less compacted syntax; (see discussion in Chapter 5). One may thus say that a syntactically complex construction is simply one in

---

[80] To offset this, early child communication takes place in—and refers to, as contents—the most immediate here–now, you–I, this–that visible object surroundings, where the context is obvious to both participants. See further discussion in Chapters 5 and 7.

[81] The relevant "bit" unit must be established for language. Lexical words, as well as NPs and VPs, are obvious possibilities, as well as "intonational groups." See some discussion in Givón (1975c).

which (a) *more information* is packed per intonational contour; and (b) *more code units* (in terms of morphemes, complex intonation and condensed syntactic pattern) are used to convey the message. One would thus expect both features to be more difficult to the child, given his condition under communicative stress. Furthermore, the seeming correlation between conceptual complexity and code complexity is in conformance with one of the most prevalent primes known to the linguist, whereby a smaller unit of meaning carries, on the average, a smaller sequence of code.[82] Finally, if the child is engaged in acquiring a communicative capacity, as clearly seems the case, then it seems reasonable that the capacity to produce the clause type via which most new information is conveyed—the main-declarative-affirmative-active clause—should develop before the capacity to produce the more presuppositional clauses. Once again, communicative necessity and psychological complexity may yet conspire to work hand in hand.

What of the classical Transformational intuition about kernels and transforms then? It is alive and well, I think, provided one realizes that

1. Its formal aspects are largely a *heuristic* for the linguist.
2. Those formal aspects cannot constitute by themselves an explanation but must rather be explained.
3. The explanation must refer to what we know about the use of syntactic structures in communication.

---

[82] Lexical morphemes are longer than grammatical morphemes, pronouns are shorter than nouns. For psycholinguistic evidence and an enlightening general discussion, see Greenfield and Dent (1978).

3
LOGIC VERSUS LANGUAGE
negation in language: pragmatics, function, ontology

3.1. INTRODUCTION[1]

> *Philosophical truth is to be sought in the presuppositions of language rather than in its expressed statements . . .*
> A. N. Whitehead, *Modes of Thought* (1938)

This chapter grew gradually out of a number of interlocking concerns set in different contexts. It began as an investigation of the use and function of negation in natural language. It was soon extended into the investigation of discourse presuppositionality and syntactic markedness as discussed in Chapter 2. Most naturally it then extended itself toward the study of language as an instrument of communication and the way discourse pragmatics interacts with syntax. This led on toward a rethinking of the relationship between the traditional treatment of negation in propositional logic as contrasted with the pragmatics of negation in natural language. As only to be expected, concerns of epistemology then led to an ontological investigation that finally set negation in a wider and seemingly more enlightening context.

In the first part I will attempt to show how negation in natural language differs, in highly specific and easily formalizable ways, from negation as traditionally treated in simple propositional logic. In the latter, the negative operator merely reverses the truth value of a proposi-

---

[1] A great number of people made helpful comments on earlier versions of this chapter, most particularly Dwight Bolinger, Erica García, Ed Keenan, Tim Shopen, Robert Hetzron, Larry Horn, Charles Osgood, Alan Timberlake, Derek Bickerton, Herbert Clark, and Robert Kirsner. I take this opportunity to thank them for their kindness and absolve them of any responsibility for the final product.

tion, without impinging upon the equal status of both [p] and [~p] as bona fide propositions *of the same sort*. This is best illustrated in the most basic logical axiom:

(1) $$\sim\sim p = p$$

In natural language, on the other hand, axiom (1) does not tell the entire story of negation and is, in fact, quite misleading as to some of the most basic properties of the negative *speech act*. Affirmatives and their corresponding negatives in language do not differ by only their truth value, but also by an additional—pragmatic—element, namely by their *discourse presuppositions*. These do not always correspond to what logicians have traditionally defined as "presupposition." Thus, for example, both types of presupposition discussed by Edward Keenan (1971) involve the *truth* of certain proposition, or—to be pragmatically looser—the speaker's *knowledge* of that truth. Now, many discourse presuppositions may indeed abide by such characterization. But others, perhaps the majority, do not always deal with what the speaker *knows to be true*. Furthermore, often they do not even deal with what the speaker knows that the *hearer* knows to be true. Rather, they involve what the speaker assumes that the hearer *tends to believe*, is *likely to be leaning toward*, or is *committed to by a probability higher than 50%*. The neat dichotomy of deductive logic thus tends, where the pragmatics of natural language is concerned, to melt in the light of *inductive*, probabilistic reasoning.

The facts of negation in language are of course a prime case in point, since if one takes presupposition in its strictly logical sense (as in Edward Keenan, 1971; Herzberger, 1971), one is bound to derive a contradiction. This is so because the discourse presupposition of a negative speech act is, as I will demonstrate below, its corresponding affirmative. Thus, from a strictly logical point of view, while the speaker asserts [~p] he presupposes [p]. Obviously this is a nonsensical conclusion which simply serves to illustrate that the facts of language as communication—once one steps beyond the artificially constructed world of the logic of atomic propositions—requires a richer, more complex, and perhaps even *open-ended* notion of presuppositional background. While one hopes that such a notion can be fleshed out with a sufficient degree of formal tightness, one must remain mindful of the real possibility that probabilistic, inductive notions may play a large—perhaps even decisive—role in the ultimate schema to be discovered.

The second part of the chapter investigates the type of predictions that one may derive from the presuppositionally *more marked* status of negative sentences. As discussed more generally in Chapter 2, these predictions involve distributional restrictions, diachronic conservatism, and psychological complexity.

In the last part I attempt to show how the pragmatics of negation as a speech act and its use in human communication all spring from a deeper *ontological* source, namely from the perceptual–conceptual strategies of *figure versus ground* by which humans construe their universe.

3.2. THE PRESUPPOSITIONAL STATUS OF NEGATIVE SPEECH ACTS

In this section I will begin by surveying the range of facts which led me initially to conclude that negative speech acts are presuppositionally *more marked* than their corresponding affirmatives. The exposition will follow an inductive rather than a deductive course. This is due in part to an aesthetic commitment, but is also a matter of necessity, since a complete range of facts on which a proper deductive exposition should be based is not yet available. In particular, I have not included many facts about embedded negation which, I believe, corroborate the analysis presented below.

3.2.1. The Restriction on Referential–Indefinites

Most object-taking verbs in language are *implicative* with respect to the *referentiality* ("existence") of their object. That is, unless the sentence is embedded under the scope of a [nonfact] modality,[2] then if the action–event described by the verb (or the entire *sentence*) is true, the referentiality (or existence) of the object must be also true. To illustrate referentiality and nonreferentiality, consider the following:

(2)   *John met a girl*

(3)   *John looked for a girl*

The verb *meet* in (2) is an *implicative* verb, and if sentence (2) is true, then the object *girl* must have existed, that is, the object is *referential*. The verb *look for* in (3), on the other hand, in *nonimplicative,* and the object *girl* of sentence (3)—even when the sentence is true—may either refer to an existing particular girl (referential) or to the *type girl* (nonreferential). Under the latter interpretation of (3), John would have been satisfied to find *any* girl.

When implicative verbs are used in an active, nonhabitual, nonrepetitive past tense, they may have *only* referential objects, though those objects could be either definite or indefinite. Thus consider:

---

[2] For a discussion of referentiality and existential opacity, see Givón (1973b), Jackendoff (1971), and Bickerton (1975b).

(4)   a. *John read a book*   (REF, INDEF)
       b. *John read **the** book*   (REF, DEF)
       c. **John read **any** book*[3]   (+NONREF)

The truth values of (4a, b, c) above may be given as in (5a, b, c) respectively:

(5)   a. *There exists a book, and John read it*
       b. *There exists a book, known to the hearer, and John read it*
       c. **There exists no book, and John read it*

Negation is one of the [nonfact] modalities in language, and nominals under the scope of such modalities may be interpreted both referentially and nonreferentially. It is thus not surprising that the negative construction corresponding to (4) should allow a nonreferential object. However, under the scope of negation—unlike the scope of the affirmative [nonfact] modality in (3)—the *referential*–indefinite interpretation of objects seems to melt away. Rather, referential objects under the scope of negation must be *obligatorily definite*:

(6)   a. *John didn't read a book*   (NONREF)
       b. *John didn't read **any** book*   (NONREF, emphatic)
       c. *John didn't read **the** book*   (REF, DEF)

The truth values of (6a, b, c) above may be given as in (7a, b, c), respectively:

(7)   a. *There exists no book such that John read it*
       b. *There exists no book such that John read it*
       c. *There exists a book known to the hearer and John didn't read it*

The referential–indefinite pattern that cannot be obtained under negation is the one whose truth value may be given as:

(8)   *There exists a book, and John didn't read it*

However, while the disallowed (5c) is logically contradictory, there is nothing *logically* wrong with (8) as an interpretation of (6a), but nevertheless it is not the preferred interpretation.

     Similar facts are reflected in the area of pronominalization. Following the introduction of an indefinite object of an implicative verb in an

---

[3] Under a [habitual] interpretation of the tense–aspect, that is, *John **used** to read any book that he could lay his hands on*, (4c) is, of course, acceptable. But the [habitual] mode is one of the [nonfact] modalities under whose scope existential opacity is possible (Givón, 1973b).

3.2. The Presuppositional Status of Negative Speech Acts

affirmative clause, pronominalization is possible under both the condition of identity of *sense* and identity of *reference:*[4]

(9)   *John met a girl yesterday,*
            {*and Fred met **one** too*   (SENSE)
            {*and Fred met **her** too*   (REFERENCE)}

But when an indefinite object is introduced in a corresponding negative sentence, only pronominalization under identity of sense is possible, but not under identity of reference. In other words, the indefinite object in the negative clause is *not* interpreted referentially:

(10)   *John didn't meet a girl yesterday,*
          {*and Fred didn't meet **one** either*   (SENSE)
          {**and Fred didn't meet **her** either*   (*REFERENCE)}

In fact, English, as well as a small number of other languages, tolerates, at the level of "grammatical competence," counterexamples to the above generalization. Consider,[5]

(11)   a. *What happened to Mary?*
      b. *Well, **she didn't read a book** that was put on the required list, and as a result she flunked her exam.*

While the grammaticality of (11) is not in doubt, there are strong grounds for suggesting that it does not really constitute a damaging counterexample to the claim made above. The argument obviously hinges on the distribution of definite and indefinite objects in discourse, that is, in live text reflecting the *true communicative choices* of speakers. Text counts of written English reveal that in main-declarative-affirmative-active clauses, on the average 50% of accusative objects are *indefinite,* and the overwhelming majority of those are *referential.* It thus seems that in actual discourse the accusative-object position is the prime environment in which *referential* arguments are introduced into the discourse *for the first time,* that is, as indefinites. These distributional facts are summarized in Table 3.1.

The distributions are radically different when one counts accusative objects of *negative* verbs in English. Of the *referential* objects counted in two fiction texts, 100% were definite. Conversely, all the morphologically indefinite accusative objects in these negative contexts were *nonreferential.* The results are summarized in Table 3.2. Thus it is apparent that even though the introduction of referential-indefinite object nouns in negative sentences is "grammatically possible" in English, at the

---

[4] For these examples I am indebted to Derek Bickerton (personal communication; but see also Bickerton, 1975c).
[5] For this example I am indebted to Tim Shopen (personal communication).

TABLE 3.1
The Distribution of Definite and Indefinite Accusative Objects in Main-Declarative-Affirmative-Active Clauses in English

Discourse type[a]	Subject				Accusative–Object			
	Definite		Indefinite		Definite		Indefinite	
	N	Percentage	N	Percentage	N	Percentage	N	Percentage
Nonfiction	43	87	6	13	24	48	25	52
Fiction	160	90	17	10	123	64	68	36
News	36	80	9	20	15	33	30	67
Sports	63	98	1	2	31	48	33	52
Total	302	91	33	9	191	56	156	44

[a] The texts counted are, respectively, Nonfiction: Chomsky (1973, pp. 3–12); Fiction: L'Amour (1965, pp. 1–25); News: *The Los Angeles Times*, 9-1-74, front page news; Sports: *The Los Angeles Times*, 9-1-74, front page of sports section.

3.2. The Presuppositional Status of Negative Speech Acts

TABLE 3.2
The Distribution of Definite and Indefinite Referential Accusative Objects in Main-Declarative-Negative-Active Clauses in English

Text[a]	Referential–Definite		Referential–Indefinite	
	N	Percentage	N	Percentage
Grey	46	100	0	0
Christie	29	100	0	0

[a] The two texts counted are Grey (1926, pp. 1–35) and Christie (1939, pp. 1–47).

level of actual attested text it is an extremely rare and largely shunned discourse strategy. Rather, it seems that speakers of English prefer to introduce referential nouns first into discourse in *affirmative* clauses, and consequently treat them only as *definites* in negative clauses. In English and a few other languages this restriction seems to hold at the level of 100% only at the level of "performance," that is, in text counts, but apparently not at the level of "grammatical competence." In most other languages, however, this restriction is imposed absolutely on the grammar.[6] As an example of such a language, consider first Hungarian:[7]

(12) a. *Jancsi olvasta a   könyvet*
       John read-it the book
       'John read the book'   (REF, DEF)

   b. *Jancsi olvasott egy könyvet*
       John read   one book
       'John read a book'   (REF, INDEF)

   c. *Jancsi könyvet olvasott*
       John book   read
       'John did some book-reading'[8] (REF, NONSPECIFIC)

Under the scope of negation, however, there is no sentence corresponding to (12b):

(13) a. *Jancsi nem olvasta a   könyvet*
       John NEG read-it the book
       'John didn't read the book'   (REF, DEF)

   b. **Jancsi nem olvasott egy könyvet*
       John NEG read   one book   (*REF, INDEF)

---

[6] For a discussion of the theoretical implications of this cross-language "difference," see Chapter 1.
[7] For the Hungarian data I am indebted to Robert Hetzron (personal communication).
[8] While logically the object of (12c) is referential, it is "nonspecified," and most languages apply to such objects the same surface marking accorded nonreferential nouns. A similar example from Hebrew was discussed in Section 1.3.3.5.

c. *Jancsi nem olvasott könyvet*
   John NEG read   book
   'John didn't read any book'   (NONREF)

Next, consider Bemba, a Bantu language employing a very different morphological system of coding the notions of definiteness and referentiality. Definiteness per se is not marked in this language. Rather, what is marked is the contrast between the referential (existential) and nonreferential interpretation of NPs. This distinction is coded by the noun-class prefix, which takes a VCV- canonic form if the noun is referential, and a CV- canonic form when the noun is nonreferential.[9] Illustrating this with an implicative verb in the past tense, one can observe the following distribution:

(14) a. *umu-ana   a-à-somene   ici-tabo*
         VCV-child he-past-read VCV-book
         {'The child read *a* book'   (REF, INDEF)}
         {'The child read *the* book' (REF, DEF) }

      b. **umu-ana   a-à-somene   ci-tabo*
         VCV-child he-past-read CV-book
         *'The child read *any* book'   (*NONREF)

Under negation, however, while a nonreferential interpretation of the object is possible, the referential object must obligatorily be interpreted as definite:

(15) a. *umuana tá-a-à-somene   ici-tabo*
         child NEG-he-past-read VCV-book
         'The child didn't read *the* book'   (REF, DEF)

      b. *umuana tá-a-à-somene   ci-tabo*
         child NEG-he-past-read CV-book
         'The child didn't read *any* book'   (NONREF)

Similar facts may be seen in Dzamba,[10] Luganda,[11] and Rwanda. In the latter two this is particularly striking because the definite object of negative verbs must obligatorily be topic-shifted to the left, a device that may be used only for definite nouns. Thus, consider the following:[12]

(16)   a. *ya-boonye umugore*
            he-past-see woman
            'He saw *a* woman'   (REF, INDEF)

[9] See further details in Givón (1973b).
[10] See Bokamba (1971) and Givón (1974b).
[11] See Mould (1975).
[12] For the Rwanda data I am indebted to Alexandre Kimenyi (personal communication).

3.2. The Presuppositional Status of Negative Speech Acts

b. *ya-**mu**-boonye umugore*
   he-past-*her*-see woman
   'He saw *the* woman' (REF, DEF)

c. *umugore ya-**mu**-boonye*
   woman he-past-*her*-see
   '*The* woman, he saw *her*' (REF, DEF, TOPIC)

d. *nhi-ya-boonye umugore*
   NEG-he-past-see woman
   'He didn't see *any* woman' (NONREF)

e. *umugore nhi-ya-**mu**-boonye*
   woman NEG-he-past-*her*-see
   ['He didn't see *the* woman.' (REF, DEF)   ]
   ['*The* woman, he didn't see *her*.' (REF, DEF, TOPIC)]

Under no circumstances can the object (16d) above be interpreted as *referential*–indefinite, though such an interpretation is quite natural in the corresponding affirmative (16a).

There exist other languages in addition to English where a referential–indefinite object following a negative verb is acceptable at the level of "competence." One of those is Israeli Hebrew, where one could indeed force this kind of interpretation by using a restrictive relative clause, the way it is done in English in (11). But the unstressed numeral *one*, which marks referential–indefinite nouns, must be present to reinforce this interpretation. Thus consider:

(17) a. *hu kaná séfer hayóm*
   he bought book today
   'He bought a book today' (REF, NONSPECIFIC)

b. *hu kaná séfer-xad hayóm*
   he bought book-one today
   'He bought *a* book today' (REF, INDEF)

c. *hu kaná et ha-séfer hayóm*
   he bought ACC the-book today
   He bought *the* book today' (REF, DEF)

d. *hu ló kaná séfer hayóm*
   he NEG bought book today
   'He didn't buy *a/any* book today' (NONREF)

e. *hu ló kaná áf séfer hayóm*
   he NEG bought any book today
   He didn't buy *any* book today' (NONREF)

f. *hu ló   kaná   et   ha-séfer hayóm*
   he NEG bought ACC the-book today
   'He didn't buy *the* book today'   (REF, DEF)

g. *hu ló   kaná   séfer-xad she-amrú lo   liknót,*
   he NEG bought book-one that-told him to-buy,
   letsaarí . . .
   unfortunately
   'Unfortunately, he didn't buy one book that he was told to buy . . .'

While I have no discourse counts from Hebrew, sentence (17g) though grammatical, is rather odd and much less preferred than the corresponding (18) in which the referential *book* is introduced for the first time—as indefinite—in an *affirmative* sentence, then appears as *definite* (here as pronoun) in the negative:

(18) *hayá séfer-xad she-amrú lo   liknót, aval hu ló   kaná   oto*
     was book-one that-told him to-buy, but he NEG bought it
     'There was a book they told him to buy, but he didn't buy *it*.'

It seems to me that precisely this kind of preference for one strategy over another underlies the facts of discourse distribution given in Table 3.2.

One should also note that a language may change the restriction on referential–indefinites under negation over a period of time, from a restriction at the competence level (as in Hungarian, Bemba, and Rwanda) to a restriction at the performance or text-count level (as in English and Israeli Hebrew). This may be illustrated by the facts of Mandarin Chinese.[13] The grammar of definiteness and indefiniteness is rather complex in this language, in a large measure as a result of ongoing diachronic change. The use of the numeral *one* to mark referential–indefinite nouns and of the distal demonstrative *that* to mark definites is a relatively recent development, and alternative devices relying on word-order differences between definites and indefinites still exist.[14] When only the old system, relying on word-order differences, is used, the language obeys the prohibition on referential–indefinites under negation at the level of grammatical competence. Thus consider

(19)   a. *wŏ dă-pò   le   zhuāngzi*
            I hit-broken ASP window
            'I broke *a* window/*some* windows'
                                    (REF, INDEF)   (SVO)

---

[13] For the Mandarin Chinese data I am indebted to Charles Li (personal communication).

[14] For an extensive discussion of the use of word order in marking the DEF–INDEF contrast in Mandarin, see Li and Thompson (1975).

3.2. The Presuppositional Status of Negative Speech Acts

b. wǒ bǎ   zhuāngzi dǎ-pò   le
   I ACC window   hit-broken ASP
   'I broke *the* window(s)'   (REF, DEF)   (SOV)

c. wǒ méi dǎ-pò   zhuāngzi
   I NEG hit-broken window
   'I didn't break *a/any* window'   (NONREF)   (SVO)

d. wǒ méi bǎ   zhuāngzi dǎ-pò
   I NEG ACC window   hit-broken
   'I didn't break *the* window(s)'   (REF, DEF)   (SOV)

In this older syntax of the language, the object noun in (19c) may only be interpreted as nonreferential. However, if the language foregoes the use of SOV syntax for definitization and instead uses the morphemes *one* and *that* (together with the numeral classifiers attached to them) to map the DEF–INDEF contrast, then at the grammatical competence level one could indeed obtain referential–indefinite objects in negative sentences:

(20) a. wǒ dǎ-pò   le   yī-ge   zhuāngzi
        I hit-broken ASP one-CL window
        'I broke *a* window'   (REF, INDEF)

     b. wǒ dǎ-pò   le   nèi-ge zhuāngzi
        I hit-broken ASP that-CL window
        'I broke *the* window'   (REF, DEF)

     c. wǒ méi dǎ-pò   yī-ge   zhuāngzi
        I NEG hit-broken one-CL window
        'There's *a* specific window that I didn't break'
                                                (REF, INDEF)

     d. wǒ méi dǎ-pò   nèi-ge zhuāngzi
        I NEG hit-broken that-CL window
        'I didn't break *the* window'   (REF, DEF)

However, while (20c)—in which the object of the negative verb is interpreted as referential–indefinite—is accepted as grammatical, the native speaker comments that it is "unpreferable," and that the construction in (21)—in which the indefinite object is introduced first in an affirmative existential construction and then appears as a zero-pronoun, that is, *definite*, in the negative—is much more preferable or "felicitous":

(21)   yǒu yī-ge   zhuāngzi wǒ méi   dǎ-pò
        be one-CL window   I   NEG hit-broken
        'There's *a* window that I didn't break'

While I do not have text-counts from Mandarin, I would predict that the speaker's preference for the strategy in (21) over that in (20c) will translate itself into text frequencies just as it does in English.

The discussion above was confined to accusative objects. However, one could easily show that it applies in equal measure to *subjects*. In most languages, the subject, unless appearing in a specialized existential construction, is obligatorily *definite*.[15] Some languages, such as English, indeed allow referential–indefinite subjects at the competence level, but as can be seen from Table 3.1, the average text frequency of this phenomenon is rather low, around 10%.[16] But even in languages such as English, which tolerate referential–indefinite subjects outside of existential constructions,[17] the status of referential–indefinite subjects in corresponding negative sentences is rather dubious. Thus consider:

(22)   a.   *A man came into my office yesterday and . . .*

         b.   **A man didn't come into my office yesterday (and . . .)*

         c.   *Someone came into my office yesterday and . . .*

         d.   **Someone didn't come into my office yesterday (and . . .)*

         e.   *No one came into my office yesterday (*and . . .)*

Later on I will discuss the *pragmatic* oddity of sentences such as (22b) and (22d) above. If one could interpret them as felicitous at all at the grammatical competence level, it is only by interpreting the subjects as *nonreferential* (i.e., *It is not true that a man came into my office yesterday . . .*), and this interpretation is rendered much more felicitously by (22e). Further below I will discuss the status of apparent counterexamples to (22d), that is, sentences such as:

(23)   *Someone didn't do the dishes yesterday*

There I will also show that the acceptability of (23) depends on the construction of a different pragmatic-presuppositional background, and that this type of counterexample corroborates rather than destroys the general restriction discussed here, which is in essence a *pragmatic* restriction.

While the restriction discussed above is thus not confined to accusative objects, its significance in actual discourse is rather marginal for subjects, since they tend to be—overwhelmingly—either definite or nonreferential. For accusative objects, however, where in affirmative sentences one finds on the average around 50% indefinites—and those mostly referential, the restriction on referential–indefinites under the

---

[15] For details and discussion see Edward Keenan (1976a), Kirsner (1973), Hetzron (1971) and Givón (1976a), as well as Chapters 1 and 2.

[16] See more discussion in Chapter 1.

[17] Even in English this freedom is illusory, since there are severe restrictions in text on the verb-type that may appear in sentences with indefinite subjects. See discussion in Chapter 2.

3.2. The Presuppositional Status of Negative Speech Acts

scope of negation is quite striking. What it means is that negative clauses are not used for introducing new referential arguments into the discourse, but rather, they are used in contexts in which a referential argument has already been mentioned in the preceding discourse,[18] and therefore in the negative clause it can only appear as definite. In purely formal terms, then, negative sentences must be *more presuppositional* than their corresponding affirmatives, since subject and object nouns tend to be *more definite* in them. In other words, when a speaker utters a negative sentence in discourse, he *assumes more* about what the hearer knows than when he utters an affirmative. In the next section I will develop this notion further and show how the restriction discussed above follows from the pragmatics and function of the negative speech act in discourse.

3.2.2. Discourse Context and Discourse Function of Negation

In this section I will present discourse evidence supporting the preliminary conclusions outlined above. Let us begin by considering the following situation: I meet a friend in the street, by accident. My friend knows that I am married. I greet him, he inquires politely *What's happening?*. I then volunteer the following information:

(24)   *Oh, my wife is pregnant.*

Now, my friend may choose to congratulate or commiserate with me, depending on further assumptions he had made about my attitude, but he will find nothing odd in our exchange. Now, consider the very same context, in which, however, rather than uttering (24) above, I volunteer instead its corresponding negative:

(25)   *Oh, my wife's not pregnant.*

My friend is most likely to balk at the felicity of this information and say (26a) or (26b) below.

(26)   a.   *Wait a minute—was she supposed to be pregnant?*
       b.   *Hold it—I didn't know she was **supposed to be** pregnant!*

My friend could of course choose not to react as in (26a,b) above but rather go ahead and congratulate or commiserate with me as before. However, this sanguine reaction on his part strongly suggests that he knew more about the context for my uttering (25), that is, that there was

---

[18] The context need not be overtly mentioned in the preceding discourse, although that is certainly one way by which speakers make sure of what hearers know. But the speakers may also assume knowledge from a previous discussion, from life experience, general knowledge of the world or its reflection in dictionary knowledge.

some *likelihood* that my wife was pregnant, that the subject has been *under discussion*, that it had been *considered as a probability*, etc. Indeed, I would not have chosen, under the normal felicity conventions of discourse, to utter the negative information in (25) unless I had reasons to assume that he had been clued into this more specific context of likelihood or previous discussion. In other words, a felicitous discourse context for the negative is the previous mention of the corresponding affirmative, or alternatively the belief by the speaker that the hearer has heard of the possibility of that corresponding affirmative being true, and in fact has *tipped his belief* toward the truth of that corresponding affirmative.

In the light of what was said above, the restriction discussed in the preceding section can now be explained in a natural way: If the speaker uttering a negative sentence assumes that the hearer knows that the corresponding affirmative was likely or has been previously mentioned, then, unless the arguments of the verb are nonreferential to begin with, the speaker must also assume that the hearer *knows the identity*[19] of those arguments, since they too must have been mentioned in previous discourse—or form part of the context assumed by the speaker. On the basis of this knowledge those arguments are definitized. To illustrate this in context, consider the same background of the situation as in (24) and (25) above, where the news I volunteer is:

(27)   *We saw a movie yesterday.*

My friend is unlikely to balk at the felicity of this information within the given context, though he could certainly seek further information, such as *Which one?*, etc. Suppose now that in the same context I volunteer instead:

(28)   *We didn't see a movie yesterday.*

In spite of what is "grammatically possible" in English, my friend's most normal interpretation of *a movie* in (28) would be nonreferential. But further, he is likely to balk and demand the missing context, as in (29):

(29)   *Oh, were you* $\begin{Bmatrix} \textit{supposed to} \\ \textit{going to} \\ \textit{planning to} \end{Bmatrix}$ *see one?*

Now, suppose the missing context—shared with my friend—was my intent to go and see a specific, referential movie whose identity was

---

[19] "Knowing the identity" of an argument is relative to a particular discourse, rather than necessarily to "the real world." Thus, if I discuss with a friend the possibility of *John's murderer was a blind man*, it is possible that neither of us may know the exact identity of the murderer, but nevertheless we can definitize him, on the basis of our shared knowledge that *Someone murdered John.*

3.2. The Presuppositional Status of Negative Speech Acts

known to my friend. Under these conditions the negative in (28) would have been inappropriate on my part, but the corresponding (30), with the object definitized, would have been appropriate.

(30)   *We didn't see that movie yesterday.*

There are thus two types of belief held by the hearer which the speaker may contradict with a negative sentence containing an object. If the corresponding affirmative involves the likelihood of performing the action with respect to "any member of the *type* x," then the noun x appears in the negative with a *nonreferential* interpretation. On the other hand, if the corresponding affirmative involves the likelihood of performing the action with respect to "a *specific token* of the type x,' then the noun x appears in the negative as *definite*. One way or another, a referential-indefinite interpretation of a previously mentioned noun is clearly inappropriate.

3.2.3. Adverbs and the Scope of Negation

It is normally assumed that in the neutral sentence pattern in language, the predicate phrase contains the asserted new information, while the subject–topic is presupposed, that is, the assertion is made with respect to it. While conceding this generalization, there remains the problem of the *scope of assertion* when the predicate phrase contains an object or an adverb in addition to the verb. For several complement types, the verb phrase containing the complement is potentially ambiguous as to whether the entire verb phrase is asserted, that is, *in focus*, or whether only the complement which follows the verb is in focus. For example, consider (31a) below, which may be given as a felicitous answer to either the wider (VP scope) question (31b), or to the narrower (COMP scope) question (31c):

(31)   a.   *He went into the bar.*
       b.   *What did he do then?*   (VP scope)
       c.   *Where did he go then?*   (COMP scope)

The use of contrastive stress may remove this potential ambiguity of (31a), but the discourse context for contrastive stress involves additional, stronger, more complex assumptions.[20] The negation of sentences such as (31a) retains the potential ambiguity of scope. Thus, it may be used to deny the wider (VP scope) assertion, as in (32), or the narrower (COMP scope) assertion, as in (33).

---

[20] See further discussion in Chapter 2.

(32) a. Where's Joe?
      b. I think he *went into the bar*.
      c. No, he didn't go into the bar, he's **sitting right there**.
         (VP scope)

(33) a. Where did Joe go?
      b. I think he went *went into the bar*.
      c. No, he didn't go *into the bar*, he went *into the lobby*.
         (COMP scope)

Again, contrastive stress on the complement tends to disambiguate the narrower scope negation, while stress on *didn't* will tend to suggest the wider (VP) scope.

Other types of complements tend to behave differently, and one could ultimately show that these differences stem from the pragmatics of what one considers to be normative action. Thus, with great many manner-adverb complements, the scope of the assertion is ambiguous in the affirmative, but unambiguously narrower in the negative. For example, (34a) may be a felicitous answer to either the wider (VP scope) question (34b) or the narrower (COMP scope) question (34c).

(34) a. He ran as fast as he could.
      b. What did he do then?   (VP scope)
      c. How did he run then?   (COMP scope)

On the other hand, the negative corresponding to (34a) tends to have only the narrower (COMP) scope:

(35)   He didn't run as fast as he could.

The difference between (34a) and (35) may be also characterized in terms of their implication properties. Thus the narrower scope interpretation of (34a) implies the wider (VP) scope, but the narrow negation scope of (35) does not imply the wider (VP) scope of negation:

(36)   He ran as fast as he could $\supset$ He ran

(37)   He didn't run as fast as he could $\not\supset$ He didn't run

Furthermore, not only does the implication in (37) fail, which is still consistent with the logical entailments of (36), but in fact the stronger inference (38) seems to hold in this case; which is—from a strict logical point of view—a contradiction:

(38)   He didn't run as fast as he could $\supset$
        He ran, though not as fast as he could

3.2. The Presuppositional Status of Negative Speech Acts

This apparent logical contradiction may be summarized as:

(39)   a. $p \supset q$
         b. $\sim(\sim p \supset \sim q)$
         c. $\sim p \supset q$

where (39b) is a correct inference from the premise (39a), but (39c) is not.[21]

The pragmatic reason why this state of affairs is tolerated in language is fairly transparent in light of the preceding discussion. Negative assertions are used in language in contexts where the corresponding affirmative has been mentioned, deemed likely, or where the speaker assumes that the hearer—erroneously—holds to a belief in the truth of that affirmative. Why then the seemingly contradictory (39c)? Consider: If one wanted to assert that no action has taken place, that is, *He didn't run at all*, the sentence (35) is wasteful, since (40) will suffice:

(40)   *He didn't run.*

Thus, if the negative in (35) is to have any independent communicative value to differentiate itself from (40), it must then exclude the verb from the scope of negation, and thus negate only the complement.[22]

Other complement types seem to impose the narrower (COMP) focus already in the affirmative. For example, consider:

(41)   a.   *John ate the glass on purpose.*
         b.   *John ate his dinner on purpose.*

Sentence (41a) is felicitous, but of the three questions in (42) below, it could be normally used as a felicitous answer only to the narrow (COMP) scope question (42c), but not to the wider (VP or OBJ) focus questions (42a, b):

(42)   a.   *What did John do then?*   (VP focus)
         b.   *What did John eat then?*   (OBJ focus)
         c.   *How come he ate the glass?*   (PURPOSE focus)

In order to understand why this is so, consider the oddity of (41b). This sentence is highly *redundant* because: (*a*) Eating one's dinner is a *normal* action one performs; (*b*) Actions *normally* performed by agents are performed *on purpose*. Thus (41b) is odd because it has no informative value, given that eating one's dinner is the normal case and given

---

[21] In fact, given the logical definition of presupposition (Edward Keenan, 1971), proposition q in (39) must be a presupposition of p, since it is true both when p is true and false. But this is precisely what is shown in (38), that is, that *He ran* is presupposed by *He ran as fast as he could*.

[22] For this suggestion I am indebted to Robert Kirsner (personal communication).

convention (b) above. On the other hand, (41a) has definite informative value, since the action of *eating glass* is *counternormative*, and therefore the question arises whether a person did it on purpose or by accident. Finally, why is the assertion scope automatically narrowed to the purpose complement in (41a)? The answer to that again hinges on the pragmatics of normative versus counternormative action. Eating glass is a counter-normative action, which by itself makes it an information-bearing event, a fact which may be seen from the informative oddity of (43c) as an answer to (43a), as contrasted with the informative felicitousness of (43b):

(43)   a. *What's new with John?*

            b. *He ate glass yesterday.*

            c. *He ate his dinner yesterday.*[23]

Thus if one says that someone ate glass on purpose, a pragmatic inference attached to this is that it is not *eating glass* per se that is in assertive focus, but rather the fact that it was done on purpose.

Further details of this phenomenon are discussed elsewhere,[24] but at any rate the facts of English are such that for some complements (*to the bar*) there is no necessary narrowing of the scope of assertion under negation, for others (*on purpose*) the scope of assertion is equally narrowed—that is, excluding the verb—in both the negative and the affirmative, while for a third group (*as fast as he could*) the scope of assertion is narrower in the negative than in the affirmative. To my knowledge no complements exist where the scope of the assertion is narrower in the *affirmative*. Thus one is again faced with a systematic bias between the affirmative and the negative in language, where the negative is consistently uttered in more presuppositional discourse contexts, thus creating the effect of "narrower scope of assertion"—which is another way of saying that the verb itself is presupposed rather than being part of the new information. As I have shown above, this phenomenon has nothing to do with the strict logic of negation, but rather with the pragmatics of the use of negation—always in context where the speaker believes that the hearer holds a certain belief in the truth of the corresponding affirmative. This belief may have arisen as a result of the preceding discourse, though quite often it is grounded in the general knowledge of the pragmatics of what is or isn't normative action.

While in English the scope of assertion is narrowed under negation

---

[23] This sentence becomes "informatively felicitous" when the speaker and hearer share the belief that John *normally* (or at least for a time) was not eating his dinner, that is, when the norm and counternorm are reversed. Similarly, (43b) becomes "informatively redundant" if John normally eats glass.

[24] See Givón (1975c).

3.2. The Presuppositional Status of Negative Speech Acts

only for some complement types, there are languages where this holds true for all complement types. I will briefly illustrate this with the data of one Bantu language, Bemba, and the reader may refer to Givón (1975c) for further details.

There are seven minimal pairs for this assertion-scope distinction in the Bemba tense–aspect system, six of those in various past tense categories and one in the habitual. I will first illustrate the distinction in the terminated, distant (before yesterday) past. In this time division, the morphological contrast is between the VP-scope morpheme *-àli-* and the COMP-scope morpheme *-à-*. When the verb phrase contains only a verb, only the VP-scope particle may be used:

(44)   a.   *ba-àli-boombele*
              'They worked'
     b.   **ba-à-boombele*

When a complement, nominal or adverbial, is present, one obtains the distinction of scope:[25]

(45)   a.   *ba-àli-boombele saana*
         'They *worked   hard*'   (VP scope)

      b.   *ba-à-boombele saana*
         'They worked *hard*'   (COMP scope)

      c.   *ba-àli-boombele mumushi*
         'They *worked   in the village*'   (VP scope)

      d.   *ba-à-boombele mumushi*
         'They worked *in the village*'   (COMP scope)

      e.   *ba-àli-boombele neemfumu*
         'They *worked   with the chief*'   (VP scope)

      f.   *ba-a-boombele neemfumu*
         'They worked *with the chief*'   (COMP scope)

      g.   *ba-àli-liile umukate*
         'They *ate bread*'   (VP scope)

      h.   *ba-à-liile umukate*
         'They ate *bread*'   (COMP scope)

The sentences with the VP scope (45a, c, e, g) may be all used to answer the wider scope WH question *What did they do then?*. The sentences with the COMP scope (45b, d, f, h) are used in contexts where the verb itself is not new information, that is, to answer the more specific WH questions such as, *How did they work?*, *Where did they work?*, *With*

---

[25] The emphasis in (45) indicate the scope of the assertion or new information.

whom did they work? and *What did they eat?*, respectively. Cleft-focusing of the complement, which leaves the verb itself as part of the presupposition, obligatorily requires the COMP-focus on the verb:

(46) a. *múúkate ba-à-liile*
 'It's bread that they ate'   (COMP focus)
 b. **múúkate ba-àli-liile*   (*VP focus)

Under the scope of negation, only the COMP-focus particle may be used:

(47) a. *ta-ba-à-boombele saana*
 'They didn't work hard'   (COMP focus)
 b. **ta-ba-àli-boombele saana*   (*VP focus)

Things are a bit more complicated, however. When the verb phrase contains only a verb, and thus the focus of negated assertion is unambiguously upon that verb, the same restriction on the VP focus particle is observed:

(48) a. *ta-ba-à-boombele*
 'They didn't work'   (COMP focus)
 b. **ta-ba-àli-boombele*   (*VP focus)

Does this represent an "analogical extension" or "grammaticalization" of the system, indicating the breakdown of the inherently semantic underlying regularity? It seems to me that one may interpret these data within the context of the same underlying regularity. As seen above, negative sentences are used in the context where the corresponding affirmative has been mentioned before or, alternatively, when the speaker assumes that the hearer tends to believe in the truth of the corresponding affirmative. While this is not, per se, a totally *presuppositional* context, it nevertheless involves a context where the verb, at the very least, could *not* be new information to the hearer. One may thus view the mapping system of Bemba as follows:

(49) Verb not new information = COMP focus
 Verb new information = VP focus

The formulation in (49) makes it easier to understand why the VP-focus particle may not be used in any negative sentence in Bemba if its function is indeed to appear in contexts where the verb is new information. This formulation also permits a unified view of other restrictions on the distribution of this particle, namely that it may not appear in relative clauses, WH questions, cleft and pseudo-cleft constructions as well as in relative-related and largely presuppositional[26] adverbial clauses such as *when, because, since, although, if, in spite of,* etc. Thus, while the negative obviously could not presuppose its corresponding affirmative, the fact that it appears in contexts where the affirmative is assumed to be known to the hearer or considered likely by him, removes the verb in the negative from the scope of strictly new information, and thus imposes on the negative in Bemba the very same scope restrictions imposed upon truly presuppositional clauses.

3.2.4. "Other Than" Ambiguity

The phenomenon discussed in this section was observed by García (1975a). It relates to the potentially ambiguous interpretation of the following two sentences, an affirmative and its corresponding negative:

(50) a. *John likes soups other than minestrone.*
      b. *John doesn't like soups other than minestrone.*

Garcia (1975a) has elicited responses to the question *Does John like minestrone?* from people given sentences (50a, b). Given the affirmative sentence (50a), 68% of the respondents answered that John *didn't like* minestrone, while 32% judged the sentence *ambiguous*, that is, that it could mean either that John liked or did not like minestrone. On the other hand, the speakers' reaction to the negative (50b) was unanimous—that John *liked* minestrone. Garcia (1975a) further observed that all speakers took, on the average, three times longer to answer the question in the context of the affirmative (50a) than the negative (50b). Garcia observes that "other than minestrone" divides the universe of soups into two groups: Minestrone versus all other soups, and that the speaker may then view the two either *disjunctively,* that is, "all soups *excluding* minestrone," or *conjunctively,* that is, "all soups *in addition to* minestrone." She then observes the following concerning the communicative appropriateness of negative sentences: "negative sentences communicate in terms of an implicit, but rejected, affirmation, which for some reason might be expected to hold, but which in fact fails to obtain . . . [1975a, p. 8]." She then explains the disparity between the interpretation of the affirmative (50a) and the negative (50b) in the following way:

> Consider, first, what "other than" does: . . . it divides the soup universe into two sets: minestrone and other soups. What does "not" tell us? It tells us that the upper set

---

[26] Of these, *if* clauses are not presupposed in the strict logical sense. However, much like negatives and yes–no questions, they appear in discourse contexts where normally the probability of the proposition embedded in the conditional expression has been entertained, discussed, or considered. Thus the verb in the *if* clause, while not strictly presupposed to be "true," cannot be new information either.

(other soups) is the one that John does *not* like. But since "not" implies a contrast with a possible affirmation, and "other than" offers us a term of reference, the conclusion is—illogically, perhaps, but unavoidably—that if we are told that he does not like the "other than" soups, the reason must be because he *does like* something else, and the only something else left is minestrone. . . . In other words: the "excluding" view taken of "other than"—as being opposed, rather than added, to the minestrone subset—is the one most congruent with the nature of negation, which—to be plausible—must be understood in terms of a contrast . . . [1975a, pp. 8-9].

Garcia goes on to show that this type of restriction of options which is brought about by the contrastive—or in my terms "presuppositional"—nature of negation does not obtain for the corresponding affirmative. While one may not subscribe to her contention that the reasoning involved in the negative case is "logically fallacious," and while one may wish to point out that the pragmatics of various presuppositions associated with speech acts in language simply involves more complex *hidden premises* which the logician in his standard analysis of negation has neglected to consider, her basic argument is perfectly sound: "From an 'objective', 'grammatical' point of view there is no fundamental difference between an affirmative and a negative sentence: a negative sentence merely denies what is affirmed in the positive sentence. But in terms of actual communication, for practical purpose, a negative sentence is, a priori, worth far less than an affirmative one . . . [1975a, p. 5]." In other words, if negative sentences are uttered in contexts where the corresponding affirmative has already been discussed, or where the speaker has reasons to believe that the hearer is familiar with that corresponding affirmative and biased toward believing in it, then obviously much of the communicative contents expressed by the negative is already part of the *presuppositions*[27] associated with negation as a speech act, and only a relatively small increment—namely, the denial by the speaker of the hearer's belief—constitutes the new communicative contribution of the negative-assertion speech act.

3.2.5. External and Internal Negation

The negation type discussed thus far is called by logicians "internal" negation, where only the assertion is negated but not the presuppositions associated with the corresponding affirmative sentence. Logi-

---

[27] One is of course tempted here to adopt Edward Keenan's (1971) distinction between "logical" and "pragmatic" presupposition and to consider the discourse-presuppositions discussed above as pragmatic. However, it is not clear to me that the distinction is either valid or necessary in natural language, since it is possible (cf. Karttunen, 1974) to define **all** presuppositions as pragmatic, that is, expressible in terms of speaker and hearer beliefs. When this is done, logical presuppositions represent the beliefs of the speaker *exclusive* of hearer's, while pragmatic presuppositions represent the belief of the speaker *about* hearer's belief.

3.2. The Presuppositional Status of Negative Speech Acts

cians also recognize "external" negation, in which the presuppositions—as well as the assertion—may fall under the scope of negation.[28] As a classical example, consider (51) and (52):

(51) *The king of France is bald*

(52) *The king of France is not bald.*

A speaker accepting (51) as felicitous must perforce presuppose that France has a king. The negative (52) may thus, according to logicians, have two readings. The first, *internal,* allows the presupposition to stand and merely negates the assertion *(he) is bald.* The second, *external,* presumably states that the sentence (51) could not be true since France has no king, that is, the presupposition is not true'

In general, while linguists and philosophers find it easy to recognize the *external* sense of negation, most speakers of human languages do not. In other words, they tend to view negative constructions almost always as *internal* operations. Thus, faced with the negative in (52), most speakers would not immediately recognize the external reading. Similarly, given the affirmative (53) below, speakers would tend to construe its negative (54) as an internal negation, while allowing a rather special form, such as (55), to represent the external interpretation in which the subject failed to have denotation:

(53) *Someone loves Mary.*

(54) *Someone doesn't love Mary,*

(55) *No one loves Mary.*

One could also show that the NP-negation pattern (55) is a more rare phenomenon in languages, and that it is in some sense a "more marked," "less likely" negation pattern, perhaps ultimately arising from a much more prevalent negative-*existential* construction, as in:

(56) *There's no one who loves Mary.*

In particular, the most overwhelming fact about the referentiality of sentential *subjects* in language, is how hard it is to suspend it even under negation.[29] This contrasts sharply with the behavior of *objects* under negation (cf. Section 3.2.1), where negation is one of the modalities which create a nonreferential interpretation of objects.

Furthermore, notice that although the external negation in (55) and

---

[28] Or, under other formulations, "allow a third value in the logic." For an extensive discussion including some historical perspectives, see Herzberger (1971).

[29] For an extensive discussion of the reference-related properties of subjects, see Edward Keenan (1976a).

(56) above suspends the presupposition of referentiality of the subject nouns, it nevertheless retains the pragmatic discourse-presuppositions associated with negation in language as noted above. For example, while the affirmative (51) may be uttered in the context "talking about the king of France," its corresponding negative (52) would have required—under either internal or external negation—additional context in order to make it felicitous, such as "talking about the possibility that the king of France is bald."

In view of the strong tendency manifested in human languages to protect the referentiality—and definiteness—of the sentential subject,[30] a number of seemingly isolated facts concerning negation in language seem to somehow converge toward a unified explanation. These facts may be summarized as such:

(57) a. Functional. *The subject of sentences is almost always referential and definite, because it serves to **link** a sentence to the preceding discourse, in the context of which a new assertion is being made. In other words, the subject functions as **topic**.*[31]

   b. Syntactic. *While in logic one most often considers negation to be a **sentential** operation, in the syntax of natural languages it is most often a **predicate-phrase** operator, excluding the subject from its scope.*

   c. Semantic. *Negation in language is overwhelmingly **internal**, with special, "marked" patterns reserved for the explicit mapping of external negation.*

   d. Diachronic. *Negative markers in language most often arise, diachronically, from erstwhile negative main verbs, most commonly **refuse, deny, reject, avoid, fail,** or **lack**.*[32]

It seems to me that these facts are obviously related. To begin with, if the subject's referentiality and definiteness is a necessary ingredient for it to perform its discourse function as "link" or *topic* (57a), then there is a certain advantage to exclude it from the scope of negation and leave it as part of the presuppositions of the sentence—since its being a topic automatically suggests that the speaker uses it to tell the hearer what he is talking about. Maintaining negation in language as largely an *internal*

---

[30] See Edward Keenan (1976a) and Givón (1976a).

[31] See Edward Keenan (1976a) and Givón (1976a). Karttunen's (1974) suggestion concerning the *incremental* nature of discourse, where assertions are made in the context of the preceding (presupposed) discourse, then they themselves become—if unchallenged—the presuppositions for the subsequent discourse, is compatible with this observation.

[32] For a discussion of the verbal origin of negative as well as tense–aspect–modal markers in language, see Givón (1973c).

operation (57c) accomplishes precisely this, since it excludes the subject from the scope of negation, which then applies only to the predicate-phrase, that is, the assertion itself. Next, if there is to be a correlation between the form and meaning in sentential structure, as is obviously desirable in any communicative system, then the syntactic–morphemic fact (57b) is precisely the kind of surface mapping which accomplishes this requirement, by making the negation marker a predicate-phrase operator. Finally, a fortunate diachronic conspiracy allows the development of negation markers to proceed, most commonly, from negative-implication verbs which have the *verb phrase* as their complement—thus excluding the subject from the scope of negation (57d). So that in *John failed to leave*, it is implied that *John didn't leave* but John's referentiality and definiteness is not challengeable.[33]

3.3. SOME CONSEQUENCES OF THE MARKED STATUS OF NEGATIVES

In the preceding sections I have shown that, with respect to their presuppositional complexity—or the richness of the assumptions which the speaker must make about what the hearer knows, negatives are more marked as compared to their corresponding affirmatives. In this section I will attempt to show how the markedness of negative sentences has a number of consequences of the type that one would like to predict, given any marked–unmarked opposition in language. The consequences I would like to discuss here are (*a*) distributional restrictions; (*b*) syntactic conservatism; and (*c*) psychological complexity. Ideally one would like to add at least one more, namely (*d*) delayed acquisition by children, and indeed there are some facts which corroborate this.

There is a certain smugness which has permeated the discussion of markedness in linguistics, at least implicitly, and it involves the tacit assumption that somehow showing that a member of a certain binary opposition is marked, constitutes an explanation of its linguistic behavior. Ohala (1974) has commented on this rather succinctly in the area of phonology, suggesting that marked, per se, is an empty notion, explaining nothing but merely *labeling* the distributional facts. Those distributional facts, that is, the wider distribution of the unmarked form, must still be explained by reference to some substantive notion that has *independent motivation*. I have made similar arguments elsewhere[34]

---

[33] Pam Munro (personal communication) suggests that in Mojave (Yuman) the negative marker may have been derived from a verb that takes the entire sentence (including the subject) under its scope, that is, a verb of the *prevent* type. This may or may not be a counterexample, but even so it is rare.

[34] See discussion in Chapter 2.

concerning the notion of unmarked or "neutral" syntax, and it seems to me, therefore, that the demonstration of behavioral consequences of markedness in syntax, while instructive, is not, by itself, enough. Rather, one must also strive to explain how the substantive, independently motivated notion of markedness involved in a particular situation *motivates* or *causes* the observed behavioral consequences. If we assume, as I suggested above, that negative clauses are more marked with respect to the complexity of the pragmatic presuppositions which characterize the discourse context in which they may be felicitously used, then we must show in what way this notion of markedness motivates the observed behavior of negative clauses in human language. Such a demonstration is indeed the purpose of this section.

3.3.1. Distributional Restrictions

As discussed in Chapter 2, a marked construction in syntax is expected to display distributional restrictions in two ways: First, it is expected to allow less distributional freedom to elements embedded in it. Second, it is expected to exhibit less freedom of embedding itself within other structure or contexts. In this subsection I will illustrate both types. As discussed in Chapter 2, in many instances distributional restrictions, while synchronically demonstrable, involve added diachronic considerations. Those will be discussed in Section 3.3.2.

3.3.1.1. RESTRICTIONS ON SCOPES AND AMBIGUITIES

In Section 3.2.3 I have shown that under the scope of negation, for at least some adverbials in English, there exists a systematic restriction in the scope of new information ("assertion"), so that scope ambiguities that are observed in the affirmative are barred from corresponding negatives. I have further shown that there was nothing in the strict *logic* of negation to motivate this behavior, and that indeed at a certain point a logical fallacy was seemingly obtained [namely, (38) and (39) above]. Rather, the explanation for the scope and ambiguity restrictions involved the *pragmatics* of negation as a speech act.

In the same vein, the restrictions on the distribution of the VP-focus markers in Bemba (see Section 3.2.3) as well as identical restrictions in Rwanda and Zulu (see Givón, 1975c), which bar these focus markers from appearing in negative clauses as well as in all presupposed and "semipresuppositional" clauses, all reflect the same pragmatic motivation as in the case of the scope-and-ambiguity restrictions in English.

Finally, the facts discussed by García (1975a; see Section 3.2.4) involve a similar situation, where again the explanation is derived from the pragmatics of negation as a speech act in discourse.

3.3.1.2. AMBIGUITY OF ADVERBS IN PERIPHRASTIC CAUSATIVES[35]

There seems to be a systematic *potential* ambiguity in the interpretation of the scope of adverbs in sentences with periphrastic *try–cause* verbs, as in:

(58)   *John told Bill to run again.*

Under more careful scrutiny, two distinct intonation patterns may be observed, each characteristic of a different interpretation of the scope of applicability of the adverb:

(58)
- a. *John told Bill to rún agàin.*
  = 'John again told Bill to run.'
- b. *John told Bill to rùn agáin.*
  = 'John told Bill to again run.'

The intonational differences are important in characterizing the balance between old and new information in the communication. This may be demonstrated by clefting sentences (59a) and (59b), as in (60a) and (60b) respectively:

(60)
- a. *What John told Bill again was to rún.*
- b. *What John told Bill was to rùn agáin.*

The relationship between the intonation contours of (59a) and (60a) as against (59b) and (60b) is rather transparent. What the intonation contours in (59) do is preserve the assertion-focus stress pattern of the *embedded* sentence. Thus in (59a) the embedded sentence has only *run* in its predicate phrase, and therefore *run* takes the normal, predicate-final assertion-focus stress characteristic of nonemphatic, neutral sentences in English. In (59b), on the other hand, *again* is the last component in the embedded sentence. Furthermore, one could easily demonstrate that in a simple sentence containing the adverb *again*, only the adverb is new information under a noncontrastive interpretation. That is, the sentence:

(61)   *Bill ran agáin.*

is normally uttered not to merely impart the new information that *Bill ran*, but rather to add, in the context of shared knowledge, that Bill had already run before, that he ran again. In this sense, the adverb *again*, is pragmatically of the same type as *on purpose*, discussed in Section 3.2.3.

---

[35] For some background see Shibatani (1973). One should point out, however, that earlier discussions focused on the syntactic significance of the presence or lack of ambiguity, rather than—as attempted here—on the possible pragmatic motivation.

At any rate, not only is *again* the last element in the embedded sentence in (59b), but it is also the only part of the predicate-phrase *run again* that is under the assertion-focus. It is thus natural that it—rather than *run*—gets the assertion-focus stress.

Under negation, however, the situation is quite different. To begin with, the negative sentence corresponding to (58) above seems to have only one reading—and one noncontrastive[36] intonation contour:

(62)   *John dídn't tell Bill to rùn agaìn.*
         *a. *John didn't **again** tell Bill to run.*
         b. *John didn't tell Bill to **again** run.*

Now, since neither *run* nor *tell* seem to receive the assertion-focus contour in (62) above, why is it that only the negation corresponding to (59b)—that is, with *again* modifying *run* in the embedded sentence—is acceptable? The answer to this lies in the interaction between the pragmatic use of stress in English, the pragmatics of negation as a contrastive speech act, and the pragmatics of the sentence-final position in English as being the one most characteristically assigned to the constituent being in assertion-focus. First, since the negative is asserted in the context of the corresponding affirmative having already been discussed (or when the speaker assumes that the hearer tends to believe in it), neither *run* nor *again* are new information in (62). Further, since only the denial in negation is really new, the assignment of assertion-focus stress to *didn't* in (62) follows the normal conventions of pragmatic stress assignment in English.[37] Now, since neither *run* nor *again* receive the assertion-focus stress in (62), the speaker is invited to generalize *positionally*. And *again* is both closer to *run* in terms of the plausibility of modifier-modified relation, and also it appears in the preferred—final—position characteristic of the assertion-focus constituent in English.

One question remains: Why could not there be another stress pattern in English, one corresponding to a negation of *again tell* as in (59a)? Suppose such a pattern existed, say as in:

(63)   *John dídn't tell Bill to rŭn again.*

The problem with this pattern is that it conveys a contrast between *run* and another possible action which Bill could have done, while leaving *again* to modify **that** action, rather than *tell*. This preference is well motivated, since if *didn't* is what occupies the assertion-focus stress in a negative sentence, then—given the principle that only one assertion-

---

[36] While (62) is noncontrastive with respect to *John, Bill, told, run,* or *again*, it is obviously contrastive in the sense that the negative speech act is **always** contrastive *vis-à-vis* the corresponding affirmative.

[37] For an extensive discussion of the pragmatics of stress in English see Schmerling (1971, 1974), Bolinger (1958, 1972) and Bickerton (1975b).

3.3. Some Consequences of the Marked Status of Negatives

focus is assigned in noncontrastive sentences of English—the stress on *run* is automatically interpreted as a *contrastive* stress. Thus the pragmatic status of the negative as a different type of speech act, uttered for a different purpose and in a more complex discourse context than its corresponding affirmative, figures crucially in restricting the range of possible interpretations of potentially ambiguous adverbial constructions of this type.

3.3.1.3. RESTRICTIONS ON
THE EMBEDDING OF NEGATIVES

In the preceding sections I have demonstrated restrictions imposed on the freedom of distribution of elements within negative clauses. Further data of this kind will be discussed in Section 3.2.3. At this point I would like to illustrate the restrictions on the embedding of negative clauses in various grammatical contexts. Without exception, these restrictions are *pragmatically* motivated, and in many cases, if the pragmatics of foreground–background is reversed, the negative rather than the affirmative is felicitous. Since the explanation of this forms the core of Section 3.4, I will forego it here and merely proceed to illustrate the phenomena.

(64) When John comes, I'll leave
      ?When John doesn't come, I'll leave

(65) The man you met yesterday is a crook
      ?The man you didn't meet yesterday is a crook

(66) Where did you leave the keys?
      ?Where didn't you leave the keys?

(67) When did John arrive?
      ?When did John not arrive?

(68) How fast did John run?
      ?How fast did John not run?

(69) How did he do it?
      ?How did he not do it?

(70) With what did he cut the meat?
      ?With what didn't he cut the meat?

(71) It's Lincoln that I'm going to talk about today.
      ?It's Lincoln that I'm not going to talk about today.

(72) What I'm going to talk about today is the Gettysburg address.
      ?What I'm not going to talk about today is the Gettysburg address.

(73) I had Mary examined by the committee.
?I had Mary not examined by the committee.
I had the doctor examine Mary.
?I had the doctor not examine Mary.

(74) I made him fall off the cliff.
?I made him not fall off the cliff.

(75) I want to work.
?I want not to work.
I don't want to work.

(76) He continued to work.
?He continued not to work.
He didn't start working.

(77) She was as fast as he was.
?She was not as fast as he was not.
She wasn't as fast as he was.

(78) A man came into my office yesterday and . . .
?A man didn't come into my office yesterday and . . .

(79) I entered, looked around—and near the bar I saw John.
?I entered, looked around—and near the bar I didn't see John.

(80) And then came John and . . .
?And then didn't come John and . . .

(81) There stood a man in front of the house.
?There didn't stand a man in front of the house.

(82) There used to be a story that went like this . . .
?There didn't use to be a story that went like this . . .

3.3.1.4. RESTRICTIONS ON REFERENTIAL-INDEFINITES

The restriction on referential-indefinites as well as their pragmatic motivation have already been discussed above, but they certainly count as another instance where a negative environment imposes more stringent distributional constraints.

3.1.5. POSSIBLE COUNTEREXAMPLES

Some phenomena are *specific to* negative clauses, and though from a purely formal point of view they constitute a body of counterexamples to our claim about the behavior of more-marked clause types, in point of fact they underscore my contention that markedness must not be treated merely at the formal level. Rather it requires specific, *substantive* explanation.

The first class of counterexamples are negative polarity items, such as *yet, at all, any more, even, give a damn*, etc., all of which tend to shun nonnegative clauses. Since they always serve to semantically—or pragmatically—amplify or quantify negation, it would be absurd to expect to find them in nonnegative clauses.

The counterexample par excellence is, of course, the negation marker itself, which appears only in negative clauses. Again, the substantive *functional* explanation of this is rather transparent. In sum, then, these apparent counterexamples merely illustrate that markedness in language is not a formal notion utterly blind to considerations of substance and function.

3.3.2. Syntactic Conservatism

Diachronic change in the areas of syntax, morphology, and meaning may be broadly divided into two types with respect to its motivation. The first type is *expressive–elaborative* change, motivated by the creative drive to elaborate more complex and subtle nuances of meaning. All semantic change falls naturally into this category. Word-order change in the area of topic-focus relations, which constitutes the very core of syntactic change, is also of this type. The second type is *simplificatory* change, motivated largely by considerations such as ease of production, ease of perception, and the need to reduce ambiguity. The claims about the syntactic conservatism of negative clauses do not pertain to simplificatory change, but only to creative–elaborative change.

In Chapter 2, I advanced a *substantive* explanation for the more innovative nature of main-declarative-active clauses so far as elaborative-expressive diachronic change is concerned. I argued that this is the clause-type which carries the bulk of the new information in discourse, and that elaborative change is therefore more crucial and more functional there. I further pointed out that Emonds's root-transformations, which are (*a*) limited to assertive clauses[38] and (*b*) involve topic-focus elaboration, are the prime source of word-order change. It is therefore reasonable to expect that negative clauses which are more presuppositional and carry less new information in discourse, will turn out to be more conservative with respect to elaborative diachronic change. In this section I will survey the evidence supporting this expectation, as well as the status of some counter examples.

3.3.2.1. ELABORATION IN TENSE–ASPECT SYSTEMS

It is widely observed that the number of tense–aspects in the affirmative paradigm is almost always larger but never smaller than in the negative. Languages thus tend to innovate tense–aspect elaboration

---

[38] For further discussion see Hooper and Thompson (1973), Givón (1973a), as well as Chapter 2.

in the affirmative, then slowly spread them on to the negative. The case of the V-focus aspect in Bemba, Rwanda, and Zulu has already been discussed in Section 3.2.3. For obvious *pragmatic* reasons, that aspect never spread to the negative paradigm.

Consider next a fairly recent elaboration in Bemba, where within the past 20 years a further elaboration in the future tense has been introduced, to give the distinction between 'tomorrow' with the low tone -*kà*- as against 'after tomorrow' with the high tone -*ká*-:[39]

(83)   a.   *n-kà-boomba*   'I will work tomorrow'

       b.   *n-ká-boomba*   'I will work after tomorrow'

In the negative the distinction has not been introduced, and the older future marker, the low-tone -*kà*-, still marks the undifferentiated 'tomorrow and beyond' future time, just as it used to do in the affirmative prior to the innovation:

(84)   a.   *nshi-kà-boomba*   'I will not work, tomorrow and beyond'

       b.   *nshi-ká-boomba

The same neutralization in the negative also occurs for the continuous aspect of the same future tenses. Thus:

(85)   a.   *n-kà-láá-boomba*   'I'll be working tomorrow.'

       b.   *n-ká-láá-boomba*   'I'll be working after tomorrow.'

       c.   *nshi-kà-léé-boomba*   'I'll not be working, tomorrow and beyond.'

       d.   **nshi-ká-léé-boomba*

The next example involves innovations in the present tense system of Swahili. At a certain time the -*na*- marker, which was probably a perfective-past marker earlier,[40] moved into the present-tense paradigm to create the potential distinction between the present-progressive and the habitual:

(86)   a.   *ni-na-fanya kazi*   'I am working'

       b.   *n-a-fanya kazi*   {'I am working' / 'I work'}

The older present marker -*a*- has become ambiguous, with some tendency to begin to specialize toward the habitual. But the old negation

---

[39] For details see Givón (1972a).
[40] For details see Wald (1973).

3.3. Some Consequences of the Marked Status of Negatives

suffix pattern of both the present tenses *-na-* and *-a-* is still the old *suffixal* negative marker—which predates *both* tenses:[41]

(87)   *si-fany-i kazi*   {'I am not working' / 'I don't work'}

Thus, while further elaboration occurred in the affirmative, it has not occurred in the negative.

The next example is again from Swahili. In this language most tense–aspect markers were innovated from modality verbs that take infinitival complements, and the infinitive prefix in the language is *ku-*, as in:

(88)   *nataka ku-fanya kazi*   'I want to work'

The old infinitive marker *ku-* has been zeroed out of the verbal-word largely as the verbs became reanalyzed as tense-aspects and fused into the following stem, though it survives in two types of 'defective' verb stems, monosyllabic and vowel-commencing ones, as in:

(89)   a.   *ni-na-ku-la*
            I-PRES-INF-eat
            'I am eating'

       b.   *ni-na-ku-enda*
            I-PRES-INF-walk
            'I am walking'

In addition it also survived in one more environment, the *negative* of the past tense *-li-* (historically 'be'), where it has assumed the function of 'negative form of *-li-*,' as in:

(90)   a.   *ni-li-fanya kazi*   'I worked'
       b.   *si-ku-fanya kazi*   'I didn't work'

The negative environment—without any special need, since a negative prefix exists and is viable in all paradigms—has thus preserved a relic of the verbal paradigm, one which has been zeroed out of the affirmative via reanalysis.

The next set of examples I owe to Robert Hetzron (personal communication). Hetzron observes that Ethiopian languages tend to have more tense–aspect–mode elaboration in the affirmative, while in the negative distinctions tend to neutralize. Thus, for example, in Amharic, the perfect *säbbärä* 'he broke' and the present perfect *säbroall* 'his

---

[41] The *-a-* "present" used to be a "recent-past" marker, perhaps with a high tone (as in Bemba). It later supplanted the "zero-present" form. The suffixal negative *-i* was probably the form corresponding to the old "zero-present."

breaking' both share the negative form of the perfect, *al-säbbärä-m*. Similarly in Chana (Gurage) one has three distinct forms in the affirmative, for the present *yisäbɨr* 'he breaks', definite-future *yisäbɨrte* 'he will no doubt break' and indefinite-future *yisbɨršä* 'he might break', but the three forms share only one negative form—*esäbir*. As Hetzron observes, the future forms in Chana (Gurage) are innovations, and the shared negative is the original negation of the present. Similarly in Amharic, the present-perfect is a more recent innovation, sharing the original negative of the perfect. Both are solid examples of how elaborative change prefers the affirmative over the negative clause. In both, the net result in terms of *synchronic* distribution is that a wider range of forms can appear in the affirmative than in the negative.

3.3.2.2. WORD-ORDER CONSERVATISM

It is not common to catch a language at the point at which changes in the neutral word-order have occurred in the affirmative but not yet in the negative, at least not at the categorial level. The result is that relatively few languages use word-order as the major clue distinguishing negative from affirmative clauses. In contrast, the syntactic conservatism of embedded clauses is much better documented.[42] Some interesting cases nevertheless exist.

Consider first the case of Kru, a Niger-Congo language. In this language the older Niger-Congo SOV syntax has largely disappeared, and in most clause-types the word order is currently SVO. However, in a number of modal environments, all of which represent historically embedded structures, SOV syntax has survived. And one of those environments is the negative.[43]

(91) *nyeyu-na bla nyino-na*
      man-the beat woman-the
      'The man beat the woman'   (SVO)

(92) *nyeyu-na si   nyino-na   bla*
      man-the NEG   woman-the beat
      'The man *didn't* beat the woman'   (SOV)

(93) *nyeyu-na jila nyino-na   bla*
      man-the want woman-the beat
      'The man *wants* to beat the woman' (SOV)

(94) *nyeyu-na mu   nyino-na   bla*
      man-the go   woman-the beat
      'The man *will* beat the woman'   (SOV)

---

[42] See discussion in Chapter 2.
[43] For more discussion of comparative Niger-Congo and Kru, see Givón (1975e).

3.3. *Some Consequences of the Marked Status of Negatives*

(95) nyeyu-na boe nyino-na bla
      man-the M woman-the beat
      'The man *may* beat the woman'   (SOV)

(96) ni-pni nyeyu-na boe nyino-na bla
      I-squeeze man-the M woman-the beat
      'I *made* the man beat the woman'   (SOV)

Thus, the embedded diachronic source of the negative construction is still reflected in the conservative word-order which it shares with embedded constructions of the same general type. And if word-order changes are, at least in part, motivated by expressive–elaboration needs—particularly in terms of topic–focus relation, then the syntactic conservatism of the more presuppositional negative is only a natural consequence of its bearing a much smaller portion of the information contents in discourse, as compared to the affirmative.

The next case pertains to innovations in the system of marking definiteness of objects in Eastern Bantu languages.[44] In these languages there is an ongoing drift toward the use of the prefixed object pronoun as a definite marker for objects. This change has progressed in Swahili to the point where it is the standard way to definitize nonhuman objects, while human objects—even indefinites—already show an obligatory pronominal agreement. An older stage of this is represented by the situation in Luganda, where topic-shifting to the left is used for definitizing objects. This device is optional in the affirmative:

(97) a. *nalaba omusajja*   'I saw *a/the* man'
      b. *omusajja na-**mu**-laba* '*The* man, I saw *him*'

In the negative in Luganda, definitization by topic-shifting is obligatory:

(98) a. *salaba musajja*
         'I didn't see *any* man'   (NONREF)
      b. *omusajja sa-**mu**-laba*
         {'I didn't see *the* man'
          '*The* man, I didn't see *him*'}   (REF, DEF)

Now, Rwanda has gone one step further and allows the use of the object pronoun for definitization without topic-shifting, that is, in the normal SVO order. However, this extension has proceeded so far only in the affirmative, while in the negative it is still obligatory to topic-shift the object in order to affect its definitization:

(99) a. *yaboonya umugabo*
         'He saw *a* man'   (REF, INDEF)

---

[44] For details see Givón (1974b, 1976a). For more on Luganda, see Mould (1975).

b. *ya-mu-boonye umugabo*
   'He saw *the* man'   (REF, DEF)
c. *nhi-ya-boonye umugabo*
   'He didn't see *any* man'   (NONREF)
d. **nhi-ya-mu-boonye umugabo*
e. *umugabo nhi-ya-mu-boonye*
   ['*The* man, he didn't see *him*']
   ['He didn't see *the* man']   (REF, DEF)

3.3.2.3. CASE REALIGNMENT IN RUSSIAN[45]

There are a number of direct-object taking verbs in Russian, including *xotet'* 'want', *iskat'* 'seek', *prosit'* 'request', *videt'* 'see', *tebovat'* 'need', 'demand', which used to take their object in the genitive rather than the accusative case. In the affirmative there is an ongoing tendency to replace the genitive with the accusative, except where a partitive reading motivates the retention of the genitive and the preservation of the part-GEN versus whole-ACC contrast. In corresponding negative clauses, however, the genitive is much slower to be replaced, even in nonpartitive readings. Thus, if one assigns four degrees of acceptability to sentences, from the most acceptable (3) to the least acceptable (0), the reaction of speakers to affirmative and negative sentences may be seen below:

(100)   (3)   a. *ja xoču boršč*   (ACC)
               'I want borscht'   (whole)

       (3)   b. *ja xoču boršča*   (GEN)
               'I want some borscht'   (part)

       (2)   c. *ja ne xoču boršč*   (ACC)
               'I don't want borscht'   (whole)

       (3)   d. *ja ne xoču boršča*   (GEN)
               'I don't want (any) borscht'

(101)   (3)   a. *ja išču sestru*   (ACC)
               'I'm looking for my sister'

       (0)   b. *ja išču sestry*   (GEN)

       (1)   c. *ja ne išču sestru*   (ACC)

       (3)   d. *ja ne išču sestry*   (GEN)
               'I'm not looking for my sister'

---

[45] For the Russian data I am indebted to Alan Timberlake (personal communication; but see also Timberlake, 1975).

3.3. Some Consequences of the Marked Status of Negatives

(102) (3)   a.   *ja išču rabotu*   (ACC)
'I'm looking for work'

(1)   b.   *ja išču raboty*   (GEN)

(0)   c.   *ja ne išču rabotu*   (ACC)

(3)   d.   *ja ne išču raboty*   (GEN)
'I'm not looking for work'

(103) (3)   a.   *ona prosila den'gi*   (ACC)
'She asked for (the) money'   (whole)

(3)   b.   *ona prosila deneg*   (GEN)
'She asked for (some) money'   (part)

(0)   c.   *ona ne prosila den'gi*   (ACC)

(3)   d.   *ona ne prosila deneg*   (GEN)
'She didn't ask for *the/any* money'

(104) (3)   a.   *ja videl etu ženščinu*   (ACC)
'I saw that woman"

(0)   b.   *ja videl etu ženščiny*   (GEN)

(0)   c.   *ja ne videl etu ženščinu*   (ACC)

(3)   d.   *ja ne videl etu ženščiny*   (GEN)
'I didn't see that woman'

(105) (3)   a.   *ja trebuju knigu*   (ACC)
'I need a book'

(0)   b.   *ja trebuju knigi*   (GEN)

(0)   c.   *ja ne trebuju knigu*   (ACC)

(3)   d.   *ja ne trebuju knigi*   (GEN)
'I don't need a book'

While the data are very straightforward as to the conservatism of the negatives, one could ask why. And I believe the answer arises as a direct consequence of the facts discussed in Section 3.2.1. The verbs involved are, with the one exception (*see*), nonimplicative verbs. That is, they could take—in the past or present tense in the affirmative—non-referential objects, in addition to referential–indefinite ones. The partitive–genitive versus accusative distinction serves in the affirmative to differentiate these two interpretations of the indefinite object, that is, "one whole specific one" as against "some member of the class, no matter which." In the negative, however, definites are marked by articles or demonstratives, so that they are sufficiently differentiated from the indefinite. And, as was seen in Section 3.2.1, the indefinite object following a negated verb could only be *nonreferential*—or "partitive." The need to differentiate the referential and nonreferential readings of indefinites thus doesn't arise in the negative. The analogical extension therefore proceeds more slowly, since it has less of a functional motivation. Thus the presuppositional markedness of negatives indirectly mediates to slow the process of analogical extension in this case.

3.3.2.4. SENSE EXTENSION OF ENGLISH MODALS[46]

Modal auxiliary verbs in English, such as *should, must, may, let,* and *have to,* are said to exhibit polysemy, so that while their older senses involved *obligation* or *speaker's preference toward action by the subject,* they have all developed *probability* senses, that is, speaker's assignment of likelihood to the proposition. Let us label the two senses "root" and "epistemic" (or R and E), respectively. In this section I would like to briefly report the results of an experiment I performed on 100 subjects. They were given the sentences with modals in the affirmative and negative as listed in Appendix 1, at the end of this chapter, and were asked, for each sentence, to assign an acceptability integer from 0 (totally unacceptable) to 3 (totally acceptable), to the R and E senses of each sentence [given as (a) and (b) in the test sheet, under each sentence]. The results for each sense of each sentence, as total aggregate score for 100 subjects, are listed in Appendix 2. In Table 3.3 the results are expressed as ratios of the acceptabilities of the R and E senses of each modal in the affirmative over their acceptability in the negative. In each case there was a *drop* in the acceptability of the E sense in the negative, a drop which averaged 37% for all five modals. In each case there was a much slighter *increase* in the acceptability of the R sense of the five modals in the negative, an increase which averaged 12%. This increase can most likely be interpreted as a result of the decreased acceptability of the epistemic senses in the negative, that is, because of less interference, indeterminancy or confusion which may exist as a result of the more viable polysemy in the affirmative. In Table 3.4 the results are presented as ratios of the acceptability of epistemic over root senses for affirmative and negatives. On the average, epistemic senses are 84% as acceptable as root senses in the affirmative, suggesting that the polysemy is quite viable. In the negative, on the other hand, epistemic senses are on the average only 47% as acceptable as root senses. In terms of ratios of the relative acceptability of epistemic over root senses in the affirmative *over* the relative acceptability of epistemic over root senses in the nega-

---

[46] For the initial idea prompting this experiment, I am indebted to Kay Hannah. My original suggestion that the phenomenon was detectable at the level of competence was rejected by a number of native speakers of English on the grounds that "upon reflection, those epistemic senses in negative sentences look perfectly acceptable."

3.3. Some Consequences of the Marked Status of Negatives

TABLE 3.3
Ratios of Acceptability Scores for Root and Epistemic Senses of Modals in the Negative over the Affirmative

Modal	Root sense	Epistemic sense
Should	1.101	.468
Must	1.218	.593
May	1.033	.819[a]
Let	1.063	.746
Have to	1.229[b]	.533
Average	1.218	.631

[a] Two epistemic senses (b) and (c) were listed on the test sheet (see Appendix 2 at the end of this chapter), and the results here represent an average of the scores of those two.
[b] Two root senses, (a) and (b), were listed, and the results are again an average of the two.

tive, the average ratio—which is an indication of the degree of polysemy of the modals, is .562 or an average drop of 44%.

In Givón (1973c) I have argued that epistemic senses of modals are diachronically natural semantic derivatives, by inductive inference, of either "ability" or "root" senses. The only problematic modal of the five used, in terms of diachronic claims, is *may*. This is so because its oldest sense was "ability," "power to act," which became obsolete after developing a "permission sense" akin to current-day's *can*. Thus, the epistemic sense of *may* may have arisen directly from the older "ability" sense, and thus possibly predated the root sense. At any rate, the experiment demonstrates in a sufficiently clear way that the creative elaboration of various senses of the modals—a process of great universality and naturalness—is carried out much more extensively in affirmative sentences than in their corresponding negatives.

There is a final note concerning epistemic senses in the negative. In the test sheet two epistemic senses were listed for *may not*, one negating

TABLE 3.4
Acceptability Ratios of Epistemic over Root Senses of Modals in the Affirmative and the Negative

Modal	Affirmative	Negative	Ratio of negative/ affirmative
Should	.769	.327	.425
Must	1.335	.650	.486
May	.822	.652	.793
Let	.666	.468	.702
Have to	.606	.267	.440
Average	.839	.472	.562

may (b), the other negating the embedded verb (c). The ratio for the second—in which the negative is *lowered* and the expression is interpreted as an affirmative probability expression rather than a denial—shows higher acceptability (.846 versus .792, see note to Table 3.3). While the increment is rather small, it may be an indication that somehow a "denial of probability of the affirmative" is less natural than an "affirmation of the probability of the negative." While for the logician these may sound equivalent, for the linguist it may not. Rather, this may represent another instance in which an expression is somehow *pragmatically less useful* in the negative.

3.3.2.5. POSSIBLE COUNTEREXAMPLES

The seeming counterexamples discussed in Section 3.3.1.5. above are also relevant here, since they involve innovation of negative-specific morphemes. In addition, I have reported elsewhere (Givón, 1977a) a case in which in the diachronic change from VSO to SVO word-order, negative clauses change earlier than affirmative clauses. When one looks at the details more carefully, however, the force of these facts as a proper counterexample is rather weak. In general, in Biblical Hebrew (where these observations were made) the change VSO-to-SVO is motivated by the *higher topicality* (presuppositionality) of the subject as compared to other arguments (see Givón, 1976a). What is also true there is that the change—all other things being equal—seems to go faster in presupposed clauses than in less-presupposed ones. This is, I believe, because the more presupposed a clause is, the more topical is its subject. Thus, since negative clauses are more presuppositional than affirmative ones, it is precisely this *substantive* basis for the markedness of negatives which motivates their seeming innovative status vis-à-vis the particular change involved here.

3.3.3. Psychological Complexity

There is a great deal of evidence suggesting that it takes speakers much longer to process negative sentences—and concepts—than to process the corresponding affirmatives. Thus, for example, Clark (1971a, 1971b, 1974) shows that processing time for inherently negative concepts is longer compared to their paired affirmative antonyms (i.e., *present–absent, remember–forget*). He further shows (1971b) that the processing time for overt negation, as in *not present*, is longer than for its logically equivalent, deeper-embedded negation as in *absent*, and further argues that the more deeply embedded the negative operator is, the easier the utterance to process. His explanation is rather illuminating: "These examples hint at the fact that a speaker usually makes an

3.3. Some Consequences of the Marked Status of Negatives

assumption about the beliefs (or apparent beliefs) of his listener whenever he utters a denial. Specifically, he normally supposes that the listener does or could well believe in the truth of what is being denied . . . [1974, p. 1312]." Finally, Clark (1969) also shows that for the whole range of antonymically paired adjectives in English, the positive member is easier to process than the negative member. Eve Clark (1971) shows that not only are the positive members of antonymic pairs easier to process, but they are also acquired earlier by children. In all these instances, structural or "syntactic–perceptual" complexity is not involved, but only *conceptual* complexity. Similar results, showing longer latencies in the processing of negative concepts as compared to their antonymically paired affirmatives, are reported by Hoosain (1973) and Hoosain and Osgood (1975). These studies again involve no factors of syntactic complexity, only conceptual. Thus, even discounting studies concerning the "late" acquisition of the *syntax* of negation as compared to the syntax of affirmative sentences, such as reported in Klima and Bellugi (1973), that is, studies which concentrate on the acquisition of the overt signalling devices for negative sentences rather than the acquisition of negation *as a speech act*, one must conclude that the psychological evidence strongly supports the view that negatives are conceptually—or in my terms presuppositionally—more complex.

A final argument will underscore the fact that the psychological complexity of negatives as compared to affirmatives has nothing to do with the mere logic of negation, but rather must arise from its *pragmatics* or use in language. This must be so for the following reason: The distinction between *same* versus *different*, "of same type" versus "of different type," "the same individual token" versus "a different individual token," "conforming with the *ground*" versus "breaking the uniformity of the ground and thus being the *figure*," is the most fundamental perceptual and conceptual primitive in cognition. This primitive is *founded* on the notion of negation in *logic*, that is, the basic axioms:

(106) $$\sim(p = \sim p)$$

But as I have already argued, these axioms do not by themselves characterize the use of negation in language. In addition, as I will argue directly, the assignment of negative versus positive values to members of antonymic pairs in human language is totally arbitrary from a strictly logical point of view. So far as logic is concerned, reversing those values would yield equally well-formed antonymic pairs. So far as human language is concerned, however, such an assignment is far from arbitrary. Rather, it reflects deep pragmatic and ontological facts about the way the human organism perceives and construes the universe.

3.4. THE ONTOLOGICAL BASIS OF NEGATION

In the preceding sections we have seen that negation is a distinct speech-act in language, that it is used largely to deny the supposed beliefs of hearers in the context where the corresponding affirmative has been assumed, rather than to impart new information in the context of the hearer's ignorance. In this section I will show how the assignment of negative valuation to certain members of antonymic pairs rather than to their antonyms, as well as the assignment of negative valuation to nonactions and nonevents (rather than to actions or events, respectively), is motivated by the perceptual opposition of *figure* versus *ground*.

3.4.1. The Ontology of Negative Properties

Suppose there was a universe in which only one distinction—*property*—existed. Additionally, suppose there were only two individuals comprising that universe, distinguished from each other by the fact that one possessed that distinguishing property and the other did not. Let us represent that universe as:

Since the two individuals are on a par except with respect to that binary property, there is absolutely no way in which one could decide which one is marked by the *presence* of the property and which one is marked by its *absence*. If one were to construe or describe this universe and the individuals within it, either strategy would net one exactly the same results, with exactly the same degree of efficiency. In other words, either individual is just as justifiably the *figure* and just as justifiably the *ground* in this universe.

Suppose now we had another universe, in which again the very same single binary distinction–property existed, but where a single individual was marked by one of its antonyms, while 24 individuals were marked by the opposite antonym, as shown below:

3.4. The Ontological Basis of Negation

In this universe, in terms of perceptual saliency or figure-ground relations, the single individual *stands out* on the background of the other 24. It is a *break in the pattern*, it has *surprise value*, it can be *singled out*. If one were now to either construe or report about this second universe, reporting the 24 individuals which constitute the perceptual *ground* as "having the property" and the single individual which constitutes the perceptual *figure* as not having it, is an uneconomical enterprise, as compared to the converse procedure. Further, in terms of retrieval strategies, if the 24 individuals were designated by the "presence" of the binary property, while the single one by its "absence," then identifying that single individual *which is different* in this universe will be an extremely costly strategy, since one would have to proceed by eliminating all the "present" 24 others first. On the other hand, if the single individual is coded with the "presence" of the property, the search procedure will be obviously much more efficient. Let us now proceed to the grammar of antonymic pairs of properties—or adjectives—in language.

Vendler (1963), Bierwisch (1967), Givón (1970a), and many others have given extensive arguments that in antonymic pairs of properties-adjectives in language one member is always designated as the positive member, the other negative. Furthermore, the positive one also acts as the unmarked member, in the sense that it gives the generic name to the property itself, has much wider distribution and by all other criteria behaves like the unmarked case. In (107) below a list of these antonymic pairs is given. The most striking thing about them is that the positive—or unmarked—member of each pair is perceptually more prominent:

(107)

Positive	Negative	Perceptual property
big	*small*	Ease of visual perception
long	*short*	Ease of visual perception
tall	*short*	Ease of visual perception
wide	*narrow*	Ease of visual perception
fat	*thin*	Ease of visual perception
high	*low*	Ease of visual perception
light	*dark*	Ease of visual perception
fast	*slow*	Ease of visual perception of rate of change
loud	*quiet*	Ease of auditory perception
sharp	*dull*	Ease of tactile perception
thick	*thin*	Ease of visual perception
hot	*cold*	Ease of temperature perception
heavy	*light*	Ease of tactile-weight perception

Both Herbert Clark (1971a) and Eve Clark (1971) have noticed the correlation between the positive value assigned in language to the unmarked member of antonymic pairs and its *perceptual prominence*. They have further suggested that precisely for this reason children acquire the *positive* members of antonymic pairs first—since they are easier to perceive.

Other investigators, such as Boucher and Osgood (1969) and Osgood and Richards (1973) have attempted to explain the psychological-processing disparity between positive and negative members of antonymic pairs by reference to *frequency of use,* which was in turn to be explained by "The Pollyanna Principle," which they give as: "humans have found believing more reinforcing than doubting, certainty more than uncertainty, plenitude more than scarcity, asserting more than denying—and congruity (and) more than incongruity (but) . . . [Osgood and Richards, 1973, p. 411]." The problem with this explanation, it seems to me, is that it picks out of all the antonymic pairs in language only the ones that have obvious *affective loading,* while leaving unexplained the very same disparity of behavior of antonymic pairs—such as measure adjectives—where no affective preference by humans can be easily postulated. As an extreme example, consider *loud* and *quiet,* where if anything the negative member has better affective loading, but humans still classify *loud*—the perceptually prominent member—as the positive. Another thing the Pollyanna Principle does not explain is the ontology of negative actions–events. Thus consider the following two sentences:

(108) *Birnboim didn't kill his wife*

(109) *Birnboim killed his wife*

Following the Pollyanna Principle, languages should consider (109) as the negative and (108) as the positive, but, in fact, they do not. As I will argue below, the very same ontology of figure–ground that explains the assignment of positive–negative valuation to properties, also explains their assignment to actions and events.

3.4.2. The Ontology of Negative Events

Events, or actions—which are events for which *responsibility* is assigned to some *agent*—are *changes* in the state of the universe across a certain time-axis.[47] A certain *State A* of the universe prevails prior to the time-axis of the event. Then, within a more or less compressed period of time[48] that state changes, and when the dust has settled a different state

---

[47] For the time-axis phenomenon, see Givón (1973c). For a more general characterization states versus events–actions, see Langacker (1975) and Chafe (1970), as well as Chapter 8.
[48] Ultimately, the judgment as to what is a "stable state," what is a "rapid–instantaneous change" and what is "slow change" depends in the fineness of *calibration* of the human perceptor–*cum*–processor apparatus. Most languages, however, make a distinction between at least three possibilities:

3.4. The Ontological Basis of Negation

of affairs prevails—*State B*. Both state A and state B are reasonably stable, otherwise they would not be considered "states," and the universe at those states is more or less *at rest*, relative to the ability of humans to perceive movement. On the other hand, during the event (or action) itself the universe is *moving*—rapidly enough so that humans, given the range of their perceptual aparatus, can perceive the change.

In Section 3.3.1.3 I have listed a great number of examples in which negative sentences seemed somehow more odd, more bizarre than their corresponding affirmatives. In this section I would like to show that the oddity of negatives in all those contexts is inherently pragmatic, and that the very same principle of figure versus ground which explained the assignment of negative valuation in the case of properties, also explains in the case of actions–events. More specifically, what is involved here is the contrast between *norm* and *counternorm*.

Consider first sentence (110):

(110)   *?When John doesn't come, I'll leave*

The function of the when-clause in its corresponding affirmative is to designate a point in time—at which the action in the main clause takes place. However, there is an infinite number of points in time at which *John doesn't come*, but only relatively few—or one—at which he does come. The negative event is thus a *background* at which no change in the state of the universe has occurred. On this background, John's coming is an event—*a change*. It is thus, statistically, much easier to fix a point in time by the occurrence of an event than by the infinite number of points in time at which it did not occur.

Consider now sentence (111) which, on the face of it, constitutes a counterexample to the claim just made above:

(111)   *When John didn't come, I left.*

However, notice that (111) does not designate a point at which *John didn't come*, but only a point terminating a whole period during which *John was supposed to come but didn't*. If in fact, had (111) designated a specific point as in (110), its interpretation would have been pragmatically odd for exactly the same reasons. Thus consider the following:

(112)   *I left at all the (nondenumerably many) points in time at which John didn't come.*

Consider now the pragmatic oddity of:

(113)   *?The man you didn't meet yesterday is a crook.*

Steady "permanent" *state* (*be a man, be tall*), a *protracted action* (*working, talking, writing*), and a *compact action* (*shoot, hit, break the window, arrive at the house*). For further discussion, see Chapter 8.

On the background of not meeting the overwhelming majority of men in the world, sentence (113) is a rather unsuccessful definite description of a man. However, suppose the ground–figure relations are reversed, and the pragmatic situation under which (113) was uttered is, instead, that you were supposed to meet a number of people, all of them showed up *except for one*. On this background, (113) would be quite a successful—and acceptable, definite description. In other words, the use of restrictive modifiers to construct definite description of nouns involves singling them out by a property or event which distinguishes them from a *larger* group. In other words, designating the individual as *figure* and the larger class as *ground* is crucial to the use of restrictive modifiers in definite description. For this reason negative events are pragmatically less useful, since most normally they do **not** single out something which occurred, that is, a *change,* on the background of the normal *inertia* of the universe.

Consider next the bizarreness of (114).

(114)   ?*A man didn't come into my office yesterday, and . . .*

Since its corresponding affirmative is used to introduce a new story, (114) is obviously a failure—unless the majority of people were normally always coming into my office, that is, unless the figure–ground relations were reversed. In fact, sentence (114) is only acceptable as a *denial* of the corresponding affirmative, that is, *It is not true that a man came into my office yesterday . . .* , and requires a very marked intonation pattern to carry through successfully.

Consider next the following sentences:

(115)   a.   *A woman with two arms came into my office and . . .*
        b.   *A woman with one arm came into my office and . . .*

In our universe (115a) is pragmatically bizarre, since it fails to distinguish the figure from the ground. In a universe where women had only one arm as a rule, (115b) would be equally bizarre, while (115a) would be a successful definite description. Similarly, consider (116).

(116)   a.   *A woman who spoke English came into my office and . . .*
        b.   *A woman who spoke no English came into my office and . . .*

In an English speaking universe, (116a) will be pragmatically bizarre, while in a non-English speaking universe, (116b) would be equally bizarre.

Consider now sentence (117).

(117)   ?*Where didn't you leave the keys?*

3.4. The Ontological Basis of Negation

It is pragmatically odd because while the place where you left one set of keys can be uniquely designated, the number of places where you did not leave the keys is nondenumerably large. However, if the figure–ground relations are shifted, and, instead, (117) was uttered on the background whereby you told me you didn't leave the keys at some place, but I didn't hear you very well; I am thus faced with the task of finding out which place—out of the very many possible ones—is the one where you said you didn't leave the keys. On this revised background, (117) is pragmatically felicitous.

Let us next consider sentence (118).

(118)   *?It's Lincoln that I'm not going to talk about today.*

Under the normal figure–ground relations, that is, that the number of things I am *not* going to talk about at any span of time is potentially infinite, (118) is indeed bizarre. However, suppose I have already mentioned a number of subjects about which I was not supposed to talk, and excluded the subject of Lincoln, which presumably was a natural member of the group. The expectations of my listeners were thus that I was deliberately eliminating the discussion of *other* subjects (probably with the tacit pragmatic inference that I might discuss Lincoln). On this new background (118) is a better speech act, though it is still strange. The strangeness arises from the fact that the normal strategy in enumerating what one intends to do is enumerating intended *actions–events*, rather than intended *absence* of actions. This is so because on the background of the nonchange or *inertia* of the universe, an action constitutes a change, that is, a figure against the ground. Thus my entire strategy of constructing an appropriate background context for (118) is still rather odd.

Consider now the bizarreness of the negative comparative in (119).

(119)   *She was as fast as he was.*
        ?She was not as fast as he was not.
        She wasn't as fast as he was.

The affirmative comparative compares the degree of presence of the same property in two individuals. The normal negative denies the affirmative. The bizarre negative-comparative would have compared, presumably the degree of absence of that property. But absence is absolute, it has no degree, and therefore is nonsensical to compare.

Finally, consider sentence (120).

(120)   *Someone didn't do the dishes yesterday.*

As it stands, (120) is a counterexample to the claim made in Section 3.2.1, that under negation, referential subjects—just like objects—will tend to be definite. However, what makes (120) a felicitous communication is that it is transacted in the context where someone was *supposed to* do the dishes but did not. Thus the affirmative is established as the *background* of expectation. And on that background, the reported non-event becomes the new *figure,* it breaks the inertia of expectation, it *stands out.* Thus, the restriction on referential-indefinites under the scope of negation is not a blind "grammatical" constraints, but rather it stems from the pragmatics of figure versus ground in communication. When the figure–ground relations are sufficiently manipulated, sentences which are normally odd becomes acceptable communication.

The ontology of negative events may be summarized as follows:

1. The normal background of the universe is *inertia, no change.* This is not a logically necessary property of the universe, but merely the consequence of the level of delicacy to which our perceptual and processing aparatus is calibrated.
2. The normal background of inertia may be designated as any one of an *infinite* number of nonevents which did not occur when the universe is at rest. From a strictly *logical* point of view, one could assign the positive valuation to any of those. But as a construction and retrieval strategy, such an assignment is of course absurd, since the designata could never be retrieved within finite time.
3. Therefore, humans consistently assign the positive valuation, that of possession of property or occurence of event, to the perceptually more prominent member of the pair, to the pole which constitutes a *change,* a *break in the routine,* a *movement,* a *rarity,* a *surprise.* In other words, they assign it to the pole for which a *finite* retrieval strategy can be constructed.
4. Negative sentences, reporting nonactions or nonevents, are used in language only when the normal figure–ground relations are reversed, that is, when the action–event is established as the background, as the *expected norm.* On this newly construed background, on this reversed inertia, the reported nonevent becomes legitimate *information,* a *rarity,* a *surprise.*

3.5. CONCLUSION

3.5.1. Logic versus Language

I have shown that negation in language is not merely negation in propositional logic, that it carries a huge pragmatic component that cannot be predicted from the strict logical properties of the truth operation involved.

3.5. Conclusion

3.5.2. Negation as a Speech Act

Negative declarative sentences constitute a different speech act than the corresponding affirmatives. Affirmatives are used to convey new information on the background of assuming the hearer's *ignorance*. Negatives are used to correct misguided belief on the background of assuming the hearer's *error*.

3.5.3. Discourse Presuppositions of Negation

Negatives are consistently more *marked* in terms of their discourse-pragmatic presuppositions. Specifically, they are uttered in contexts where the corresponding affirmative has been discussed, or else when the speaker assumes that the hearer's bias toward or belief in—and thus familiarity with—the corresponding affirmative. This notion of presupposition diverges strongly from the normal logic notion, since it is not the *truth* of the affirmative or the hearer's *knowledge* of that truth that is at issue, but rather the hearers *familiarity* with a certain affirmative proposition, or the *probability* of his *belief* in it. As in many other instances where one examines language carefully and without a logic-derived bias, the system turns out to be much more *induction-based*, much less deductive.

3.5.4. Consequences of Discourse Markedness

I have shown that a number of behavioral consequences of markedness, such as distributional restrictions, diachronic conservatism, and psychological complexity are all characteristic of negative sentences. I have also attempted to show how these behavioral consequences of the markedness of negatives are **not** purely formal, but rather may be explained via reference to the substantive nature of the markedness phenomenon involved, that is, the discourse-pragmatics of negation.

3.5.5. The Ontology of Negation

It is not altogether unexpected that a serious epistemological investigation would soon lead into pragmatics, and that pragmatics would then lead to ontology. The process of explanation is but a series of concentric circles. That the phenomena under scrutiny are embedded at the inner core is merely a consequence of the *contingently*-assembled heuristics of a particular investigation. It was thus a pleasant surprise for me to discover that at the bottom of negation lay a general principle of human perception and cognition, that of *figure* versus *ground*. Indeed, the entire system of human communication and information processing, as is evident from the study of discourse pragmatics, is founded upon this principle. Our system of communication is thus founded on the very same general principle which underlies our perception and construction of our universe, namely that continuity, inertia, no-change, familiarity, is the background which need not be reported, which can be ignored. On that background, properties and events *stand out;* they constitute a *change* in the inertia, *information.*

I have already commented above on the fact that the distinction between *inert state* and *change* is not a logically necessary distinction, but merely reflects the level of delicacy at which our perceptual apparatus is calibrated. I doubt it very much that this level of calibration is totally accidental in all other respects. Rather, it seems to me, it may be strongly determined by the survival needs of the species. It may also be that every organism calibrates its perception–construction system—however rudimentary, in such a way that a foreground–background differentiation of the phenomenological universe is obtained. But this may be simply another way of defining cognition at its most basic level, that is, as a system which imposes a *nonrandom* construction upon its universe.

It is probably far from accidental that at the bottom of the figure–ground opposition lies a simple *probabilistic* principle: the *ground* is a phenomenon with over 50% frequency, the *figure* is under 50%. Given a hypothetical universe with a single binary distinction, having a perceptual system calibrated at a level such that the frequency of presence or frequency of absence of that single property is exactly 50%, would be the biological equivalent of having no perceptual system at all. This is because when calibrated at such a level, the system yields results that do not transcend the *random order.* Now, while we have no evidence the universe per se is anything **but** random, we also have no evidence of the universe per se. The apparently vast nonrandomness we perceive all around us may simply be another way of conceding that our perceptual and constructive tools are—by definition—calibrated at a level which allows us the rare privilege claimed by all organisms, that of living in a nonrandom universe.

In light of the role of inertia in Newtonian physics, its role in the structure of both our perception and cognition is less than surprising. Nor is it surprising in the light of Taoist philosophy. In his *Tao Teh Ching,* Lao Tse marks the active, large, light, hard, loud pole as the positive or *Yang,* and the passive, small, dark, soft, quiet pole as the negative or *Yin.* The concept of *Tao* itself is, in turn, analogous to inertia or *entropy.* While *Tao* differentiates into the pair of *Yin* and *Yang,* the *Yin* properties of passivity, inertia, not-doing are those which conform with *Tao,* going with it rather than resisting it. It is thus comforting to note that this independent investigation has yielded results which recapitulate both Newton and Lao Tse.

3.5.6. Epistemological Closure

This study also underscores the fundamental unity of perception and cognition, since both seem to abide by the same overriding principle of figure versus ground. One may thus project toward a unified theory of perception–cognition in which the traditional Western epistemological dispute between rationalist and empiricist has been, to quite an extent, preempted.

APPENDIX 1: TEST SHEET FOR AN EXPERIMENT ON THE INTERPRETATION OF ENGLISH MODALS

Instructions: The 10 sentences below are said to be *potentially ambiguous.* That is, some speakers of English find that they can understand them in more than one way. This test attempts to find out how you, as a native speaker of English, accept the interpretations most commonly assumed as "possible"—*in your own ordinary everyday speech.* Under each of the sentences 1-10 below two possible interpretations are listed, (a) and (b). Would you please mark each (a)/(b) interpretation as to the degree to which you can recognize it as a legitimate interpretation of the sentence above it. Mark in the following way:

        0 = a very unlikely interpretation for me
        1 = bad but maybe possible for me
        2 = sound OK for me, sort of
        3 = perfectly OK for me

Thank you.

1. John should get married next year.
   (a) I would prefer that he got married.
   (b) I think it is likely that he'll get married.

2. John shouldn't get married next year.
   (a) I would prefer that he didn't get married.
   (b) I think it isn't likely that he'll get married.

3. John must be there.
   (a) I would prefer that he should be there.
   (b) I think it is likely that he is there.

4. John mustn't be there.
   (a) I would prefer that he not be there.
   (b) I think it is likely that he's not there.

5. John may enter the house alone.
    (a) John is permitted to enter the house alone.
    (b) I think it is likely that he will enter the house alone.
6. John may not enter the house alone.
    (a) John is not permitted to enter the house alone.
    (b) I think it not likely that he will enter the house alone.
    (c) I think it is likely that he won't enter the house alone.
7. Let John be their leader, then . . .
    (a) I prefer that John becomes their leader, . . . (please don't block him)
    (b) Suppose John becomes their leader, then . . .
8. Don't let John be their leader, then . . .
    (a) I prefer that John doesn't become their leader, . . . (so do block him)
    (b) Suppose John doesn't become their leader, then . . .
9. John has to finish soon.
    (a) I strongly prefer that he finish soon.
    (b) John is obligated to finish soon.
    (c) I think that it is likely that he'll finish soon.
10. John doesn't have to finish soon.
    (a) John is not obligated to finish soon.
    (b) I think it is not likely that he'll finish soon.

APPENDIX 2: TOTAL SCORES FOR 100 SUBJECTS OF THE RESULTS OF THE EXPERIMENT ON ENGLISH MODALS

Modal	Affirmative		Negative	
	Root sense	Epistemic sense	Root sense	Epistemic sense
Should	247	190	272	89
Must	197	263	240	156
May	270	222	279	176(b)
				188(c)
Let	237	158	252	118
Have to	212 (a)	148	295	79
	276 (b)			
Average	239	196	267	124

4

SEMANTIC CASE AND PRAGMATIC FUNCTION
promotion, accessibility, and the typology of case marking

4.1. INTRODUCTION[1]

This chapter is a preliminary investigation into a number of interdependencies which rest at the very core of the typological definition of a language. I will be first concerned with the interplay between the case-marking *cum* word-order typology of the language and its so-called transformational behavior. I will also deal with the interaction—within case-marking systems—between semantic and pragmatic function. To a lesser extent I will also probe into the way in which semantic, pragmatic and complexity considerations conspire to determine transformational behavior.

The range of facts to be discussed is by now familiar. It involves first the generalizations made by Keenan and Comrie (1972, 1977) concerning the *Accessibility hierarchy* of the various case-functions to transformational rules, most specifically to relativization. This hierarchy has been given by Keenan and Comrie (1977) as:

(1) SUBJ > DIR OBJ > IND OBJ > OBLIQUE > GEN > COMPAR

They have then observed that the SUBJECT case cross linguistically is the most accessible to relativization. And further that within a particular language, when a certain strategy$_i$ of relativization is used, an implicational relation obtains among the case-function such that if case x is accessible to strategy$_i$, then case y must also be accessible if it is higher

---

[1] I am indebted to Ed Keenan, Alexandre Kimenyi, David Perlmutter, Edith Moravcsik, Joseph Greenberg, and Judy Gary for comments and suggestions on earlier versions of this chapter.

on the accessibility hierarchy than case x.² In this chapter I will deal with two restrictions on relativization. The first involves languages which obligatorily promote nonsubjects to subject (i.e., *passivize* them) before they are accessible to relativization. The second involves languages in which prepositional (or "indirect") objects must be first promoted to direct-object (i.e., undergo *dative-shift*) before they can be relativized. With respect to both restrictions, I will argue that they are motivated by considerations of case-marking, specifically by the need to *recover the semantic function* of the deleted coreferent argument in relativization.

The second set of facts have been observed over the past few years by Perlmutter and Postal (1974), Johnson (1974), Chung (1975), Gary and Keenan (1975), and Kimenyi (1976) among others, within the general framework of *relational grammar*. Among others, these facts concern languages in which prepositional (indirect) objects cannot be passivized directly, but must be first promoted to direct-object (i.e., dative-shifted). I will argue that these restrictions are again motivated by the need to recover the semantic function of the promoted ex-object argument.

In the course of the investigation I will suggest that one must take into account the two-level nature of case systems, that is, the fact that they mark both the *semantic* function of the various arguments vis-à-vis the verb ("event," "action"), and—in well-defined cases—their *pragmatic* or discourse function. With respect to the SUBJECT–NOMINATIVE case this observation is of course quite familiar, since it has long been identified as the argument which carries the TOPIC function.³ In the case of DIRECT-OBJECT, a category of considerably narrower currency, I will argue for considering it a pragmatic case as well. It involves, in languages where it can be observed, *relative topicality* relations between various object cases. I will thus argue that the dative-shift rule involves, at the very least, increasing the topicality of the shifted nonaccusative object vis-à-vis the accusative. And that this function of dative-shift may help explain its interaction with other transformational processes in the grammar.⁴

---

² The formulation in Keenan and Comrie (1977) is couched in terms of "hierarchy constraints," which I have attempted to render here more accessible.

³ For an extensive discussion of the relationship between the notions "subject" and "topic," see various papers in Li (1976).

⁴ While passivization involves the promotion of a non-agent argument to the pragmatic case of TOPIC–SUBJECT, dative-shift involves the topicality relations of the objects vis-à-vis each other, leaving the topicality of the SUBJECT–AGENT unaffected. Thus, in languages in which the pragmatic case "direct object" is a demonstrable phenomenon, the arguments are ranked as follows in terms of their pragmatics of topicality: SUBJECT > DIRECT OBJECT > OTHERS. There are grounds for believing that all languages, at the discourse level, differentiate between objects—when more than one appears per sentence—as to which is more "focus" of new information and which is more "topical." See further discussion in Givón (1975c).

4.2. THE CASE-RECOVERABILITY PROBLEM

One may choose to argue that no absolute need exists in language for marking by overt morphological means the semantic or pragmatic function of the various arguments vis-à-vis the verb. Both the semantic specificity of the various arguments and the pragmatic knowledge of the shared universe and the specific discourse context constitute an immense body of informational *redundancy* from which the case-functions of the various arguments may be presumably recovered. This is indeed attested by the fact that many languages have only a partial system of morphological case marking, and a number of languages, such as Classical Chinese or some relatively young Creoles, exhibit no case morphology. At the same time it is also true that the very same languages, given sufficient time, develop case-marking morphology via universally established diachronic routes, de-nominal or de-verbal.[5] Furthermore, word-order strategies of a language interact with its case-marking morphology, and it is quite common in languages in which the order SVO has become rigidly grammaticalized to find both the SUBJECT, and ACCUSATIVE or DIRECT-OBJECT unmarked morphologically. One may thus say that in such languages the position of the argument vis-à-vis the verb—preverbal for SUBJECT and postverbal for ACCUSATIVE–DIRECT OBJECT—constitutes the perceptual clue necessary to convey the semantic or pragmatic function of that argument. The fact that over time all languages seem to gravitate toward developing either morphological or syntactic or combined strategies of case-marking is by itself a strong attestation that semantic–pragmatic–contextual redundancy is not enough, not even in the *neutral*[6] sentence pattern of the language.

While one may not wish to commit oneself to any particular model of describing the relationship between the neutral and transformed sentence patterns of language, one may still refer to the difference between a neutral and transformed pattern as a *transformational operation*. Again, regardless of how these operations are formulated ultimately, they tend to always interfere with the neutral strategy of assigning case-functions to the arguments. The interferance may be due to deletion (most commonly under coreference), order scrambling, or changes in the case-marking morphology (via various promotion, demotion, raising, or lowering). Pronominal substitution may on occasion involve all three.[7] Transformational operations thus create the case-recoverability problem, which I shall define as follows:

---

[5] For discussion of the diachronic rise of case morphology, see Givón (1975e).

[6] It is traditionally assumed that the syntactic topology exhibited in the main, declarative, affirmative, active clause is the neutral pattern. For further discussion, see Chapter 2.

[7] Thus, if pronouns tend to exhibit more case-marking than nouns, as often seems to be true, then a

(2) *When the strategy used in the neutral sentence pattern for recognizing the case-function of arguments vis-à-vis the verb is tampered with by transformations, the language resorts to **remedial strategies** for recoding those case-functions.*

There are two clarifications which must be added to the formulation in (2). First, it is not the case that **every** language in **every** instance must have a remedial strategy to counter the disruptive effect of transformations. The alternative of relying, at least to some extent, on semantic–pragmatic–contextual redundancies, remains ever present, as is the alternative of tolerating lesser communicative efficiency and higher potential ambiguity. Since alternative strategies are often available and languages often employ a mixture of those, one could not predict that a language will actually use a remedial strategy at all, but only assess the *efficacy* of various strategies once they are used. Second, one must remember that the processing difficulty or psychological *complexity* presumably involved in each transformational tampering with the neutral pattern must be viewed as *relative to that neutral pattern*. As a correlate, the efficacy of various remedial strategies of case-function recoverability must also be viewed as relative to the neutral pattern. These are complexities which I am in no position to resolve, but which one must bear in mind when a resolution to the entire riddle of grammatical typology is contemplated.

4.3. RELATIVIZATION

In this section I will consider restrictions on relativization which were summarized in the accessibility hierarchy of Keenan and Comrie (1977). I will begin by outlining the most common case-recoverability strategies used in the formation of relative clauses in language.

4.3.1. Strategies of Relativization

Some of the data that will be discussed can also be found in Comrie (1975a) and Keenan and Comrie (1977), though my presentation is likely to differ in detail as well as emphasis. In defining restrictive relative clauses I will follow the essentially semantic definition given by Keenan and Comrie (1975):

---

fronted object relative pronoun such as *whom* exemplifies all three types of tampering with the neutral strategy. In terms of morphology, it shows an *increase* of marking–transparency and thus represents an *improvement* over the neutral pattern. One may wish to consider the general tendency of pronouns to be more case-marked than nouns as a *compensation* for the deletion and (often) movement "tampering" involved in pronominalization.

4.3. Relativization

(3) "Any syntactic object [is] a relative clause if it specifies a set of objects (possibly a one-member set) in two steps: A larger set is specified, called the *domain* of relativization, and then restricted to some subset of which a certain sentence, the *restricting* sentence, is true. The domain of relativization is expressed in surface by the *head NP*, and the restricting sentence by the *restricting clause*, which may look more or less like a surface sentence depending on the language . . . [p. 1]."

The following relativization strategies are most commonly used in language. Many language, probably most, use a mixture of strategies. Furthermore, a language may use an ambiguous recoverability strategy, in which case the function of two or more cases is coded the same way and disambiguation must presumably rely on various available redundancies. Additionally, a language may have a recoverability strategy for some case-arguments and none for others, for the latter again relying on available redundancies.

4.3.1.1. THE NONREDUCTION STRATEGY

This strategy is used partially in Hindi and Bambara (Keenan and Comrie, 1977), is also reported at least to some extent in Diegeño (Gorbet, 1974), Navajo (Gorbet, 1974) and Mojave (Munro, 1974), among others. Its most extreme case is probably that of Hittite (Justus, 1976a). There are two related features to this strategy. The first involves the fact that the neutral pattern of the restricting sentence remains intact, so that no recoverability problem arises. The second is that the restricting sentence, which, in some abstract sense, also "includes" the head noun, appears at a *topic* or *preposed* position vis-à-vis the matrix sentence (main clause), and the coreferent noun within the *main* clause is pronominalized or even deleted. Thus consider the following sentence from Hittite (Justus, 1976a):

(4) kw-iš šaga-iš kišari, ta lugal-i
which-NOM sign-NOM appears, PRT king-DAT
sallugal-ga tarueni
queen-AND report-we

{ 'Whichever sign appears, we shall report it to the king and queen'
'If any sign appears, we shall report it to the king and queen'
'We shall report to the king and queen any sign that appears' }

Consider next the following case from Bambara,[8] where the coreferent noun in the restricting sentence is marked by a special morpheme. The restricting sentence remains intact ("unreduced"), and may be embedded, as in:

---

[8] For the Bambara data I am indebted to Ibrahima Coulibali (personal communication).

(5)   n ye ce **min** ye muru san ye
       I past man REL past knife buy see
       'I saw the man who bought the knife'

or unembedded, as in:

(6)   ce **min** ye muru san, n ye o ye
       man REL past knife buy, I past *him* see
       'The man who bought the knife, I saw him'

These two variants may be seen in object relativization as well:

(7)   ce be   n ye   so   **min** ye dyɔ
       man PROG I past house REL see build
       'The man is building the house that I saw'

(8)   n ye   so   **min** ye, ce be   o dyɔ
       I PAST house REL see, man PROG *it* build
       'The house that I saw, the man is building it'

4.3.1.2. THE GAP STRATEGY

At its most extreme, this is a strategy in which the coreferent noun within the restricting clause is deleted without trace. Thus consider the following data from Japanese:[9]

(9)   otoko-ga   onna-ni   tegami-o   kaita
       man-SUBJ woman-DAT letter-ACC wrote
       'The man wrote a letter to the woman'

(10)   onna-ni   tegami-o   kaita otoko-wa
       woman-DAT letter-ACC wrote man-TOP
       'the man who wrote a letter to the woman'

(11)   otoko-ga   onna-ni   kaita tegami-wa
       man-SUBJ woman-DAT wrote letter-TOP
       'the letter that the man wrote to the woman'

(12)   otoko-ga   tegami-o   kaita onna-wa
       man-SUBJ letter-ACC wrote woman-TOP
       'the woman to whom the man wrote a letter'

In judging the efficacy of such a strategy, in which no seeming morphological means is visible for recovering the case-function of the deleted noun, one must assume that full use is made of redundant semantic–pragmatic–contextual information. But it may very well be that, particularly in a language with a relatively rigid neutral word order, the pres-

---

[9] For the Japanese data I am indebted to Katsue Akiba. The topic case-suffix *-wa* is uniformly used here for the out-of-context head of relative clauses.

4.3. Relativization

ence of a gap by itself is a perceptual clue contrasted with the neutral word-order strategy. One would expect, in a language employing this strategy to the full, a rigid word-order in the relative clause as well. The interaction between word-order and gap strategies in relativization may be thus discussed as another recoverability strategy.

4.3.1.3. WORD-ORDER STRATEGIES

This is a strategy used partially in dialects of present day English. Thus consider the dialect in which both object and subject relative subordinators are dispensed with, and the relative clause is differentiated from main clauses by intonation:

(13) the man saw John yesterday is a crook (NP–V–NP . . .)
      (SUBJ)

(14) the man John saw yesterday is a crook (NP–NP–V–. . .)
      (OBJ)

This strategy is used for only subject and direct-object relativization, in a language in which the position of these to argument before and after the verb is rigidly grammaticalized. One may just argue that English can afford to dispense with case-marked relative pronouns here precisely because the syntactic order NP–V . . . is a clue to the case SUBJECT as it is in the neutral pattern. While the syntactic order NP–NP–V . . . is a clue to the case DIR-OBJECT—in sharp contrast to the neutral pattern . . . V–NP.[10]

4.3.1.4. THE NOMINALIZATION STRATEGY

In a number of languages, such as Turkish or Yaqui, relative clauses appear as nominalizations, in which at least one of the arguments is marked by a *genitive* affix. The verb in the clause usually appears in a nominalized, non-finite form. In Yaqui, for examples, the nominal-relative suffix on the verb is different for subject and object relativization. And the subject and object in object relative clauses appear as genitives. Thus consider:[11]

---

[10] While one cannot predict that all languages with a rigid SVO order will avail themselves of this strategy, some added facts seem to underscore its availability. In spoken Israeli Hebrew, for example, the normal recoverability strategy involves the use of anaphoric pronouns, see below. The word-order in the main clauses may be either VS . . . or SV . . . But in accusative relativization, the order is rigidly SV, the anaphoric–resumptive object pronoun may be optionally deleted, and thus—as in English—the difference between object and subject relative clauses is signaled by word order:

    ha-ish   she-Yoav raa etmol
    the man that-Yoav saw yesterday
    'The man that Yoav saw yesterday'   (O–S–V = object rel.)
    ha-ish   she-raa et-Yoav   etmol
    the-man that-saw ACC-Yoav yesterday
    'The man who saw Yoav yesterday'   (S–V–O = subject rel.)

[11] For details see Lindenfeld (1973).

(13′) hu o?oo tuka im yepsa-k
       this man yesterday here arrive-AUX
       'The man arrived here yesterday'

(14′) hu o?oo tuka im yepsa-k-*ame*
       this man yesterday here arrive-AUX-*REL*
       'the man who arrived here yesterday'

(15)   empo hu kari hinu-k
       you-NOM this house buy-AUX
       'You bought the house'

(16)   *hu-ka kari-ta* em hinu-k-a?u
       this-*GEN* house-*GEN* your buy-past-*REL*
       { 'the house that you bought' }
       { 'the house of your buying' }

(17)   in-acai hu kari hinu-k
       my-father this house buy-AUX
       'My father bought the house'

(18)   hu kari *in-acai-ta* hinu-k-a?u
       this house my-father-*GEN* buy-AUX-*REL*
       { 'the house that my father bought' }
       { 'the house of my father's buying' }

The word order in main clauses in Yaqui is most commonly SOV, and both subject and accusative are morphologically unmarked. The effect of the nominalization–genitive strategy in relativization is to increase case differentiation by markings on both the nouns and the verb.

4.3.1.5. ANAPHORIC PRONOUN STRATEGY

Within the framework of embedding plus reduction in relativization, this is in a sense the least disruptive strategy, involving the replacement of the coreferent NP within the restricting clause with the anaphoric pronoun marked for the appropriate case, and often at the same syntactic position as the deleted NP. Hebrew and Arabic, among others, employ this strategy almost fully, though many languages use it partially, under certain grammatical conditions or with particular case-functions. As an illustration consider the following data from Israeli Hebrew:[12]

(19)   a. *Miryam natna et-ha-sefer le-Yosef*   (neutral)
          Mary gave ACC-the-book to-Joseph
          'Mary gave the book to Joseph'

---

[12] For details see Givón (1973a, 1975a).

4.3. Relativization

b. *ha-isha **she**-natna et-ha-sefer le-Yosef* (SUBJ)
the-woman *that*-gave ACC-the-book to-Joseph
'the woman who gave the book to Joseph'

c. *ha-sefer **she**-Miryam natna oto le-Yosef* (ACC)
the-book *that*-Mary gave *it* to-Joseph
'the book that Mary gave to Joseph'

d. *ha-ish **she**-Miryam natna lo et-ha-sefer* (DAT)
the-man *that*-Mary gave *to-him* ACC-the-book
'the man to whom Mary gave the book'

The subject relative clause in (19b) appears to have no anaphoric pronoun, but this is misleading since the verb is inflected for subject agreement (in this case third person singular feminine) which thus functions as an anaphoric pronoun.

4.3.1.6. RELATIVE PRONOUN STRATEGY

This strategy is well known in Indo-European languages such as English or Spanish, and involves case-marked pronouns which most normally get attracted to a position between the head noun and the restricting clause.[13] The relative pronoun thus serves a double function: It carries the case-marking of the deleted NP and also separates the head noun from the embedded sentence. The case-marked relative pronoun may be akin to or include the corresponding interrogative pronoun. This strategy is often used partially, mixed with others.

4.3.1.7. THE EQUI-CASE STRATEGY

Under the most stringent application, if a language confined itself to use only this strategy in relativization, it could only modify subjects of the matrix sentence with subject relative clause, objects with object relative clauses etc. This provision would automatically insure the recovery of the case-function of the deleted coreferent noun from that of the head. Obviously this would also be a disastrous limitation in terms of *expressive power*, and it is no great wonder that no language relies on this strategy exclusively. Many languages take advantage of this provision partially, however, and some cases of this type will be discussed further presently.[14]

4.3.1.8. THE VERB-CODING STRATEGY

This strategy as used in the Philippine and other West-Malayo-Polynesian languages will be discussed at great length later in this chapter. One variant of this strategy involves the appearance of the

[13] For a discussion of possible motivation for this attraction, see Givón (1972b).
[14] In the relativization of prepositional objects in Hebrew, the anaphoric pronoun may be optionally deleted if its preposition is identical with that of the head noun (Givón, 1975a).

case-marking morpheme of the deleted NP as an affix on the verb within the relative clause, as in English:

(20)   a.   *I worked **with** the boy*
                b.   *the boy I worked **with***

It characterizes the relativization of locatives in Bantu languages, as in Bemba:

(21)   a.   *naaliile **ku**-mushi*
                    I-went *to*-village
                    'I went to the village'

                b.   *umushi **uo**   naaliile-**ko***
                    village *that* I-went-*to*
                    'the village I went to'

This and other Bantu variants will be discussed further in great detail in connection with promotion rules.

4.3.2. Relativization and Promotion to Subject

In this section I will deal with languages of the type which restricts relativization to subjects only, and are thus in a large measure responsible for the first segment of Keenan and Comrie's accessibility hierarchy. Put another way, in these languages a rule of subjectivization, that is, passivization, is a prerequisite *feeder* to relativizing any nonagent argument. Data of this type can be found in Keenan (1972b, 1976b) for Malagasy, in Bell (1974) for Cebuano, or in Schachter (1976) for Phillippine languages in general. To my knowledge this type of restriction has been reported only for Malayo-Polynesian languages of similar type. I will illustrate it by data from a Philippine language closely related to Tagalog and Cebuano, Bikol.[15]

In this language the *semantic* case of the SUBJECT-TOPIC argument is coded on the verb. In the neutral pattern the SUBJECT-TOPIC carries only its *pragmatic* case-marking as a prefix. All non-TOPIC arguments are marked for their *semantic* case by a prefix, though a certain range of ambiguity is tolerated in the semantic case-marking.[16] The result of this system is that the TOPIC argument is verb coded for its *semantic* case, and passivization or topicalization involves switching the coding system of an argument from noun-coding to verb-coding of its semantic case-function. As an example consider the following:

---

[15] For the data I am indebted to Manuel Factora (personal communication).
[16] Most commonly the AGENT and GENITIVE markers are identical, the DATIVE and LOCATIVE-DIRECTIONAL are identical (often including the BENEFACTIVE) and a number of OBLIQUE cases may also share their marking.

4.3. Relativization

(22) a. Agent-topic:

    nag-ta ʔó   ʔang-laláke ning-líbro sa-babáye
    AGT-give TOP-man   ACC-book DAT-woman
    'The man gave a book to the woman'

b. Accusative-topic:[17]

    na-ta ʔó   kang-laláke   ʔang-líbro   sa-babáye
    ACC-give AGT-man   TOP-book DAT-woman
    {'The man gave the book to the woman'
    'The book was given to the woman by the man'
    'As for the book, the man gave it to the woman'}

c. Dative-locative-topic:[18]

    na-ta ʔo-(h)án   kang-laláke ning-líbro ʔang-babáye
    DAT-give   AGT-man   ACC-book TOP-woman
    {'The man gave the woman a book'
    'The woman was given a book by the man'
    'The woman, the man gave her a book'}

d. Instrumental-topic:

    (i) Agent:

        nag-putúl ʔang-laláke ning-tubú
        AGT-cut   TOP-man   ACC-sugar-cane
        gamit- ʔang-lanséta
        INST-knife
        'The man cut sugar-cane with a knife'

    (ii) Instrument:[19]

        pinag-putúl kang-laláke ning-tubú
        INST-cut   AGT-man   ACC-sugar-cane
        ʔang-lanséta
        TOP-knife
        {'The man cut sugar-cane with the knife'
        'The knife was used by the man to cut sugar-cane'
        'As for the knife, the man cut sugar-cane with it'}

e. Benefactive-topic:[20]

[17] In addition to the accusative-topic marker *na-*, the preverbal infix *-in-* is also used when accusatives are promoted via definitization.

[18] The DATIVE–DIRECTIONAL verb coding involves adding the suffix *-an* to whatever codes the accusative-topic.

[19] The INSTRUMENTAL verb-coding prefix *pinag* is made of the causative prefix *pag-* plus the definite-accusative infix *-in-*.

[20] The verb coding for a BENEFACTIVE topic involves adding the suffix *-an* to the verb prefixed with the INSTRUMENTAL *pinag-*.

(i) Agent:

nag-bakál *?ang-laláke ning-kandíng*
AGT-buy TOP-man ACC-goat
para-sa-babáye
BENEF-woman
'The man bought a goat for the woman'

(ii) Benefactive:[21]

pinag-bakal-án *kang-laláke ning-kanding*
BENEF-buy AGT-man ACC-goat
?ang-babáye
TOP-woman
{'The man bought the woman a goat'
'The woman was bought a goat by the man'
'The woman, the man bought her a goat'}

As is evident from the glosses in (22), promoting a nonagent to the status of topic in Bikol is not equivalent to passivization in English. It covers roughly the range of passivization, topic-shift, contrastive topic, and definitization of the accusative. The frequency in discourse of non-agent topic constructions in Philippine languages is much higher than that of passives in English.[22] From our point of view, however, the most salient feature of this promotional system is that it results in *verb-coding* the semantic case-function of the topic argument.

Relativization in Bikol is restricted to topic–subject arguments. In other words, promotion to topic status is an obligatory feeder to relativization of any nonagent argument. Thus, compare the relative clauses in (23) below to the corresponding neutral patterns in (22):

(23) a. Agent:
marái ?ang-laláke na nag-ta?ó ning-líbro sa-babáye
good TOP-man that AGT-give ACC-book DAT-woman
'The man who gave a book to the woman is good'
**marái ?ang-laláke na na-ta?ó ?ang-líbro sa-babáye*
(*ACC-topic)
**marái ?ang-laláke na na-ta?o-hán ning-líbro ?ang-babáye*
(*DAT-topic)

---

[21] The description of the semantic case markers as given in (22) is a bit simplified. The *ning-* indefinite-accusative marker may on occasion be used to mark indefinite dative or agents. The *sa-* dative marker may also mark the definite accusative as an alternative to topicalization with *-in-*. The topic-marker *?ang-* is always definite, unless the argument is generic.

[22] For an extensive discussion of the subject–topic in Philippine languages, see Schachter (1976). In English, the percentage of passive sentences in written text is between 0% and 18% (see Chapter 2), and probably very low in informal, less-educated speech.

4.3. Relativization

b. Accusative:
marai ʔang-libro na na-taʔó kang-laláke sa-babáye
good TOP-book *that* ACC-give AGT-man DAT-woman
'The book that the man gave to the woman is good'[23]
*marái ʔang-líbro na nag-taʔó ʔang-laláke sa-babáye
(*AGT-topic)
*marai ʔang-líbro na na-taʔo-hán kang-laláke ʔang-babáye
(*DAT-topic)

c. Dative-locative:
marái ʔang-babáye na na-taʔo-hán kang-laláke ning-líbro
good TOP-woman *that* DAT-give AGT-man ACC-book
{'The woman to whom the man gave a book is good'
'The woman who was given a book by the man is good'}
*marái ʔang-babáye na nag-taʔó ʔang-laláke ning-líbro
(*AGT-topic)
*marái ʔang-babáye na na-taʔó kang-laláke ʔang-libro
(*ACC-topic)

d. Instrumental:
marái ʔang-lanséta na pinag-putúl kang-lakáke ning-tubú
good TOP-knife *that* INST-cut AGT-man ACC-sugar-cane
{'The knife with which the man cut sugar-cane is good'
'The knife used by the man to cut sugar-cane is good'}
*marái ʔang-lanséta na nag-putúl ʔang-laláke ning-tubú
(*AGT-topic)
*marái ʔang-lanséta na na-putúl kang-laláke ʔang-tubú
(*ACC-topic)

e. Benefactive:
marái ʔang-babáye na pinag-bakal-án kang-laláke
good TOP-woman *that* BENEF-buy AGT-man
ning-kandíng
ACC-goat
{'The woman for whom the man bought a goat is good'
'The woman that was bought a goat (for) by the man is good'}
*marái ʔang-babáye na nag-bakál ʔang-laláke ning-kandíng
(*AGT-topic)
*marái ʔang-babáye na na-bakál kang-laláke ʔang-kanding
(*ACC-topic)

The Bikol data above represent a clear case of the *verb-coding* strategy of relativization. The language embeds relative clauses and

---

[23] Also glossed: 'The book given to the woman by the man is good'.

deletes the coreferent NP, so that the nonreduction strategy is inapplicable. While the gap strategy is universally available, one must note that except for a strong verb-initial constraint and a weak preference for the order V–AGT–DAT–ACC, the language allows considerable syntactic freedom in ordering the arguments following the verb. These order variations are presumably used to indicate more subtle nuances of relative topicality of the arguments, given that the main topic is established via the *ʔang*-prefix. As I have noted above, the use of the gap strategy most often involves word-order rigidity as compensation. The language does have case-inflected anaphoric pronouns equivalent to *ʔang-, kang-, ning-,* and *sa-* (topic, agent, accusative, and dative, respectively), but they are not used in relativization. Further, in addition to the case-marking ambiguities noted above (cf. footnote 16), the anaphoric pronominal system represents further reduction, since only pronouns representing the *semantic* cases of agent, accusative and dative are available. A complete anaphoric pronoun recoverability strategy is therefore impossible.[24] Furthermore, languages of the Bikol type have not developed case-inflected relative pronouns, and the relative subordinator is invariant. But given all these "deficiencies," these languages have a built-in verb-coding strategy used in their system of promotion to topic-subject. Given that this element exists *independently* in the grammar, its use in relativization is mere exploitation of the existing grammatical resources of the language. The restriction on subject-only in relativization is thus best viewed within the context of case-recoverability. In terms of typological predictability, one could now make two observations, couched in terms of a stronger and a weaker condition:

(24) TYPOLOGICAL CONDITION I *(stronger). If a language has no other viable recoverability strategy in relativization, and if in addition it has a promotion to subject device which involves coding the semantic case of the subject on the verb, then the language will tend to exploit this device in relativization by imposing a subject-only constraint and thus resorting to verb-coding recoverability strategy.*

(25) TYPOLOGICAL CONDITION II *(weaker). Only languages in which promotion to subject results in coding the verb for the semantic case of the topic/subject will have the subject-only constraint in relativization.*

To my knowledge the prediction couched in the less ambitious CONDITION II (25) has no exception. Within Western-Malayo-Polynesian, only languages in which the verb-coding in passivization is more extensive

---

[24] Compare this with Hebrew, where *all* the case-functions in the neutral pattern have corresponding anaphoric pronouns that are used in relativization.

4.3. Relativization

have imposed the subject-only relativization constraint. The stronger CONDITION I (24) is both more interesting and more problematic. First, it is hard to define the notion of "viable alternative strategy," which is unavoidably a matter of degree. It is equally hard to define the extent to which verb coding in passivization has to be extant before it is considered "available." We so far have no clear notion of assessing the perceptual or psychological efficacy of conding strategies in grammar, especially when comparing different strategies.[25] I nevertheless feel that the ultimate goal for the typologist is to elaborate and flesh out stronger predictions of the type given in CONDITION I.

4.3.2.1. OTHER FUNCTIONAL EXPLANATIONS

Given that the promotional apparatus in Philippine languages is best described as a discourse-dependent advancement of nonagents to status of *main topic* of the sentence, Schachter (1976) has suggested that given the function of relativization in definite description and thus its association with topicality, perhaps the coreferent (deleted) NP within a relative clause is also *more topical* and this would reflect in the subject-topic-only constraint. While attractive, this explanation has a number of drawbacks. To begin with, relative clauses also modify indefinite heads, and in that case (a) the head itself is low in topicality and (b) the restrictive clause cannot be said to even be presupposed. Furthermore, while relative clauses modifying definite nouns are presupposed, one finds within them indefinite and thus presumably less topical NPs. However, to the extent, that the head noun is definite and the relative clause presupposed, the coreferent noun within the clause must be of high topicality. Schachter's suggestion may thus have considerable merit, in which case the explanation for the subject-only constraint on relativization must involve a fortuitous conspiracy of two different functional explanations. However, since TYPOLOGICAL CONDITION II (and perhaps ultimately also CONDITION I) seems to obtain, the functional explanation suggested by Schachter could not by itself be the typologically crucial one, since it holds true for all languages. The explanation just offered and involving case-marking typology must in this case be decisive.

4.3.2.2. OTHER PSYCHOLINGUISTIC EXPLANATIONS

Keenan and Comrie (1977) have argued that processing subject relative clauses is psychologically less complex than processing object relative clauses. They cite experimental evidence from Hawkins and Keenan (1974), Legum (1975), Hatch (1971), Brown (1971), Sheldon

---

[25] It is much easier to assess the degree of efficiency within the *same* strategy. The ultimate determination must be experimental and psycholinguistic.

(1974), Cook (to appear), and Valli, Achard-Boule, and Beretti (1972). There are a number of difficulties with this explanation. To begin with, the studies cited involved only French and English, both strong SVO languages. In both languages subject relativization preserves the neutral strategy SVO, while object relativization involves a word-order which is not attested in the neutral pattern—OSV. Thus while the recoverability of the subject function in relativization requires no change from the neutral pattern, the recoverability of the object function requires a jarring readjustment vis-à-vis the neutral strategy. But neither French nor English, nor any other SVO language exhibits, to my knowledge, the subject-only constraint in relativization. It is not clear to me that in the verb-initial languages which do exhibit the relativization constraint, processing difficulties are going to hierarchize along the same lines. Complexity, as Kennan and Comrie (1975) note, is not an independent parameter but rather must be viewed *relative* to the neutral pattern.

Comrie (1975a) has discussed the following Swahili data as possible support for the greater psychological complexity of object relativization as compared to subject. When the relative pronoun is verb-bound in Swahili, in object relativization the subject of the relative verb must be postposed obligatorily. One gets then a well-known potential ambiguity when both the subject and object are of the same gender (1/2) and number:

(26)   *mtoto a-li-ye-m-penda   Hamisi*
        child he-past-*REL*-him-love Hamisi

   a. 'the child that loved Hamisi'   (Subj. rel.)
   b. 'the child that Hamisi loved'   (Obj. rel.)

Comrie observes that while in principle (26) is ambiguous, in fact most speakers queried prefer the *subject* interpretation (26a), and would rather render the object interpretation (26b) as the passivized:

(27)   *mtoto a-li-ye-pend-wa   na Hamisi*
        child he-past-*REL*-love-*PASS* by Hamisi
        'the child loved by Hamisi'

While the facts are not to be doubted, the argument is far from conclusive. First, Swahili has an alternative relativization in which the relative pronoun is free (and attached to the carrier *amba-*) and the subject of the relative clause need not be postposed:

(28)   *mtoto amba-ye Hamisi a-li-m-penda*
        child *REL*   Hamisi he-past-him-love
        'the child that Hamisi loved'

And the preference for the passivized (27) was not compared with that of (28). Furthermore, Swahili tends toward the neutral syntactic strategy

SVO,[26] though not to the same degree as English and French. Thus, while the subject relative interpretation in (26a) would have retained that neutral strategy, the object relative interpretation (26b) requires the nonneutral strategy OVS, and the object relative in (28) requires the nonneutral strategy OSV, as in English. This enough may be cause for greater processing complexity, but this complexity again is relative to the neutral pattern and so far says nothing about the verb-initial languages in which the subject-only constraint is actually found. To sum up then, while I think the experimental evidence cited by Keenan and Comrie is valid, it is not clear that it explains the subject-only constraint in the languages which actually show it. Finally, if the explanation is universally valid, then it certainly cannot explain why only languages of a certain typological character seem to exhibit the constraint.

4.3.3. Relativization and Promotion to Direct Object

In this section I will discuss the type of data which provided the motivation for the second link in the accessibility hierarchy, that is, DIR OBJ > INDIR OBJ. The data involves languages which, to a greater or lesser degree, require the promotion of a prepositional object onto "direct object" before it is available for relativization. In other words, the rule of *dative-shift* become an obligatory feeder in the relativization of non-ACCUSATIVE objects. I will attempt to show that, just as happens in the case of the subject-only constraint, languages exhibiting the *direct-object-only* constraint in nonsubject relativization are those which gain verb-coding of the semantic case of the relativized prepositional object as it is dative-shifted into the unmarked case "direct-object." I will argue, further, that one must consider the case direct-object—which is much less universally attested as subject—as another *pragmatic* case, involving relative topicality of the object arguments. The leftmost object, as per the universal tendency (see Bolinger, 1952), is the more topical one. Here again a conspiracy may exist between case-marking and topicality considerations. I will attempt to formulate the same type of typological predictions as in (24) and (25) above. I will also attempt to show how within the same language—or a closely related group—variations in the availability of noun-coding and verb-coding case morphology determine the applicability or inapplicability of the direct-object-only constraint.

---

[26] Swahili, somewhat like Spanish (Bolinger, 1954) and Hebrew (Givón, 1976b), allows both VS and SV in its neutral pattern, with the variation governed by discourse-pragmatics. The preference for VS is particularly striking when nonsubjects are topicalized or relativized. Thus the OVS order is actually available in Swahili main-clauses, though it is a "more marked" pattern, if one assumes subjects are more likely to be topical than objects (Edward Keenan, 1976a; Givón, 1976a).

4.3.3.1. THE DATIVE-SHIFT RULE

One may choose to define the dative-shift rule formally as one changing an indirect or prepositional object into a direct object (as in Keenan and Comrie, 1977; Gary and Keenan, 1975; Perlmutter and Postal, 1974; or Kimenyi, 1976; among others). Two criterial features in the case-marking system are usually taken to be associated with this change:

1. The erstwhile indirect object looses its case-marking morpheme during the promotion.
2. The order ACC-INDIR is reversed.

For example:

(29) *John gave the book to Mary*   (V–ACC–DAT)   →
      John gave Mary a book   (V–DAT–ACC)

The "demoted" accusative object may remain unmarked, as is usually the case when the prepositional object was DATIVE or BENEFACTIVE. But it may also acquire a preposition as it moves away from the verb. Thus consider:

(30) *John sprayed the paint **on** the wall*   (V–INST–LOC)
      *John sprayed the wall **with** paint*   (V–LOC–INST)
      *He supplied the ammunition **to** the troops* (V–INST–LOC)
      *He supplied the troops **with** ammunition*   (V–LOC–INST)

One of the variant orders may involve verb-coding of the semantic case-function of the object NP *closer* to the verb, see the Bantu and Indonesian data presented later is this chapter. The order switch between the two objects may involve no change at all in the case-marking situation, see Hebrew and Spanish data further below. While one may choose to call some of these variants "promotion to direct object" and dismiss the others as mere order switch, the evidence suggests to me that in terms of *function* all variants share a common core.

The dative-shift rule is most commonly described for SVO languages in which the SUBJECT and ACCUSATIVE are unmarked for their case. Their being morphologically unmarked is not altogether divorced from this particular word-order typology, since one could argue that their position vis-à-vis the verb—NP–V . . . versus . . . V–NP, respectively—constitute their case-marking. But in terms of function, *verb-initial* languages such as Bikol allow order variations between the ACCUSATIVE and DATIVE–BENEFACTIVE–INSTRUMENTAL objects, and it is most sensible to assume that these variations perform an identical function. What one does not find associated with these variations in verb-initial languages, however, are changes in the case-marking morphology either on the NPs or the verb. Similarly, SOV

4.3. Relativization

languages such as Amharic or Sherpa also allow ACC–DAT versus DAT–ACC order variations, and there is no reason to assume that they do not perform similar functions. But again, most commonly in this typology, no changes in the case-marking morphology are involved.

I would like to argue here that the most common function of the dative-shift rule involves changing the *relative topicality* of the accusative vis-à-vis the prepositional object. This involves the universal word-order principle that the left-most constituent is the *more topical* one, that is, the one more likely to *not* constitute new information, while the right-most constituent is the *focus* of the new information (see Bolinger, 1952).[27] Let me illustrate this first with a few examples from English. Consider the situation when one of the object NPs is made topical via previous mention in a preposed–topical adverbial clause:[28]

(31)   a.   *When he found it, John gave the book to Mary.*

         b.   *?When he found it, John gave Mary the book.*

Thus, when the ACCUSATIVE object is established as topical, the order ACC–DAT as in (31a) is more natural, and DAT–ACC as in (31b) less so. Consider now the opposite case:

(32)   a.   *When he found her, John gave Mary the book.*

         b.   *?When he found her, John gave the book to Mary.*

Here the DATIVE object is established as topical, and as a result the order DAT–ACC is more natural.

The converse of this may be shown when the *focus* is preestablished via a WH question. Consider first:

(33)   a.   *To whom did John give the book?*   (DAT focus)

                b.   *He gave the book to Mary.*

                c.   *?He gave Mary the book*[29]

(34)   a.   *What did John give to Mary?*   (ACC focus)

                b.   *He gave Mary the book.*

                c.   *?He gave the book to Mary.*[29]

---

[27] There is no full overlap between the dichotomies topic/focus, definite/indefinite and presupposed/asserted. Quite often a definite object can constitute the focus of new information in a particular communication. See some discussion in Chafe (1976), Bolinger (1954), and Givón (1976b).

[28] There is evidence to suggest that adverbial clauses are "more topical" when preposed and "more focus" when postposed. Further, in New Guinea languages in which adverbial clauses are obligatorily marked with a *topic* modality, they can only *precede* the main clause (Thurman, 1978).

[29] Both (c) variants in (33) and (34) become acceptable under contrastive stress placed on the object closer to the verb. English thus makes use of either word-order or stress to impart relative topicality relations. Other SVO languages (Spanish, Hebrew, Indonesian) cannot freely move the focus-stress from the sentence-final position. See Shir (1979) for further discussion of the pragmatic nature of dative-shifting.

A related fact in English is the reluctance to move the accusative anaphoric pronoun away from the verb:

(35)   a. *He gave it to her*
          b. **He gave her it*

While this constraint is not fully symmetrical and is most commonly described in "syntactic" terms, it seems to me that it must reflect the general tendency to keep the accusative near the verb if it is highly topical, as anaphoric pronouns surely are.

An interesting—and converse—reflection of the same principle is found in English idioms formed on the V–ACC–DAT verb type. Thus consider:

(36)   a. *He gave her a kiss*
          b. **He gave a kiss to her*
          c. *He gave her a kick*
          d. **He gave a kick to her*
          e. *He gave them a lecture*
          f. **He gave a lecture to them*

Even though *give a kiss, give a kick, give a lecture* are just about lexicalized, the tendency to keep the indefinite—and thus less topical—accusative away from the verb is maintained.

Evidence of this type abounds cross-linguistically. At this point let me cite only two pieces of evidence from Rwanda, a Bantu language with an SVO typology. Kimenyi (1976) has observed that when the order V–ACC–INDIRECT is maintained, the indirect–prepositional object could be either definite or indefinite. While if the indirect object is promoted via dative shift, it must be obligatorily *definite* (or generic):

(37)   a. *umugabo a-ra-tema   igiti n-umupaanga*
             boy   he-ASP-cut tree *with*-iron
             'The boy cut the tree with {an iron / the iron}'

          b. *umgabo a-ra-tem-eesha   umupaanga igiti*
             boy   he-ASP-cut-INST iron   tree
             {'The boy cut the tree with {the iron / *an iron}'
              'The boy used the iron to cut the tree'}

Another observation made by Kimenyi (1976) is that if the accusative object is an anaphoric pronoun—and thus high in topicality—the promotion of prepositional objects to direct object via the dative-shift rule is blocked. Thus:

4.3. Relativization

(38) a. *umugabo y-a-taa-ye   igitabo **mu**-maazi*
           boy   he-past-throw-ASP book   *in*-water
           'The boy threw the book into (the) water'

     b. *umugabo y-a-taa-ye-**mo**   amaazi igitabo*
           boy   he-past-throw-ASP-*LOC* water   book
           'The boy threw the/a book into the water'

     c. *umugabo y-a-**gi**-taa-ye   **mu**-maazi*
           boy   he-past-*it*-throw-ASP *in*-water
           'The boy threw it into (the) water'

     d. **umugabo y-a-**gi**-taa-ye-**mo**   amaazi*
           boy   he-past-*it*-throw-ASP-*LOC* water

One can also show that the same rule of dative-shift, in functional terms, may also exist in an SOV language where no morphological changes in the case marking are associated with it, but only the relative order change. Thus, in Sherpa, a Tibeto–Burmese language with strong SOV syntax, one finds the consistent order variation of accusative and prepositional objects, as in:[30]

(39) *tiki   kitabi   čoxts-i-kha-la   žax-sung* (S–ACC–DAT–V)
       he-ERG book   table-GEN-on-DAT put-AUX
       'He put the book on the table'

(40) *tiki   čoxts-i-kha-la   kitabi žax-sung* (S–DAT–ACC–V)
       he-ERG table-GEN-on-DAT book put-AUX
       'He put on the table a book'

If the preceding context topicalizes the ACCUSATIVE, as in *I asked him what he did with the book, so he said that* . . . , the order ACC–DAT is preferred. While if the preceding context topicalizes the dative, the order DAT–ACC is preferred.

One qualification must be made at this point. Anderson (1970) has pointed out in connection with a special case of dative-shift variation, the one in which case-marking switches are involved, that in addition to the pragmatic variation ("what one is talking about"), *semantic* differences of various kinds may also appear. Thus, consider:

(41)   *What did you do to the wall?*
                  a. *I sprayed it **with** paint.*
                  b. ?*I sprayed paint **on** it.*

(42)   *What did you do with the paint?*
                  a. *I sprayed it **on** the wall.*
                  b. ?*I sprayed the wall **with** it.*

---

[30] For the data I am indebted to Konchchok Lama (personal communication).

Anderson (1970) has observed that in (41), where *wall* is mentioned as topic, variant (a) with the order WALL–PAINT is preferable. While presumably in (42), where *paint* is the topic, variant (a) with the order PAINT–WALL is preferable. In addition, however, the two variant orders also differ in their semantic entailment. *Spraying paint on the wall* does not entail covering the *entire* wall with paint, while *spraying the wall with paint* seems to entail spraying the *entire* wall. Conversely, *Spraying the paint on the wall* entails spraying **all** the paint, while *spraying the wall with paint* does not. At this point I will merely refer the reader to an illuminating general discussion in Bolinger (1952) where it is shown that when inherently pragmatic word-order variations exist, semantic variation quite often sets in as a result. In our particular case, I believe, it is the fact of "talking about x" which gives rise to the inference of "talking about *all of* x," rather than vice versa.

4.3.3.2. LANGUAGES WHICH DO

In this section I will outline the data from languages which require the application of dative-shift as an obligatory feeder to relativization of a nonaccusative object. I will show that two main typological parameters single these languages out:

1. Dative-shift results in *verb-coding* of the semantic case of the nonaccusative object which has lost its noun-bound marking.
2. The strategy of relativization in the language does **not** provide for another way for differentiating the nonaccusative from the accusative in relativization.

I will also demonstrate how within the same language one may find alternative strategies for different nonaccusative objects, pending on whether case-coding is available. And that again, the case-functions which require dative-shift as a prerequisite feeder to their relativization are characterized by exactly the same two parameters (1) and (2) above.

4.3.3.2.1. Indonesian[31]

Indonesian is a SVO language with the SUBJECT and ACCUSATIVE unmarked morphologically and the nonaccusative objects marked by prepositions. Dative-shift is an independent rule in this language, and results in verb-coding of the semantic case of either DATIVES or BENEFACTIVES on the verb. The language thus satisfies condition (1) above. As an example consider the following data from Chung (1975):

(43) a. *Hasan mem-beli badju* **untuk** *wanita itu*
Hasan ACT-buy clothes *for* woman the
'Hasan bought clothes for the woman'

---
[31] A more extensive example of similar data is found in a related language (Fijian; Foley, 1976).

4.3. Relativization

b. *Hasan mem-beli-kan wanita itu badju*
   Hasan ACT-buy-*BEN* woman the clothes
   'Hasan bought the woman clothes'

c. *Hasan meng-irim-kan*[32] *seputjuk surat* **kepada** *wanita itu*
   Hasan ACT-write-*BEN*   a letter *to* woman the
   'Hasan wrote a letter to the woman'

d. *Hasan meng-irim-i wanita itu seputjuk surat*
   Hasan ACT-write-*DAT* woman the   a letter
   'Hasan wrote the woman a letter'

In relativization Indonesian uses the invariant subordinator *jang*, uninflected for semantic case. Subject relativization preserves the neutral SVO strategy of the language, as in (again from Chung, 1975):

(44) *wanita jang mem-beli badju* **untuk** *Hasan*
   woman *that* ACT-buy clothes *for* Hasan
   'the woman who bought clothes for Hasan'

Accusative relativization is differentiated from subject relativization first by the word-order strategy OSV, and second by the fact that the verb loses its ACTOR prefix.[33] But neither of these differentiate the accusative from nonaccusative objects, which share the same strategy up to this point. Thus, for accusative (Chung, 1975):

(45) a. *badju jang Hasan beli* **untuk** *wanita itu*
    cloth *that* Hasan bought *for* woman the
    'the clothes that Hasan bought for that woman'

  b. *surat jang Hasan kirim-kan kepada wanita itu*
    letter *that* Hasan write-*BEN to* woman the
    'the letter that Hasan wrote to the woman'

The differentiation of either the dative or benefactive object from the accusative in relativization is achieved via the verb-coding strategy that is available by making dative-shift an obligatory feeder to relativization. Thus consider (data again from Chung, 1975):

(46) a. *wanita jang Hasan beli-kan badju*
    woman that Hasan buy-*for* clothes
    'the woman for whom Hasan bought clothes'

---

[32] The benefactive verb-coding suffix -*kan* does not only appear in the promotion of benefactives to direct-object, as in (43b), but also when the dative object is construed as "beneficiary" rather than mere locative–goal. The preposition *kepada* 'to' by itself indicates the directional–locative goal.

[33] I suspect the *meN*- prefix in Indonesian is cognate to the AGENT-focus prefix in Philippine languages (see preceding Bikol data). Its loss during relativization suggests that the Indonesian strategy used to be similar to that of the Philippine one, namely a "subject only" restriction. In time, Indonesian shifted to SVO with an unmarked subject and accusative, and the subject only restriction was relaxed, as the language readjusted to a new case-marking typology. The passivization–topicalization system of Indonesian (see following) is probably a later development, following the loss of the Philippine-type voice-change system.

b. *wanita **jang** Hasan beli badju (**untuk**)
woman that Hasan buy clothes (for)

c. wanita **jang** Hasan kirim-i surat
woman that Hasan write-DAT letter
'the woman to whom Hasan wrote a letter'

d. *wanita **jang** Hasan kirim surat (**kepada**)
woman that Hasan write letter (to)

The direct-object-only restriction thus serves to rescue the semantic case-marking of nonaccusative objects in relativization via verb-coding. An added proof that this is indeed the function of the promotion rule here may be seen in the following data. Indonesian has recently developed—most likely via borrowing from English—an alternative relativization strategy in which the case-marked WH particles are used *plus* the neutral pattern prepositions. And when that strategy is employed,[34] not only is the direct-object-only restriction relaxed, but it is in fact impossible to use this strategy on the dative-shifted variant. Thus compare (46a) above to (47a) (data from Sandy Chung, private communication):

(47) a. wanita **untuk-siapa** Hasan mem-beli badju
woman for-who Hasan ACT-buy clothes
'the woman for whom Hasan bought clothes'

b. *wanita **untuk-siapa** Hasan beli-kan badju
woman for-who Hasan buy-BEN clothes

Thus, when an alternative recoverability strategy is available, the verb-coding strategy which motivated the direct-object-only restriction is discarded.

4.3.3.2.2. Bantu

Another major source of data substantiating the segment DIR > INDIR in the accessibility hierarchy comes from various Bantu languages. As in Indonesian, the general typology of these languages is SVO with subject and accusative (or "direct object") unmarked morphologically. As in Indonesian, the coding capabilities involving word order and relative pronouns can adequately code the difference between subject and object relativization but cannot go further in distinguishing the semantic case of various object types. As in Indonesian, the partially imposed restriction of direct-object-only achieves further case differentiation of those objects via *verb-coding*. There are two striking themes running through the Bantu data. First, the verb-coding or promotion strategy within one language is used only for the cases for which an

---

[34] This borrowed strategy is not yet considered "standard," and the preferred native strategy is still via promotion to direct-object and verb-coding.

4.3. Relativization

alternative coding strategy is **not** available. And second, as languages lose one type of coding, they make greater use of the verb-coding–promotion alternative.

4.3.3.2.2.1. Bemba[35]

The dative-shift rule is functional in Bemba, but the promotion involved does not create, in the neutral pattern, increased verb coding. Thus for some dative–benefactive objects the BENEFACTIVE verb suffix appear obligatorily in either word-order variant:

(48)   a.   *umukashi a-a-tum-**in**-e   icitabo **ku**-muana*
            woman   she-past-send-*BEN*-ASP book   *to*-child
            'The woman sent the book to the child'
                                                                                 (ACC–DAT)

         b.   *umukashi a-a-tum-**in**-e   umuana icitabo*
            woman   she-past-send-*BEN*-ASP child   book
            'The woman sent the child a book'
                                                                                 (DAT–ACC)

In other verbs the BENEFACTIVE verb suffix appears in neither variant:

(49)   a.   *umukashi a-a-moneshya icitabo **ku**-muana*   (ACC–DAT)
            woman   she-past-show book   *to*-child
            'The woman showed the book to the child'

         b.   *umukashi a-a-moneshya umuana icitabo*   (DAT–ACC)
            woman   she-past-show child   book
            'The woman showed the child a book'

Nonhuman locatives do not lose their preposition in dative-shifting, and in general dative-shifting seems less natural here:

(50)   a.   *umuana a-a-shya   icitabo **mu**-ngaanda*   (ACC–LOC)
            child   he-past-leave book   *in*-house
            'The child left the book in the house'

         b.   *?umuana a-a-shya   **mu**-ngaanda icitabo*   (?LOC–ACC)
            child   he-past-leave *in*-house   book
            'The child left in the house a book'

         c.   **umuana a-a-shya   ingaanda icitabo*   (*LOC–ACC)
            child   he-past-leave house   book

When a clear BENEFACTIVE object is present, one which does *not* blend with the DATIVE, it is unmarked, must appear next to the verb, and the verb obligatorily takes the benefactive suffix:

---

[35] The Bemba data are derived from my own field notes (1968). Some of the material may be found in Givón (1972a). The information came initially from Peter Chilufya of Malolo, Chief Chiti Mukulu, Kaasama district.

(51) a. umuana a-a-shit-**ila**   umukashi icitabo   (BEN–ACC)
       child   he-past-buy-*BEN* woman   book
       ['The child bought a book for the woman']
       ['The child bought the woman a book']

   b. *umuana a-a-shit-**ila**   icitabo (**ku**)mukashi (*ACC–BEN)[36]
      child   he-past-buy-*BEN* book   (*to*) woman

Dative-shift is perhaps possible but less natural with either the associative or instrumental objects, both marked with the preposition *na*:

(52) a. umuana a-a-lya   umukate **no**-omunaankwe (ACC–ASSOC)
       child   he-past-eat bread   *with*-friend-his
       'The child ate (the) bread with his friend'

   b. ?umuana a-a-lya **no**-omunaankwe umukate   (?ASSOC–ACC)

   c. umuana a-a-lya   umukate **ne**-ecimuti   (ACC–INST)
      child   he-past-eat bread   *with*-stick
      'The child ate (the) bread with a/the stick'

   d. ?umuana a-a-lya **ne**-ecimuti umukate   (?INST–ACC)

In the case of the ASSOCIATIVE object, it can be promoted to conjoined-*subject*, a process resulting in verb-coding its semantic function with the suffix -*na*, as in:

(53)   umuana **no**-omunaankwe ba-a-lya-**na**   umukate
       child   *and*-friend-his   they-past-eat-ASSOC bread
       'The child and his friend ate (the) bread together'

Dative shifting of the type "spray x *on* y" versus "spray y *with* x" discussed earlier [cf. (41), (42)] is also found in Bemba, as in:

(54) a. *aa-cimine inama **ne**-omuele*
         he-stabbed animal *with*-knife
         'He stabbed/pierced the animal with a/the knife'

      b. *aa-cimine umuele **mu**-nama*
         he-thrust knife   *into*-animal
         'He thrust the knife into the animal'

      c. *aa-fwaanta umuana **ne**-ecimuti*
         he-bruised child   *with*-stick
         'He bruised the child with a/the stick'

      d. *aa-fwaanta icimuti **pa**-muana*
         he-stuck   stick   *at*-child
         'He stuck the stick at the child'

---

[36] Since the dative-directional *ku*- also codes 'from', this sentence without the benefactive -*il*- suffix is acceptable under the interpretation: 'The child bought a/the book from the woman'.

4.3 Relativization

    e. *aa-kaaka umuti **ne**-ekaamba*
        he-tied   tree   *with*-rope
        'He tied the tree with a rope'

    f. *aa-kaaka ikaamba **ku**-muti*
        he-tied   rope   *to*-tree
        'He tied the rope to a/the tree'

In relativization in general, the language maintains the SVO strategy for subject and OSV for object relatives. Subject relativization involves in addition also a tonal change on the subject-agreement pronoun, as in:[37]

(55)   a. *umuana á-a-lya   umukate*
           child   *he*-past-eat bread
           'the child ate (the) bread'

        b. *umuana ù-a-lya   umukate*
           child   *who*-past-eat bread
           'the child who ate (the) bread . . .'

In relativizing objects, a demonstrative pronoun is used as a subordinator, together with the OSV word-order strategy. Most commonly that demonstrative pronoun is inflected for gender–number of the deleted noun, *not* for case. Thus consider relativization of the accusative:

(56)   *umukate **uo**   umuana à-a-lya*
         bread   *that* child   he-past-ate
         'The bread that the child ate . . .'

The relativization of nonaccusative objects illustrates how a language mixes strategies pending on the availability of case marking. For the locative cases *pa-*, *ku-*, *mu-*, demonstratives inflected for the normal noun-genders are available.[38] Two alternative strategies are then possible. If an equi-case situation is available, that is, when the *head* noun is also prepositional in the *same* case, the demonstrative pronouns inflected for the prepositional gender are used, as in:

(57)   a. *naa-laandile **ku**-muana **uko**   umukashi àa-peele icitabo*
           I-spoke   *to*-child   *to-whom* woman   she-gave book
           'I spoke to the child to whom the woman gave a/the book'

---

[37] While the tonal change is "phonemically" on the pronoun, it results in a complex tonal displacement over the entire verbal word. For all noun classes with the exception of human-singular, the subject agreement pronoun is the same (minus the tonal difference) in main and relative clauses. The human-singular (class 1) shows, on top of tonal differences, also the *a/u ariation*.

[38] These prepositional cases in Bantu tend to behave like the noun-genders, in terms of the pronominal agreement system, but only up to a point. The demonstratives corresponding to them cover the semantic range of *'here'*, *'there'*, *'in here'*, *'to here'*, etc., though the deictic space is richer (in its coding) than in English.

b. *naa-li mu-ngaanda **umo** umunaandi àa-keele*
   I-lived *in*-house *in-which* friend-my he-lived
   'I lived in the house where my friend lived'

If the head noun is in a different case than the coreferent noun in the restricting clause, however, this strategy is not available, since in Bemba the relative object pronoun must agree with gender, number *and* case with the *head* noun. Rather, the prepositional case of the coreferent noun is marked via a verb-coding strategy as a suffix, in a pattern reminiscent of similar variations in English:[39]

(58) *naa-mweene umuana **uo** umukashi àa-peele-**ko** icitabo*
      I-saw   child *that* woman   she-gave-*to* book
      'I saw the child that the woman gave the/a book to'

(59) *naa-mweene ingaanda **iyo** umunaandi àa-keele-**mo***
      I-saw   house   *that* friend-my he-lived-*in*
      'I saw the house that my friend lived in'

In relativizing the instrumental and associative cases, the coding of the semantic case of the coreferent (deleted) noun is achieved via the anaphoric pronoun strategy, as in:

(60) a. *umuana áa-lya na-o*
         child he-ate with-*him/her*
         'The child ate with him/her'
      b. *umuntu **uo** umuana àa-lya na-o*
         person *that* child he-ate with-*him/her*
         { 'the person with whom the child ate'
         { 'the person that the child ate with'

(61) a. *umuana áa-lya na-o*
         child he-ate with-*it*
         'The child ate with it'
      b. *umuele **uo** umuana àa-lya na-o*
         knife *that* child he-ate with-*it*
         { 'the knife with which the child ate'
         { 'the knife that the child ate with'

Finally, the *same* verb-coding strategy used for the benefactive in the neutral pattern is also used in relativization:

(62) *umuana **uo** umukashi àa-shit-**ila** icitabo*
      child *that* woman she-bought-*BEN* book
      { 'the child for whom the woman bought a/the book'
      { 'the child that the woman bought a/the book for'

---

[39] In English this variation appears "optional" when only competence data are examined. That is, *The child **to** whom I gave the book* versus *The child I gave the book **to**.*

4.3 Relativization

To sum up the Bemba data, the language uses verb-coding of the semantic case in two instances, benefactive (complete) and locative–dative (partial, alternating with the equi-case strategy), but in neither is there a good argument for considering this a case of promotion to direct object, since the pattern is either independent of dative-shift (as BENEFACTIVE), or simply does not at all appear in the neutral pattern (as in LOCATIVE–DATIVE). The Bemba data could nevertheless serve as an excellent point of departure for discussing both Rwanda and Swahili, to follow. This is because in the latter two an erosion in the case-morphology of the object nouns, coupled with a rise in verb-coding in dative-shift, creates a situation—most strikingly in Rwanda—where by making dative-shift an obligatory feeder for nonaccusative object relativization, the language gains in terms of case recoverability.

4.3.3.2.2.2. Swahili

In Swahili the use of the prepositions *pa-*, *ku-*, *mu-* on nouns disappeared, and as a compensation the use of the BENEFACTIVE verb-coding suffix has assumed additional functional load. In no event is this change linked to dative-shift or promotion to direct-object. Consider first the use of the benefactive suffix in signaling PURPOSE cases, as in:[40]

(63)   a. *a-li-tia   mayai bakuli-ni*
              he past-put eggs basin-*LOC*
              'He put the eggs in the basin'

        b. *bakuli ya ku-til-ia   mayai*
              basin of to-put-*BEN* eggs
              'a basin for putting eggs in'

        c. *a-li-kula   **kwa** kisu*
              he-past-eat *with* knife
              'He ate with a knife'

        d. *kisu cha ku-l-ia*
              knife of to-eat-*BEN*
              'a knife for eating (with)'

The semantic specificity of the benefactive suffix in these cases is rather low, since it could cover a wide range of nonaccusative object relations. Furthermore, the pattern in (63b, d) is *not* the bona fide relative pattern. In both cases, however, there is a trade-off between the nominal case marking in the neutral pattern and the verb-coding strategy in the transformed pattern.

Another case of verb-coding in Swahili, this time within the neutral pattern, may be seen in:

---

[40] The data here and in (64) are patterned after Ashton (1944).

(64) a. *a-li-tupa   mawe*
       he-past-throw stones
       'He threw stones'

   b. *a-li-wa-tup-i*a   *watoto   mawe*[41]
       he-past-*them*-throw-*BEN* children stones
       'He threw stones **at** the children'

   c. *a-li-panda   ile mibuyu*
       he-past-climb the Baobabs
       'He climbed the Baobab trees'

   d. *a-li-pand-i*a   *ile   mibuyu*
       he-past-climb-*BEN* the Baobabs
       'He climbed **up** the Baobab trees'

   e. *a-li-kimbia*
       he-past-ran
       'He ran'

   f. *a-li-m-kimbil ia   mama   wake*
       he-past-*her*-run-*BEN* mother his
       'He ran **to** his mother'

Finally, Swahili also exhibits the use of the benefactive verb-suffix in coding the DATIVE case function in relativization, although this pattern is lexical specific. Thus, the verb *-pa* 'give' admits the BENEFACTIVE suffix neither in the neutral nor in the relative pattern, and the dative–benefactive object must be adjacent to the verb, as do benefactives in general:[42]

(65) a. *a-li-m-pa   mwanamke kitabu*
       he-past-her-give woman   book
       'He gave the woman a book'

   b. **a-li-m-p-ea*   *mwanamke kitabu*
       he-past-her-give-*BEN* woman   book

   c. *mwanamke a-li-ye-m-pa   kitabu*
       woman   he-past-*REL*-her-give book
       'The woman to whom he gave a book'

   d. **mwanamke a-li-ye-m-p-ea   kitabu*
       woman   he-past-*REL*-her-give-*BEN* book

With the verb *-tuma* 'send' one gets a bona fide case of both dative-

---

[41] In this case, the prepositional object must be adjacent to the verb, as would the BENEFACTIVE (see preceding Bemba data). The obligatory human object agreement is evident, as it is also in (64f).

[42] For the rest of the Swahili data, I am indebted to Mrisho Kivugo (personal communication).

shifting and the obligatory use of the benefactive suffix in relativization. Thus consider:

(66) a. *a-li-m-tuma   baruwa **kwa** mwanamke*
he-past-her-send letter to   woman
'He sent a letter to the woman'

b. *a-li-m-tum-ia   mwanamke baruwa*
he-past-her-send-*BEN* woman   book
'He sent the woman a letter'

c. *mwanamke a-li-ye-m-tum-ia   baruwa*
woman   he-past-*REL*-her-send-*BEN* letter
'the woman to whom he sent a letter'

d. **mwanmke a-li-ye-m-tuma   baruwa*
woman   he-past-*REL*-her-send letter

Thus the dative case marking in the neutral pattern alternates between the preposition *kwa* (a Swahili innovation that may also mean 'by', 'at') when the dative object is remote from the verb (66a) and the BENEFACTIVE verb suffix when the dative object is near the verb (66b). Since the preposition *kwa* is morphologically barred from being used in the relative pronoun position or as a relative anaphoric pronoun, the only way to rescue the dative case marking is by making the verb-suffix variant obligatory in relativization. A similar situation is found in the relativization of directional-locative objects, where (*a*) the order ACC–LOC is rigid in the neutral pattern, and (*b*) the use of the benefactive verb suffix is obligatory in relativization:

(67) a. *a-li-tuma   baruwa ofici-ni*   (ACC–LOC)
he-past-send letter office-*LOC*
'He sent a letter to the office'

b. *?a-li-tuma ofici-ni baruwa*   (?LOC–ACC)

c. *ofici a-li-yo-tum-ia   baruwa*
office he-past-*REL*-send-*BEN* letter
'the office to which he sent a letter'

d. **ofici a-li-yo-tuma baruwa*

To sum up the Swahili situation, we have seen that the loss of the locative–dative prepositions on the noun has resulted in increased functional load on the BENEFACTIVE verb-coding suffix in both the neutral pattern and in relativization. But since this suffix is not involved in dative-shifting per se, there is no obligatory feeding of the relativization of nonaccusative objects via promotion to direct object.

4.3.3.2.2.3. Rwanda[43]

In terms of the use of verb-coding as a strategy of marking the semantic case of nonaccusative objects, Rwanda represents an extreme case within Bantu, probably even within its closer subgroup of Lake-Bantu. This is evident in **both** parameters which together constitute the typological characterization of a language with a direct-object-only constraint on object relativization:

1. In dative-shifting of most prepositional object to a position near the verb, the object noun becomes morphologically unmarked and the verb gains a verb-coding suffix which indicates the semantic case of the nonaccusative object.
2. The verb-coding strategy, thus made available in the neutral pattern, is extensively used in relativizing nonaccusative objects.

Let us consider the neutral pattern and dative-shift possibilities first.

Subject to a number of lexical-specific and other constraints, dative-shift in the case of locative objects is used in Rwanda, whereby the preposition becomes a verb suffix, as in:

(68) a. *umugore y-ooher-eje   umubooyi ku-isoko*   (ACC–LOC)
       woman   she-sent-ASP cook   *to*-market
       'The woman sent the cook to the market'

   b. *umugore y-ooher-eje-ho   isoko   umubooyi*   (LOC–ACC)
       woman   she-sent-ASP-LOC market cook
       'The woman sent to the market the cook'

The use of the *ku*- preposition for dative object NPs has been eliminated in this language, though in related languages such as Luganda it is still attested. As a result, the language has just about collapsed the DATIVE and BENEFACTIVE case-marking system, with a tendency to keep the dative–benefactive object closer to the verb, though presumably the order ACC–DAT is also acceptable. Thus consider:

(69) a. *Yohani y-ooher-er-eje   Maria ibaruwa*   (DAT–ACC)
       John   he-sent-BEN-ASP Mary a/the letter
       'John sent Mary a/the letter'

   b. ?*Yohani y-ooher-er-eje ibaruwa Maria*   (?ACC–DAT)

A similar pattern is observed for the benefactive, where the tendency to keep the benefactive object closer to the verb is even stronger, and the verb-coding suffix is used in either order:

---

[43] Most of the data on Rwanda, called by its speakers KinyaRwanda, are from Kimenyi (1976, personal communication), but see also Gary and Keenan (1975).

(70) a. *Maria y-a-tek-e-ye*   *abaana inkoko*
        Mary she-past-cook-BEN-ASP children chicken
        'Mary cooked (the/a) chicken for the children' (BEN–ACC)

     b. ?*Maria y-a-tek-e-ye inkoko abaana*   (?BEN–ACC)

A case of true promotion-type alternation occurs with the purpose–goal object, where when the non-accusative object is away from the verb it takes the preposition *ku-* (directional-dative), while when it is close to the verb it is unmarked but the verb gains the BENEFACTIVE suffix. Thus:

(71) a. *Karooli y-a-fash-ije*   *abaantu **ku**-busa*
        Charles he-past-help-ASP people *for*-nothing
        'Charles helped the people for nothing'   (ACC–GOAL)

     b. *Karooli y-a-fash-**ir**-ije*   *ubusa abaantu*
        Charles he-past-help-*BEN*-ASP nothing people
        'Charles helped (the) people for nothing'   (GOAL–ACC)

A similar variation between NP-coding and verb-coding in dative-shifting is seen with instrumental objects:

(72) a. *umualimu a-ra-andika*   *ibaruwa **n**-ikaramu*
        teacher   he-ASP-write letter   *with*-pen
        'The teacher is writing the letter with a/the pen'
                                                        (ACC–INST)

     b. *umualimu a-ra-andik-**iisha***   *ikaramu ibaruwa*
        teacher   he-ASP-write-*INST* pen   letter
        'The teacher is writing a/the letter with the pen'
                                                        (INST–ACC)

In manner adverbs a similar promotional behavior is seen between the noun-coding preposition *na-* and the verb coding suffix *-na:*[44]

(73) a. *Maria y-a-tets-e*   *inkoko **n**-agahiinda*
        Mary   she-past-cook-ASP chicken *with*-sorrow
        'Mary cooked the chicken with regret'   (ACC–MANN)

     b. *Maria y-a-tek-**an**-ye*   *agahiinda inkoko*
        Mary   she-past-cook-*ASSOC*-ASP sorrow   chicken
        'Mary cooked a/the chicken with regret'   (MANN–ACC)

---

[44] The verb suffix *-na* is probably etymologically of the same source as the preposition *na-*, and is the most common reciprocal–associative suffix in Bantu.

As compared to both Bemba and Swahili, then, Rwanda has developed an extensive system of verb-coding the semantic case of the nonaccusative object, especially when it is dative-shifted to a position adjacent to the verb—and thus stripped of its original case marking (if any). While this system is by no means complete or unambiguous, it nevertheless represents the gradual evolution of a coherent new strategy.

In relativization (as well as in passivization, to be discussed later), Rwanda makes a similar use of this case-marking bonus as does Indonesian, by imposing—in many cases—the same direct-object-only constraint.

Subject relativization in Rwanda involves the same type of tonal changes and reliance on the neutral SVO word-order strategy as in Bemba, above. The relativization of accusative objects (and object NPs in general) involves the OSV word-order strategy, but no use of any relative subordinator is made. This feature must be considered as a decrease in the redundancy features of relativization (as compared to Bemba or Swahili), since the relative subordinator-pronoun in Bantu normally agrees in gender and number—and in the case of the locative *pa-*, *ku-*, *mu-* also with case—with the head noun. Thus consider:

(74) a. Subject: *umugabo u-a-kubis-e abagore*
man who-past-strike-ASP women
'the man who struck the women'

b. Accusative: *abagore Yohani y-a-kubis-e*
women John he-past-strike-ASP
'the women that John struck'

The verb-coding strategy, and as a correlate the promotion of indirect to direct-object as prerequisite to relativization, comes into play in relativizing all nonaccusative objects. Thus, of the two variant orders in (68) above, only the variant (68b) with the order LOC–ACC and the locative suffix on the verb can undergo relativization:

(75) a. *isoko umugore y-oohere-je-ho umubooyi*
market woman she-sent-ASP-*LOC* cook
'the market to which the woman sent the cook'

b. **isoko umugore y-oohere-je umubooyi* **ku**

The benefactive verb suffix must be used obligatorily in relativizing either DATIVE or BENEFACTIVE objects, though in this case one does not need to consider this a promotion to direct object, since the suffix is obligatorily used in the presence of these object types in either order. Thus for dative objects [compare to (69)]:

4.3 *Relativization*　　177

(76)　　a.　*umugore Yohani y-ooher-er-eje　　ibaruwa*
　　　　　　woman　John　　he-sent-*BEN*-ASP　letter
　　　　　　'the woman to whom John sent the letter'

　　　　b.　**umugore Yohani y-ooher-eje ibaruwa*

Similarly for benefactive objects [compare to (70)]:

(77)　　a.　*abaana　Maria y-a-tek-e-ye　　　　　inkoko*
　　　　　　children Mary she-past-cook-*BEN*-ASP chicken
　　　　　　'the children for whom Mary cooked (the) chicken'

　　　　b.　**abaana Maria y-a-tek-ye inkoko*

In the relativization of instrumental objects, only the variant involving the INST–ACC order and verb-coding can be relativized. Thus compare (72) to:

(78)　　a.　*ikaramu Yohani y-andik-**ish**-ije　　ibaruwa*
　　　　　　pen　　John　　he-wrote-*INST*-ASP letter
　　　　　　'the pen with which John wrote the letter'

　　　　b.　**ikaramu Yohani y-andik-ije ibaruwa (**na-yo**)*

In relativizing the ASSOCIATIVE object, which in the neutral pattern takes the same *na-* preposition when not dative-shifted, another recoverability strategy is used, that of *anaphoric pronoun*. Thus consider:

(79) a.　*umuhuungu a-ra-ririimba(-**na**)　　urururiimbi **n**-umugore*
　　　　boy　　　　 he-ASP-sing(-*together*) song　　　with-woman
　　　　'The boy is singing a song with the woman'

　　　b.　*umugore umuhuungu a-ririimba(-**na**)　urururiimbi **na-ye***
　　　　woman　boy　　　　he-sing(-*together*)　song　　　with-her
　　　　'the woman with whom the boy is singing a song'

The INSTRUMENTAL and ASSOCIATIVE thus differentiate themselves in relativization, where the anaphoric pronoun strategy cannot be used for instrumentals [cf. the inacceptability of (78b)]. The direction of this differentiation may be shifting, however, since the use of the associative *-na* verb-suffix is already optional in both the neutral and relative pattern [cf. (79)] and could in time replace the anaphoric pronoun strategy and thus further expand the use of verb-coding.

In relativizing manner adverbs constructed with the preposition *na-* which alternates with the verb-suffix *-na*, only the variant with the MANN–ACC order and verb-coding can be relativized. Thus compare (72a,b) to the following:

(80) a. *agahiinda Maria y-a-tek-**an**-ye   inkoko*
 sorrow   Mary she-past-cook-ASSOC-ASP chicken
 'the regret with which Mary cooked the chicken'

 b. **agahiinda Maria y-a-tek-ye inkoko **na-ko***

Finally, a conflicting behavior is seen in the case of relativizing goal-purpose objects, where neither variants in (70) can be used for relativization, but rather a morphologically unmarked one is used, so that the semantic case GOAL–PURPOSE must be inferred. Thus compare (70) to the following:

(81) a. *imhaamvu Karooli y-a-fash-ije   abaantu* (no coding)
 reason   Charles he-past-help-ASP people
 'the reason why Charles helped (the) people'

 b. **imhaamvu Karooli y-a-fash-**ir**-ije abaantu*
  (*verb-coding with BEN)

 c. **imhaamvu Karooli y-a-fash-ije-**ho**-abaantu*
  (*verb-coding with LOC)

One could speculate why this inconsistent behavior is possible. To begin with, the semantic case "reason–purpose" is already coded by the *head noun* itself. Furthermore, the BENEFACTIVE suffix is already overloaded in relativizing other functions, and the same is true for the locative *-ho* suffix.[45]

4.3.3.3. LANGUAGES THAT DO NOT

In this section I will briefly contrast the Indonesian and Rwanda data presented above with a number of languages, all of which can shift the relative order of objects following the verb to achieve the pragmatic effect of dative-shift. In none of these languages does dative-shift result in verb-coding of the semantic case of the shifted nonaccusative, and in none is dative-shift an obligatory feeder to relativization.

---

[45] One may note a similar situation in English, where *for* is used in the neutral pattern to code both the BENEFACTIVE and REASON–PURPOSE clauses, as in *He did it for Joe* versus *He did it for money*. But the two functions split in relativization, as in *the reason/why he did it . . .* versus *the person for whom he did it. . . .* I think two universal principles govern this behavior: (a) Relativazation introduces more complexity in recoverability of case functions, and this is compensated by less-ambiguous case-marking; (b) Oblique adverbials cases, such as "manner," "purpose," "condition," and "time," can, in general, tolerate less-explicit case marking, since their lexical membership is extremely limited and by itself tends to give strong semantic clues as to the likely case-function. In contrast, the lexical potential membership of subject, direct-object, benefactive, dative, and instrumental (and to a lesser extent the locative) is much larger and the case-specificity is much lower (i.e., a noun could be either one of many case-functions), so that predictability is lower.

4.3.3.3.1. English

Dative shifting through which the erstwhile prepositional object loses its case-marking is limited in English to only a few verbs such as *give, send, bring, present, tell,* and *show*. The object is most commonly also the BENEFACTIVE, in addition to being the directional-goal. It is obligatorily human. No case-marking on the verb is gained in dative-shifting, it merely leaves two object NPs unmarked. Recoverability of the case-function of the nonaccusative in relativization is assured via WH-prepositional pronouns, such as *to whom, for whom, with whom, with which,* etc. Nothing would be thus gained by a direct-object-only constraint in relativization, and in fact no such constraint is evident.

4.3.3.3.2. Hebrew

This language is again close to the SVO typology of Indonesian and Rwanda, though the accusative is case-marked when definite. Dative shifting is functional, but involves neither loss of case marking nor gain in verb-coding, but only word-order variation, as in:

(82) *hu natan et-ha-sefer le-Yosef* (ACC–DAT)
he gave ACC-the-book to-Joseph
'He gave the book to Joseph'

(83) *hu natan le-Yosef et-ha-sefer* (DAT–ACC)
he gave to-Joseph ACC-the-book
'He gave Joseph the book'

The ACC–DAT order in (82) is an appropriate answer to the DAT-focus question *Who did he give the book to?*, while the DAT–ACC order in (83) is an appropriate answer to the ACC-focus question *What did he give Joseph?*. In relativization, the recoverability of semantic cases of all object NPs is assured via the case-marked anaphoric pronoun strategy, so that nothing would be gained by a direct-object-only constraint on relativization of objects, and indeed such a constraint is not evident.

4.3.3.3.3. Sherpa[46]

This is a strict SOV language with all cases marked suffixally. In the past tense the marking system is *ergative*, with the accusative unmarked and the subject of transitive marked by the GENITIVE case. But even the unmarked subject of nonpast or intransitive verbs is well differentiated from the unmarked accusative. This is because the subject normally carries either a suffixal topic-marking (*-ti*, 'sg.', *-tua* 'pl.') most often together with a demonstrative. Since subjects are most often definite, they thus contrast both with the indefinite accusative that is

---

[46] For the Sherpa data I am indebted to Konchhok Lama (personal communication).

marked by the numeral *one* or the definite accusative that is simply unmarked.

As we have seen above [(39), (40)], dative shifting is functional in Sherpa but involves no changes in case-marking on the NPs, nor any verb-coding gain. While the language has the relatively inefficient *gap* strategy in relativization, nothing would have been gained by a direct-object-only constraint, and in fact that constraint does not exist. Thus consider the following:

(84)   a.   *pumpetsa-ti-ki   mi-la   tyeŋka bin-sung*
           woman-TOP-ERG man-DAT   money give -AUX
           'The woman gave the money to the man'   (neutral)

      b.   *mi-la   tyeŋka   bin-dup   pumpetsa-ti*
           man-DAT   money   give-ING   woman-TOP
           'The woman who gave the man money
                                       (subject rel., DAT–ACC)

      c.   *tyeŋka mi-la   bin-dup   pumpetsa-ti*
           money   man-DAT   give-ING   woman-TOP
           'The woman who gave the money to the man'
                                       (subject rel., ACC–DAT)

      d.   *tii   pumpets-i   mi-la   bin-dup   tyeŋka-ti*
           that woman-ERG man-DAT give-ING money-TOP
           'The money that the woman gave to the man'
                                                   (ACC rel.)

      e.   *tii   pumpetsa-ti-ki   tyeka bin-dup   mi-ti*
           that woman-TOP-ERG money give-ING man-TOP
           'The man to whom the woman gave (the) money'
                                                   (DAT rel.)

4.3.3.4. EXPLANATIONS

4.3.3.4.1. Case-Marking Typology

To my knowledge, the direct-object-only constraint on object relativization appears only in SVO languages. They are, furthermore, SVO languages in which the *accusative* object is unmarked. Further, they are languages in which the rule of dative-shift strips the nonaccusative object of its case-marking morpheme, thus in effect neutralizing its case with that of the accusative. Finally, they are languages where the loss of case-marking of the nonaccusative in dative shifting is compensated by a gain in verb-coding of the semantic case of the promoted nonaccusative object. While the connection between SVO typology and unmarked

4.3 Relativization

accusative is probably an independent natural process,[47] the other typological parameters defining languages which observe this constraint may again be expressed in two alternative—strong and weak—conditions:

(85) TYPOLOGICAL CONDITION III *(strong). If a language has no viable recoverability strategy for differentiating the accusative from nonaccusative objects in relativization, and if in addition it has a promotion-to-direct-object (or "dative-shift") rule which results in coding the semantic case of nonaccusative objects on the verb, then the language will tend to exploit this device in relativization by imposing a direct-object-only constraint on the relativization of nonaccusative objects, thus in effect resorting to a verb-coding strategy in the relativization of object arguments.*

(86) TYPOLOGICAL CONDITION IV *(weak). Only languages in which (a) the accusative object is unmarked, (b) the promotion of nonaccusative objects results in loss of their case-marking, and (c) that promotion results in verb-coding of the semantic case of the nonaccusative, will have the direct-object-only constraint in the relativization of object arguments.*

As in the case of TYPOLOGICAL CONDITIONS I and II [see (24), (25)], the stronger and more vulnerable CONDITION III (85) is of greater interest, since it would predict the diachronic evolution of the constraint as well as make reference to its function. The weaker CONDITION IV (86) is, to my knowledge, without exception.

4.3.3.4.2. The Topicality Explanation

If Schachter's (1976) suggestion recounted previously (Section 4.3.2.1.) is correct, then by the same token of explaining the functional raison d'être of the subject-only constraint on relativization, it also explains the direct-object-only constraint on object relativization. But again, while suggestive, this explanation is universal and thus cannot predict which language will or will not follow this natural-seeming possibility.

---

[47] Most commonly SVO languages take advantage of the position of subjects and objects vis-à-vis the verb and leave them morphologically unmarked, while other object cases are marked with prepositions or postpositions. SOV languages more frequently tend to have either the object or the subject or both morphologically marked, quite often within an Ergative pattern, as in Sherpa, see above. The situation with V-first languages is not clear, in the sense that many different subtypologies exist and a simple correlation between the gross typological feature of word-order and the degree of case-marking of objects and subjects does not really exist.

To further suggest that two types of functional explanations may be involved here, I would like to cite the following data from Amharic.[48] In this SOV language, topic-shifting of nonsubjects to the left of the subject results in obligatory *object agreement* on the verb. Thus:

(87)   a.   *Almaz bet-u-n*   *bä-mätrăgiya-w*   *tärrägä-cc*
            Almaz house-the-OBJ with-broom-the cleaned-*she*
            'Almaz cleaned the house with the broom'
                                                 (SUBJ agreement)

        b.   *bet-u-n*   *Almaz bä-mätrăgiya-w*   *tärrägä-cc-iw*
            house-the-OBJ Almaz with-broom-the cleaned-*she-it*
            'The house Almaz cleaned with the broom'
                                                  (ACC agreement)

        c.   *bä-mätrăgiya-w Almaz bet-u-n*   *tärrägä-cc-ibb-at*
            with-broom-the Almaz house-the-OBJ cleansed-*she-with-it*
            'With the broom Almaz cleaned the house'
                                                    (INSTR agreement)

The very same constraint is observed in object relativization, so that one could quite plausibly argue that *topicalization* of the object is an obligatory feeder to its relativization. Given that both passivization and dative-shift increase the topicality of the left-moved object, the Amharic constraint may be viewed within the same functional framework as suggested by Schachter's (1976) explanation. The relevant Amharic data for the relativization of objects corresponding to (87) are:

(88)   a.   *Almaz bä-mätrăgiya-w yä-tärrägä-cc-iw*   bet
            Almaz with-broom-the *REL*-cleaned-*she-it* house
            'The house that Almaz cleaned with the broom'

        b.   **Almaz bä-mätrăgiya-w yä-tärrägä-cc bet*

        c.   *Almaz bet-u-n*   *yä-tärrägä-cc-ibb-at*   *mätrăgiya*
            Almaz house-the-OBJ *REL*-cleaned-*she-with-it* broom
            'The broom with which Almaz cleaned the house'

        d.   **Almaz bet-u-n yä-tärrägä-cc mätrăgiya*

One must note, however, that the object agreement pronouns in (88a) and (88c) also involve *case marking*. In other words, the linking of object agreement—or topicalization—as an obligatory feeder to object relativization has effectively resulted, once again, in *verb coding*. Since the relative subordinator *yä-* in Amharic is invariant, object agreement in relativization thus becomes the recoverability strategy in Amharic. Once

---

[48] For more details see Haile (1970) and more data in Fulas (1974).

again we are faced with a seeming conspiracy between two functional explanations, that of topicality and that of case-typology.

4.3.3.4.3. Complexity and diachronic source

Apart from restricting object relativization to direct-objects and its linking to dative-shift as a feeder, Keenan and Comrie (1977) also note that in general oblique prepositional cases sometimes resist relativization altogether. In Givón (1975a) I have suggested that in Modern Hebrew the relativization of objects must be hierarchized according to perceptual complexity, with the hierarchy being:

(89)   ACCUSATIVE > OBJECT MARKED WITH
             SMALL PREPOSITIONS
         > OBJECT MARKED WITH
             LARGE PREPOSITIONS

I suspect the issue involved here is the following: Case-marking morphemes are diachronically derived from either nouns or verbs. In the case of the nominal source, they most commonly arise as reanalysis of genitival compounds (*on top of the house*). In the case of verbal source they may either rise directly from verb serialization (as in Mandarin or Kwa) or via the mediation of N–N compounds (*concerning John*).[49] Now, while these complex case-marking morphemes lose their complexity in time and shrink in size, when they are still close to the point of innovation they behave to quite an extent as complex structures. Thus, in relativizing them languages must resort to strategies which apply to complex structures, and those may not be available in some languages or for some cases. Take as an example case markers arising from genitival N–of–N compounds. In English they are relativizable by two patterns:

(90)   a. *I stood on top of the house*

    b. *The house on top of which I stood*

    c. *The house on whose top I stood*

In Hebrew equivalent constructions are relativized via the anaphoric pronoun device which allows relativization out of a possessive modifier. Thus:

(91)   a. *raiti   et-ha-isha   shel-o*
            I saw ACC-the-wife of-*him*
            'I saw his wife'

    b. *ha-ish   she-raiti   et-ha-isha   shel-o*
            the-man that-I-saw ACC-the-wife of-*him*
            'the man whose wife I saw'

---

[49] For discussion see Givón (1975e).

c. *amadti al-yad   ha-bayit*
   I-stood on-hand-of the-house
   'I stood near the house'

d. *ha-bayit she-amadti al-yad-o*
   the-house that-I-stood on-hand-of-*it*
   'the house near which I stood'

There are languages which (*a*) have complex case markings which have not yet been reduced and (*b*) possess no viable device for relativizing out of complex genitival expressions, and in such languages one expects difficulties in relativizing objects whose case-marking morphology is still complex. Let me cite one example from Sherpa, which actually manages to wiggle out of the difficulty, though not quite elegantly. The normal relativization strategy in this language is simply a *gap*, with much of the burden of recoverability loaded on *semantic redundancy* involving the verb and arguments. Thus, the differentiation between the ACCUSATIVE and INSTRUMENT relativization in the following is based mostly on such redundancies:

(92) a. *tii   mi-ti-ki   daa kimbok-**thwani** soo-sung*
        that man-TOP-ERG rice spoon-*with*   eat-AUX
        'The man ate (the) rice with a/the spoon'   (neutral)

   b. *tii-mi-ti-ki   kimbok-**thwani** so-up   daa-ti*
       that-man-TOP-ERG spoon-*with*   eat-ING rice-TOP
       'the rice that the man ate with a/the spoon'   (ACC rel.)

   c. *tii-mi-ti-ki   daa so-up   kimbok-ti*
       that-man-TOP-ERG rice eat-ING spoon-TOP
       'the spoon with which the man ate (the) rice' (INST rel.)

Some simple cases may, on occasion, be actually coded in relativization. Thus consider the associative case:

(93) a. *tii-mi-ti-ki   daa pumpetsa-tan-**mula** soo-sung*
        that-man-TOP-ERG rice woman-CONJ-*with* eat-AUX
        'The man ate (the) rice with the woman'   (neutral)

   b. *tii-mi-ti-ki   **mula** daa soup   pumpetsa-ti*
       that-man-TOP-ERG *with* rice eat-ING woman-TOP
       'the woman with whom the man ate (the) rice'
                                                       (ASSOC rel.)

Complex case markings, on the other hand, cannot be accommodated in such manner, and thus allow potential ambiguities. Thus consider:

(94) a. *tii-mi-ti   khaŋp-i-naŋ-la   no*   (neutral)
        that-man-TOP house-of-*inside*-DAT be
        'The man is inside the house'

b. *tii-mi-ti*   *khaŋpa-la*   *no*   (neutral)
   that-man-TOP house-*DAT* be
   'The man is at the house'

c. *tii-mi*   *wo-tup khaŋpa-ti*   (LOC rel.)
   that-man be-ING house-TOP
   'the house where (at which/in which) the man is'

The only way to obtain complete case specificity is by repetition, which is possible but not considered elegant:

(95) *tii-mi*   *khaŋp-i-naŋ-la*   *wotup*   *khaŋpa-ti*
     that-man house-of-*inside*-DAT be-ING house-TOP
     'the house inside which the man is'   (INSIDE rel.)

All other things being equal, the accusative is the least-marked object case in language, and innovations of case morphology, particularly via the genetival compound channel, are likely to involve the "indirect" or "oblique" object cases. They thus stand a better chance of involving greater complexity of structure and ultimately of presenting greater difficulties in relativization.

4.4. PASSIVIZATION AND PROMOTION TO DIRECT OBJECT

In this section I will deal with languages which restrict the subjectivization of nonagents to direct objects only, and in addition promote indirect to direct objects before they can be passivized. As it turns out, the very same languages requiring this promotion for relativization also require it for passivization, and I will argue that the same *case-typology* explanations must be invoked here. In addition I will also sketch out a number of more general functional explanations involving *topicality*, and will argue that the more general restriction of passivization to "direct" or accusative objects must be viewed within the context of those functional explanations. Since the function of passivization will be invoked repeatedly, I will begin by arguing for a functional definition of passivization.

4.4.1. On Defining "Passive"

Both Perlmutter and Postal (1974) and Keenan (1975) argue against a purely syntactic definition of passive and substitute a *relational* definition instead. The one suggested by Perlmutter and Postal (1974) is "(i) The active SUBJECT case ceases to bear any grammatical relation to its verb, and (ii) the DIRECT OBJECT becomes subject."

This definition involves a number of drawbacks. To begin with, it is just as purely formal as the traditional transformational definition. It does not accommodate cases where a nondirect object can be *directly* passivized. As Keenan (1975) points out, it leaves out a great number of passivization types known in various languages. Edward Keenan (1975) views passivization primarily as a process of *demotion of the agent* from the subject position, with the promotion of a nonagent to subject status viewed as a consequence. While this definition is much more general in terms of cross-linguistic passivization types, it again disregards the function of passives. Further, it ignores the complete gradation—both synchronic in some languages and diachronic in others—between topicalization, definitization, and passivization.

Since I am primarily concerned here with functional explanations, I will consider passivization as a functional rule defined somewhat loosely as:

(96)   *Passivization is the process by which a **nonagent** is promoted into the role of **main topic** of the sentence. And to the extent that the language possesses coding properties*[50] *which identify main topics as **subjects** and distinguishes them from topics, then this promotion may also involve subjectivalization.*

4.4.2. The Typology of Passives

In this section I will briefly survey the most common *nonstandard* types of passivization found in language, in the main following the typology given by Edward Keenan (1975). The purpose of this exercise is to illustrate why the functional definition given in (96) above is more adequate for a universal characterization of these various types, as well as for understanding their diachronic rise.

4.4.2.1. THE PHILIPPINE TYPOLOGY

The Bikol data cited in (22) above illustrate this typology, in which no positional adjustment occurs but only various morphological or case-coding adjustments. All nonagents may be promoted via the very same mechanism, and the concept of *direct-object* is not viable in the grammar. In terms of function, this type covers three rules of English: *passive, topic-shift,* and (in the case of accusatives) *definitization.* Thus consider:

---

[50] Edward Keenan (1975) list these coding properties as position, case-marking, and verb-agreement, of which the first is said to be more easily acquired, while the other two may lag behind. As I shall argue later, a nonagent can be considered "promoted to topicality" even without assuming the characteristic position of the subject–agent. Thus, when the agent is deleted, the nonagent standing closest to it "wins by default." For an extensive discussion of how hierarchic principles determine the subject of passives in Austronesian languages, see Foley (1976).

(97) a. *nag-ta?ó ?ang-laláke ning-líbro sa-babáye*
AGT-give TOP-man ACC-book DAT-woman
'The man gave a book to the woman'

b. *t-in-a?ó kang-laláke ?ang-libro sa-babáye*
ACC-give AGT-man TOP-book DAT-woman
{'The man gave *the* book to the woman'   } (DEF ACC)
{'*The book*, the man gave it to the woman'} (TOP SHIFT ACC)

c. *na-ta?ó kang-laláke ?ang-líbro sa-babáye*
ACC-give AGT-man TOP-book DAT-woman
{'The man gave *the* book to the woman'   } (DEF ACC)
{'*The book*, the man gave it to the woman'   } (TOP SHIFT ACC)
{'*The book* was given to the woman by the man'} (PASSIVE ACC)

The TOPIC (*?ang-*) phrase in Bikol exhibits the same general restriction which topic-shift constructions do: It can be definite or generic, but *never* referential-indefinite.[51]

4.4.2.2. THE TOPIC-SHIFT TYPOLOGY

Aside from the facts of Philippine languages discussed above, there are other grounds for believing that a discrete separation between passive and topic-shift rules is not always tenable, even in subject prominent languages. Let me cite here a few examples. Consider first passivization in Bhasa Indonesian. (See further discussion in Givón, 1976a. The data is taken from Chung, 1976b.) In this language two passive rules arose historically from topic-shift constructions (which still exist in the language). The older pattern is unrestricted as to agents and allows both definite and indefinite promoted subjects, as in:

(98) a. *Ali mem-batja buku itu*
Ali ACT-read book the
'Ali read the book'

b. *buku itu di-batja (oleh) Ali*
book the PASS-read (by) Ali
'The book was read by Ali'

The passive prefix *di-* is etymologically the third-person-singular *subject* pronoun, attesting to the topic-shift origin of the construction. Topic shifting by itself in Indonesian precipitates the removal of the active prefix from the verb,[52] and requires definitization:

(99) a. *Ali mem-batja buku itu*
Ali ACT-read book the
'Ali read the book'

[51] See Givón (1977b, 1976a).
[52] Topic shifting and passivization also share the constraint of "direct-object-only," see following.

b. *buku itu Ali batja* (DEF topic)
   book the Ali read
   'The book, Ali read it'

c. **buku Ali batja* (*INDEF topic)
   book Ali read

Later on Indonesian developed another passive via topic-shifting, this one restricted to first and second person agents. This pattern retains the constraint on definiteness, characteristic of topic-shift constructions:

(100) a. *buku itu saja-batja* (DEF)
          book the I-read
          {'The book, I read it'
          {'The book was read by me'}

       b. **buku saja-batja* (*INDEF)
          book I-read

This second passive is thus an intermediate between passivization and topic-shift.

A similar case may be seen in a Bantu dialect group of the Zambia–Congo–Angola border, involving languages such as Lunda–Ndembu, Lovale, Kimbundu, and probably others. This group has lost the Bantu verb suffix passivization pattern, and has resurrected a passive pattern via topic-shifting. Thus consider the following data from Kimbundu:[53]

(101) Topic Shifting:

       a. *aana a-mono Nzua*
          children *they*-saw John
          'The children saw John'

       b. *Nzua, aana a-mu-mono*
          John, children *they-him*-saw
          'John, the children saw him'

       c. *Nzua, ngi-mu-mono*
          John, *I-him*-saw
          'John, I saw him'

       Passivization:

       d. *Nzua a-mu-mono kwa meme*
          John *they-him*-saw by me
          'John was seen by me'

       e. *meme a-ngi-mono kwa Nzua*
          I   *they-me*-saw by John
          'I was seen by John'

---

[53] See Givón (1976a). For the data I am indebted to Charles Uwimana (personal communication).

f. *Nzua **a-mu**-mono   kwa aana*
   John *they-him*-saw by   children
   'John was seen by the children'

In this pattern the **plural** third-person subject pronoun *a-* (rather than the singular as in Indonesian) has become the invariant passive marker on the verb. While the erstwhile object pronoun, obligatory in topic-shifting in Bantu, has become, effectively, the new subject agreement of the passive.

Consider next the case of a group of Bantu languages of the Congo, such as Dzamba, Lingala, and Likila. In these languages the topic-shifting of nonagents precipitates *postposing* of the agent, thus in effect realigning the word-order (for SVO languages) AGT–V–ACC to the characteristic passive order (for SVO languages) ACC–V–AGT. Another adjustment which brings the pattern closer to passivization involves the loss of the subject-agent agreement in this topic-shift. Thus consider the following data from Dzamba:[54]

(102) a. *oPoso a-tom-aki   mukanda*   (neutral)
         Poso *he*-send-past letter
         'Poso sent a letter'

   b. *oPoso a-**mu**-tom-aki*   (Pronominal object)
       Poso he-*it*-send-past
       'Poso sent it'

   c. *i-mukanda **mu**-tomaki oPoso*   (Topic-shift/passive)
       the-letter *it*-sent   Poso
       {'The letter, Poso sent it'
       {'The letter was sent by Poso'}

   d. **i-mukanda oposo **mu**-tomaki*   (*No subject postposing)

   e. **i-mukanda a-mu-tomaki oPoso*   (*No loss of subject agr.)

Given Edward Keenan's (1975) criteria for passives, the topic-shift pattern in (102) clearly shows a number of features of passives: (*a*) The word order is OBJ–V–AGT, and (*b*) the only agreement on the verb is controlled by the new *topic*. The field is further muddied by the fact that Dzamba also has a "more normal" left-dislocation topic-shift pattern in which (*a*) the agent retains its preverbal position and (*b*) it also retains subject agreement:

(103)   *i-mukanda oPoso a-mu-tomaki*
             the-letter   Poso *he*-it-sent
             'The letter, Poso sent it'

[54] For the data and more discussion, see Bokamba (1976). Both the subject postposing and the loss of subject agreement are also found in object relativization, again suggesting a link between object topicalization and object relativization.

Other languages also exhibit some passive properties in topic-shift constructions. Thus I have shown (Givón, 1976b) that in both Israeli Hebrew and Spanish the left-shifting of objects tends to be accompanied by *postposing* the agent to the right of the verb. A truly mind-blowing instance of blurring the line between passive and topic-shift (or perhaps even definitization) has been reported by Trithart (1976) for a Bantu language called ChiCewa. In this language the promotion of an object to topic via either passivization or topic-shifting makes it eligible to raising to object, a process normally reserved for subjects only. Thus consider:

(104) a. *Joni a-ma-lima cimanga* (neutral)
John he-ASP-plant corn
'John plants corn'

b. *Joni a-ma-ci-lima* (Pronoun object)
John he-ASP-*it*-plant
'John plants it'

c. *a-ma-ci-lima* (Pronoun subject and object)
he-ASP-*it*-plant
'He plants it'

d. *cimanga a-ma-ci-lima* (Topic shifted object)
corn *he*-ASP-*it*-plant
'The corn, he plants it'

e. *cimanga ci-na-lim-wa ndi mkazi* (Passive)
corn *it*-ASP-plant-*PASS* by woman
'The corn was planted by the woman'

f. *ndi-m-ganiza (mkazi) kuti a-a-lima cimanga*
I-*her*-think (woman) that *she*-ASP-plant corn
{'I think that the woman plants corn'
 'I think the woman to have planted (the) corn'}

(Raised AGT-subject)

g. *ndi-ci-ganiza (cimanga) kuti ci-na-lim-wa ndi mkazi*
I-*it*-think (corn) that *it*-ASP-plant-*PASS* by woman
{'I think that *the* corn was planted by the woman'
 'I think the corn to have been planted by the woman'}

(Raised PASS-subject)

h. *ndi-ci-ganiza (cimanga) kuti (mkazi) a-na-ci-lima*
I-*it*-think (corn) that (woman) *she*-ASP-*it*-plant
{'I think that the woman planted *the* corn'
 'I think that, *the* corn, the woman planted it'
 'I think that *the* corn was planted by the woman'}

(Raised TOPIC-object)

4.4. *Passivization and Promotion to Direct Object*   *191*

The raised object in either (104g) or (104h) is obligatorily *definite*, and the data once again illustrates the difficulties involved in laying down discrete boundaries between passive and topic-shift, and thus also between subject and topic.⁵⁵ Raising to object in ChiChewa must be defined upon the functional notion "topic" rather than the grammatical "subject."

4.4.2.3. THE AGENT DELETION TYPOLOGY

Edward Keenan (1975) cites a number of languages where in what is equivalent to passivization the agent gets demoted or deleted while no other changes take place. These languages constitute the best support for his *demotional* definition of passivization. Some of his examples are:

(105) *Latin:*   curritur
                    run-PASS-3sg
                    'there was running'

(106) *Turkish:* a. *Ahmet kadin-la   kunuş-tu*
                      Ahmet woman-with talk-past
                      'Ahmet talked with the woman'

                   b. *kadin-la   kunuş-ul-du*
                      woman-with talk-PASS-past
                      'The woman was talked with'

(107) *Dutch:*   a. *De jongens fluiten*
                      the boys   whistle-3pl
                      'The boys whistle'

                   b. *Er wort door de jongens gefloten*
                      it was by   the boys   whistle-PARTICIPLE
                      'There was whistling by the boys'

(108) *Mojave:*   *injep ny-tapuy-c-m*
                    I-ACC 1sg-kill-PASS-past
                    'I was killed'

In all these cases the verb shows some passive morphology, the agent has been demoted either by total deletion or relegation to *by*-phrase, but the new topic retains its nonagent case morphology. Subject agreement most commonly neutralizes to third-person singular or plural, though in Mojave it is adjusted to agree with the new topic. For the definition of passive as "raising to grammatical subject" this analysis is presumably injurious since the nonagent does not acquire all coding properties of the subject and may not even acquire its characteristic syntactic position. The data is much less problematic for the definition of passive as "pro-

---

⁵⁵ For the interplay between "subject" and "topic," see Li (1976).

motion of nonagent to topic" (96), since as Kirsner (1973, 1976 for Dutch) and Foley (1976, for a similar type of Malayo-Polynesian passive) argue, topicality is assigned by a very general rule of *preemption*, by which the argument *highest on the topicality hierarchy* gets interpreted as the topic–subject. The deletion (or removal to an oblique case) of the agent automatically vacates the main topic slot, thus leaving it to be overtaken by the higher bidder, so to speak.[56]

There is an interesting piece of data from Ute, a language with an agent-deletion passivization type, which further supports this view of passivization. In this language the "passive" verb is marked by the suffix *-ta* and the deletion of the agent. No changes in the case-marking of the other arguments are observed, and the semantic interpretation of the construction is "impersonal-active," that is, *Someone killed John* rather than *John was killed (by someone)*. This active interpretation is obvious from the fact that the passive can be embedded under command verbs (*tell, force*) or be used in the imperative. At any rate, passivization can occur as long as there is *another argument left* after agent deletion. Thus:

(109) ta'wóci tųpųyci tiráabi-kya   (ACTIVE)
       man-SUBJ rock-OBJ throw-PAST
       'The man threw the rock'

(110) tųpųyci tiáabi-ta-x̂a   (PASSIVE) (DIR-OBJ)
       rock-OBJ throw-PASS-PAST
       'Someone threw the rock'

(111) pǫzǫ́-qwati tiká'napų-'ubwán 'abí-kya   (ACTIVE)
       book   table-on   lie-PAST
       'The book lay on the table'

(112) tika'napų-'ubwán 'abí-ta-x̂a   (PASSIVE) (INDIR-OBJ)
       table-on   lie-PASS-PAST
       'Something lay on the table'

(113) ta'wóci pųka wųų́ka-x̂a   (ACTIVE)
       man-SUBJ hard work-PAST
       'The man worked hard'

(114) pųka wųų́ka-ta-x̂a   (PASSIVE) (ADVERB)
       hard work-PASS-PAST
       'Someone worked hard'

(115) *wųų́ka-ta-x̂a
       work-PASS-PAST   (*PASSIVE, NO TOPIC)

---

[56] For more on the *topicality hierarchy,* see Hawkinson and Hyman (1974) and Givón (1976a).

4.4. *Passivization and Promotion to Direct Object*   193

Thus, in this type of passive, as long as there is *any* argument, be it oblique or adverbial, to fill in the topic function, passivization is possible, regardless of the transitivity or active–stative properties of the verb. The only item that cannot be left as topic is the *verb* itself. But in fact, in some languages this also is possible, as in the Latin example in (105) above. In fact, the Dutch example (107b) is of the same type, although rather than being deleted completely the agent has only been removed to an oblique, nontopical case.

Passive morphology is not an essential ingradient in this typology. Thus, for example, Israeli Hebrew has lost the old morphological passives as productive rules, though they are still found lexically. To express nonagent promotion to primary topic, one of the devices involves neutralizing the verb agreement to third-person plural, with an added option of topic-shifting:

(116) a. *hi   raata   et-Yoxanan barxov*   (active)
           she   saw-3rd-f-sg   ACC-John   in-the-street
           'She saw John in the street'

       b. *rau   et-Yoxanan barxov   etmol . . .*
           saw-3pl   ACC-John   in-the-street yesterday . . .
           'John was seen in the street yesterday . . .'
                                                          (agent deletion)

       c. *et-Yoxanan rau   etmol   barxov*
           ACC-John   saw-3pl yesterday in-the-street
           'John was seen in the street yesterday'
                                       (agent deletion plus contrastive topic)

       d. *Yoxanan, rau   oto   etmol   barxov*
           John,   saw-3pl him   yesterday in-the-street
           'John, he was seen yesterday in the street'
                                           (agent deletion plus topic-shift)

Similar processes may be said to exist in English (*they say that . . .*), German (*Mann sagt . . .*) or French (*on dit . . .*).

4.4.2.4. THE REFLEXIVE-PASSIVE TYPOLOGY

This variant is found in Romance, Slavic and probably many others. It involves a diachronic reanalysis of the reflexive-active into a pragmatic equivalent of passive. The erstwhile reflexive morphology plus third-person (singular in Spanish) agreement on the verb code the passive form. And the erstwhile reflexive subject—at least in Spanish—reverts to an *object* case. Thus consider:[57]

---

[57] For further discussion of the Spanish data see Givón (1976a). For an interesting diachronic twist on similar Slavic data see Comrie (1975b).

(117) a. *se-curaron   los brujos*   (Reflexive)
        REF-cured-3pl the sorcerers
        'The sorcerers cured themselves'

   b. *se-curó   a   los brujos* ("Passive", "Impersonal")
      REF-cure-3sg DAT the sorcerers
      {'The sorcerers were cured'
       'Someone cured the sorcerers'}

The "impersonal passive" in (117b) would certainly qualify under our definition (96), since in the absence of an overt agent the object is next in line for being interpreted as topic. One may further wish to argue that under such circumstances dative-shift may assume the function of passivization, since without an agent the most topical object is also the primary topic of the sentence. Thus consider:

(118) a. *se-dió   a   Juan un libro*   (DAT–ACC)
         REF-gave-3sg DAT John a   book
         {'John was given a book'
          'Someone gave John a book'}

   b. *se-dió   un libro a   Juan*   (ACC–DAT)
      REF-gave-3sg a   book DAT John
      {'A book was given to John'
       'Someone gave a book to John'}

While in Spanish this is only a possibility, the advancement of dative-shift to the status of *primary* promotion rule in the language has in fact been reported for a number of Malayo-Polynesian languages, such as Mota (SVO) or Fijian (VOS) (Foley, 1976), where the origin of this development clearly involves (*a*) an agent-deletion passive type; (*b*) an active form of the verb; and (*c*) neutralized verb agreement to third-person plural or singular.[58]

4.4.3. The Recoverability Problem in Passivization

For languages in which passivization involves recoding of the promoted nonagent with all the subject coding properties defined by Edward Keenan (1975), such as case, position, and verb-agreement, the recoverability problem arising in passivization may be defined as such:

---

[58] This again underscores the pragmatic nature of the dative-shift rule. Foley (1976) sketches out a paradoxical situation in languages where the direct-object position assumed a great number of Edward Keenan's (1976a) "subject properties," such as left-most position among the arguments, obligatory definiteness and a wider quantifier-scope than the agent. Whether this is a stable typology or a drift toward ergativity remains to be seen.

(119) *While being advanced into the **pragmatic** case of subject–topic, the nonagent loses its **semantic** case-function marking, which cannot be recovered from the word-order or morphology of the passive sentence per se.*

The severity of such a recoverability problem is universally mitigated by pragmatic–semantic–contextual redundancies. Furthermore, the recoverability problem is the severest in languages where the promoted nonagent acquires **all** of Keenan's subject coding properties, but may be less severe in languages where the promoted nonagent retains some of its original case-coding properties. Thus Edward Keenan (1976a, 1975) reports that in Kapampangan (Philippine) the promoted object, while acquiring subject agreement, also retains its original *object* agreement on the verb. The Kimbundu (Bantu) passive sketched out in Section 4.4.2.2 represents a similar case.[59] In the following sections I would like to show that languages which require advancement of a nonaccusative object to direct-object as prerequisite feeder for its passivization are characterized by two crucial typological features:

1. They are all languages in which the promoted nonagent does **not** retain any of its *semantic* case-coding morphology.
2. They are all languages in which dative-shifting results in *verb-coding* the semantic case of the promoted nonagent.

The direct-object-only constraint may be thus viewed primarily as a *recoverability strategy,* as it was viewed in relativization. But in addition other factors which may explain more universal motivation for such a constraint will also be discussed.

4.4.4. Languages Which Do Not

While to quite an extent similar, the direct-object-only constraint on passivization should not be confused with the much more common *accusative*-object-only constraint. While the former allows nonaccusative objects to be passivized after first promoting them via dative-shift (and thus restricts passivization to the *pragmatic* case if DIR OBJ), the latter restricts passivization to the *semantic* case ACCUSATIVE.

In general, no language whose passive typology is of the agent-deletion type exhibits this constraint, and the reason is obvious: The semantic case of the nonagent topic remains coded as it was in the neutral active pattern.

In the Philippine typology, the semantic case of the promoted nonagent is coded on the verb, so that no recoverability problem exists. Further, advancement to topic–subject does not involve changes in

---

[59] On the use of grammatical agreement in enriching the case-marking system, see Givón (1976a).

word-order but only in morphology, and to the extent that a fixed word-order exists, it is better characterized *semantically* as V–AGT–ACC–DAT or V–ACC–DAT–AGT.

In languages where passivization may be synchronically characterized as being of the topic-shift typology, such as Kimbundu or Dzamba (see Section 4.4.2.2), the presence of object agreement to some extent expresses the semantic case of the promoted object.

The bulk of languages with "classical" passivization, that is, those in which the verb gets marked by passive morphology and all the coding properties of the subject get acquired by the promoted nonagent, restrict passivization mostly to *accusative* objects, with small allowances here and there. One may indeed wish to view this restriction in the context of a *recoverability strategy:* Since these languages do not code the semantic case of the promoted nonagent in any recoverable fashion, the effect of the accusative-only constraint on passivization is to identify the union of subject coding properties plus passive verb morphology as an instance of coding the semantic case *accusative.* In contrast, the union of subject coding properties plus active verb morphology then codes the semantic case *agent.* This is not to say that these languages cannot advance nonaccusative objects to topicality, since most of them have the topic-shift avenue of advancement open, and many have the agent-deletion avenue open as well. They thus divide the promotion of objects to topicality according to coding. Accusatives get coded as subjects plus passive verb morphology, while other objects retain their original semantic case marking when promoted.

An interesting variation is reported by Keenan (1975) for German, where passivization of the "standard" type is restricted to accusatives, while datives may be passivized via the following procedure:

1. The verb shows passive morphology.
2. The verb agrees with the promoted dative.
3. The promoted dative *retains* its dative case marking.

The relaxation of the accusative-only restriction here may be viewed in terms of recoverability: Only an object which retains its semantic case marking breaks the constraint. In the same way, most of the exceptions to the accusative-only constraint in English and Bantu passivization may be viewed as instances in which the semantic case of the promoted nonaccusative object is somehow retained. Thus consider:

(120) a. *John is listened **to** by his peers*
       b. *This house was broken **into** yesterday*
       c. *This matter has been looked **at** carefully*
       d. *The lock has been tampered **with***
       e. *John is spoken for*

4.4. Passivization and Promotion to Direct Object

All these prepositional cases become unrecoverable in passivization when an accusative object exists as well. Thus compare:

(121) a. *The office was sent to a letter
       b. *The box was put into a letter
       c. *The station was left at Sheila
       d. *The knife was cut with the meat
       e. *John was written for a letter

The inacceptability of passives in (120) as against (121) may be viewed in terms of *case confusion:* The surface pattern SUBJ–V–PREP–NP tends to be interpreted according to the *neutral* pattern, that is, with the preposition coding the semantic case of the *following* NP rather than that of the promoted object.

A similar situation in a conservative Bantu language, such as Bemba,[60] produces a different result altogether. Thus consider:

(122) a. *a-a-pona   icitabo mu-sanduku*
          he-past-put book   *in*-box
          'He put the book in the box'   (neutral)

       b. *icitabo ci-a-pon-wa   mu-sanduku*
          book   *it*-past-put-PASS *in*-box
          'The book was put in the box'   (ACC-passive)

       c. *mu-sanduku mu-a-pon-wa   icitabo*
          in-box   *there*-past-put-PASS book
          'in the box was put a book'
                                        (LOC-PASSIVE, NP-coding)

       d. *isanduku li-a-pon-wa-mo   icitabo*
          box   *it*-past-put-PASS-*in* book
          { 'The box was put-into a book' }
          { 'In the box was put a book' }
                                        (LOC-passive, verb-coding)

The pattern in (122b) is the normal passivization for accusatives. The pattern in (122c) is analogous to the DAT-passive in German, discussed above. The pattern in (122d) is the equivalent of the impermissible English pattern in (121,) and the reason why Bemba allows it and English does not is easy to discern: The verb-suffix preposition in Bemba is not a separate word, and had a different phonological shape (closed with the vowel *-o*) than the prepositional pre-noun form, so that no possible

---

[60] The passivization of locatives (including datives, if they are marked by *pa-*, *ku-*, or *mu-*) has been retained in all Bantu languages which retain these prepositions **and** the pronominal forms corresponding to them. Thus I believe Bemba represents a conservative situation in Bantu. As we shall see further below, a decrease in the functional load on these prepositions often results in an increased use of the *verb-coding* suffixes, as in Rwanda.

case confusion may arise. In Bemba the nonaccusative passive patterns in (122c, d) are confined to the three locative prepositions *pa-*, *ku-*, *mu-*. As we shall see below, by increasing its verb-coding capacity, a Bantu language could passivize more nonaccusative objects.

4.4.5. Languages Which Do

4.4.5.1. INDONESIAN

As in relativization, nonaccusative objects may passivize in Indonesian, but only if they are first promoted to direct-object. And this promotion results in verb-coding of the semantic function of the promoted object. Thus consider (data from Chung, 1975):[61]

(123)   a. *Hasan mem-beli badju* **untuk** *wanita itu*
           Hasan ACT-buy clothes *for*   woman the
           'Hasan bought clothes for the woman'   (neutral)

    b. *Hasan mem-beli-kan wanita itu badju*
           Hasan ACT-buy-*BEN* woman the clothes
           'Hasan bought the woman clothes'   (Dative-shifted)

    c. *badju itu di-beli* **untuk** *wanita itu (oleh Hasan)*
           clothes the *PASS*-buy *for*   woman the (by   Hasan)
           'The clothes were bought for the woman (by Hasan)'
                                               (ACC-passive)

    d. *wanita itu di-beli-kan*   *badju (oleh Hasan)*
           woman the PASS-buy-*BEN* clothes (by   Hasan)
           'The woman was bought-for clothes by Hasan'
                                           (BEN-passive, shifted)

    e. **wanita itu di-beli*   *badju (untuk) (oleh Hasan)*
           woman the PASS-buy clothes *(for)*   (by   Hasan)
                                   (*BEN-passive, nonshifted)

(123')   a. *Hasan meng-irim-kan seputjuk surat* **kepada** *wanita itu*
           Hasan ACT-write-*BEN* a   letter *to*   woman the
           'Hasan wrote a letter to the woman'   (neutral)

    b. *Hasan meng-irim-i*   *wanita itu seputjuk surat*
           Hasan ACT-write-DAT woman the a   letter
           'Hasan wrote the woman a letter'   (Dative-shifted)

---

[61] For other Austronesian languages with a similar typological behavior, see Foley (1976).

c. *surat itu di-irim-kan kepada wanita itu*
   letter the PASS-write-BĒN to woman the
   'The letter was written to the woman' (ACC-passive)

d. *wanita itu di-irim-i seputjuk surat*
   woman the PASS-write-DAT a letter
   'The woman was written-to a letter'
   (DAT-passive, shifted)

e. **wanita itu di-irim(-kan) seputjuk surat*
   woman the PASS-write(-BEN) a letter
   (DAT-passive, nonshifted)

4.4.5.2. BANTU

I have already illustrated how in more conservative Bantu dialects such as Bemba, objects marked with the prepositions *pa-*, *ku-*, and *mu-* may be directly passivized via two alternative strategies: (*a*) retaining the prepositional case on the new subject and thus affecting prepositional subject agreement, or (*b*) resorting to a verb-coding strategy, with the subject agreement then controlled by the gender–number of the new subject. In languages such as Bemba, LuGanda, or Shona, which use *ku-* to mark dative-human objects, the same two strategies are also available for passivizing datives. In Rwanda, on the other hand (see preceding discussion), dative objects are morphologically *unmarked*, normally remain adjacent to the verb, and most commonly require the verb suffix BEN (*-ir-/-er-*). In other words, they have effectively merged with the *benefactive* case which exhibits these characteristics in all Bantu languages. While one may not wish to characterize the BEN suffix as "promotional" in this case, because only the DAT/BEN–ACC order is attested, the same obligatory use of this suffix in passivization as in relativization is seen in Rwanda:[63]

---

[62] For more data again see Kimenyi (1976) and Gary and Keenan (1975).

[63] When the accusative object is present, the passivization of "goal" objects is blocked even if the BENEFACTIVE suffix is present. There are other "preemption" constraints of this type in Rwanda and other Bantu languages; for example, sometimes when both objects are present, the one higher on the topicality hierarchy preempts passivization, topicalization, pronominalization or definitization. For some Shona details, see Hawkinson and Hyman (1974). Another case is shown in Rwanda (Kimenyi, 1976), where if the dative is a pronoun (i.e., "highly topical"), the accusative cannot be promoted to subject via passivization. Thus:

*y-a-**mu**-haye inkoko*
she-past-*him*-give chicken
'She gave him a chicken'

inkoko y-a-mu**-ha-we*
chicken it-past-*him*-give-PASS
*'The chicken was given to him'

(124) a. *Yohani y-ooher-er-eje*   *Maria ibaruwa*
John   he-past-send-*BEN*-ASP Mary   letter
'John sent Mary a letter'   (neutral)

b. *ibaruwa y-ooher-er-eje*   *Maria*
letter   it-past-send-*BEN*-ASP Mary
'The letter was sent to Mary'   (ACC-passive)

c. *ibaruwa y-ooher-eje*
letter   it-past-sent-ASP
'The letter was sent'   (ACC-passive, no dative present)

d. *Maria y-ooher-er-ej-we*   *ibaruwa*
Mary   she-past-send-*BEN*-ASP-*PASS* letter
'Mary was sent a letter'   (DAT-passive)

e. **Maria y-ooher-ej-we*   *ibaruwa*
Mary   she-past-send-ASP-*PASS* letter
                      (*DAT-passive without BEN suffix)

(125) a. *Yohani y-a-tek-e-ye*   *Maria inkoko*
John   he-past-cook-*BEN*-ASP Mary   chicken
'John cooked a chicken for Mary'   (neutral)

b. *inkoko y-a-tek-e-y-we*   *Maria*
chicken it-past-cook-*BEN*-ASP-*PASS* Mary
'The chicken was cooked for Mary'   (ACC-passive)

c. *inkoko y-a-tets-e-we*
chicken it-past-cook-*ASP-PASS*
'The chicken was cooked'   (ACC-passive, no BEN suffix)

d. *Maria y-a-tek-e-we*   *inkoko*
Mary   she-past-cook-BEN-ASP-PASS chicken
'Mary was cooked-for a chicken'   (BEN-passive)

e. **Maria y-a-tets-e-we*   *inkoko*
Mary   she-past-cook-ASP-PASS chicken
                     (*BEN-passive, no BEN suffix)

In contrast, an accusative pronoun does *not* block the passivization of the dative object:

      umugabo y-a-gi-ha-we
      boy   he-past-*it*-give-PASS
      'The boy was given it' (the chicken)

We have here an interaction between the topic-hierarchy and two processes of promotion to higher topicality: passivization and pronominalization.

4.4. Passivization and Promotion to Direct Object

The passivization of locative objects in Rwanda exhibits the same two coding patterns as in Bemba (see (122) above), except for two provisions: (a) The locative suffixes are used in dative-shifting locative objects and may be thus considered "promotional," and (b) when the NP-coding pattern is used, the verb suffix may be also used optionally, as in (126):

(126)   a.   *umugore y-ooher-eje*   *umuooyi **ku**-isoko*
             woman   she-past-send-ASP cook   *to*-market
             'The woman sent the cook to the market'   (neutral)

         b.   *umugore y-ooher-ee-**ho***   *isoko   umubooyi*
             woman   she-past-send-ASP-*to* market cook
             'The woman sent the cook to the market'   (dative-shifted)

         c.   ***ku**-isoko   k-ooher-ej-we(-**ho**)*   *umubooyi*
             to-market *there*-past-send-ASP-*PASS*(-*to*) cook
             'To the market was sent the cook'
                                                    (LOC-passive, NP-coding)

         d.   *isoko   ry-ooher-ej-**we-ho***   *umubooyi*
             market it-past-send-ASP-*PASS*-*to* cook
             'The market was sent-to the cook'
                                                    (LOC-passive, verb-coding)

         e.   **isoko ry-ooher-ej-we umubooyi*
                                           (*LOC-passive, no LOC suffix)

While the NP-coding recoverability strategy in (126c) is possible, it is not frequently used, and the optional use of the promotional verb suffix -*ho*/-*mo* there strongly suggests that Rwanda is moving toward the use of the verb-coding strategy alone. Given that it has also developed verb-coding in dative-shifting locatives—and thus extended the conservative Bemba pattern, this development is not unexpected.

Bantu languages in general cannot passivize instrumental objects. But Rwanda—together with other Lake-Bantu languages, which have developed the use of a promotional suffix in dative-shifting instrumentals—can passivize them. But dative-shift is an obligatory feeder to passivization of instrumentals:

(127)   a.   *y-a-andits-e*   *ibaruwa n-ikaramu*
             he-past-write-ASP letter   *with*-pen
             'He wrote the letter with a pen'   (neutral)

         b.   *y-a-andik-**ish**-i je*   *ikaramu ibaruwa*
             he-past-write-*INST*-ASP pen   letter
             'He wrote the letter with the pen'   (dative-shifted)

    c. *ikaramu y-a-andik-**ish**-ij-we   ibaruwa*
        pen   it-past-write-*INST*-ASP-*PASS* letter
        'The pen was written-with the letter'   (INST-passive)

    d. **ikaramu y-a-andits-we   ibaruwa*
        pen   it-past-write-ASP-*PASS* letter
        (*INST-passive without INST suffix)

The extension of dative-shift and verb-coding to other object cases has them accessible to passivization as well. Thus for *manner*:

(128)   a. *y-a-koz-e   akazi n-inkweeto mbi*
            he-past-work-ASP work *with*-shoes bad
            'He did work using dirty shoes'   (neutral)

         b. *y-a-kor-**an**-ye   inkweto mbi (akazi)*
            he-past-work-*ACCOMP*-ASP shoes   shoes (work)
            'He used dirty shoes to do work'   (dative-shifted)

         c. *inkweto z-a-kor-**an**-w-e   akazi*
            shoes   they-past-work-*ACCOMP-PASS*-ASP work
            'The shoes were used to do work'   (MANNER-passive)

         d. **inkweto z-a-koz-w-e   akazi*
            shoes   they-past-work-*PASS*-ASP work
            (*MANNER-passive without ACCOMP suffix)

Finally for *goal*:

(129)   a. *Karoli y-a-koz-e   **ku**-mafaranga*
            Charles he-past-work-ASP *for*-money
            'Charles worked for money'   (neutral)

         b. *Karoli y-a-kor-e-ye   amafaranga*
            Charles he-past-work-BEN-ASP money
            'Charles worked for the money'   (dative-shifted)

         c. *amafaranga ya-a-kor-e-w-e*
            money   it-past-work-*BEN*-PASS-ASP
            'The money was worked for'   (GOAL-passive)

         d. **amafaranga ya-a-koz-w-e*
            money   it-past-work-PASS-ASP
            (*GOAL-passive without BEN suffix)

4.4.6. Case-Marking Typological Explanation

Following the previous discussion, the typological definition of languages which impose either the accusative-only constraint or the direct-object-only constraint in passivization may now be given:

(130)   TYPOLOGICAL CONDITION V *(accusative-only constraint). Languages in which (a) passivization involves complete loss of the semantic case-coding of the object—and thus assumption of all coding properties of the subject—and (b) in addition no other provisions are made for coding the semantic case of nonaccusative object on the verb, will tend to exhibit the accusative-only constraint in passivization. Conversely, languages—or object cases—who break the constraint are those in which either (a) the object does not lose its semantic case-marking in passivization, or (b) alternative verb-coding provisions are made for preserving the semantic case of the promoted object.*

The predictions made by CONDITION V above are good either for languages—if they treat their object cases uniformly, or alternatively for individual object types in a single language.

(131)   TYPOLOGICAL CONDITION VI *(direct-obj. only constraint). Only languages in which (a) passivization involves a complete assumption of the case-coding properties of the subject by the promoted object (and thus complete loss of the semantic case-coding of that object), and in addition (b) promotion of nonaccusative objects to direct-object status results in verb-coding of the semantic case of the promoted object, will exhibit the direct-object only constraint on passivization.*

CONDITION VI again applies either to languages when all object cases are uniformly treated, or to individual cases within a language in case they are not treated uniformly. I believe both conditions characterize reasonably well the classes of languages which obey or do not obey these constraints. The gist of the argument is that since neither of these constraints is universal, an explanation of either is good only if it manages to make reasonably confirmable typological predictions. The only context in which such predictions can be made, in my mind, is that of case-typology and case-function recoverability.

Given typological CONDITION VI, English may at first appear to be a counterexample to it, given cases (admittedly limited) of the following type, where it seems that the dative-shifted variant gets passivized:

(132)   a. *John gave a book to Mary*
        b. *John gave Mary a book*
        c. *Mary was given a book*
        d. *?Mary was given to a book*
        e. *?Mary was given a book to*

However, we have already noted [cf., (120), (121) above] that English can passivize many indirect objects leaving their preposition stranded behind, as in (132d, e), and that possibility is blocked in the presence of an unmarked accusative object, most likely due to *case confusion*. It is thus possible to view (132c) as an attempt to avoid this case confusion, and one might as well note that only a small semantic range of verbs, such as *give, show*, allow this pattern, and that even with *bring* and *send* which allow dative-shift of the same type, this passivization is odd. Furthermore, this oddity increases when the other object is semantically close to the dative. Thus compare:

(133)   a. *?She was brought two pictures and was asked to . . .*
        b. *??She was brought two men and was asked . . .*

The limitations on this pattern in English may be viewed as a reflection of the fact that it does *not* involve verb-coding of the promoted object, and is thus extremely vulnerable in terms of case recoverability.

4.4.7. Functional Explanations in Terms of Topicality

Since it is clear that both passivization and dative-shift involve promotion to higher topicality, their coupling in passivization of course makes sense: If the accusative is higher in topicality than the dative, then it seems strange that the dative rather than accusative is promoted via passivization. On the other hand, if dative shift already promotes the nonaccusative one step, it is more natural to use the dative-shifted variant for further promotion to subject–topic. Instances of *preemption*, as in Rwanda (see footnote 63.) or Shona (Hawkinson and Hyman, 1974) tend to reinforce this view, which is also compatible with the preemptive interpretation of passives of the agent-deletion type (see discussion in Section 4.4.2.3, Kirsner, 1973, 1975; Foley, 1976). While acknowledging the plausibility of this explanation, one must also note that it is again entirely universal and by this virtue typologically neutral. That is, it cannot help us predict which languages will and which will not make dative-shift an obligatory feeder to passivization. One may again view this explanation as a "conspiratorial extra bonus," and perhaps also note that it predicts at least the *absence* of one type of grammatical behavior:

In no language is the case found where an accusative object gets first *demoted* via dative-shifting as a prerequisite to its passivization.

4.5. SUMMARY

I have shown that within the framework of case-recoverability strategies one could make highly specific prediction as to what features in the case marking typology of a language determine its dependence a promotional rule such as passive or dative-shift as a prerequisite to another rule, such as relativization or passivization. The typological conditions are restated here:

CONDITION I/II *(passive and relativization)*. *Only languages in which promotion to subject via passivization results in verb-coding the semantic case of the promoted nonagent exhibit the subject-only constraint on relativization.*

CONDITION III/IV *(dative-shift and relativization)*. *Only languages in which (a) the accusative is unmarked, (b) in addition when a nonaccusative is dative-shifted it loses its nominal case marking, and (c) in addition the dative-shifted nonaccusative gains verb-coding of its semantic case via dative-shift, will exhibit the direct-object-only constraint on object relativization.*

CONDITION V *(accusative-only constraint on passive)*. *Only languages in which (a) passivization involves complete loss of the semantic case-coding properties of the object and an assumption by it of all the case-coding properties of the subject, and (b) no additional provisions exist for coding the semantic case of promoted nonaccusative objects on the verb, will exhibit the accusative-only constraint on passivization.*

CONDITION V also applies to cases within an individual language, and would predict that if for some object case alternative coding procedures are available, the constraint on its passivization will be broken.

CONDITION VI *(dative-shift and passivization)*. *Only languages in which passivization involves (a) the complete assumption of the coding properties of the subject by the promoted object (and thus complete loss of its original case-coding), and in addition (b) promotion of nonaccusative objects to direct-object via dative-shifting results in verb-coding of the semantic case of those objects, will exhibit the direct-object-only constraint on passivization.*

In effect, then, the direct-object-only constraint on passivization constitutes one type of *relaxation* of the accusative-only constraint, which is much more general. Agent-deletion or topic-shift types of passivization may be also viewed as coding strategies which in effect break the accusative-only constraint. The Philippine verb-coding typology of passivization–topicalization may be also viewed as another coding strategy which allows breaking the accusative-only constraint.

I have also assessed other possible explanations of the various constraints in terms of the function of passive, dative-shift, and perhaps relativization in promotion to *topicality* in language. While these considerations are universal and thus cannot by themselves predict the class of languages which will obey these constraints, they may still *reinforce* the naturalness of these constraints once the case-typology factors are present. At the very least, topicality functional considerations may partially motivate the following *negative* predictions:

1. No language exists in which the subject must be first demoted (via passivization) before it can be relativized.
2. No language exists in which an accusative object must be first demoted via dative-shift before it can be relativized.
3. No language exists in which an accusative object must first be demoted via dative-shift before it can be passivized.

That these negative predictions are not wholly independent of case-marking considerations is only to be expected.

While the subject–topic case-function has long been recognized as a *pragmatic* case, the direct-object function quite often gets confused with the accusative or somehow labeled "grammatical." While this is a much less universal case than subject–topic, it shares some of its properties in languages where it exists: (*a*) Nonaccusative objects lose their semantic case marking when promoted to direct-object, as they often do in passivization; (*b*) dative-shift involves promotion to higher topicality, though not to *primary* topic–subject as is done in passivization; (*c*) much like some types of passives, dative-shift may apply without any changes in the case-marking of the two objects. One other striking feature of the direct-object is that it shares the case-marking properties of the accusative, but only when the accusative is *unmarked*. No language exists, to my knowledge, where the accusative is a marked case and non-accusative objects gain that marking in dative-shifting. Thus, it seems, that it is the unmarkedness of the accusative which makes it such a natural promotional case, and this is only natural: By promoting other objects into the same case of the unmarked accusative, they lose their original semantic case marking but do not gain another *semantic* case. But this is precisely what happens in promotion to *subject:* The subject case is a purely *pragmatic* case, and involves no gain in semantic marking, but only loss. The two promotion rules are in that sense quite similar, and this may reinforce our view of both as birds of the same *pragmatic* feather.

5

SYNTACTICIZATION
from discourse to syntax: grammar as a processing strategy

5.1. INTRODUCTION[1]

Given the discussion in Chapter 2 concerning the relation between discourse and syntax and the explanatory role played by discourse-pragmatics in our understanding the syntax of human language, one is prompted to ask: Does syntax have any independent existance apart from discourse? As I have suggested earlier, the traditional transformationalist approach to "independent syntax" is untenable on two grounds: First, it is derived from a set of data that is restricted and presanitized. Second, it does nothing to further our understanding as to why the grammar of human language is the way it is. On the other end of the ideological scale, it has been suggested by García in her "Discourse without syntax" (1977) that syntax per se does not exist at all, and that human language can be described exhaustively by reference to *communicative principles* which underlie the structure of discourse. While pursuing the research that formed the basis for Chapters 2, 3, and 4, I found myself slowly gravitating towards precisely that position, of rejecting the existence of syntax altogether and viewing it as a complex *artifact,* arising from the interaction of various communicative principles and strategies, such as those discussed in the preceding chapters. The artifact itself seemed *stable enough,* I thought, because the underlying

---

[1] An earlier version of this chapter was presented at the *Symposium on Discourse and Syntax,* University of California, Los Angeles, November 1977. I have benefited greatly from comments and suggestions made by the Symposium's participants and would like to record my indebtedness here. In particular, I would like to thank Elinor Keenan, Manny Schegloff, Patricia Greenfield, Edward Keenan, David Zubin, Bob Longacre, and Pete Becker for their many helpful suggestions. The title of the chapter owes much to Sankoff and Brown's (1976) "The origins of syntax in discourse."

strategies as well as their interactions were themselves stable. What I am proposing to do in this chapter is in a sense a *tactical retreat* from that extreme position. What I hope to illustrate below is that (*a*) there are many facts supporting the existence of some *structural* level called syntax, but (*b*) in order to explain the formal properties of that *structural* level, one must make reference, once again, to a number of *substantive* explanatory parameters of language. Rather than winding up with an independent, formal, and *autonomous* level of structural organization in language, we indeed find syntax to be a *dependent,* functionally motivated entity, whose formal properties reflect—perhaps not completely but nearly so—the properties of the explanatory parameters which motivate its rise.

The range of data upon which I will build the argument involve four sources whose underlying unity is not hard to perceive. For reasons that will be made apparent later on, it is easy to interpret all four as processes:

(1) a. *Diachronic:*   Loose parataxis → Tight syntax
     b. *Ontogenetic:*   Early pragmatic mode → Later syntactic mode
     c. *Pidgins–Creoles:*   Nongrammar → Grammar
     d. *Register level:*   Unplanned–informal speech → Planned–formal speech

Per se, several of the processes listed above have been dealt with in the recent literature. Thus, (1c) was discussed in Sankoff and Brown (1976), the parallels between (1b) and (1d) were discussed by Elinor Keenan (1977), and the parallels between (1a), (1b), and (1c) were discussed in Slobin (1977). This chapter is thus intended as a synthesis.

5.2. THE DIACHRONIC PROCESS OF SYNTACTICIZATION

In this section I will describe a number of recurring themes in diachronic syntax. I would like to suggest that all of them represent processes by which loose, paratactic, "pragmatic" discourse structures develop—over time—into tight, "grammaticalized" syntactic structures. For each one of these processes one could prepare a balance sheet of communicative *gains* and communicative *losses*. The principles which control the balance of gain and loss here are, presumably, what we are investigating.

If language constantly takes discourse structure and condenses it—via syntacticization—into syntactic structure, one would presumably

5.2. The Diachronic Process of Syntacticization

expect human languages to become increasingly syntacticized over time. In fact, this is not the case. Rather, syntactic structure in time *erodes*, via processes of *morphologization* and *lexicalization*. I have dealt with this end of the cycle elsewhere,[2] and the principles motivating the erosion of syntax are not necessarily indentical to those which motivate its rise. Nevertheless, one must keep in mind that we are dealing here with cyclic *waves*, which may be characterized roughly as:

(2)   Discourse → Syntax → Morphology → Morphophonemics → Zero

The last two steps are motivated largely by phonological attrition and will not be discussed further here. The first two steps, which are often *coupled* (i.e., occur simultaneously), are motivated by various *communicative needs* and will form the bulk of the cases to be discussed.

5.2.1. From Topic to Subject

Quite a few recent works have dealt with the relation between the discourse-functional notion *topic* and the "syntactic–grammatical" notion *subject*.[3] Thus, Keenan (1976a) has shown that most of the properties of subjects can be understood in terms of topic properties.[4] Li and Thompson (1976) and Schachter (1976, 1977) illustrated the considerable difficulties involved in deciding whether in a particular language one deals with subject or topic. Following Li and Thompson (1976), the possibility is still open that some languages may have more grammaticalized subjects while others may have more discourse-pragmatic topics, although only a serious distributional study of texts—of both formal and informal registers—can settle this issue conclusively.

In Givón (1976a) I pointed out that one of the most acclaimed properties of subjects, that of *grammatical agreement* on the verb, is fundamentally a *topic* property, and that it arises diachronically via the reanalysis of topic into subject and—simultaneously—of an anaphoric pronoun into a (normally verb-bound) agreement morpheme. As an illustration, consider the following example from noneducated American English, where this process is currently endemic:[5]

(3)   *My ol' man, he rides with the Angels* →
        TOPIC   PRO V
              My ol' man he-rides with the Angels
              SUBJECT   AG-V

[2] See Givón (1971, 1975e, 1976a).
[3] See various papers in Li (1976).
[4] And a small residue of *agent* properties.
[5] This example was heard in a waiting room of County General Hospital, Los Angeles, by Jean Tremaine. Only the grammaticalized form on the right was attested, though its source on the left is transparent.

One must remember, however, that English has both SUBJECT and TOPIC constructions, and that they serve normally different discourse functions (see Chapter 2). Thus the grammaticalization of topics into subjects does not mean that the language has lost the topic construction, but only that it has gained grammatical agreement as an added morphological *coding property* for its grammatical subject.[6] As we shall see further below, there are reasons to believe that every language has a wide range of *discourse registers*, for the loose-informal-pragmatic to the tight-formal-syntactic.

As I have also shown in Givón (1976a), unrelated and typologically diverse languages undergo the development schematized in (3) above in very much the same fashion, leaving the same indelible marks in terms of grammatical agreement. In one case, Sankoff (1976) showed three consecutive cycles of the same process occuring in one language (Tok Pisin, a Pidgin language in the New Guinea Highlands) within a hundred years. The communicative balance sheet for such a process may be divided as follows:

1. *Time of delivery.* Subject constructions are delivered faster and without an intonational break, while topic constructions typically take more time.
2. *Coding.* Subject constructions are typically *better coded* morphologically than topic constructions (see Keenan, 1976a), with verb agreement being one typical instance of such coding, but case marking possibly another one and rigidity in word-order another.
3. *Resolution.* In terms of identifying the topic of discourse, topic constructions obviously exhibit 100% correlation between form and function. While it is true that subjects in discourse are *most commonly* also the topic, there is probably a residue of between 10–20% in which the topic does not coincide with the grammatical subject.[7]

Whether or not the communicative loss (3) is real remains problematic, since the pragmatic and lexical redundancies present in the discourse context presumably could offset such a loss. Furthermore, since most languages retain both topic and subject constructions, a certain division of labor between the two is normally observed (see discussion in Chapter 2). Thus subject constructions are typically used when the topic is

---

[6] As Pete Becker (personal communication) points out, the diachronic process is really from *topic + subject* to *subject + agreement*.

[7] The 10–20% figure is based on a rough estimate derived from the fact that, in general, in connected human narrative, equi-subject chains are about 5–10 verbs long. In some languages (New Guinea), these chains tend to be much longer (up to 50 verbs per chain ending with a finite verb). Thus human discourse tends to be multipropositional and topic-maintaining. This makes the strategy of using well-coded and faster-processed subjects a viable means to render equi-topic chains. See the further discussion in this chapter as well as Chapter 7.

maintained *the same*, that is, when it is reasonably easy to identify; topic constructions are typically used when the discourse topic is *changed*, that is, when it is harder to identify.[8] Thus, one may conceive of the SUBJECT strategy as that of *automatic processing*, to be used when the going is easy, when one maintains the same subject over a chain of clauses, and when time saving is thus possible and further facilitated by the enhanced coding properties of SUBJECT. Finally, as we shall see later, the coupling of syntacticization with the rise of morphology (coding) is a recurring theme in diachronic change and exhibits many parallels in other areas of the data base, specifically in the development of child language towards the adult mode of communication.

5.2.2. From Topicalization to Passivization

In Givón (1976a) I cited two examples of this diachronic process, one from Kimbundu, the other from Indonesian. It is obviously a closely related process to the one just discussed. However, here an *object topic* (left-dislocated object) becomes grammaticalized into the *subject-of-passive*, with certain coding consequences arising simultaneously. As an illustration, consider this process in Kimbundu, a Bantu language:

(4)   OBJECT–TOPIC   PASSIVE
      CONSTRUCTION   CONSTRUCTION
      Nzua, a-mu-mono   →   *Nzua a-mu-mono   (kwa meme)*
      John they-him-saw   John they-him-saw (by   me)
      'John, they saw him'   'John was seen by me'

The balance sheet of communicative gain and loss is very much the same as in Section 5.2.1. The morphological adjustment in the agreement system is more complex, however. The left-dislocated topic construction on the left in (4) has a third-person-plural subject agreement that may be totally viable (though it may be also "impersonal"), a fact that may be demonstrated from inserting a fully specified subject:

(5)   *Nzua, a-ana   a-mu-mono*
               John children they-him-saw
               'John, the children saw him'

In the passive construction on the right, on the other hand, the *a*-morpheme in the subject-agreement position is frozen and agrees neither with the new subject–patient nor with the agent, a fact that is obvious from the ungrammaticality (indeed the absurdity) of (6):

(6)   **Nzua a-ana   a-mu-mono   kwa meme*
            John children they-him-saw by me

---

[8] For further detail see Keenan and Scheffelin (1977) and Duranti and Keenan (1979).

Furthermore, the erstwhile object agreement (*-mu-* 'him') of the neutral pattern has in fact become the subject-of-passive agreement, thus contributing to special morphological coding of the new passive construction.

5.2.3. From Topic Sentences to Relative Clauses

Many languages[9] have or used to have what is often refered to as unembedded–unreduced relative clauses.[10] Those are basically *topic* sentences, roughly arranged before or after the main clause much like adverbial clauses. I will illustrate this pattern schematically by paraphrasing the Hittite examples given in Justus (1976a, 1976b):

(7)   a   *If we see **any** man, we'll report **him** to the king*
                                                                                                           (OBJ REL)

   b.   *If **a** man comes, we'll report **him** to the king*
                                                                                                            (SUBJ REL)

Justus (1976b) has suggested that a certain relative-clause type in Germanic, Romance, and Indic, where a *relative marker* precede the head noun but the clause itself follows, is diachronically derived from the Hittite-type topic-sentence construction as paraphrased in (7). For subject relative clauses—the most common type cross-linguistically and least-complex psycholinguistically[11]—such a development may be schematically outline as:

(8)   a   *man comes, we'll report **him** to the king*   →
      INDEF   PRO

           a   *man **comes** we'll report to the king*
           Whatever NP   REL
         '*Whatever man comes we'll report to the king*'

In Hittite, an SOV language, such reanalysis will involve no dislocation whatever in the neutral syntactic pattern. In later Germanic and Romance dialects, a reanalysis as in (8) would place the object NP at a topicalized position, a relatively mild dislocation.[12] And in subject relativization where the head noun is also the subject of the *main* clause, no disruption of the neutral pattern occurs at all:[13]

---

[9] This has been reported in Hittite (Indo-European), Bambara (Mendeic, Niger-Congo), Hindi-Urdu (Indo-European), Wappo, Navajo (Athabascan), Diegeño (Yuman), Japanese (Altaic), and New Guinea, among others, and is probably quite extensive elsewhere.

[10] This pattern has been discussed in Chapter 4, as one of the available patterns of relativization.

[11] See discussion in Keenan and Comrie (1977).

[12] See comments in Chapter 4, about the possibility that head nouns modified by relative clauses tend to be "more topical."

[13] Hawkins and Keenan (1974) also cite evidence that subject relative clauses are psycholinguistically easier to process, but the evidence is not altogether conclusive.

(9)   *a man comes, he'll visit the palace*   →
       ***whatever** man comes will visit the palace*

Finally, Justus (1976a, 1976b) point out that the prenominal "relative" marker in Hittite (*ku-*), Romance (*qu-*), and Germanic (*wh-*) is etymologically a *cataphoric* element related to *indefinite* pronouns. This supports the paraphrases given on the left in (8) and (9).

A reanalysis of this type is also reported for Yuman (Langdon, 1977), for Tok Pisin (a Pidgin-Creole; Sankoff and Brown, 1976), and for Wappo (Li and Thompson, private communication). The actual morphological consequences (or "coding gains") of the reanalysis may vary. In Bambara, for example, the topic sentence may be either left-dislocated or embedded. When it is left-dislocated, an anaphoric pronoun appears in the main clause. When it is fully embedded, no anaphoric pronoun appears. But in both cases the coreferent noun within the topic-sentence/relative-clause is marked by a special suffix (reminiscent of the *ku-* element in Hittite):[14]

(10)   cę **min** ye mùru sàn, n ye o   ye
       man REL past knife buy, I past him see
       'The man who bought the knife, I saw him' (UNEMBEDDED)

(11)   n ye cę̀ **min** ye mùru sàn ye
       I past man REL past knife buy see
       'I saw the man who bought the knife'   (EMBEDDED)

With the exception of the *min* morpheme, the pattern in (10) is a loose, paratactic pattern, indistinguishable from sentence concatenation. While this cannot be documented for all languages, it is still possible that *all* embedded, "syntactic" relative clauses in language arose diachronically from loose, paratactic concatenations.

The communicative balance sheet is here again rather obvious: One gains automatic, fast, morphologically coded processing, while the loss presumably involves the effects of deletion under coreference and the rise of the recoverability problem (see discussion in Chapter 4). Again, lexical, contextual, and general pragmatic redundancies are likely to pick up the communicative slack, especially since restrictive relative clauses are overwhelmingly background–presupposed information.

5.2.4. From Conjunction to Subordination in the Verb Phrase

The first type of case to be discussed here involves the infinitival complements of verbs imposing an equi-NP condition, either those with an equi-subject condition (*want, try, begin*) or those with an equi-object

---
[14] For the Bambara data I am indebted to Ibrahima Coulibali (personal communication).

condition (*order, force, ask*). The complement verb in many languages is *nonfinite*, as in English, and this involves a marked reduction in the tense–aspect morphology, lack of subject agreement, and often some special infinitival–nominal morphology. In many other languages, however, the complement verb is either *finite* or at least exhibits subject pronominal agreement on the verb. This may be seen in Arabic, Greek, some Slavic languages, and Icelandic,[15] among others. Thus consider the following, from Palestinian Arabic:

(12)   ana biddi   i-mshi
          I   I-want I-go
          'I want to go'

Now, since the subject agreement pronoun marking the complement verb is the very same type used in simple subject *anaphora* in equi-subject concatenations, it is most likely that the current subordinate, syntactic construction in those languages in fact arose from a loose, paratactic concatenation via syntacticization. In fact, the possibility is still open that *all* equi-NP verb complements in language arose via such a process, which may be thus schematized as:

(13) a. For equi-subject verbs:

          I want I-go   →   *I want to-go*
          SUBJ-FINITE   SUBORD-INFINITIVE

      b. For equi-object verbs:

          I tell you you-go →   *I tell you to-go*
          OBJ SUBJ-FINITE   OBJ SUBORD/INFINITIVE

Another type of condensation from a looser paratactic to a tighter, subordinate pattern in the verb phrase was described, for Mandarin Chinese, in Thompson (1973). It involves resultative verb compounds, as in:

(14)   tā lā-kāi   le   mén
          he pull-open ASP   door
          'He pulled the door open'

(15)   tā lā-de-kāi   mén
          he pull-can-open   door
          'He can pull the door open'

While Thompson (1973) points out that a synchronic transformation derivation of sentences such as (14) and (15) from looser conjunctions is

---

[15] For the latter, see Andrews (1976), where the presence of pronominal traces on the complement verb is used as an argument for a *synchronic* derivation. As in many synchronically oriented transformational arguments, I think the real import of the data is *diachronic*.

untenable, it is most likely that in fact that very derivation happened diachronically, roughly along the schematic pattern:[16]

(16)   *he pulled the door, and (it) opened* → *he pulled the door open*

Lexicalized and semilexicalized verb compounds of this and other types are highly prevalent in the Sino-Tibetan, Southeast Asian, and Niger-Congo linguistic areas. The most likely source of such condensations is more loose, concatenated structures.

Similar cases are common elsewhere. Thus, for example, Akiba (1978) suggested that the tightly-bound constructions of auxiliary verb plus verb in Japanese developed historically from looser, *conjoined* structures.[17] Hyman (1971) suggested that the tightly-bound serial verb constructions in Niger-Congo (specifically in Kwa) arose historically from loose consecutive conjunctions.[18]

5.2.5. Causativization and the Rise of Complex Verbs

Another common process by which looser, sentential constructions get condensed into tighter "syntacticized" verb phrases, and as a result more simple predicates become more complex,[19] is the process of lexical causativization. This process involves, diachronically, *predicate raising* by which two verb phrases ("clauses") carrying their own case-marked arguments become condensed into a single verb phrase. The two verbs become a single lexical-causative verb, and the subject of the lower clause gets accommodated as an *object* of the resulting compound verb.[20] This process may be represented schematically as:

(17)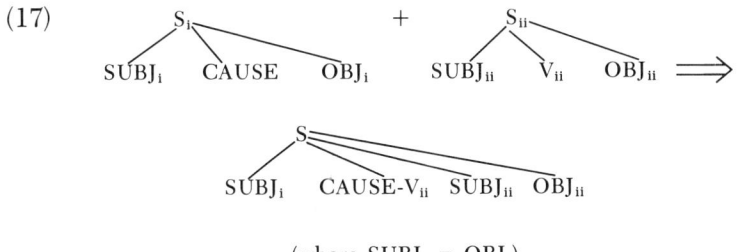

(where $SUBJ_{ii} = OBJ_i$)

---

[16] In Chinese, the anaphoric pattern in such a close concatenation (i.e., where the coreferent argument is both syntactically and pragmatically rather transparent) is deletion ("zero pronoun"). See Li and Thompson (1979).

[17] For the condensation involved in the development of auxiliary verbs into tense–aspect–modal markers, see further below.

[18] The condensation of serial-verb constructions and its role in the rise of case-marking will be discussed later in this chapter.

[19] Complexity can be measured here in terms of the number of nominal arguments per verb. For an extensive discussion of synchronic semantic and pragmatic aspects of causativization, see Shibatani (Ed., 1976) and Givón (1975d). For more diachronic aspects, see Givón (1971, 1976c).

[20] For the principles governing such and accomodation cross-linguistically, see Comrie (1976) and Cole (1976).

This type of condensation, as well as the one arising from the reanalysis of serial verb constructions (see further below), are both major contributors to the diachronic rise of syntacticized, complex verb phrases. They both increase the number of nominal arguments per lexical verb in a clause. They both, in a sense, create the real problem of case marking, that is, the fact that an increasing number of nominal arguments are present per verb, so that the verb itself cannot serve as indicating the function of the noun. The language then must resort to case-marking morphology on the nouns themselves (see later discussion). This general phenomenon is an illustration of how the loose, paratactic mode–level of language is transparent enough to require relatively little morphological coding. The rise of the grammatical morphology in language may be thus seen as *coupled to* the rise of the syntactic mode.

5.2.6. The Rise of Some Complex Genitive Constructions

In a number of languages there exist a seemingly complex genitive construction that must have arisen via syntacticization of a looser paratactic construction. As an illustration, consider the normal possessive construction of Krio, a Creole language:[21]

(18)   Jɔn **hin**-ós
         John *his*-house
         'John's house'

Since the history of Krio, a relatively recent English-lexicon-based Creole, is rather transparent, the syntacticized construction in (18), in which the normal anaphoric genitive pronoun is used obligatory (and the intonation contour is unified), must have arisen from a looser, topicalized (left-dislocated) construction, namely:

(19)   *John, his house*

A parallel situation may be shown in the more literary level of Modern Hebrew, except that here the order is different:[22]

(20)   bet-o   shel   Yoav
         house-*his* *that-to* Yoav
         'Yoav's house'

The genitive particle *shel* is a composite of the relative subordinator *she-* (full–older form *asher*) plus the dative preposition *l*. Here the paratactic

---

[21] For the data I am indebted to Sori Yilla (personal communication).

[22] I could find no attestation of this construction in Biblical Hebrew, and tend to suspect that it may have arisen during the Mishnaic or Talmudic period. In Modern Hebrew it is not used at the most colloquial register.

source was more likely either an afterthought topic (right dislocation) or an emphatic construction of the type:

(21)   *bet-i*   *she-l-i*
         house-*my* that-to-*me*
         'my *own* house'

If the afterthought topic construction was the source, then (20) may be viewed as the condensation–syntacticization of the looser construction in (22):

(22)   *bet-o,*   *shel*   Yoav
         house-*his* that-to Yoav
         'His house, the one belonging to Yoav'

The naturalness of this process is not difficult to discern: In possessive constructions, the possessor—normally human—is *more topical* than the possessed, and therefore quite often it winds up being topicalized if the construction to begin with has it at a less topical position.[23]

5.2.7. The Rise of Cleft and WH-Question Constructions

One of the most puzzling universals of word order is that of the left-attraction of the focus–assertional–emphatic constituents in cleft and WH-questions. It is particularly puzzling to find it in many subject-first languages, where it is reasonably clear that the general pragmatic principle governing word-order is that more topical material precedes and more assertional material follows. In the past I have attempted to explain this glaring discrepancy by pointing out that in cleft sentences the focus constituent is at the same time both topical and assertional.[24] It seems to me, however, that a much more simple and straightforward explanation can be constructed, one which makes reference to the *diachronic* rise of these constructions via syntacticization of a looser, paratactic construction.

It is well known that in both cleft and WH-question constructions, one element—most commonly a nominal—is in the assertion (or interrogation) *focus*, while the rest—the material which often resembles the syntax of a *relative clause*—is presupposed. Thus:

(23)   *It's John who left*
                  FOCUS   PRESUPPOSED

---

[23] For a general discussion as well as more examples of similarly motivated reanalysis of existential and possessive expressions, see Givón (1976a).

[24] See Givón (1974a). This is another example where a diachronic explanation of the details of synchronic syntactic properties turns out, I think, to be more insightful. This general phenomenon is the theme of Chapter 6.

(24)   *Who   left?*
                             FOCUS PRESUPPOSED

Now, in actual discourse contexts in the informal conversational register, most often there is no need to pronounce the entire construction in (23) or (24), since the presupposed portion is not only known to both participant but quite often has been mentioned in the directly preceding discourse. The more prevalent conversational strategy is thus much more likely to be:

(25)   A: *Mary did it.*

                        B: *No,* **it was John.**

(26)   A: *. . . . did it*

                        B: **Who?**

If that is a reasonable argument, then one may view the rise of the syntactic patterns in (23) and (24) as a result of tacking the presupposed portion onto the focus constituent (25), and (26) as an afterthought, paratactic construction, as in (27) and (28), respectively.

(27)   **It was John,** *(the one) who did it.*

(28)   **Who (was it),** *(the one) who did it?*

The correlation to relative clauses observed by Schachter (1973) and Takizala (1972) thus finds a diachronic—that is, a solid—motivation. Furthermore, the relative clause phenomenon associated with focus–WH constructions in many languages is pragmatically of the *nonrestrictive* kind, that is fully compatible with the parenthetic, afterthought nature of those presupposed clauses.[25]

5.2.8. The Biblical Hebrew Sentential Complements

In Givón (1974c) I have shown that the verb-complement constructions in Late Biblical Hebrew which use the erstwhile relative-clause subordinator *she-/asher*, must have arisen via the reanalysis of a more paratactic "blend" construction. What was apparently involved is the fact that verbs such as *see, think* or *know* can in language in general—take both direct-object nominal complements as well as a sentential complement. In Early Biblical Hebrew already one finds the following kinds of blends, where such a verb takes both a nominal and a sentential complement. The sentential complement, in turn, may be of the normal

---

[25] That is, there is no way in which one could conceive of them synchronically as "narrowing the domain of the head NP," or "functioning to establish definite description," which is the normal function of restrictive relative clauses.

5.2. The Diachronic Process of Syntacticization

V-comp type in Early Biblical Hebrew, that is, with the subordinators *ki* or *vehine*, as in:

(29)   va-yar? ?elohim ?et ha-?or **ki** tov   (Gen. 1:4)
        and-saw GOD   ACC the-light *that* good
        'And God saw the light, that it was good'

But the blend pattern can also exhibit the sentential complement in a relative-clause form. And that form may be "headless," as in (30).

(30)   shama'nu ?et   ?asher hovish Jhwh   ?et   mey   (Josh. 2:10)
        we-heard ACC *that*   dried   JHWH ACC water-of
        yam   suf
        sea-of Suf
        'We heard it, that God dried up the water of the Red Sea'

But it can also be a "headed" form, as in (31).

(31)   ?al   tir?u-ni   **she**-?ani   shxaxoret   (Song of Solomon 1:6)
        don't you-see-*me that*-I   swarthy
        ['Don't see me, who is dark-skinned']
        ['Don't see that I am dark-skinned']

The data strongly suggests that the later V-comp constructions, fully syntacticized as in (32):

(32)   yada'ti **she**-gam   hu? r'ut   ruax   (Eccl. 1:17)
             I-knew *that*-also it   folly-of spirit
             'I knew that it too was folly'

in fact arose from the looser, paratactic blends described earlier. In those, the speaker in fact *hedges*: He first expresses the nominal object; then, on realizing that it is not that nominal per se but rather a proposition about that nominal (i.e., in which that nominal is an argument) that he intended to express, he adds that preposition as an *afterthought*. One of the most natural patterns to be use in such an afterthought is naturally a nonrestrictive relative clause, since one argument of the proposition has already been mentioned and can thus be deleted under coreference.

It is likely that the type of reanalysis just described is much more widespread. For example, in Aramaic the subordinator for both relative clauses and verb complements is the same demonstrative *di*, and it may well be that it spread into the V-comp paradigm via a similar blend pattern. A similar situation is observed in Germanic, and Vennemann (personal communication) has suggested that the reanalysis proceeded along similar lines, schematically:

(33)   *I know **that**, (i.e.,) it is true*   →   *I know **that** it is true*
              OBJ   SUBORD

5.2.9. The Rise of Grammatical ("Inflectional") Morphology

In the preceding sections I have shown that in almost every case where loose, paratactic structure is condensed historically into tight, syntactic structure, the condensation involves the simultaneous rise of grammatical morphology to better code the emergent syntax. In this section I would like to pursue this theme further. By way of illustration, I will cite two major subsystems of inflectional morphology, one usually arising as noun inflection, the other as verb inflection. While in the past[26] I have looked at these processes in a narrower context, dealing with the rise of morphology per se, it seems to me now that it may be more revealing to treat syntacticization and the rise of grammatical morphology as two mutually dependent parts of the same process. Via syntacticization the language loses message transparency while it gains processing speed. The concomitant rise of morphology offsets the losses by adding *coding* to the construction, thus facilitating the emergent mode of automatic processing.

5.2.9.1. FROM SERIAL VERBS TO CASE MARKERS

This subject has been surveyed in great details in the past few years. Some works dealt with the synchronic status of serial verbs.[27] Others dealt with several diachronic aspects.[28] In Givón (1975e) I surveyed the subject from the perspective of the rise of case-marking morphology via the de-verbal channel of serial verbs. What is involved, diachronically, is a slow process of reanalysis, by which the description of an event—that is, a proposition—is first assembled as a concatenation of small propositions in which, roughly, a one-to-one correlation is maintained between verbs and nominal arguments, so that in essence the function of each nominal argument is marked by the verb which precedes or follows it.[29] In the course of time, however, a slow and gradual reanalysis occurs, by which the verbs *except for one* become grammaticalized as case-markers, eventually becoming bound to their respective nominal arguments. The loosely concatenated, paratactic expression then becomes a single sentence, falling under a single intonational contour, with *one* complex verb. As an illustration, consider the following examples:[30]

(34) ū lá dùkū là
he *take* pot *break*
'He broke the pot' (ACCUSATIVE, Nupe)

---

[26] As in Givón (1971, 1973c, 1975a).
[27] Stahlke (1970), Li and Thompson (1973b, 1973c), Hyman (1971).
[28] Lord (1973), Li and Thompson (1973a).
[29] The subject–agent argument is normally the only one to break this generalization, and one may argue that it is marked *positionally*. All known serial-verb languages are subject–first languages (SVO or SOV).
[30] These examples are cited from Givón (1975e), where the original sources are acknowledged.

(35) iywi awá òtsi ikù utsì
boy took stick shut door
'The boy shut the door with a stick'   (INSTRUMENTAL, Yatye)

(36) ū bìcì lō dzūká
he ran go market
'He ran to the market'   (LOCATIVE, Nupe)

(37) iywi awá ínyahwè awa ìtywi
boy took book went house
'The boy brought the book home'   (LOCATIVE, Yatye)

(38) mo mú ìwé wá fún ọ
I took book come give you   (DATIVE–BENE-
'I brought a book for you'   FACTIVE, Yoruba)

(39) Zhāng-sān bèi Lĭ-si piping le
Zhang-san submit Li-si criticize ASP   (AGENT-OF-PAS-
'Zhang-san was criticized by Li-si'   SIVE, Mandarin)[31]

The type of verb eventually giving rise to a particular case marker is amazingly consistent over wide areas of Africa and Southeast Asia, where this phenomenon is recorded at its most elaborate. Furthermore, it illustrates in the clearest fashion the intimate connection between syntacticization and the rise of grammatical morphology. The original, paratactic, loosely concatenated expression has no need for case marking, since each nominal argument is sufficiently identified, in terms of its case-function, by the verb to which it is paired in a small atomic clause. When the serial chain is reanalyzed as a single sentence with one complex verb, the problem of case marking then arises. This is so because the verb can mark only two arguments—topic-agent and object—positionally. But the syntacticization added more object arguments, and they need to be marked with respect to their case-function. Hence the "extra" verbs, which in a sense already had been functioning, in part, to mark the case-role of their paired arguments, now assume this case-marking function as their major raison d'être. The development of grammatical morphology thus becomes necessary when the language shifts from the paratactic to the syntactic mode.

5.2.9.2. FROM AUXILIARY VERBS TO
TENSE-ASPECT-MODALITY MARKERS

There is a small group of "auxiliary" verbs which, in an amazingly uniform fashion across languages, develop into highly specific tense–aspect modality markers, with the latter most commonly becoming—sooner or later—bound to the verb. The most common changes, cross-linguistically, are[32]

---

[31] This example is from Li and Thompson (1973a).
[32] For further discussion, see Givón (1973c).

(40)   *want* → FUTURE
        go → IRREALIS → FUTURE
        come → PERFECTIVE → PAST
        finish → PERFECTIVE → PAST
        have → PERFECTIVE → PAST
        be → PROGRESSIVE-HABITUAL → FUTURE
        start → FUTURE
        know → *can* → HABITUAL-POSSIBLE-PERMISSIBLE
        lack–fail–refuse → NEGATION
        done → PERFECTIVE → PAST

In most cases, the construction in which such changes take place is the equi-subject construction discussed in Section 5.2.4. Diachronically, the process thus involves the condensation–syntacticization of two loosely concatenated clauses, with the second one exhibiting subject anaphora under coreference (by either *zero*, an anaphoric pronoun or subject-agreement pronoun on the verb) into a single clause under a single intonation contour. Invariably the "main" verb becomes morphologized, most commonly as a tense–aspect–modal marker, while the second verb—semantically much more specific or "weighty"—remains the sole verb of the syntacticized construction. Once again, then, syntacticization and the rise of grammatical morphology seem to go hand in hand.[33]

5.3. AN INTERIM SUMMARY

In the preceding sections we have covered virtually all the major syntactic, tightly-bound, "subordinated" construction in language. In each instance, I have shown that many languages present evidence that such constructions arose diachronically, via the process of *syntacticization*, from looser, conjoined, paratactic constructions. Thus the entire process labeled by transformationalists as *embedding transformations* turns out to be a mere recapitulation of attested diachronic changes. I would like to suggest now that these diachronic processes should be properly viewed in the context of **the genesis of syntax ex-discourse**. Furthermore, I would like to posit two extreme poles of *communicative mode*: the *pragmatic* mode and the *syntactic* mode. In the cases surveyed above, we have been then dealing with the rise of the latter out of the former. That every human language known to us has *both* extremes—as well as any intermediate in between—will become

---

[33] It is most likely that the main–auxiliary verb already carried—as one of its functions—the signal for some tense–aspect–modal notion. The amazing universality of this process and the high semantic specificity of the verbs contributing to it, point in that direction. But in the syntacticized construction, the erstwhile verb has shed its other (earlier) functions and has become specialized.

5.3. An Interim Summary

rapidly obvious from the discussion further below. The extreme poles can, nevertheless, be characterized as such, in terms of their structural properties. This characterization is an *interim* one, and will be further elaborated below. In particular, I will attempt to probe in the following sections into the *functional parameters* which constrain the use of these two communicative modes.

(41)

	Pragmatic Mode	Syntactic Mode
a.	Topic–comment structure	Subject–predicate structure
b.	Loose conjunction	Tight subordination
c.	Slow rate of delivery (under several intonation contours)	Fast rate of delivery (under a single intonational contour)
d.	Word-order is governed mostly by one *pragmatic* principle: old information goes first, new information follows	Word-order is used to signal *semantic* case-functions (though it may also be used to indicate pragmatic–topicality relations)
e.	Roughly one-to-one ratio of verbs-to-nouns in discourse, with the verbs being semantically simple	A larger ratio of nouns-over-verbs in discourse, with the verbs being semantically complex
f.	No use of grammatical morphology	Elaborate use of grammatical morphology
g.	Prominent intonation–stress marks the focus of new information; topic intonation is less prominent	Very much the same, but perhaps not exhibiting as high a functional load, and at least in some languages totally absent

In the following sections I will attempt to show that to quite an extent this dichotomy also characterizes three other contrastive pairs of human communication: Pidgin versus Creole, Child versus Adult, and Informal versus Formal language.

5.4. PIDGINS AND CREOLES

It is appropriate to discuss this topic next, since in a way it involves similar *diachronic* developments as the ones shown above, although in this case they are much more rapid. The difference between Pidgin and Creole languages has often been obscured in earlier studies. More recently it has been shown[34] that the two types of language contrast sharply in some rather fundamental ways. Briefly, it seems that Pidgin languages (or at least the most prevalent type of Plantation Pidgins) exhibit an enormous amount of internal variation and inconsistency both within the output of the same speaker as well as across the speech community. The variation is so massive to the point where one is indeed justified in asserting that the Pidgin mode has *no stable syntax*. No consistent "grammatical" word-order can be shown in a Pidgin, and little or no use of grammatical morphology. The rate of delivery is excruciatingly slow and halting, with many pauses. Verbal clauses are small, normally exhibiting a one-to-one ratio of nouns to verbs. While the subject–predicate structure is virtually undeterminable, the topic–comment structure is transparent. Virtually no syntactic subordination can be found, and verbal clauses are loosely concatenated, usually separated by considerable pauses. In other words, the Pidgin speech exhibits almost an extreme case of the *pragmatic* mode of communication.

In contrast, the Creole—apparently a synthesis *di novo* by the first generation of native speakers who received the Pidgin as their data input and proceeded to "create the grammar"—is very much like normal languages, in that it possesses a syntactic mode with all the trimmings described in (41) above.[35] The amount of variation in the Creole speech is much smaller than in the Pidgin, indistinguishable from the normal level found in "normal" language communities. While Creoles exhibit certain uniform and highly universal characteristics which distinguish them, in degree though not in kind, from other normal languages,[36] they certainly possess the entire range of grammatical signals used in the syntax of natural languages, such as fixed word order, grammatical morphology, intonation, embedding, and various constraints.

The most fascinating feature of Pidgin speech is the fact that while it seems "not to have any syntax," its pragmatics at the discourse level is virtually intact. Thus, while identifying subject and predicate is a tantalizingly difficult task, identifying the message—and in particular the topic and comment—is much easier. Let me illustrate this peculiar quality of the Pidgin by an example taken out of transcripts collected by D. Bickerton from a Japanese Pidgin-English speaker in Hawaii.[37]

---

[34] Bickerton (1975a, 1977), Bickerton and Odo (1976, 1977), Bickerton and Givón (1976).

[35] Bickerton and Odo (1977) claim that Hawaiian Creole has a higher frequency of topicalized (as against grammatical) subjects than "normal" natural languages. However, they compare an extremely *informal* register of Hawaiian Creole with Standard Educated American English. See discussion in Section 5.6.

[36] See Bickerton (1975a), Givón (1975g), Kay and Sankoff (1974), Traugott (1977), and Slobin (1977).

[37] The speaker was a Japanese male, age 90, recorded in the island of Hawaii where he had lived since 1907—close to 70 years. The data is courtesy of Derek Bickerton and his tape collection. I have marked with [. . .] interclausal intonation breaks and with wider spacing more major breaks. The spelling has been adjusted closer to standard English.

(42)   . . . *Oh me?* . . .
       Oh me over there . . .
       nineteen-twenty over there say come . . .
       store me stop begin open . . .
       me sixty year . . .
       little more sixty year . . .
       now me ninety . . .
       na ehm . . .
       little more . . .
       this man ninety-two . . .
       yeah, this month over . . .
       me Hawaii come [desu] . . .
       nineteen-seven come . . .
       me number first here . . .
       me-[wa] *tell* . . .
       You sabe guruméru? . . .
       You no sabe guruméru? . . .
       yeah, this place come . . .
       this place been two-four-five year . . .
       stop, ey . . .
       then me go home. . . .
       Japan . . .
       by-m-by wife hapái ('carry') . . .
       by-m-by . . . little boy . . . come . . .
       by-m-by he been come here . . . ey . . .
       by-m-by come . . .
       by-m-by me before Hui-Hui stop . . .
       Hui-Hui this . . .
       eh . . . he . . . this a . . . Manuel . . . you sabe [ka]? . . .

The creation of a Creole language out of the Pidgin thus represents another instance of syntacticization. The Pidgin mode of communication is essentially our pragmatic mode (41). The Creole went on to develop the syntactic mode out of it. The important question to raise at this point is: What are the conditions which, in the Pidgin, govern the exclusive use of the pragmatic mode only? At this point I would like to suggest three of those:

(43)   a. Communicative stress. *The Pidgin-speaking community is thrown together **without a common language** but has urgent tasks to perform.*

       b. Lack of common pragmatic background. *Members of the Pidgin community come from different cultural and racial communities, they **share relatively little of the general,*** *pragmatic presuppositional background which forms the general context for human communication.*[38]

c. Immediately obvious context. *The tasks or topics of communication in the Pidgin-using society are immediate, obvious and nonremote. They are **right there** in both time and space, involving various–largely physical–tasks to be performed on the plantation.*

The communicative stress and the lack of common pragmatic background are the chief contributors to the *slow rate* of communication. But to some extent the obviousness of the *immediate context* and *tasks* is what makes this mode of communication possible at all.

The Creole society, on the other hand, grew slowly out of the Pidgin situation. Children took the normal 5–7 years to create a grammar, the range of subjects, contexts and tasks to be dealt with has expanded to the normal social range. Years of living together have created an increasing body of common pragmatic background and common cultural assumptions, as well as a growing knowledge of members of the community, their personality and motivation. On this facilitating background, the syntactic mode of communication, with its condensation, time-saving and structuralized, automated coding procedures, can evolve.

5.5 CHILD VERSUS ADULT LANGUAGE

Some hints suggesting that early child language is basically of the pragmatic mode come as early as Gruber (1967b), with his now forgotten observation that early child language seems to abound with *topics* at the expense of subjects. For a while this pioneering insight was buried under a veritable avalanche of purely syntactic studies, purporting to document the acquisition of *structure* without reference to communicative skills. By now the pendulum has swung the other way, and a growing number of studies show that children first acquire a *communicative system,* and that in all fundamental ways this early communicative system exhibits the characteristics of our *pragmatic* mode (41).[39] Its rate of delivery is slow, it is concatenated rather than embedded, it lacks grammatical morphology, the noun-to-verb ratio approaches one-to-one, topics prevail over subjects, word order is mostly

---

[38] As suggested in Chapters 2 and 3, communication takes place on a vast background of a shared (presupposed) universe of knowledge, including real-world knowledge, cultural conventions, social structure, the likely motivation of one's interlocutor(s), etc. Knowledge of the preceding discourse is a subset of this background.

[39] Some of the studies in this rapidly growing field include Elinor Keenan (1974a, 1974b, 1975a, 1975b, 1977), Keenan and Schieffelin (1976), Bates (1974, 1976), Sconlon (1974, 1976), Greenfield and Smith (1976), and Bloom (1973).

5.5. Child versus Adult Language

pragmatic, and one of the earliest discernible principles is that of assigning higher intonation contours to the focus of new information.

In terms of the characteristics of the communicative situation prevailing at the early stages of child language, we find a striking parallel with what was described for Pidgins (43) above:

(44) a. Communicative stress. *The child is thrown into the world with urgent functions to be taken care of and no mode of communication to be shared with the surrounding human community.*

b. Lack of common pragmatic background. *The child obviously lacks the shared common background of knowing the world, the culture, the social structure, and the probable motivation of his interlocutors.*

c. Immediately obvious context. *Early child communication involves immediately obvious topics, tasks, and contexts of the here-and-now, the most immediate and obvious of which is of course the child himself.*

As Elinor Keenan (1977) has pointed out, what follows in the subsequent development of the adult linguistic skills from the child's mode is a gradual change in the parameters which govern the communicative situation (44). The communicative stress slowly eleviates, as the child acquires language skills. Larger and larger portions of the common pragmatic background are acquired. The range of topics, tasks, and contexts slowly enlarges itself from the immediate to less immediate, from the obvious to less obvious, from the concrete to the more abstract. This is paralleled by the shift in communicative mode, from the early child's totally *pragmatic* mode toward the gradual acquisition of the *syntactic* mode. The child never loses the early mode, and as an adult he controls an entire *scale*, from the extreme pragmatic to the extreme syntactic. The epitome of the latter is the formal, *written* mode (see discussion in Section 5.6). But the adult may always, under the appropriate communicative situation, revert back to a largely *pragmatic* mode. The type of communication used by adults learning a *second language* is largely of the pragmatic mode, as is the *Pidgin* register. This earliest-acquired type of communication, then, remains with us through life. In some fundamental ways, it must be considered our *embryonic, rudimentary* form of communication.[40] Furthermore, while the study of universals of language has confined itself, under both transformational and nontransformational schools, almost exclusively to the syntactic mode, it is quite likely that the pragmatic mode is actually the *most* universal component

---

[40] The obvious phylogenetic implications of this, in terms of the evolution of human language, will be discussed in Chapter 7.

of our communicative skills, the bottom-line register shared by all humans.

To sum up, then, in the development of the adult linguistic mode out the the child's, one observes a striking parallel to the diachronic processes discussed in Sections 5.2 and 5.3 as well as to the development of the Creole mode out of the Pidgin. In each case the syntactic mode evolved over time out of the pragmatic mode. The process of syntacticization is strikingly similar in those three. In the following section I will discuss the consequences of such development in the adult, non-Pidgin speaker, that is, the coexistance of a *range* of registers or communicative modes, with the extremes being our syntactic and pragmatic modes.

5.6. INFORMAL VERSUS FORMAL SPEECH

One of the greatest shocks administered to the psyche of a devout generative linguist is likely to come on that rare day when he makes the unfortunate move toward tackling natural, live, informal, and unsolicited speech. Such an experience may result in the total collapse of the intricate frame of grammaticality and competence, an edifice which was erected initially in order to insulate the generative linguist from precisely such a discouraging confrontation with the real world of language data. If a linguist is honest about his empirical responsibilities, then at some point in his/her career he/she has to face the profound—and disturbingly *scalar*—difference between the formal and informal registers of adult language. The first, the formal register, has been the traditional stock in trade of the linguist and almost his sole data input. In this sense the transformationalist and the traditional grammarian have shared a common prejudice, though while the traditionalist tends to ignore the informal register because of deep-seated *prescriptive* prejudices, the transformationalist dismisses the data as chaotic, degenerate, and reflecting "performance" factors. The seemingly chaotic, nongrammatical nature of unplanned,[41] informal speech tends to parallel the situation found in early child language, and studies dealing with the structural properties and communicative constraints on informal speech are relatively recent. Earlier studies tended to dwell upon the social-interactional aspects of the transaction, while paying less attention to the information transaction and the grammatical structure.[42] More recently, a number of related studies focused on the difference between the informal and formal register.[43] These studies have been summarized by Elinor

---

[41] The terms "planned" versus "unplanned" discourse were introduced by Elinor Keenan (1977a). They overlap with my "formal" versus "informal" distinction.

[42] See Sacks, Schegloff, and Jefferson (1974), Schegloff (1973, 1979), Schegloff, Jefferson, and Sacks (1977).

[43] In a collection edited by Keenan and Bennett (1977), with the relevant papers being Elinor Keenan (1977), Bennett (1977), Kroll (1977), Shimanoff and Brunak (1977).

Keenan (1977, 1979), where she comments on the amazing parallelism between the child versus adult and the planned versus unplanned discourse registers.[44] In summary, informal–unplanned discourse tends to:

1. Show more topicalized (left-dislocated) constructions; these are almost entirely absent in the formal–planned register
2. Favor loose coordination over tight subordination, that is, less embedding
3. Involve more repetition, pauses, and in general an increased time of delivery
4. Involve a considerable reduction and simplification of the grammatical morphology, that is, reduced tense–aspect systems, less complex case morphology, dispensing with subordinating morphemes for both verb complements and relative clauses, an increased use of zero anaphora over anaphoric pronouns
5. Exhibit shorter verbal clauses, with fewer nominal arguments per verb
6. Exhibit a much more prominent topic–comment structure, as against the more prominent use of grammatical subjects in the planned–formal register

As Elinor Keenan points out in her summary, the adult has never forgotten his first-acquired communicative skill, our *pragmatic mode*. He simply added onto it, via the gradual rise of the *syntactic* mode. While it is unlikely that an adult, in relaxed informal conversation among people sharing his cultural and linguistic code, will revert *all* the way to the *extreme* pragmatic mode, the similarities are nevertheless quite striking. Furthermore, under situations of extreme communicative stress, such as those prevailing in the Pidgin situation or under a pressing need to communicate in a foreign language, the adult in fact reverts almost all the way[45] to the extreme pragmatic register on the scale.

When one turns to consider the communicative situation under which informal–unplanned discourse is used, a much more complex picture is found, with many parameters interacting with each other in a complex fashion. At the moment it seems to me that at least the following may be said:

1. *Communicative stress.* One very common type of informal communication is under relaxed conditions without time pressure, where planning is simply *not necessary*. On the other hand, under extreme

---

[44] Apparently, the research underlying this chapter and Elinor Keenan's work were carried on independently along similar lines. I am more than delighted to acknowledge this happy convergence.

[45] Given that the adult is already a mature speaker of *some* language, with a vast lexicon, an organized and coded world view, and many presuppositions about the universe and society, human motivation, and interaction, it is unlikely that he will revert *all* the way to the child's mode of communication.

emergency conditions, where there's no time for planning at all, pragmatic (unplanned) rather than syntactic speech is also used.[46]

2. *Time pressure.* While the most common pragmatic mode seems to involve *no time pressure,* emergency situations—including perhaps to a lesser degree the Pidgin and foreign-language situations—also seem to precipitate the use of the pragmatic mode.

3. *Degree of planning.* Here Elinor Keenan's characterization is quite apt. The pragmatic mode is, for whatever reason (too much time or no time at all), an unplanned mode, that is, *you plan as you go;*[47] the ultimate example of the planned mode is tight, educated written language.

4. *Face to face monitoring.* As Manny Schegloff (personal communication) has pointed out, face-to-face communication can afford to be less planned, less tightly organized, more repetitious, and seemingly more slapdash *precisely* because of the constant monitoring of the interlocutor, his following the topic, his degree of comprehension, and his reaction to the presuppositions upon which the communication floats. This affords the speaker the opportunity for instant repair, for repetition, for slowing down, for simplification and clarification as he follows the facial, gestural, and interjectional clues emitted by the hearer. Such repetition, repair, and slow-down are part of the characteristics of pragmatic speech.

5. *Shared general pragmatic background.* Here again we find a complex interaction with another factor, namely the *degree of immediately obvious context.* In general, informal speech is found first among *familiars* who share a large background of their pragmatic presuppositions about the universe and themselves. Under such conditions, the topic, context, or task for the communication may be less immediately obvious. On the other hand, this mode is also found among *strangers,* in superficial encounters. But there the topic, task, or context tend to be much more immediately obvious. These two factors tend to thus form an aggregate of shared background. The child's case and that of the Pidgin speaker fall at the same extreme here. That is, while the general pragmatic background is minimal, the communication is strictly face-to-face and involves mostly the immediately obvious, the here-and-now, the interlocutors themselves, thus tending to *preclude* third persons, past–future time and nonvisible space.

The extreme instance of the formal–planned pole is educated, book-written language, and it is therefore of great interest to assess the communicative parameters under which it is used. Those may be summarized as:

[46] For this suggestion I am indebted to Patricia Greenfield (personal communication).
[47] In terms of the overall time spent on planning *and* delivery, one may suspect that a certain balance prevails, so that the more time one spends on *pre*-planning, the less one spends on actual delivery. The extreme emergency situations (*fire!*) corresponds to neither extreme here, since there is little time for either preplanning or delivery.

1. There is extremely careful planning, with corrections, rewriting and reformulation.
2. Considerable time-pressure is, on the one hand, obvious in terms of saving space and reducing printing costs. On the other hand, a much longer time is spent on preplanning.
3. There is an almost total lack of communicative stress, since the message usually is written for delayed reading.[48]
4. There is a total absence of face-to-face monitoring.
5. A relatively small body of presuppositional background is assumed at the very onset, since one is then in fact writing *for strangers*.[49] However, the presuppositional background is then built up gradually, in a carefully-planned manner, with each new line increasing it, to the point where the expository portion gives way to the main body of the narrative.
6. There is virtually no immediately obvious context, topic, or task. Typically, one writes about other times, other places, and nonpresent people.

The written register, much like the formal public-address register, is thus the utmost mode of communication in the *mass society of strangers*. It is a product of need; it is there for a purpose. Conversely, since language evolved as an oral tool, initially in immediately obvious contexts, dealing with immediately obvious topics and tasks, involving face-to-face communication among small groups of intimates who shared much of the pragmatic presuppositions about their universe and its social and motivational structure, an inescapable conclusion is that in the evolution of language, the pragmatic mode was the *earlier* type of human communication, while the syntactic mode is a later outgrowth from it.[50] I will return to this topic in Chapter 7.

5.7. DISCUSSION

5.7.1. Diachrony and Child Development

There seems to be an inescapable connection between diachrony and child development in the sense that processes that seem to occur as the child modifies its early communicative mode via syntacticization are

---

[48] In writing under time-pressure, the characteristics of the register veer sharply toward the pragmatic mode, as may be seen in Janda (1976).

[49] Obviously the reduction could not be complete here, since as the context, task, and topic are not immediately obvious, communication could not proceed unless there was *some* shared background.

[50] There are no linguistic communities known to me in which *only* the pragmatic mode is used. So obviously, the human species wherever it be has evolved to the point where nonimmediately-obvious contexts, topics, and tasks can be dealt with, and where one may communicate with strangers as well as with—sometimes overwhelmingly—with familiars. To the extent that written language represents the apex of the syntactic mode, the majority of societies (and speakers) do not exhibit that extreme.

identical to processes which create syntactic structures in language over time. This probably involves an active, creative interaction between the corrective, instructive adult input and the evolving needs of the communicative situation. But the causal relation is far from clear, and it may well be that language evolves diachronically the way it does *precisely* because children indulge in syntacticization under specific communicative constraints, needs, and requirements.

5.7.2. The Diachronic Cycle

While pragmatics gives rise to syntax, syntax in turn gives rise to grammatical morphology, which then decays via phonological attrition.[51] At least at their present stage, it seems, human languages keep renovating their syntax via syntacticizing discourse.

5.7.3. Universality and Evolution

It seems rather clear that the pragmatic mode of human communication, as previously defined in (41), is ontogenetically and phylogenetically earlier, and, in terms of cross-language attestation, more universal than the syntactic mode. At the syntactic level, languages tend to diverge enormously. At the pragmatic level, they tend to be amazingly similar. The fact that this mode is always used under the stressful conditions of no common language—as in Pidgins or foreign-talk—simply underscores its status as the *universal common denominator*.

5.7.4. Coexisting Registers

A mature speaker has not lost his earlier mode, but rather has slowly acquired progressively more syntacticized registers. While the extremes on this scale are attested in early child speech and in formal, educated written language, a complex interaction of communicative parameters—as discussed earlier—determines the choice (or necessity) of the appropriate point on the register scale.

5.7.5. Coding Modalities in Syntax

Out of the four major coding modalities used in the syntactic mode—rigid word-order, grammatical morphology, constraints,[52] and intonation—the first three arise together via the process of syntacticiza-

---

[51] Here the *semantic bleaching* of lexical words into grammatical morphemes goes hand in hand with the phonological bleaching (reduction), that is, destressing, cliticization, and assimilatory erosion.

[52] By "constraints" I mean conditions such as coreference, case-identity, parallel structure, etc., which are normally associated with so-called syntactic transformations.

tion, and should be viewed as its necessary correlates. Intonation, on the other hand, remains largely pragmatic and may or may not be used in the syntactic mode.[53]

5.7.6. On Explaining Synchronic Syntax

Quite often it turns out that the structure of synchronic syntax cannot be understood without reference to either diachronic or developmental processes. In either case the process of syntacticization, which brings syntax into being, cannot be understood without reference to its initial departure point, the pragmatic mode, as well as to the communicative parameters which govern its evolution, ontogenetically and diachronically.

5.7.7. Grammar as an Automatic Processing Strategy

One may view the rise of rigid word-order, condensed—tight, subordinate—syntactic constructions, rich grammatical morphology, and tight syntactic constraints–rules, as the rise of *automatic processing* of speech. The pragmatic mode is analytic and slow, and it has a high degree—for all practical purpose 100%—of communicative fidelity, a one-to-one correlation between code and message. But it is also a cumbersome mode, requiring a high degree of face-to-face interaction and often limited to topics, tasks, and context that are not too far removed from here, now, and us. In the syntactic mode one may view the more evolved coding devices as the *tools* of automatic processing. But while one gains speed, one loses resolution, since in syntax the correlation between form and meaning is typically somewhere *below* 100%. The syntactic mode is thus used only when other parameters which govern the communicative situation make it possible to *offset* such a loss. Does syntax exist, then? Yes and no. It does exist as a mode of linguistic communication, and it does have highly specific structural properties. Therefore the extreme position as represented by García (1977) seems rather untenable. On the other hand, syntax can neither be understood nor can it be explained without reference to *both* its evolution ex-discourse as well as to the communicative parameters and principles which govern both its rise out of the pragmatic mode and its selective use along the register scale of human communication. Therefore the other extreme position, that of the transformational-generative orthodoxy, seems even more untenable.

---

[53] Most typically, languages with a highly productive lexical tone, as well as those with a highly productive use of the pragmatic word-order principle of topic–comment, tend to make less use of intonation as a signal for topic–focus relations. Mandarin Chinese and Yoruba are examples of the first type, and current Spanish of the second. English, on the other hand, is one of the most extreme examples of rigid word-order and a highly evolved use of pragmatic intonation. For more details, see Bolinger (1958, 1972, 1977a, 1977b, 1977c).

6

LANGUAGE CHANGE
where does crazy syntax come from: diachronic constraints on synchronic grammars

6.1. INTRODUCTION[1]

In Chapter 5, it was suggested that the synchronic characteristics of syntactic structures cannot be understood without some reference to the diachronic processes which gave them rise. The syntactic structures whose origin ex-discourse we investigated there were all of a very general sort. They are, in fact, the most standard *universal,* run-of-the-mill syntactic structures found in human language. The data I propose to investigate in this chapter, on the other hand, are from a purely synchronic point of view a bit crazy. That is, in every case they involve a glaring infringement upon general principles which govern human communication, such as message transparency, one-to-one correlation between form and meaning, consistency of coding conventions, or ease of processing. These principles, one must add, seldom manifest themselves in the structure of any language in an *absolute* fashion. In fact, we have already seen that syntax (or "the grammar") at its best is a flawed instrument of communication, with less than 100% fidelity. The type of "crazy syntax" discussed here is therefore *relative* to the attested level of communicative efficacy found in language at its best. What I will argue here is that, in each instance, a *crazy* synchronic state of the grammar has arisen via diachronic changes that are highly *natural* and, presumably, motivated independently by various communicative factors.

[1] I am indebted to Dwight Bolinger, Robert Hetzron, and Winfred Lehmann for suggestions and comments on an earlier version of this chapter. I would also like to acknowledge Larry Hyman's paper (LSA Winter, San Diego, 1973) "How do natural rules become unnatural?," which prompted me to see the obvious parallels between phonology and syntax.

Given that a language—any language—is at any given point in time in the middle of numerous ongoing diachronic changes in its grammar, one must now raise a fundamental question concerning our notion of *naturalness* in linguistics: If synchronic grammar is, indeed, forever a function or reflection of diachronic change, and if, furthermore, crazy or unnatural[2] synchronic states in grammar can and do arise in a massive way out of natural, communicatively motivated diachronic change, then from what area of our language data should we derive our understanding of what is natural in human language?

The question posed above lies at the very heart of a complex interaction between the steady-state object that language presumably is to its *speaker* at any given point during communication, and language as a phenomenon in the middle of flux within the *very same* speaker at the *very same* time during communication. It is of course not an accident that the data of synchronic variation within the speech of both an individual and a community turn out to overlap with the data of diachronic change. These rather embarrassing facts have a way of intruding, again and again, on the secure world of the structuralist. Thus Saussure and the Bloomfieldians insisted that facts concerning diachronic change, that is, how the language arrived at its present synchronic state, should be studied in a separate subdiscipline, namely, via diachronic linguistics. So far as one can tell, there was nothing dogmatic about this separation in Saussure's *Course,* where he acknowledges that the separation between the "flux" and "state" in language can be only achieved via a certain measure of abstraction.[3] In fact, Saussure comes close in some of his comments to recognizing the fundamental unity of synchronic and diachronic linguistics.[4] In practice, however, he was responsible for separating the two subfields of linguistics, a separation adopted by the Bloomfieldian as a significant, a priori methodological stricture and as such swallowed whole-hog by the transformationalists.[5] Under the ensu-

---

[2] The notion "unnatural" in language may have two distinct readings: (*a*) "Less commonly found in languages," and (*b*) "Communicatively disruptive." For reasons that will be made apparent later in this chapter, the two senses do not *always* coincide.

[3] "In practice a language-state is not a point but rather a certain span of time during which the sum of the modifications that have supervened is minimal. . . . Studying a language-state means in practice disregarding changes of little importance. . . . In static linguistics, as in most sciences, no course of reasoning is possible without the usual simplification of the data [Saussure, 1915, pp. 101–102]." Saussure does not make it explicit whether the simplification is only a methodological preliminary upon which a permanent *theoretical* edifice should not be constructed.

[4] In referring to the synchronic identity of the same form as representing the same meaning, as against the diachronic identity of one form-meaning element with its diachronic antecedent, Saussure writes: "That is why I could state that knowing how *Gentlemen!* retains its identity when repeated several times during a lecture is just as interesting as knowing why *pas* (negation) is identical to *pas* (noun) in French, or again, why *chaud* is identical to *calidum*. . . . The second problem is really but an extension and a complication of the first. . . . [1915, p. 182]."

[5] Again, there is nothing in Bloomfield's *Language* itself to suggest the irrelevance of synchronic and diachronic analysis to each other. Rather, he seems to be arguing for a practical shift of emphasis,

ing tradition, it is assumed that "the language" is a static object manipulated or "learned" by speakers (i.e., Saussure's *langue* or Chomsky's *competence*), rather than a dynamic system of communication where one strategy is always in the process of being modified into another.

The relevance of the history of the language to its present state depends, rather obviously, on the goals adopted by the linguist. If his analysis confines itself to *describing* what the speaker knows about his/her language, chances are high that diachrony is irrelevant to the speaker's ability to manipulate his communicative system. However, if the linguist strives to *understand* why the structure of language is the way it is,[6] then—as I will attempt to show—the diachronic rise of that structure as well as the communicative principles which govern it become enormously germane.

6.2. CRAZY SYNCHRONIC PHONOLOGY

In this section I would like to illustrate briefly how in other areas of the grammar, for example, phonology, precedents exist—rather massively—for natural diachronic change giving rise to bizarre synchronic states. The argument follows Hyman (1973), and I will illustrate it by data from Swahili. In this language, a gliding rule that is rather widespread in Bantu is observed, and one of its attestations is:

(1) $\qquad i \rightarrow y\ /\ \text{\_\_\_\_}V$

The motivation for this rule, a rather universal one, is a transparent *dissimilatory* motivation, namely, the resolution of VV sequences into WV sequences (when the two vowels are different), and falls within the framework of the idealized CVCV distribution of vowels and consonants in language, a distribution with both acoustic and articulatory motivation. Next, another change occurred in the language, this time of an *assimilatory* nature, of palatalization:

(2) $\qquad k \rightarrow c\ /\ \text{\_\_\_\_}y$

The natural articulatory motivation for rule (2) is quite transparent, and it is one of the most common assimilatory changes in language. Finally, a third change occurred, with probably a combination of assimilatory *and* dissimilatory motivation, one that can be labeled "glide swallowing":

---

from the largely diachronic preoccupation of the neogrammarians toward more descriptive work: "We can study linguistic change only by comparing related languages or different historical stages of the same language . . . (1933, pp. 16–17)."

[6] One could of course say, after Chomsky, that the structure of language is *innate*, that is, prewired into our neural apparatus. But that amounts to terminating the investigation rather prematurely, with all the interesting questions left unanswered, indeed unasked.

(3) $\quad cy \to c\ /\ \text{\underline{}}V$

The rule (3) may be viewed as a cluster simplification rule, that is, converting CGV sequences into CV sequences and thus motivated by the universal idealized CVCV distribution. However, it has an assimilatory component, namely that only if the glide and the preceding consonant are articulated at the same point will rule (3) occur. Such a restriction is of course familiar from English, and may have to do with the need to insure recoverable deletion.[7] The result of the application of all three rules in historical order to /ki-V/ sequences in Swahili may be illustrated in:

(4)
Old form	New form	Gloss
*ki-engo	c-engo	'dwelling'
*ki-ama	c-ama	'association'
*ki-upa	c-upa	'bottle'
*ki-o ki-ote	c-o c-ote	'any' (class 7/8, sg.)
*ki-ini	ki-ini	'kernel'

Since many of the changes are attested in stem-internal positions, what we have here in effect is a phonemic split, where the old phoneme /k/ gave rise to /k/ and /c/. But the distribution of the two phonemes synchronically is rather bizarre: /k/ appears before all five vowels, that is, sequences such as /ka, ko, ku, ke, ki/ are attested. But /c/ appears only before four of the vowels, so that sequences such as /ca, co, cu, ce/ are attested. But no sequences such as /*ci/ or /*cy/ are now attested. The synchronic craziness of this state of affairs is rather obvious, with /ki/ attested and /*ci/ unattested. In a rather glaring fashion it goes against universal predictions as to which vowels will palatalize consonants and which will not. But nevertheless, such an unnatural synchronic state arose from the concatenation—in historical order—of three highly natural phonetic changes. If a linguist took the synchronic facts of Swahili at face value as representing naturalness in phonology, he would draw rather bizarre conclusions. On the other hand, by studying the diachronic sequence of changes which led to the current state of affairs, the linguist is bound to gain better understanding of what is natural and universal. What I propose to do in the rest of this chapter is illustrate the viability of a similar argument in syntax.

6.3. TYPOLOGICAL INCONSISTENCIES BETWEEN MORPHOLOGY AND SYNTAX

In his pioneering article, Joseph Greenberg (1966) observed a correlation between the morphemic and syntactic order of languages,

---

[7] See Hudson (1974) for further discussion.

whereby OV languages tended to exhibit *suffixal* bound morphology and VO languages *prefixal* morphology. As I have pointed out elsewhere,[8] this correlation is in essence of a diachronic origin. That is, certain word types within specific syntactic constructions tend to give rise to specific morpheme types, and the syntactic order prevailing within those constructions at the time of cliticization perforce determines the morphotactic order within a compound arising from that construction.[9] Greenberg also observed that many VO languages, with English being a representative example, do not abide by this correlation very consistently, and exhibit mostly suffixal morphology. As I pointed out (Givón, 1971), such inconsistencies arise because of a sequence of natural diachronic changes:

1. A layer of morphology arises and at that time "conforms" to the prevailing syntactic typology of the languages.
2. Due to highly natural processes[10] the syntax of the language changes, while the old morphology—being bound—remains as a frozen relic.

As a result of such concatenation of independent diachronic changes, all presumably motivated by communicative factors, a language thus becomes synchronically "of mixed typology." There is no solid psycholinguistic evidence that speakers of a VO language with a predominantly suffixal morphology are aware of that "inconsistency." Nor is there solid evidence to suggest that, somehow, because of the VO word order, they expect to process speech via the use of prefixal morphemic signals rather than the "inconsistent" suffixes. With crucial experiments yet to be designed and carried out, there are nevertheless reasons for assuming, in a rather tentative way, that when the *same* phenomenon in the grammar is *coded inconsistently* by the morphology, such a situation may in fact constitute an instance of "communicatively crazy" syntax. In this section I would like to discuss two illustrative examples of this type.

6.3.1. Frozen Object Pronouns

In a number of language groups which are currently VO or drifting toward VO but used to be typologically OV at some earlier time, one finds the phenomenon of OV syntax for pronominal objects but VO syntax for nominal objects. In all cases, the pronouns involved are clitics, that is, bound as prefixes to the verbal word and thus without freedom. Since there are grounds for believing that nominal direct objects are the

---

[8] Givón (1971, 1975e).
[9] For some examples, see Section 5.2.9.
[10] For a discussion of natural causes of syntactic change, see Vennemann (1973a), Givón (1975e), Hyman (1975), Ard (1976), and Givón (1977a).

neutral pattern in syntax,[11] one may well argue that a situation of this kind merely exhibits the utilization of word-order differences to code the more-marked pattern of pronominal object as against the unmarked pattern of nominal direct objects. Furthermore, in VO language that used to be OV, such as Romance, Bantu, or Iroquois, the preverbal position of clitic object pronouns in fact conforms to a very general pragmatic principle governing word order, by which *more topical* ("old," "presupposed") information goes first.[12] This principle can be illustrated independently in English, where object pronouns are *not* bound, but nevertheless have a tendency to precede nominal objects and thus come closer to the verb. Thus consider:[13]

(5)   a. *John gave a book to Mary*
       b. *John gave her a book*
       c. *John gave a book to hér*
       d. **John gave a bóok to her*
       e. *John gave it to Mary*
       f. **John gave Mary it*

While there is a difference between accusative and dative pronouns, the seemingly acceptable pattern (5c) is only acceptable under *contrastive* stress, that is, a more-marked pattern. Now, while the Spanish, Bantu, or Iroquois object pronouns are *frozen* preverbally, one could nevertheless assert that they got frozen at their *natural* pragmatic position, so that the current discrepancy between VO nominal syntax and OV pronominal syntax in those languages is actually communicatively justified and thus not crazy at all. In order to show that this is not the case, let us observe what languages with such a discrepancy are currently doing with their pronominal syntax.

In Spanish, under simple, nonemphatic anaphoric situations, only the preverbal clitic object pronoun is used:

(6)   *la ví a María*
             PRO saw PREP Mary
             'I saw Mary'

(7)   *la ví*
             'I saw her'

Furthermore, for human direct objects as well as for (human) dative

---

[11] See Chapter 2.
[12] For a general discussion, see Bolinger (1952).
[13] For further discussion of this phenomenon in English and more support for viewing it as governed by discourse-pragmatic features, see Shir (1979).

6.3. Typological Inconsistencies between Morphology and Syntax 241

objects, the clitic preverbal pronoun is obligatory, and thus in fact has become an object agreement marker on the verb:[14]

(8)   a. *vi a María
              b. *le dí el libro a Juan*
                  'I gave the book to John'
              c. **dí el libro a Juan*

Emphatic pronouns conform to the VO pattern:

(9)   a. *la dí el libro a élla*
                  'I gave the book *to hér*'
              b. **dí el libro a élla*

Thus, if a pronoun is not bound, it conforms to the unmarked nominal VO syntax. Here one could still argue that this fact is still consonant with the discourse-pragmatic principle already mentioned, since emphatic–contrastive pronouns are more "new information" than unstressed anaphoric pronouns. There is a good reason to believe that when an anaphoric pronoun becomes cliticized as grammatical agreement on the verb, and then the more emphatic independent pronoun is used emphatically, sooner or later the anaphoric function of the clitic–agreement morpheme recedes, due to phonological attrition, and the erstwhile emphatic–independent pronoun then becomes *de-marked* toward simple-anaphoric function. I have reported such a process for Biblical Hebrew *subject* pronouns, where in Early Biblical Hebrew the independent subject pronouns are used only emphatically–contrastively, but in Late Biblical Hebrew as well as in Modern Hebrew there is less and less use of the subject-agreement conjugation in anaphora, and consequently the independent pronouns now serve as both anaphoric and emphatic.[15] A similar phenomenon may be reported for the object pronouns of Hebrew, where in Biblical Hebrew the bound suffix pronouns are used for anaphora, but in Modern Hebrew that usage is considered *archaic*, and only the independent object pronouns are used anaphorically.[16] To some extent one could predict this development in Spanish, where when an ambiguity of interpretation is possible, the independent

---

[14] See discussion in Givón (1976a). In some dialects of Spanish this may be a "less obligatory" process. That is, it may not be totally categorial, in other words, at the level of analysis of "competence." But even there it is of very high frequency in "performance," that is, in actual texts.

[15] See Givón (1977a).

[16] Hetzron (personal communication) has pointed out that in Biblical Hebrew one can find also the intermediate state—as in Spanish—where the object pronoun suffixes cooccur with the independent, emphatic personal pronouns (and probably also with the emphatic full noun). This represents, at least in principle, a potential for the development of obligatory object agreement—at least for definite ("more topical") objects. The more modern dialects do not show such a development, and in fact such data seem to be rare in the Old Testament. One may thus say that this potential was somehow "aborted."

object pronoun becomes almost obligatory with a less-than-emphatic interpretation.[17] Thus consider:

(10) a. *la ví sentanda en el jardín*
PRO saw sitting in the garden
{ ?'I saw her as she was sitting in the garden'
'I saw her as I was sitting in the garden' } (woman speaker)

b. *la ví a ella sentando en el jardín*
PRO saw PREP she sitting in the garden
{ 'I saw her as she was sitting in the garden'
?'I saw her as I was sitting in the garden' } (woman speaker)

c. *lo ví ayer hablando con María*
PRO saw yesterday talking with Mary
{ 'I saw him yesterday as he was talking to Mary'
'I saw him yesterday as I was talking to Mary' }

d. *lo ví a el ayer hablando con María*
PRO saw PREP he yesterday talking with Mary
{ 'I saw *him* yesterday as he was talking with Mary'
?'I saw him yesterday when I was talking with Mary' }

Facts such as (10) above represent the slow, gradual move to transfer the anaphoric function from the preverbal clitics to the postverbal independent pronouns, eventually bringing the language back to typological consistency.

A similar tendency may be currently observed over the Bantu dialect area. The more conservative situation may be demonstrated in Swahili, where the postverbal independent pronouns are used only emphatically:

(11) a. *ni-me-mu-ona* (ANAPHORIC)
I-ASP-him-see
'I saw him'

b. *ni-me-mu-one yéye (mwenyewe)* (EMPHATIC)
I-ASP-him-see he (himself)
'I saw *him*'

A more advanced situation is found in Zulu.[18] Here the contrast between the anaphoric preverbal clitics and the emphatic independent pronouns is still evident, as in:

---

[17] This suggestion was first made to me by Hector Morales (personal communication).
[18] For the data see Kunene (1975).

(12)   a. *u-ya-yi-shaya*   (ANAPHORIC)
            he-ASP-it-hit
            'He hit it'

        b. *u-shaya yona*   (EMPHATIC)
            he-hit *it*
            'He hit *thát one*'

In addition, however, one finds several other combinations with "more subtle" contrastive use of the independent postverbal pronoun. Thus:

(13)   a. *u-shaya yona imbongolo*
            he-hit *it* donkey
            'He hit it, *the dónkey*'

        b. *u-ya-yi-shaya yona*
            he-ASP-*it*-hit *it*
            '. . . (but) he hit *ít* (instead)'

        c. *u-ya-yi-shaya yona imbongolo*
            he-ASP-*it*-hit *it* donkey
            '. . . (but) he hit *ít*, *the dónkey* (instead)'

The situation in Zulu is thus an intermediate, reminiscent of Spanish, where the rising frequency of cases in which the clitic pronoun cooccurs obligatorily either with the independent pronoun or the nominal object itself creates the background for reanalysis, whereby (*a*) the clitic pronoun will be analyzed as an automatic object-agreement marker (as is already the case for human and definite objects in both Zulu and Swahili[19]), and (*b*) the anaphora function will transfer from the clitic pronoun to the independent, erstwhile emphatic pronoun.

Finally, one finds in the Northwestern Bantu area the most advanced situation, where the clitic object pronouns do not exist any more and anaphoric (as well as emphatic) functions are carried out by the erstwhile independent pronouns—that appear in a *postverbal* position. Thus consider the following data from Duala:[20]

(14)   a. *esukudu y-emedi   wa*
            school   it-accepted *you*
            'The school accepted you'

        b. *a-sengan-e   mo*
            he-listen-DAT *him*
            'He listens to him'

---

[19] See discussion in Givón (1976a).
[20] The data are from Epée (1975).

c. *diboa di-bó mó*
    ailment it-kill *him*
    'An ailment killed him'

It thus seems that, regardless of the soundness of the discourse-pragmatic principle discussed previously, when VO languages renovate their object pronouns, they bring them back in line with the nominal VO word-order. Such diachronic evidence strongly supports the suggestion that the typological inconsistency between OV pronominal syntax and VO nominal syntax is not only glaring to the linguist, but also in some sense "communicatively uncomfortable" to the speakers, who eliminate that inconsistency from their grammar over time.

The next example involves Amharic, an ex-VSO language which changed via contact with its massive Kushitic substratum to SOV. Here we find, with respect to object pronouns, the opposite situation, whereby nominal objects are preverbal while the anaphoric clitic pronouns are postverbal. Thus consider:[21]

(15) a. *Kassa borsa wǝssǝdǝ*
        Kassa wallet took
        'Kassa took a wallet'

   b. *Kassa borsa-w-n   wǝssǝdǝ-w*
       Kassa wallet-the-OBJ took-*it*
       'Kassa took the wallet'

   c. *Kassa wǝssǝdǝ-w*
       Kassa took-*it*
       'Kassa took it'

   d. *Kassa borsa-w-n   lǝ-Mulu sǝtṭa-at*
       Kassa wallet-the-OBJ to-Mulu gave-*her*
       'Kassa gave the wallet to Mulu'

   e. *Kassa borsa-w-n   sǝtṭ-at*
       Kassa wallet-the-OBJ gave-*her*
       'Kassa gave her the wallet'

When an emphatic independent pronoun is used in Amharic, however, it conforms to the unmarked SOV order of nominal syntax. Thus:

(16)   *Kassa borsa-w-n   lǝ-sswa sǝtṭa-at*
        Kassa wallet-the-OBJ to-*her* gave-*her*
        'Kassa gave the wallet to *hér*'

And since the object-clitic pronouns function as an almost[22] obligatory

---

[21] Some of the data were summarized in Givón (1976a), but see also Haile (1970) and Fulas (1974).

[22] Hetzron (personal communication) has pointed out that the agreement of suffix object pronouns is obligatory only if the definite–topical object noun is "presentative," that is, if it is to be talked about as

agreement for definite (or topical) objects, the situation is all set toward the eventual de-marking of the independent pronoun, as in Spanish, Hebrew, or Bantu. Here, however, the new pronoun, in spite of being emphatic, conforms to the current OV syntax of nominal objects, rather than to the discourse-pragmatic principle discussed above. In other words, the speakers of the language are once again—slowly but surely—bringing the pronominal object syntax in line with the nominal object syntax. Whatever natural communicative principle motivating such a pull, it is obviously independent of the OV-VO typological distinction, as well as of the general pragmatic principle which favors an earlier position for anaphoric pronouns in discourse. Therefore, the typological inconsistency of pronominal and nominal object syntax indeed constitutes an instance of synchronically crazy syntax arising via diachronically natural change.

6.3.2. Morphologically Mixed Coding of Case Function

Here one could again cite Amharic as one of many examples where case function is coded by a mixed array of prefixes and suffixes.[23] In all instances the prefixes data back to the VSO stage of pre-Amharic, while the suffixes are more recent innovations accomplished during the current SOV stage. In general, one would expect a situation like that to create processing difficulties relative to a situation where all case notions were marked by the same coding strategy, say only suffixes (as in Japanese) or only prefixes (as in Hebrew). Similar examples in the other typological diachronic direction abound, as in Latin or German, with the older suffixes combining with the newer prepositions to create a complex coding system. Niger-Congo, Classical Arabic, and Akkadian also present situations of this type. In all cases, a synchronically less-natural situation[24] has arisen via natural diachronic change. In all cases the language slowly eliminates the irregularities via the phonological attrition of the old morphology and the simultaneous rise of new morphology that is typologically consistent. If one were then to derive one's ideas about what is natural or communicative preferred in case-coding

---

an important topic in the following discourse (Haile, 1970). However, since human–dative objects tend to be high on the topicality scale and thus likely to be talked about over long stretches of narrative (Givón, 1976a), the agreement with topic–definite dative objects—while not 100% categorical—is likely to be of a very high frequency in discourse.

[23] For details see Hetzron (1970), Givón (1971).

[24] There is good psycholinguistic support for viewing morphological inconsistency of case-role coding as representing processing complexity to the speaker. Thus, Slobin and Bever (1978) report that Turkish children acquire the highly consistent case-morphology of their language with relative ease, while having much harder time with the word-order. On the other hand, Serbo-Croatian children have a much harder time generalizing on the complex, mixed case-morphology of their language, while their word-order generalizations stabilize much earlier.

strategies in language from the rather prevalent synchronic facts summarized above, one would obtain a highly tainted perspective of the communicative principles that govern human language.

6.4. CLEFT AND WH-QUESTION REVISITED

One of the most widely observed patterns in syntax is the so-called "WH-movement" of questions particle, via which—regardless of the original position of various case arguments in the neutral sentence pattern—WH-pronouns corresponding to nominal or adverbial arguments seem to be "attracted to the beginning of the WH-question." At one time or another, this "movement rule" has been touted as a *formal universal* of language, and its parallel with a similar rule in cleft constructions duly noted. Various attempts have been made to explain the correlation between the two constructions in this regard, by noting the similarities in presuppositional structure.[25] In both cases, the explanation is somewhat lame, since the order of elements in clefts and WH-questions indeed violates the universal pragmatic order, with the focus element *preceding* the presupposed portion. Similar attempts by Hudson (1972) and Creider (1979) stumble on precisely the same contradiction.

In Section 5.2.7, I suggested that the naturalness of this left-movement rule in clefts and WH-questions can only be understood in the context of the diachronic process of syntactization which gives rise to them, as well as to the original paratactic construction that served as point of departure for that diachronic change. Briefly recapitulating:

(17) *It's John, the man who killed Mary* →

                                              It's John *who killed Mary*

(18) *Who is it, the man who killed Mary?* →

                                              Who *killed Mary?*

The intermediate stages in the process of syntactization are not attested in all languages. In some, however, one finds the entire range. One of those in Kihung'an, a Bantu language (see Takizala, 1972). In this language one finds the following range of alternatives for cleft-focus constructions:

(19)   a.   *kwe Kipés, muut wu ka-knoonin ku-suum kit*
               BE   Kipes person who he-failed to-buy chair
               zoono
               yesterday
                 'It was *Kipes*, . . . the person who didn't buy a chair yesterday'

---
[25] See, for example, Takizala (1972) or Schachter (1973).

b. *kwe Kipés, wu ka-khoonin ku-suum kit zoono*
   BE Kipes who he-failed to-buy chair yesterday
   'It was *Kipés*, . . . who didn't buy a chair yesterday'

c. *kwe Kipés wu ka-khoonin ku-suum kit zoono*
   BE *Kipes-who* he-failed to-buy chair yesterday
   'It was *Kipés* who didn't buy a chair yesterday'

d. *kwe Kipés ka-khoonin ku-suum kit zoono*
   BE Kipes he-failed to-buy chair yesterday
   'It was *Kipés* who didn't buy a chair yesterday'

e. *Kipés ka-khoonin ku-suum kit zoono*
   Kipes he-failed to-buy chair yesterday
   '*Kipés* didn't buy a chair yesterday'

Sentence (19a) is a paratactic structure, with a "headed" nonrestrictive relative clause. Sentence (19b) is again paratactic, but with a "headless" nonrestrictive clause. Sentences (19c,d,e) are all "condensed" or syntacticized, under the same intonation contour, with progressive elimination of the relative-clause morphology as well as the copula characteristic of the focus constituent. As Takizala (1972) point out, two facts remain constant across all variants: (*a*) the intonation pattern characteristic of focused Hp's; and (*b*) the special negation pattern (with the auxiliary verb *fail*) that is found in relative clauses but not in main clauses. Otherwise, sentence (19e) may be likened to the stress-focus pattern in English, which does not tamper with the neutral word-order.

A similar gradation may be observed for object clefting:

(20) a. *kwe kít, kiim ki ka-swiimin Kipes zoon*
   BE chair thing that he-bought Kipes yesterday
   'It's a *chair*, . . . the thing that Kipes bought yesterday'

b. *kwe kít, ki ka-swiimin Kipes zoon*
   BE chair that he-bought Kipes yesterday
   'It's a *chair*, . . . what Kipes bought yesterday'

c. *kwe kít Kipés ka-swiimin zoon*
   BE chair Kipes he-bought yesterday
   'It's a *chair* that Kipes bought yesterday'

d. *kit Kipes ka-swiimin zoon*
   chair Kipes he-bought yesterday
   'It's a *chair* that Kipes bought yesterday'

e. *Kipes ka-swiimin kít zoono*
   Kipes he-bought chair yesterday
   'Kipes bought a *chair* yesterday'

Here an added rule of *subject postposing* is seen in (20a,b), a rule characteristic of object topicalization and relativization in several Bantu languages (see discussion to follow later). As the morphology of relativization is eliminated (20c), the subject postposing rule is dropped, another vestige of the simplification occurring here. The tone structure and the negation pattern (when used) remain the ones characteristic of relative clauses, even when other morphological vestiges of the original paratactic construction have been eliminated.

Finally, a similar gradation is also seen with WH-questions. Thus:

(21) a. *kwe khí, kiim ki ka-swiimin Kipes zoon*
BE what thing that he-bought Kipes yesterday
'*What* is it, . . . the thing that Kipes bought yesterday?'

b. *kwe khí, ki ka-swiimin Kipes zoon*
BE what that he-bought Kipes yesterday
'*What* is it, . . . what Kipes bought yesterday?'

c. *kwe khí ki ka-swiimin Kipes zoon*
BE what that he-bought Kipes yesterday
'*What* is it that Kipes bought yesterday?'

d. *kwe khí Kipes ka-swiimin zoon*
BE what Kipes he-bought yesterday
'*What* is it that Kipes bought yesterday?'

e. *Kipes ka-swiimin khí zoon*
Kipes he-bought what yesterday
'Kipes bought *what* yesterday?'

Now if the suggestion concerning the origin of the left-movement of the focus constituent in WH-questions and clefts is indeed correct, then the naturalness of the synchronic order—which is admittedly bizarre—does not derive from any *synchronic* universal principle. Rather, the current frozen syntactic order reflects an older, paratactic *pragmatic* order. That is, the fact that the presupposed portion of the eventual construction was tacked on at the end as an *afterthought,* as a nonrestrictive relative clause.[26] And while both the paratactic original order and the process of syntacticization are natural universals, the synchronic order—however prevalent—is to some extent crazy.[27,28]

[26] It is still clear that the presupposed part of the cleft and WH-question construction does not act as a *restrictive* relative clause on the "head" element in focus. That is, it does not "narrow down the domain" for the purpose of establishing unique definite description, as restrictive relative clauses normally do.

[27] In a number of Bantu languages where intermediates as in Kihung'an cannot be found, a frozen relic suggests nevertheless a similar diachronic development of the WH-question left-movement pattern. This is a reflex of the old copula **ni* as a prenasalized element on many WH-question words. For further discussion, see Givón (1974b).

[28] For some reason, it is harder to find cleft constructions (and WH-question left-movement) in SOV languages. But they are clearly not totally barred from that typology. Thus Hetzron (personal communication) suggests that in Amharic, a strict SOV language, the normal focusing device "recognized by the grammarians" is the *pseudo-cleft,* that is, where the focus element comes *last,* as in:

6.5. PRONOUN ATTRACTION AND OBJECT RELATIVIZATION

In an earlier work (Givón, 1972b) I suggested that there was a universal synchronic principle pertaining to the morphology of relative clauses, the *pronoun attraction* principle, by which relative pronouns or relative-clause subordinating morphemes tend to appear *adjacent* to the head noun modified by the clause, and thus *separate* the head noun from the relative clause. I suggested that a plausible explanation for this phenomenon involved the need for *case recoverability*, that is, the fact that the case-function of the head noun may be different from the case of its coreferent noun within the relative clause, and therefore if the head noun was not kept apart from the clause, its main-clause case marking may interfere with the recoverability strategy via which the case-function of the deleted noun within the relative clause is determined.[29] In support of this argument I cited the following type of data from Bantu languages. In object relativization in a number of Bantu languages, the subject noun within the relative clause is *postposed,* so that instead of the SV order of main clauses one obtains a VS order in object relative clauses. As an example, consider the following data from Kihung'an:[30]

(22) MAIN: *kipes ka-swiimin kit zoon* (SVO)
Kipes he-bought chair yesterday
'Kipes bought a chair yesterday'

(23) REL: *kit ki-a-swiimin Kipes zoon* (VS)
chair REL-he-bought Kipes yesterday
'The chair that Kipes bought yesterday . . .'

I further observed that subject postposing in Bantu seemed to occur only in languages in which the relative pronoun–subordinator was bound to the verb, either prefix or suffix. Then I suggested that subject postposing must be motivated by the need to separate the head noun from the relative clause, that is, the *pronoun attraction* principle. The argument

---

maryam-ɨn yǝ-gǝddǝl-at yohánnɨs nǝw
Mary-OBJ REL-killed-her John is
'The one who killed Mary is *John*'

However, Hetzron goes on to observe, at the colloquial register one can already find the cleft version:
yohánnɨs nǝw (,) maryam-ɨn yǝ-gǝddǝlǝ-w
John is Mary-OBJ REL-killed-DEF
'It's *John* (, the one) who killed Mary'

Since there is no formal difference between a restrictive and a nonrestrictive relative clause in Amharic, and since the cleft sentence above is acceptable equally well with a pause—and with the relative clause interpreted as "headless" and nonrestrictive vis-à-vis *John*, I believe this data represents another example of the diachronic rise of cleft constructions via the condensation of looser discourse structure.

[29] See discussion in Chapter 4.
[30] For the data see Takizala (1972).

may have rested there with a seemingly neat synchronic explanation. But further facts soon came into the fore. First, Bokamba (1971, 1976) observed that in Dzamba, Likila, and Lingala, Bantu languages typologically close to Kihung'an [see (22) and (23)], not only does subject postposing (and thus VS order) occurs in object relativization, but also in object *topicalization*. Next, a similar parallel between a VS word-order in object relativization and object topicalization (fronting) was observed in Spanish and Hebrew (Givón, 1976b, 1977a) as well as in Arabic (Russell, 1977), all languages in which the relative subordinator is not bound to the verb and thus where the pronoun attraction principle could not be invoked as explanation to subject postposing. It was now apparent that the explanation was inherently *pragmatic,* and that the VS word-order represented a demotion of the subject from *higher*-topical position when another—nonsubject—element was promoted to higher topicality. I then argued (see Chapter 4) that there are good grounds for believing that in relativization the coreferent noun within the relative clause is enhanced in topicality,[31] and the VS order observed in object relativization in all those languages thus reflects a demotion of the subject under such conditions. On this background, consider the following facts of relativization in Modern German.

On the face of it, it seems that German abides by the pronoun attraction principle in relativization. Thus:[32]

(24) a. Subject: *der Mann der kamm*
the man *who* came
'The man who came . . .'

b. Accusative: *der Mann den ich schon lange keene*
the man *whom* I already long knew
'The man that I've long known . . .'

c. Dative: *der Mann dem ich das Buch*
the man *to-whom* I the book
gegeben habe
given have
'The man to whom I gave the book . . .'

d. Genitive: *der Mann dessen Frau mitkamm*
the man *whose* wife with-came
'The man whose wife came along . . .'

The relative pronouns used in (24) above are not the traditional WH

---

[31] Similar arguments, over different data, may be found in Kuno (1976b, for English and Japanese data), Schachter (1976, for Philippine data), and Russell (1977, for Arabic data).
[32] For the data I am indebted to Theo Vennemann (personal communication).

6.5. Pronoun Attraction and Object Relativization

pronouns used in relativization in many Indo-European languages. Rather, they are the demonstrative pronouns. Vennemann (personal communication) has suggested that the syntacticized relative clause pattern of German as seen in (24) above arose diachronically from a *paratactic*, topicalized pattern in which the demonstrative pronoun is in fact at a *topicalized* ("thematized") position. That is, respectively:[33]

(25)
  a. Subject: *der Mann, der kamm*
                          'The man, he came, . . .'
  b. Accusative: *der Mann, den Ich schon lange keene*
                          'The man, him I've long known, . . .'
  c. Dative: *der Mann, dem ich das Buch gegeben habe*
                          'The man, to him I gave the book, . . .'
  d. Genitive: *der Mann, dessen Frau mitkamm*
                          the man, his wife came along, . . .'

If Vennemann's suggestion is correct, as I believe it is, then what we see here is a classical case of the ultimate advantage of a diachronic over a synchronic explanation: On the face of it one may indeed invoke the synchronic principle of *pronoun attraction* in order to explain the position of the relative pronoun adjacent to the head noun in German. However, the diachronic facts suggest that the relative pronouns do not occupy their position because of the pronoun attraction principle, but rather because of a *pragmatic* principle of *topic fronting*. Furthermore, this pragmatic principle has exerted its influence *diachronically*. That is, first it operated within a parenthetic, paratactic expression as in (25) above. Then that construction was syntacticized to yield the current pattern of restrictive–embedded relative clauses (24). Thus the synchronic, universal, pragmatic principle of topic fronting must indeed be invoked in order to explain the synchronic facts of relativization in German. But in order to understand how this universal principle actually exerted its influence in this particular case, we must resort to diachronic explanation.

Hetzron (personal communication) has pointed out to me that Hungarian must have undergone a similar diachronic development as hypothesized above for German. This is evident from the etymology of the current relative subordinators, such as *a-ki* 'who', which is etymologically **that-who*, that is, 'the one who'. In other words, the relative clause was originally *nonrestrictive*, with the "pronoun attraction" possibly motivated, originally, by topicality–focus considerations.

---

[33] The data here are hypothetical and not necessarily grammatical or meaning the same thing in present-day German.

6.6. SOME PUZZLES IN SWAHILI RELATIVIZATION

Swahili represents a certain bewildering complexity in the morphology and syntax of relativization. Three different strategies seem to apply:[34]

(26) a. *mtu amba-ye a-me-kuja*
man say-*who* he-PERF-come
'The man who sleeps'

b. *mtu a-li-ye-kuja*
man he-past-*who*-come
'The man who came'

c. *mtu a-soma-ye*
man he-read-*who*
'The man who reads'

In (26a) the relative clause is subordinated by a reflex of the verb 'say' (-*amba*), to which the relative pronoun is suffixed. That strategy thus abides by the attraction principle. In (26b) the relative pronoun is infixed in the verbal word between the tense marker and the verb, thus neither opening nor closing the relative clause. In (26c) the relative pronoun is a verb suffix. Furthermore, synchronically, strategy (26a) can be used for all tenses, strategy (26b) can be used for only the past (-*li*-), future (-*ta(ka)*-) and progressive (-*na*-) tenses. Strategy (26c) is confined to the habitual (-*a*-/-*ϕ*-). This is admittedly a rather confusing synchronic situation, and there is even some evidence that language learners—in both first and second language acquisition—find strategy (26a) the easiest to manipulate. The diachronic story is much more straightforward, however, and may be summarized as follows:

1. The Proto-Bantu relative pronoun position was most likely at the *verb-suffix* position.
2. The subordinator *amba-* in (26a) is a verb ('say').
3. The tenses which require the "infix" relative pronoun in (26b) are all ex-verbs:

   -*li* *'be' → 'past'
   -*na* *'have' → 'progressive'
   -*ta(ka)* *'want' → 'future'

4. Bantu as a whole carries much evidence for an older, pre-Niger-Congo stage of SOV syntax.[35]

---

[34] For more details, see Givón (1972b, 1975e).
[35] See discussion in Givón (1975e) and Hyman (1975).

6.7. Mixed Typologies in Verb Phrase Syntax

Thus, the confusion of present-day relativization in Swahili derives from a succession of natural diachronic changes:

1. The cliticization of the relative pronoun postverbally at the old SOV stage
2. The drift from SOV to SVO
3. The development of tense–aspect markers from verbs
4. The cliticization of the de-verbal tense–aspect markers as verb prefixes during the current stage of SVO syntax
5. The development of the verb 'say' as a subordination marker, probably first in verb complements (still attested as *ku-amba* 'to say') and then extended to relative clauses

Once again, one could not hope to understand or explain the synchronic state without reference to its diachronic origins.

6.7. MIXED TYPOLOGIES IN VERB PHRASE SYNTAX

In Section 6.3.1 I discussed cases of mixed VP syntax where the position of clitic object pronouns did not conform to the position of object nouns. In this section I will discuss somewhat similar cases of "crazy" VP syntax arising from various types of diachronic change, all involving discrepancies between the syntactic positions of various types of *nominal* objects.

6.7.1. Direct versus Indirect Object

In the Niger-Congo family, where the drift from SOV to SVO is evident in all subbranches, a number of groups, most particularly within the Mendeic and Voltaic branches, exhibit SOV syntax for direct object nouns but SVO for all other objects.[36] Thus, consider the following examples from Kpelle:[37]

(27) è kâli kaa
      he hoe saw
      'He saw the hoe'

(28) è lì naa
      he went there
      'He went there'

---

[36] See further details in Givón (1975e).
[37] The data are originally from Bill Welmers (personal communication).

(29) è wúru tèe à bóa
he stick cut with knife
'He cut the stick with a knife'

(30) è sęŋ-kâu tèe kâloŋ-pí
he money sent chief-to
'He sent the money to the chief'

Such a situation is far from rare, although it is not always stable. Thus, for example, both Rybarkiewicz (1975) and Canale (1976) have noticed that in the drift from SOV to SVO in Old English, the direct object is the last to move to postverbal position. Bickerton and Givón (1976) have noted the same statistical tendency in the English-based Pidgin spoken by Japanese speakers in Hawaii as it drifts from the SOV syntax of Japanese toward to SVO syntax of English. A similar situation is reported for Persian and Modern Armenian.[38] One is thus tempted to suggest that this type of situation is characteristic of the SOV to SVO drift continuum, and Hyman (1975) among others has attempted to explain the naturalness of this phenomenon. But regardless of the ultimate explanation, it is a very complex synchronic situation for speakers, but one which cannot be understood without reference to the natural diachronic change which brought it about.[39]

6.7.2. Nominalized versus Free Object

This is again a situation typical of ex-SOV languages, where one finds OV order in lexical, frozen VP nominalizations, but the more progressive VO order in sentences, as in English:

(31)

OV	VO
lion-tamer	He tames lions
street-cleaning	They clean the streets
fly-fishing	They fish with a fly
etc.	

The same can be seen in the Kwa (Niger-Congo) language Nupe, currently an SVO language:[40]

---

[38] Galust Mardirussian (personal communication). The Armenian situation is intriguing since Classical Armenian was already predominantly VO, so that in the drift back toward acquiring some OV features (motivated either internally or by contact with Persian), the direct object moved back to a preverbal position while the indirect object remained postverbal. Thus, while drifting "backwards" as compared to the more common drift (SOV to SVO), Armenian nevertheless wound up at a coherent intermediate stage normally found on the OV-to-VO continuum.

[39] One could of course choose—as Heine (1975) did—to disregard the need for explanation and simply label this "another major word-order type."

[40] For more data see Madugu (1978), as well as Hyman (1975) and Givón (1975e).

6.7. Mixed Typologies in Verb Phrase Syntax

(32)   *gbè elo*   *elobbè*
                hunt deer   deer-hunt
                'to hunt a deer'   'deer-hunting'

                pá eya   *eyapá*
                drive car   car-drive
                'driving a car'   'car-driving'

This situation is motivated to quite an extent by the fact that:

1. All lexical OBJECT–VERB compounds of this type involve *non-referential* objects.[41]
2. In general, nonreferential objects tend more to *incorporate* into the verb, while referential objects do not. Furthermore, accusatives, instrumentals, and manner-adverbs are normally the least referential objects to move from OV to VO syntax.
3. The syntax of the language changed from OV to VO *after* the frozen, object-incorporation pattern was established.

The opposite case may be seen in Akkadian, which changed from an earlier VO to a later OV syntax, presumably via contact with the Sumerian substratum. However, lexical VP nominalizations retain the frozen, older VO pattern:[42]

(33)   Sentential (OV)   Lexical (VO)

a.   *ina idi   umma-nīya illakū*   *ālikūt did umma-nīya*
      at side-of troops-my   they-go   goer(s) side troops-my
      'They go at the side of my troops'   'the goers at the side of my troops',
                                                      'helpers'

b.   *ana šarr-im   ikrub*   *ikrib   sarr-i*
      for king-GEN he-prayed   prayer-of king-GEN
      'He prayed for the king'   'prayer for the king'

c.   *dull-am   ippeš*   *epīš   dull-im*
      work-ACC he-does   doer-of work-GEN
      'He does work'   'workman'

d.   *abull-am inaṣṣar*   *maṣṣar   abul-im*
      gate-ACC he-watches   watcher-of gate-GEN
      'he watches the gate'   'gate-keeper'

Since situations of this type are common, the linguist is often tempted to assume that a synchronic permutation "rule" for VP nominalizations can be formulated, such as VO → OV (for English, Niger-Congo) or OV → VO (for Akkadian). The linguist then goes on to discuss such a

---

[41] Thus a "street cleaner" could not mean someone who on a particular day cleaned our *particular* street, but only someone who habitually cleans *streets*. See further discussion in Section 6.7.3, as well as Mardirussian (1975).

[42] The Akkadian data are originally from Bucellati (1970), and for further discussion see Givón (1977c).

"rule" in terms of its formal properties, naturalness and putative language universals. But once again, the real story of natural universals of human language lies in the sequence of diachronic processes—object incorporation (lexicalization) and word-order change—which gave rise to such a synchronic "rule."

6.7.3. Referential versus Generic Object

This case is closely related to the one discussed above. In a number of languages nonreferential objects (including instrumentals and manner adverbs) are incorporated into the verb. As an example consider Southern Ute, where the morphology—loss of nominal suffix—indicates clearly which objects are incorporated and which are not. In addition, the language is in the middle of drifting from OV to VO syntax. Referential objects may appear either pre- or postverbally. But nonreferential objects may only appear preverbally, which is also the obligatory position for adverbs of manner, regardless of their etymology. Thus:

(34) a. ta²wóci mamáci pyníkyaay-kya (REF-object, SOV)
man woman-ACC see-PAST
'The man saw a/the woman'

b. ta²wóci pyníkyaay-kya mamáci (REF-object, SVO)
man see-PAST woman-ACC
'The man saw a/the woman'

c. ta²wóci mamá-²ásti²i (NONREF-object, SOV oblig.)
man woman-want
'The man wants/is looking for a woman'

d. ta²wóci mamáci ka-²ásti-wa (REF-object,
man woman-ACC NEG-want-NEG SOV)
'The man doesn't want the woman'

e. ta²wóci ka-²ásti-wa mamáci (REF-object, SVO)
man NEG-want-NEG woman-ACC
'The man doesn't want the woman'

f. ta²wóci kac-á mamá-²ásti-wa (NONREF-object,
man NEG-he woman-want-NEG SOV oblig.)
'The man doesn't want a/any woman'

g. máa ta²wóci mamá-paĝáywa-ri- (MANNER, SOV oblig.)
that man woman-walk-HABIT
'That man walks like a woman'

Now, since Ute, like many other members of the Uto-Aztecan family, is steadily drifting from OV to VO syntax,[43] the end result of this drift,

---

[43] In text counts of natural, unsolicited narrative, over 50% of the referential objects are already at a

which follows the incorporation of nonreferential objects in a preverbal position, would be a synchronic situation in which referential objects appeared only postverbally and nonreferential objects preverbally. But once again, in order to understand the naturalness of such a synchronic state, one must resort to diachronic explanation.

6.7.4. Definite versus Indefinite Objects

In Mandarin Chinese, as a result of the reanalysis of serial verb constructions as case-markers (see discussion in Section 5.2.9.1), a certain restructuring of the word-order has also occured. Briefly, from a prevailing SVO syntax prior to the syntacticization of serial verbs, one arrives at many SOV constructions, at least with respect to many direct-objects. However, the preverbal object with or without the *ba-* marker (the ex-verb 'seize') can only be definite, while indefinite objects follow the verb. Thus:[44]

(35) a. wǒ bǎ zhuāngzi dǎ-pò le   (DEF-object, SOV)
        I ACC window   hit-broken ASP
        'I broke *the* window'

   b. wǒ dǎ-pò le zhuāngzi   (INDEF-object, SVO)
        I hit-broken ASP window
        'I broke *a/some* window'

   c. wǒ yīnyuè tīng le   (DEF-object, SOV)
        I music   hear ASP
        'I heard *the* music'

   d. wǒ tīng le yīnyuè le   (INDEF-object, SVO)
        I hear ASP music   PART
        'I listened to *some* music'

Synchronically, Chinese is then of mixed SOV/SVO syntax. Furthermore, the distribution seen in (35) above abides by a universal pragmatic rule of ordering, namely that more topical elements (DEF) tends to precede less topical elements (INDEF). In fact, the same ordering principle may be also seen in the subject position in Chinese:

(36) a. kèrén zhùo-gōng
        guest work   (DEF-GENERIC-
        {'The guests work'   subject, SV)
        {'Guests always work'}

---

postverbal position (VO), as are many—if not most—subject nouns. Thus at the text-count level, at the very least, the language is beginning to manifest VSO syntax.

[44] The synchronic situation is highly complex, and for further discussion see Li and Thompson (1973a, 1973b, 1973c, 1975) and Givón (1977b). For the data here I am indebted to Charles Li (personal communication).

b. *yŏu kèrén zhùo-gōng*   (REF-INDEF-subject, VS)
   be guest work
   'There's some guest(s) who work(s)'

c. *kèrén lái   le*   (DEF-subject, SV)
   guest come ASP
   'The guest(s) arrived'

d. *lái   kèrén le*   (REF-INDEF-subject, VS)
   come guest ASP
   'A/some guest(s) arrived'

What we are faced with here is rather common and may be summed up as follows:

1. A certain succession of natural diachronic changes has produced a potentially "crazy" synchronic state in syntax.
2. However, it turns out—felicitously—that by another universal principle that may be totally unrelated to the original changes, the resulting synchronic state is actually not crazy at all, it is rather natural and, in fact, conforms with other areas of the synchronic grammar of the language.
3. Most likely, the speakers capitalize on such a situation by stabilizing a new generalization.
4. Presumably, the resulting synchronic state is potentially more stable than other "crazy" products of diachronic change.

So far as the linguist is concerned, he may choose to conclude that the explanation for the functional OV/VO variation in Chinese is purely synchronic. It may very well be, however, that Chinese would never have arrived at this variation without the diachronic changes of grammaticalizing the serial *ba*-construction. So that what may seem to the linguist who confines his observation to synchronic data as a highly plausible universal of language (i.e., the use of the OV/VO variation to mark the contrast between DEF–INDEF objects), may indeed turn out to be a rather rare case which never occurs unless a particular chain of specific and natural diachronic changes gives it rise. This seems indeed to be the case here. The synchronic situation found in Chinese is rare, unlike the much more common use of the OV–VO variation (including incorporation–cliticization) to mark the NONREF–REF contrast. Furthermore, there are grounds for believing that Chinese is in the process of eliminating this feature from its grammar by developing an alternative system which uses the numeral 'one' and the demonstrative 'that' to code the same distinction in an invariant SVO syntax (see Givón, 1977b). The only other linguistic area where a remotely similar contrast can be found is Niger-Congo, where in the Kwa subgroup the *very same* diachronic chain of events (i.e., the grammaticalization of serial-verb constructions) has given rise to the phenomenon. Thus consider the following data from Nupe:[45]

(37) a. *Kúta wã   nyika bè   foma **nyi***   (SVO)
        Kuta caught fish   *with* net   *with*
        'Kuta caught the fish with a net'

   b. *Kúta lá   foma wã   nyika*   (SOV)
      Kuta *took* net   caught fish
      'Kuta used the net to catch a fish'

Sentence (37a) may be an answer to the INSTRUMENT-focus question: *What did Kuta catch the fish with?*. While (37b) may be used as an answer to the ACCUSATIVE-focus question: *What did Kuta use the net to catch?*. In summary, then, even when a synchronic state may look natural, it may turn out that in order to understand the complexity involved with such naturalness one may have to resort to diachronic explanation.

6.7.5. Main Clause versus Subordinate Clause Object

As a result of various types of natural diachronic change, the synchronic syntax of main clauses—normally more innovative—may grow out of whack with the syntax of subordinate clauses which is normally more conservative.[46] In Chapter 3, I cited one example of this type from Kru, a Niger-Congo language, where the conservative SOV order has survived in embedded modal clauses (under *order, want,* and IMPER, as well as *possible* and NEG), while otherwise the more innovative SVO syntax prevails. At least at the statistical level,[47] one could observe in Old English during the early stages of the drift from SOV to SVO a higher preponderance of SOV syntax in subordinate clauses. A more intriguing case is that of modern German. On the face of it, it is usually claimed that SOV syntax was reintroduced back into its subordinate clauses after an earlier period of more consistent VO syntax. The current synchronic situation is then described as OV in subordinate clauses and VO in main clauses. Thus:[48]

(38)   a. *Der Mann isst den Apfel*   (MAIN, SVO)
           'The man eats the apple'

        b. *Der Mann der den Apfel isst*   (REL, SOV)
           'The man who eats the apple'

---

[45] See Madugu (1978), as well as Isaac George Madugu (personal communication).
[46] For some discussion of the naturalness of such a development, see Chapter 2.
[47] See text counts in Rybarkiewicz (1975), Canale (1976), and Stockwell (1977).
[48] For the German data I am indebted to Anna Meyer (personal communication).

	c.	*Der Mann **will** den Apfel essen* 'The man wants to eat the apple'	(V-COMP, SOV)
	d.	*Ich weiss dass der Mann den Apfel isst* 'I know that the man eats the apple'	(V-COMP, SOV)
	e.	*Wenn der Mann den Apfel isst* 'When the man eats the apple'	(ADV-CLAUSE, SOV)

In a way, however, the description of German as an SVO-in-main-clause type is rather misleading. In colloquial speech, most of the tense–aspects are marked by various auxiliary verbs. And this situation automatically precipitates OV syntax in the "complement" of those auxiliaries. Thus:

(39)   a. *Der Mann ass den Apfel*   (PAST, not in
          'The man ate the apple'   colloquial, SVO)

       b. *Der Mann **hat** den Apfel gegessen*   (PAST, SOV)
          'The man *ate* the apple'

       c. *Der Mann **wird** den Apfel essen*   (FUTURE, SOV)
          'The man *will* eat the apple'

       d. *Der Mann **ist** den Apfel am Essen*   (PROGRESSIVE, SOV)
          'The man *is* eating the apple'

       e. *Der Apfel **wurde** von dem Mann gegessen* (PASSIVE, SOV)
          'The apple *was eaten* by the man'

The specific auxiliaries used to render tense–aspects in German represent universal, natural developments (*have* → PERFECTIVE → PAST; *will–want* → FUTURE; *be* → PROGRESSIVE; *be* → PASSIVE). But here this natural development has—serendipity again—conspired to *regularize* the synchronic syntax of colloquial German, in fact rendering it, at the text level, an almost consistent SOV type. Now here is the rub:

1. In general, the drift from SOV to SVO is a widely attested natural process in language, while the opposite drift is rare and in most cases may involve contact.
2. In general, the syntax of main clauses is more innovative and that of subordinate clauses more conservative.

But in German both (1) and (2) above are violated. In other words, via one highly natural set of diachronic changes (auxiliary verbs going into tense-aspect markers) two much less natural diachronic change also take place. Without a careful examination of the complex interaction of all three diachronic changes, the linguist may be tempted to interpret the "re-regularization" of German syntax as an instance of some *abstract principle* such as "languages tend to gravitate toward typological consistency in their word-order."[49] But while such an abstract principle may be the fortuitous *result* seemingly emerging after a complex chain of diachronic changes, it turns out in fact to be the wrong explanation if one is interested in understanding what universal principles *in fact* played the crucial role in determining the synchronic syntax of colloquial German.

6.8. FROZEN SYNTACTIC CONSTRAINTS

In many languages the coordinating conjunction *and* arises historically from the subordinating preposition *with* (and ultimately from a serial verb *be at, be with, join,* etc.). While the reanalysis from subordination to coordination can be demonstrated on semantic grounds, quite often the syntactic constraints applying to the coordination still reflect the earlier situation of the subordination. One such example is cited in Lord (1973), discussing the situation in Gã, a Kwa language. There, the conjunction *kè* 'and' is etymologically derived from 'with' and ultimately from 'be at' or 'join'. The verb agreement situation, however, treats coordinated NPs conjoined by *kè* as singulars, that is, as if the second conjunct is subordinated by 'with':

(40)   *mì tá*
         I   SG-sit
         'I sit'

(41)   *wò trà*
         we PL-sit
         'we sit'

(42)   *mì kè lè tà*
         I   and he SG-sit
         'I and he sit'
         (Historically: 'I sit with him')

Furthermore, Lord (1973) also notes that the conjunction *kè*, when used to conjoin pronouns, is always followed by an *object* pronoun and pre-

---

[49] Similar abstract principles have been suggested at various times as "explanation" of syntactic change, an explanation somewhat akin to "analogy." See for example Lehmann (1973), Vennemann (1973b) and Hawkins (1977), among others. There is nothing in Greenberg (1966) to suggest such an "explanation."

ceded by a *subject* pronoun, regardless of whether the coordinate NP functions as subject or object within the sentence. Furthermore, Lord (1973) also notes that it is possible in Gã (as well as in other Kwa languages with a similar conjunction derived out of a subordinating preposition or verb) to violate Ross's (1967) Coordinate NP Constraint and cleft-front either one of the two members of the conjunction. That is, in these languages one can obtain sentences equivalent to the unacceptable English sentences:

(43)   a. *It's John who and Mary came*
       b. *It's Mary who John and came*

Historically, such sentences in Gã are derived from, respectively:

(44)   a. *It's John who came with Mary*
       b. *It's Mary who John came with*

A similar situation can be seen in most Bantu languages, where the subordinating conjunction *na* ('with', PNC *'be-at') has also developed the sense of the coordination 'and'. Thus consider the following case of topicalization (left-dislocation) and clefting in Luganda:[50]

(45)   a. *omukazi y-a-laba   omusajja **ne** omuana*
          woman she-past-see man   *and* child
          'The woman saw the man and the child'

       b. *omusajja **ne** omuana, omukazi y-a-**ba**-laba*
          man   *and* child   woman   she-past-*them*-see
          'The man and the child, the woman saw them'

       c. *omusajja, omukazi y-a-**mu**-laba   **ne** omuana*
          man   woman   she-past-*him*-see *and* child
          { 'The man, the woman sáw hìm with the child' }
          { *'The man, the woman saw hím and the child' }

       d. *omusajja **gwe** omukazi y-a-laba   **ne** omuana*
          man   *who* woman   she-past-see *and* child
          { 'It's the mán that the woman saw with the chíld' }
          { *'It's the mán that the woman saw, and the chíld' }

       e. *omuana **gwe** omukazi y-a-laba   omusajja **ne-yo***
          child *who*   woman   she-past-see man   *and*-him
          'It's the child that the woman saw the man with'

Another case of frozen constraints was reported by Elimelech (1973)

---

[50] The data are from Givón (1970b).

6.8. Frozen Syntactic Constraints

for Yoruba. In this language, the sentence conjunction ´sì arose diachronically from the verb *join–add*. This is still evident by the fact that it takes the high tone of subject pronominal agreement in front of it. It is also evident by its postsubject position in the conjoined sentence:

(46)   a.   *yémisi ´lè kọrin, yémisi ´sì lè jó*
            Yemisi can sing   Yemisi *and* can dance
            'Yemisi can sing, Yemisi can also dance'

       b.   *Yémisi ´lè kọrin, Barúk ´sì lè jó*
            Yemisi can sing   Baruch *and* can dance
            'Yemisi can sing, and Baruch can dance'

       c.   *Yémisi ´lè kọrin, ó ´sì lè jó*
            Yemisi can sing   he *and* can dance
            'Yemisi can sing, and he can also dance'

Sentence (49c), however, is as far as Yoruba can go with VP conjunction, and full VP conjunction is not possible:

(47)   **Yémisi ´lè kọrin ´sì (lè) jó*
           Yemisi   can sing   *and* (can) dance

Thus the synchronic conjunction ´sì still retains the constraint that it can only be inserted following a subject, a behavior characteristic of a verb. For a similar reason gapping is also impossible in Yoruba:

(48)   *Yémisi jẹ ẹwà, Barúk ´sì jẹ ẹran*
           Yemisi ate beans Baruch *and* ate meat
           'Yemisi ate beans, and Baruch ate meat'

(49)   **Yémisi jẹ ẹwà, Baruk ´sì ẹran*
           Yemisi   ate beans Baruch *and* meat

Thus the conjunction *sì* must not also follow a subject like a verb, but as a *serial* verb—its diachronic origin—it must also *precede* a verb. For this reason the conjunction of two object NP is also barred in Yoruba:

(50)   a.   *Yémisi jẹ ẹwà, ó ´sì jẹ ẹran*
            Yemisi ate beans he *and* ate meat
            'Yemisi ate beans, he also ate meat'

       b.   **Yémisi jẹ ẹwà, ´sì ẹran*
            Yemisi ate beans *and* meat

A reminiscent situation may be seen in Amharic, where the sentential conjunction *dǝgm-* is a participial form of the verb *dǝggǝmǝ* 'repeat', and it requires pronominal–possessive agreement with the subject preceding it. Thus consider:[51]

---

[51] For discussion and clarification of the data, I am indebted to Robert Hetzron (personal communication).

(50') a. *Kassa wǫmbǫr-u-n   ayya, Mɨhrǫt dǫgm-a   ayyǫ-cc-iw*
       Kassa chair-the-OBJ saw   Mɨhrat repeating-*her* saw-she-*it*
       'Kassa saw the chair, and Mɨhrat saw it too'

   b. *Kassa wǫmbǫr-u-n   ayyǫ,   ɨne dǫgɨmm-e   ayyǫ-hu-t*
      Kassa chair-the-OBJ saw   I   repeating-*my*   saw-I-*it*
      'Kassa saw the chair,   and I saw it too'

   c. *Kassa wǫmbǫr-u-n   ayyǫ,   Tǫklu dǫgm-o   ayyǫ-w*
      Kassa chair-the-OBJ saw   Taklu repeating-*his*- saw-*it*
      'Kassa saw the chair, and Taklu saw it too'

In all of the instances cited above, the synchronic facts are both bizarre and incomprehensible. But they are rather straightforward when one has access to the diachronic processes which lead—rather universally—to the slow, gradual reanalysis of verbs as subordinating prepositions and onward to coordinating conjunctions. And while at the semantic–functional level the reanalysis may be complete, quite often at the morphological, syntactic and constraint level one finds—as frozen relics—the footprint of earlier diachronic states.

6.9. FROZEN LEXICAL PATTERNS

In many Bantu languages, and most likely also in Proto-Bantu, the noun-class prefixes on adjectives are identical to those on nouns, but the pronominal-agreement prefixes on verbs, numerals, quantifiers, relative-clauses and possessive modifiers are different to some degree and for some noun classes.[52] For example, consider the following Swahili data:

(51)   *m-ji   u-angu m-kubwa u-me-jaa   watu*   (class 3/4, sg.)
       CL-city CL-my CL-big   CL-PERF-fill   people
       'My big city was full of people'

(52)   *mi-ji   i-angu mi-kubwa i-me-jaa   watu*   (class 3/4, pl.)
       CL-city CL-my CL-big   CL-PERF-fill   people
       'My big cities were full of people'

Bantu adjectives are a curious word-class. The number of inherent (nonderived from other words) adjectives that can be reconstructed for Proto-Bantu is very small, no more than 10. They all code inherent–permanent properties, such as *big, small, male, female, bitter, good,*

---

[52] The variation applies only to noun classes with nasal prefixes, that is, *mu-/mi-/ma-/n(i)-*, and is phonetic in origin, most likely as the result of the *weakening* of the nasal consonants in certain intravocalic environments, later to be interpreted as a morphophonemic variation.

6.9. Frozen Lexical Patterns

bad, long, short, green–unripe, wild. This situation conforms to Dixon's (1970) observation that the most likely properties to be coded by the class "adjective" are more *time-stable* properties (as contrasted with *temporary states*). In many Bantu languages, (cf. Bemba; Givón, 1972a), all other stative modifiers (*hot, cold, brave, white, black, red,* etc.) are formally verbs. In others, they are formally adjectives derived from verbs (*broken, bent, dirtied,* etc.). In fact, a number of the supposed "original" Proto-Bantu adjectives can be traced to a similar de-verbal derivation via a PERFECTIVE–PASSIVE aspect, such as: *-kulu* 'big' < *-kula* 'to grow', *-bisi* 'unripe/green' < *-bisa* 'be raw/green', *-ipi* 'short' < *-ipa* 'be short', *-lulu* 'bitter' < *-lula* 'be bitter'). The small irreducible residue of "original" adjectives seem most likely to have initially come from *nouns*, via the process of *semantic bleaching*, for example:

(53)   **-bi* 'child' > 'young' > *-pya* 'new'
        *-lume 'man' > 'male'

One may thus arrive at the following explanation for the similar morphological behavior of adjectives and nouns: Adjectives started as nouns, taking the characteristic noun prefix (as against the modifier–predicate prefix of verbs, possessives, numerals, quantifiers, etc.). Eventually, via semantic bleaching, these stems lost some of their semantic specificity, so that the erstwhile *child* could modify animal nouns and thus become *young*, and later modify also inanimates and thus become *new*. Similarly, the erstwile *man* can modify animate nouns and thus become *male*. But by generalizing in this fashion, these stems also lost their *inherent nominal gender*, since animates and inanimates are not in the same Bantu noun-class as humans, and modifiers must exhibit pronominal agreement with their heads, much like predicates agree with subjects. We thus wind up with the seeds of a new word-class, "adjective", which (a) has no inherent gender but "agrees with the gender of subject or head nouns"; (b) has the characteristic predicate–modifier syntactic distribution of an adjective; (c) requires a verb *be* to carry tense–aspects; but (d) exhibits a *nominal* rather than modifier–predicate prefix form.

In approaching this phenomenon *synchronically*, in the best know-nothing transformational tradition, Heny (1972) suggested that "deeply" Bantu adjectives are really nouns, since they display noun-type prefixes. The fact that adjectives otherwise didn't behave like nouns syntactically or semantically was not deemed significant. Neither was a *diachronic* explanation of the phenomenon considered of interest, although in this particular case diachrony was the most obvious explanation. Heny then proceeded to make grand universal claims about lexical structure on the basis of the Bantu situation.

There are a number of facts that bear on the legitimacy of Heny's endeavor. First, the class "adjective" can arise diachronically either out of the class "noun," as in Bantu, or out of the class "verb," as in some Nilotic languages (Creider, 1976). The first diachronic channel results in frozen *nominal* relics in the adjectival morphology, while the second results in frozen *verbal* relics. But, as is discussed in further detail in Chapter 8, the lexical membership of word-classes is amazingly stable cross-linguistically, and may be summarized as follows:

1. Phenomena which do not tend to change their identities over time tend to be lexicalized as *nouns;* they are thus considered *entities.*
2. Phenomena which change rapidly over time tend to be lexicalized as *verbs.* That is, they are coded as *events–actions.*
3. Phenomena which change over time at a certain intermediate rate are those which have the highest potential of lexicalizing as *adjectives;* that is, they are considered *states.*
4. Among states, more *permanent–inherent* states (size, shape, color, goodness–badness, taste, smell, texture) are more likely to pioneer the class "adjective," while the more *temporary–contingent* states (*hot, cold, angry, sad, sick, broken, bent,* etc.) may either remain (stative) verbs or are late to move into the "adjective" class.

The diachronic rise of the word-class "adjective" is thus motivated, cross-linguistically, by stable, universal considerations having a considerable measure of predictability. But the blind synchronic "analysis" à la Heny (1972) tends to obscure this.

Another relevant range of facts is to be found in the subsequent history of the morphology of the class "adjective" in many Bantu languages. This involves a tendency to bring the prefixal series in line with that of other predicates–modifiers, thus shifting it from the nominal prefix type. Thus, in Bemba, for example, this is achieved by simply dropping the nasal consonants out of most of these prefixes (with class 1/2 singular being the conservative exception), as in:

(53′) *umu*-kate *u*-suma *u*-li kuno (class 3/4 sg.)
CL-bread CL-good CL-be here
'The good bread is here'

imi-ti *i*-kalaamba *i*-li kulya (class 3/4 pl.)
CL-tree CL-big CL-be yonder
'The big trees are there'

ama-sabi *ya*-suma *ya*-li kuno (class 5/6 pl.)
CL-fish CL-good CL-be here
'The good fish are here'

in-koko *i*-bi *i*-li kuno (cl. 9/10 sg.)
CL-chicken CL-bad CL-be here
'The bad chicken is here'

> in-koko ši-bi ši-li kuno   (class 9/10 pl.)
> CL-chicken CL-bad CL-be here
> 'The bad chicken are here'

A different strategy to achieve the same end—that is, bringing the prefixal morphology of adjectives into line with other predicates–modifiers—may be seen in Lunda-Ndembu, Kimbundu, Nyanja/Chewa (partial), and Rwanda/Rundi (partial). This strategy involves nominalizing the adjective (*good* → *goodness*) and then using it in the *possessive* pattern (*a good man* → *a man of goodness*), thus shifting the prefixal agreement of adjectives to the possessive pattern, which is a modifier–predicate pattern. Thus, from Nyanja:[53]

(54) a. *ci-manga ci-a-bwino*   (class 7/8 sg.)
          CL-maize CL-of-goodness
          'good maize'

      b. *n-kuni y-a-iwisi*   (class 9/10 sg.)
          CL-wood CL-of-green
          'green wood'

      c. *mw-ana w-a-mng'ono*   (class 1/2 sg.)
          CL-child CL-of-small
          'a small child'

      d. *zi-patso z-a-zing'ono*   (class 9/10 pl.)
          CL-fruit CL-of-small
          'small fruit'

In fact, (54b,c,d) exhibit certain intermediate characteristics with respect to this development. In (54b) the adjectival stem *-wisi* is preceded by the modifier–predicate prefix *i-*; in (54c) the adjective stem *-ng'ono* is preceded by the nominal prefix *m(u)-*; and in (54d) the adjectival stem *-ng'ono* is preceded by the prefix *zi(n)-* interpretable as either a nominal or modifier/predicate prefix.[54] So that in fact in those three instances the adjectival construction exhibits *double agreement* with the head noun, and this is certainly an intermediate situation.

To sum up, then, while the synchronic "analysis" of the Bantu adjectival prefix situation yields neither insight nor explanation, the diachronic investigation illuminates the process of rise of the word-class "adjective," traces its subsequent development and places the morphological peculiarities of synchronic structure in their rightful natural context. We have tracked here both how natural diachronic change gave rise to a crazy synchronic state, as well as how subsequent diachronic change eliminated that craziness.

[53] The Nyanja data are from Price (1966).
[54] The noun prefix *zi-n-* of class 9/10 pl. exhibits the complete assimilation of the nasal element either before voiceless consonants (**zi-m-patso* > *zi-patso*) or before nasals (**zi-n-ng'ono* > *zi-ng'ono*), so that the surface for *zi-ng'ono* is diachronically–derivationally ambiguous.

6.10. DISCUSSION

As we have seen in Chapter 2, the fundamental structural and "behavioral" properties of syntax are not arbitrary, but rather reflect the use of various syntactic constructions in communication, that is, in discourse. It is hard to see how one could expect it to be otherwise. Furthermore, as was shown in Chapter 5, while being communicatively motivated, syntax is neither an ideal communicative mode nor does it bear a strict one-to-one correlation to discourse. Rather, it is a communicative mode which arises—diachronically, ontogenetically, and most likely also phylogenetically—as a result of grammaticalization–syntactization of the pragmatic mode of discourse. That process of syntacticization is itself motivated by a number of communicative factors pertaining to the immediate situation in which communication takes place, the degree of time pressure, the degree of preplanning, the amount of shared presuppositional background etc. Still, given the data discussed in Chapter 5, one may view synchronic syntax as reflecting communicative requirements in a reasonably clear fashion, although that reflection is mediated via the various developmental processes involved in syntacticization. The data discussed in this chapter, however, are, in a way, of a radically different kind, and are thus brought up in order to stretch the anti-diachronic argument of the structuralist *ad absurdum*. In each case we have discussed, the diachronic processes which gave rise to a particular synchronic state of affairs had unimpeachable communicative motivation of one kind or another. That is, the principles which governed the documented diachronic change were run-of-the-mill universal principle which govern human communication wherever it takes place—in speech *production,* in speech *perception,* in the *acquisition* of first or second language and in the constant modification of the communicative instrument which goes on endlessly during production, perception, and acquisition. They are principles such as "ease of delivery," "maximal differentiation," "ease of perception-processing," "reduction of ambiguity," "maximization of clarity of the code-meaning correlation" or "creative elaboration." Nevertheless, quite often—perhaps more often than not—such transparently sane principles, via the diachronic changes motivated by them, wind up producing crazy or countercommunicative synchronic results. How could that be? The answer can be made obvious by reverting to the comparable situation in phonology, where the parameters are fewer and relatively more transparent. What one sees there is the concatenation of changes motivated by *conflicting* communicative principles. Roughly speaking, assimilatory rules are motivated by "ease of speech production," namely, speed and smoothness of articulatory transitions. Their end result is, most commonly, the eradication of sharp coding distinctions. On the other hand, dissimilatory rules are motivated primarily by "ease of speech perception," namely, clarity of auditory–acoustic processing. Their end result is most commonly an increase in coding distinction. Assimilatory changes thus increase ambiguity as they increase delivery speed. Dissimilatory changes increase message fidelity as they decrease delivery speed. Furthermore, often subsequent changes—by themselves of unimpeachable communicative motivation—conspire to destroy the original (assimilatory or dissimilatory) motivation for preceding changes (see Section 6.2). The resulting synchronic state is thus a *mixed* entity, a *communicative compromise* between conflicting communicative requirements, reflecting the frozen imprints of successive swings and counterswings of the communicative pendulum.

While the communicative principles which govern morphology and syntax may be more complex and—for the moment—less obvious to the linguist, the situation there is essentially of the same kind. Thus the data cited in this chapter represent the mere tip of a mammoth iceberg. Data such as this are everywhere; it is absolutely impossible to study any area of the grammar (or lexicon) of any human language without having to confront the staggering mass of such data. While some of the resulting synchronic states in grammar are relatively rare, many others are both common and *stable*. Here lies a major pitfall for a methodology that attempts to derive our notions of *naturalness* in human language on the basis of *only* synchronic data. Let us suppose that a certain sequence of diachronic changes is highly natural and therefore wide-spread, for example, the cliticization of object pronouns followed by word-order change from OV to VO. The naive linguist will then discover many languages in which, synchronically, the very same discrepancy exists between the pronominal and nominal syntax. Soon he is at work formulating a universal rule of *pronoun hopping*,[55] which he deems to be one of the (formal?) universals of object pronominalization in human language. Such an example is not offered here as a caricature. Indeed, the transformational-linguistic literature of the past two decades is full to the brim with such scenarios, where stable diachronic processes have produced *equally* stable and widely attested (i.e., "universal") synchronic phenomena in grammar, and where those synchronic phenomena then serve as the sole input in the formulation of dubious—most often absurd—"linguistic universals." Real linguistic universals, however, must be principles which explain *why* the grammar is synchronically the way it is. Those, I believe, will turn out to be largely *mediated by* or *manifest in* the ever-present process of diachronic change.

---

[55] Shades of affix hopping....

7
LANGUAGE AND PHYLOGENY
the SOV mystery and the evolution of discourse

7.1. INTRODUCTION[1]

> It is quite senseless to raise the problem of explaining the evolution of human language from more primitive systems of communication that appear at lower levels of intellectual capacity . . .
>
> Noam Chomsky (1968, p. 59)
>
> It strains credulity to pretend that language as we know it suddenly sprang up intact as a cultural invention in the absence of extensive cognitive and communicative preadaptation . . .
>
> John Lamendella (1976)

In Chapters 5 and 6 I suggested that there are strong grounds for believing that the synchronic structure of human language cannot be understood without reference to the prior developmental stages that gave rise to it. I first demonstrated that this must be the case so far as diachronic change in any language is concerned. I further suggested that it must also be true in reference to the gradual development of communicative skills by the child during first-language acquisition. Both *diachrony* and *ontogeny*, it thus seems, leave their imprints on the extant adult human language.

---

[1] I am indebted to Harry Whitaker, Dwight Bolinger, Elinor Keenan, and John Lamendella for many helpful suggestions, comments, and criticisms of an earlier version of this chapter. Mostly, I would like to record my indebtedness to Shaggy-Dog Givón (1969–1976), who prompted my interest in language evolution, supplied much relevant data and gave me the initial idea of writing this chapter. *Requiescat im pacem*, charmed prince.

What I propose to do in this chapter is pursue the least supported and most controversial link in the chain of evidence and argument developed thus far. That is, I propose to show that *phylogeny* too has left its imprint on extant human language. In so doing, I will raise—as forcefully as I can—objections to Chomsky's Cartesian bias concerning the legitimacy of viewing human language as the latest link in a long, gradual development of communicative systems via many intermediate stages in hominid evolution.

There are two striking things about Chomsky's facile dismissal of serious investigation of the phylogeny of human language: First, it was accomplished *by fiat,* in an empirical vacuum, with no shred of evidence. Second, it flies in the face of extensive evolutionary evidence in all other functional–structural subsystems of the human organism *including* neurology and cognition. Chomsky has thus invited us, tacitly, to accept human anatomy, physiology, and neurology as the products of a complex, protracted, and gradual evolutionary process, but on the other hand reject a similar developmental view of cognition and language. If taken seriously, such a position is nothing but a resurrected version of the body–mind dualism of bygone eras.[2]

While inviting the linguist to reject the Cartesian bias concerning the phylogenetic evolution of human language, one must confront openly the difficulties involved in deciding what evidence is admissible and supportive of a phylogenetic interpretation of at least *some* features of extant human language. First, we have no *direct* evidence of the cognitive capacity and communicative behavior of the hominid intermediates that spanned the evolutionary gap between the common ancestor of pongids and hominids, and extant *Homo sapiens.* We do, however, have direct evidence concerning the anatomy, physiology, social structure, *and* neurology of the intermediate hominid stages. We do have a great body of evidence about the behavior, social structure, neurology, cognition, and communication of our closest relatives, the pongids ("great apes"). Finally, we also have a growing body of relevant evidence concerning the neurological, cognitive, and communicative *ontogeny* of humans. And while some of the evidence is tentative, indirect, and requires considerable *extrapolation,* it is nevertheless hard to imagine why, given the present state of our knowledge, one should accede to Chomsky's anti-evolutionary bias a priori.

In this chapter I will discuss several aspects of the available evidence, concentrating primarily on three:

1. Evidence from child language development (ontogenesis)

---

[2] Descartes' religiously inspired doctrine of the uniqueness of Man among sentient beings is admittedly a clearer version of this dualism. A more updated version with essentially the same bias may be found in Adler (1967).

2. Extrapolations from the communicative behavior of higher mammals and, subsequently, of pongids
3. Possible frozen relics ("vestiges") of phylogenetically older communicative systems that have survived in the attested data of extant human language.

In the important areas of human behavioral, cognitive, communicative, and neurological evolution, as well as in the area of pongid cognition and communication, I will rely primarily on the admirable summaries given in Dingwall (1979) and Lamendella (1976, 1977a, 1977b, in press, in preparation), as well as on a number of other published reports. While the entire range of data is somewhat fragmented, and while the chain of arguments leading from data to conclusion is often fragile, I see no reason for suspending a serious discussion. This chapter is neither a complete nor final treatment of the subject, and should be taken simply as one more link in a chain eventually to be closed.

7.2. ARGUMENTS FOR A NEO-RECAPITULATIONIST VIEW

If one is to cite the ontogenetic development of human language in the child as supportive, indirect evidence bearing upon the phylogenesis of language, one must justify *some* version of a recapitulationist thesis. The arguments summarized below are taken from Lamendella (1976). They involve a refocusing of Haeckel's (1874) observation that stages in the ontological development of organisms bear evidence—in both sequence and kind—to stages in the phylogenetic evolution of the species. Lamendella first points out that three features of Haeckel's original formulation have been empirically disconfirmed:

1. The assumption that ontogenetic stages recapitulate phylogenetic stages in the *adult* ancestor: It turns out that actually they recapitulate stages in the *immature* ancestor at the *corresponding level* of maturation.
2. The assumption that the correspondence between ontogeny and phylogeny is *complete*: In fact, while many traits recapitulate, some do not (de Beer, 1951).
3. The assumption that recapitulation is expressed at the level of the *entire organism*: The evidence suggests that the relevant domain for tracing recapitulation is *each functional subsystem* per se.

Lamendella then observes: "Most scholars have no problem accepting the notion of phylogenetic recapitulation for basic *anatomical* and *physiological* systems in the *embryo,* but there seems to be a general distaste for entertaining the idea of *postnatal* stages of human *cognitive* or *linguistic* information processing might also be a repetition of our species' history . . . [Lamendella, 1976; all italics mine]. He then points out that postnatal maturation that recapitulates phylogeny in the areas of anatomy, physiology, neurology, and sensory development has been observed in higher mammals, who share with humans the trait of immature birth[3] (Noback and Moscowitz, 1963; Noback and Montagna, 1970). Furthermore, there are strong grounds for believing that motor-skills, cognitive, sociocultural, and communicative evolution occured together "in a series of mutually supportive stages . . . [Lamendella, 1976; see also Geertz, 1962; D'Aquili, 1972]." The argument is then summarized:

> The existence or nonexistence of postnatal recapitulative sequences is an empirical question which must be asked and answered for each developmental domain. Whatever the difficulties in obtaining clear evidence, phylogenetic recapitulation plays such a strong role in the ontogeny of all other functional systems that it would be unwise to ignore its possible role in the cognitive and linguistic domains simply because the time of birth has passed . . . [Lamendella, 1976].

One more aspect of the problem that must be emphasized (Lamendella, personal communication), is the interaction between the development—both phylogenetic and ontogenetic—of neural systems relevant to the support of cognition and communication, on the one hand, and the development of the culturally created communicative system that is sustained by the relevant neurological substructures. Both ontogenetically and phylogenetically these two rise together, *interactively,* though it may well be that at any particular stage one may *outpace* the other—and, in fact, *stimulate* or *facilitate* its further development. In this context, one must take into account the crucial significance of postnatal maturation in making room for the process of *culturally mediated learning*:

> The explanation of the biological utility of immature developmental stages lies partially in the further inverse relationship existing between the state of maturity at birth (or hatching etc.) and the potential of a species to rise above *stereotyped, automatic responses* to a limited range of specific sensory stimuli. Immaturity of Neuro-Functional Systems which are nonetheless functional, provides the developing individual with *flexibility* and the chance to successfully adapt as an individual to an ecological niche in a *highly variable environment* which may not be predictable in advance. Maturation concomitant with *individual experience* directing or-

---

[3] "If we examine the phylogenetic scale, we observe a general inverse relationship between the level of organizational complexity achieved by the adult form of a given species and the degree to which the new individual approximates the adult. Some lower invertebrates go through no maturational period at all, and for many of those which do, only growth—the mere accretion of tissue—is involved . . . [Lamendella, in prep., p. 47]."

ganizational growth in appropriate direction, not only relieves the genetic code of a heavy burden of detailed specificity, but allows *learning* to assume a prime role in the adaptation of both the individual and the species . . . [Lamendella, in prep., p. 47; emphasis added].

7.3. THE SOV MYSTERY

In this section I shall introduce a range of facts about human languages which, I will claim, represent a likely instance of a *relic* of an earlier evolutionary stage of human language which has survived into the present era. In most human languages extant today, the particular feature in question is still attested. In the majority of all others, it can be reconstructed via a judicious use of internal and comparative methods, to a period usually not earlier than 6000–7000 B.C. Only for a very small minority of the world's languages is evidence for this relic not clearly present, and so far as one can tell these may represent languages with an earlier time of departure from the putative earlier stage, or perhaps a faster rate of change. The facts as I see them may be summarized as follows:

1. It seems that the majority of language families known to us exhibit SUBJECT–OBJECT–VERB (SOV) syntax, and so far as one can tell they were always SOV[4] (Altaic, Turkic, Caucasian, Dravidian, Sino-Tibetan, all Papua-New-Guinea phylums, Kushitic, Khoi-San, Athabascan, Uto-Aztecan, Hokan, and many others).

2. The overwhelming majority of languages and language families which do not show actual SOV syntax currently,[5] can be nevertheless reconstructed via internal and comparative methods back to an earlier SOV stage. In other words, either their syntax or—at the very least—their bound morphology exhibit coherent relics of the earlier SOV stage (Indo-European, Semitic,[6] Fino-Ugric, Mandarin, Niger-Congo,[7] Nilo-Saharan, Afro-Asiatic,[8] Iroquois, Mayan, and in fact all currently non-SOV Amerindian languages with perhaps one exception).

3. Only very few language families seem to show no solid evidence

---

[4] That is, there is no surviving relic evidence embedded in the bound morphology of the language (where relics survive longest), to give grounds for any internal reconstruction other than SOV. For discussion of the methodology of internal reconstruction of syntax via bound morphology, see Givón (1971), as well as more recent refinements in Givón (1977c).

[5] In a family some members may be currently SOV while others may not, or some or all members may exhibit SOV relic features while their syntax is already non-SOV.

[6] See Givón (1977c).

[7] See Givón (1975e) and Hyman (1975).

[8] Kushitic is SOV and Semitic can be reconstructed to SOV. The entire Afro-Asiatic group must have been SOV, as a detailed analysis of the bound morphology Chadic, Berber, and Old Egyptian is bound to show.

for an earlier SOV stage [Austronesian, Salish(?)]. Even in those the evidence is not by any means conclusive.

4. The most common natural drive in word-order change seems to be SOV > VSO > SVO, with a much more restricted drift of SOV > VSO > VOS also attested in a number of cases. The drift *toward* SOV from any other typology is relatively rare.[9]

The more recent pieces of the SOV puzzle, in particular studies of the various pathways of natural drift from SOV, are slowly becoming available. Thus there is a growing body of evidence that the drift from OV to VO word-order, most likely via an intermediate stage of V-first or V–S syntax, is *pragmatically* motivated (Hyman, 1975; Stockwell, 1977). There is fairly conclusive evidence that the drift from VSO to SVO is pragmatically motivated (Vennemann, 1973a; Givón, 1977a). There are also some indications that the drift from VSO to VOS may be motivated by a shift in the underlying pragmatic principle of word-order, from "topic goes to the left" to "topic goes to the right" (Creider, 1975; Foley, 1976; and discussion of both in Givón, 1977a).

While the evidence is by no means conclusive, it nevertheless suggests that natural, internally motivated drift from SOV to various typological targets is motivated primarily—though perhaps not exclusively—by *discourse-pragmatic* considerations. Put another way, somehow the SOV word-order, though seemingly the *earliest* attested in human language, is *not* the one most *compatible* with the currently extant discourse-pragmatic evolutionary stage of human language.[10] And if this is indeed the case, it is a fact demanding explanation. Apart from this, however, the central question remains: Why is it that the oldest word-order that can be reconstructed in human language is SOV? Is this a mere artifact of time-dependent erosion of all vestigial relics of earlier-yet stages?

While the latter question raises a possibility that cannot be ruled out on a priori grounds, I have chosen for the purpose of the discussion here

---

[9] So far, most of the strongest demonstrable instances of change *toward* SOV (Ethiopian-Semitic, Akkadian, New-Guinea Austronesian) seem to have been motivated by massive substratum contact. But some cases of *partial* natural drift toward SOV have been reported where an *internal* motivation is plausible, such as German (see discussion in Section 6.7.5), Mandarin (Li and Thompson, 1973a), and Armenian (Mardirussian, 1978).

[10] Since the majority of extant human languages are to this day SOV, obviously the incompatibility is not absolute. There are some indications that the most stable SOV language (cf. New-Guinea major phylums or some Sino-Tibetan languages) may have actually developed a *discourse type* that may have *stabilized* the SOV word-order or capitalized on it. This involves the use of verb-final particles which control the flow of discourse, such as topic-maintaining–switching particles, evidentiary particles, sequence versus simultaneity particles, presupposed versus asserted modal particles, etc. The final position of a finite verb in the thematic paragraph (or "verb chain") in these languages becomes a crucial strategic necessity in the processing of discourse. (For a description of such a language, see Thurman, 1978.) We are thus faced with the possibility that different discourse-processing strategies may evolve side by side in human language.

to disregard it. Instead, I would like to rephrase the original question more boldly: How come we seem to have arrived at the current[11] evolutionary stage of the neurological, cognitive, and linguistic capacities of *Homo sapiens* all speaking SOV languages? Why have we been drifting away from the SOV typology? Discussing such questions in a coherent and responsible fashion is a delicate enterprise, not always supported by a complete body of facts and air-tight proofs, often involving inferential leaps. I see no reason why this should deter us, as long as more complete data are not available, and as long as something of interest may be gained from leaping.

7.4. EXTRAPOLATION NUMBER 1: THE COMMUNICATIVE SYSTEM OF CANINES

The material reported in this section represents the cumulative product of seven years of continuous observation of one male Belgian Shepherd dog between 1 October 1969 and 20 August 1976. The observation was informal but extensive, and the subject's communicative behavior with both humans and other canines was noted. I have no wish to justify the method of data gathering, short of suggesting that what it lacked in formal design and explicit controls was more than offset by the gains accruing from observing the natural pragmatics of the communicative context, as well as by the great amount of intimate personal contact.

What is summarized below represents only the most global, obvious, stable features of the canine communication system, features which every person who has ever interacted with a dog over a long period of time would recognize immediately. Nevertheless, since I will argue that such data can be legitimately used as a point-of-departure for *extrapolating* toward the early communicative behavior of humans, it is certainly incumbent upon me to justify the choice of a distant evolutionary point which is not directly in the evolutionary path of hominids (canines) rather than choosing to cite our closest extant relatives, the pongids.[12]

---

[11] Paleontological evidence and concomitant neurological reconstruction suggests that the "current" stage of cognitive and intellectual evolution of *Homo sapiens* may be pushed back 50,000–100,000 years (Lamendella, in prep., Dingwall, 1979). This is not to suggest that necessarily communicative evolution proceeded at the *exact* same pace. As I shall argue further below, socialcultural development—which *motivates* the rise of specific communicative systems—may either lag behind or outpace neurological evolution. Thus, for example, chimpanzees and canines are roughly at the same social and communicative stage of evolution, although the former have been demonstrated *capable* of a much more sophisticated cognitive and communicative behavior than the latter, and are known to be neurologically much more evolved.

[12] Dingwall (1979) voices a strong injunction against the practice of citing evidence such as I am citing below as *homolog* of a comparable stage of human communication: "only data from living representatives of a common evolutionary lineage . . . can provide a foundation for inference about the phylogenetic development of behavior. . . ."

Except for the fact that these are the data available to me, it also turns out that my observations about canine communication match closely the reports of the communicative behavior—and social structure—of pongids *in the wild,* and further, there are grounds for believing that canine and pongid communication *chez eux* is based upon the same *limbic* neurological subsystem (Lamendella, in press, in preparation, personal communication).[13] I will therefore summarize briefly, following this section, some of the literature on pongids.

7.4.1. Here-and-Now, You-and-I, This-One-Here and That-One-There

The most striking feature of canine communication is that it is seldom, if ever, about anything except the immediate, perceptually accessible situation and environment, where time is the time of speech—namely, *now*[14]—the subjects–agents are only *you* or *me,* and the objects to be talked about or manipulated are *concrete, perceptually accessible* object right at the scene of the communicative interaction. Each of these features will be dealt with separately.

7.4.1.1. TIME

As will be made obvious in Section 7.4.2, canine behavior suggests that they must have some mental representation—however vague—of *future,* or at least *immediate* future. Observation of some of their long-range planning behavior—unless one dismisses it as instinct governed[15]—suggests that perhaps they also have some notion, probably even more vague, of less-than-immediate future. Observations of what

---

[13] Lamendella (in press) also points out that the human child's communication system during the first year after birth is based upon the same *limbic* neurological subsystem, and that limbic communication patterns—and the neurological structure supporting them—persist in playing an important role in the communicative behavior of human adults.

[14] Lamendella (personal communication) points out that "now" here should be interpreted as "timeless." This remains to be verified. Certainly one of the striking features of canine (as well as pongid and early child) communication is that there is little evidence to support inference about the coding of time-concepts removed from the time of speech. To that extent, then, one may suggest that the concept of time itself has not yet differentiated in canines. As I shall argue below, *some* notion—however vague—of both immediate past and future must be posited, at least tentatively, for canines, although the argument may in fact turn on semantics rather than substance. It is certainly true in adult human communicative behavior, in particular in the data of tense–aspect systems, that in some sense "time of speech" is the least marked, most obvious underlying parameter of the system, and that both "past" and "future," as well as "always," are more complex psycholinguistic elaborations (see some discussion, albeit formal, in Givón, 1972a, Chapter 4).

[15] There is an unfortunate tradition of dismissing many complex behavioral patterns of higher vertebrates as instinct governed, that is, automatic circuitry reflexes, without sufficient neurological justification. While the older neurological subsystems in mammals (and the human neonate) are of this type, the neurology of canines has much more advanced components, supporting both intentional behavior and some planning.

dogs remember suggest that they may possibly have some representation—however vague—of *past* (see Section 7.4.3). What is clear, however, is that if canines do have some internal, differentiated notions of nonpresent time, those notions are left *uncoded* and play no significant role in communicative transactions. Communication thus deals exclusively with the present or the most directly extendable future.

7.4.1.2. PLACE

It is clear, both from observing intentional behavior and from the implications of memory, that dogs have some notion—however vague and ill-coded—of places *not here* (*invisible, over the hill, inside the house*, etc.). In some sense, then, they must have some of the neurological foundations for generalizing about *object permanence* is Piaget's (1954) sense.[16] It is equally clear, however, that, by and large, most of canine communicative behavior is about objects right at the communicative scene, perceptually accessible to both interlocutors.[17]

7.4.1.3. OBJECTS

As far as one can ascertain, dogs communicate about concrete objects directly accessible to their perceptual modalities at or near the communicative scene. It is clear that they have some *object concepts* in Lamendella's (in prep.) terms. That is, they do not only react to the perception of *movement*, but also observe *properties* and thus generalize, at least to some extent, about *types* of objects. Furthermore, it is reasonably clear that canines differentiate between *animate* and *inanimate* object, and that, further, their initial criterion for animacy is *motion*. In addition, after an initial investigation of an object at motion, dogs seem to be capable of differentiating between motion *under one's own volition* and passive–caused or random ("wind caused," "water caused") motion. As Lamendella (in prep.) points out, these are the very same criteria (motion and motion-under-internal-cause) that underlie the

---

[16] Lamendella (in prep.) points out that "object permanence" is a necessary component for propositional representation of events or "change of state," involving both change of *place* and change in *perceptible properties*. While it is clear that dogs exhibit some notion of object permanence as far as change of place is concerned, it is not clear how much perceptual modification they accommodate before ceasing to treat an object as being "the same." As Lamendella points out, the latter type of "object permanence" concept involves a considerable amount of sophistication in inference, propositional conceptualization, memory and the concept of time. My own observations suggest that dogs have a relatively small capacity for this sophistication, and that a drastic alteration in the perceptible properties of concrete objects, even over a short time-span and within the immediate perceptual field, makes it impossible for them to infer "sameness." Much of this inability correlates with their relatively low ability to process "cause" and "sequence" at a level beyond the most immediate, and it is reasonable to assume that this in turn correlates with neurologically based memory limitations.

[17] Most of my observations are about objects accessible visually or auditorily, though one must concede that olfactory accessibility may be just as germane in the communication of canines *chez eux*. In terms of frequency, my observations suggest that so far as *communication* is concerned, these three modalities are hierarchized as follows: visual > auditory > olfactory.

human child's evolving concept of animate entities. As argued in Chapter 8, these are the criteria that must underlie the category "animate" in adult human language.

7.4.1.4. PARTICIPANTS

It is clear that the *agent* and *recipient* within the communicative system of canines are always *you* and *I* but never a third person. In other words, in coding and transmitting messages about actions–events, dogs deal exclusively with transactions performed by the two interlocutors, "speaker" and "hearer," and if a third animate party is present, he/she is relegated to the status of "object." Thus, while (1) is a plausible canine speech act, (2) and (3) are not:

(1)   *(you) give me this bone.*

(2)   **(you) make him give me this bone.*

(3)   **(you) give her this bone*

Furthermore, so far as I can ascertain, the *beneficiary* of a canine-coded speech act is never anyone except the "speaker," so that (4) below is also an implausible canine speech-act:[18]

(4)   **I want to give you this bone*

7.4.2. Illocutionary Force of Canine Speech Acts

In the speech of human adults, there are three most common speech acts: declarative, interrogative, and imperative. I refer to them here as *functions*, not *structures*, since it is well known in linguistics that a performative function can be disguised in a structure that is *more commonly* used to code another performative function.[19] The last two speech acts are *manipulative*, that is, designed to elicit *action* on the part of the hearer. Interrogative manipulations are most commonly used to elicit *verbal action*, most specifically to obtain *information*. Imperative manipulations are most commonly used to precipitate *action*, though presumably the action could also be verbal. The declarative function, on the other hand, is used most *directly* to convey *information*, although there are grounds for suspecting that the ultimate purpose may not necessarily

---

[18] Dogs are prone to coming home with "treasures" and proudly lay them at your feet; thus they are clearly capable of generous *behavior*. But in their coded *communicative* systen, the recipient–beneficiary assignment seems to be 100% egocentric.

[19] Thus, for example, *I'd like you to bring me an apple* is, in terms of structure, a declarative sentence, although in terms of function it is a request or command, that is, a manipulative. Similarly, *I'd like to know who did it!* may be a declarative structure masking an interrogative. It is much less common to mask a declarative function in a manipulative structure.

7.4. The Communicative System of Canines

be the gain of information per se, but rather, information is a means to a more remote end.

Of the three major speech acts used in adult human language, canines seem to use primarily one—the imperative. That is, most of their speech acts are manipulations, designed specifically to obtain nonverbal (noninformational) action. Now, this is not to suggest that some level of "information" does not play a role in canine cognitive structure ("memory," "retrieval") and communicative behavior, as is discussed in section 7.4.3, But most of what one may consider "information conveying" speech acts of canines, turn out to be disguised manipulatives, as in:

(5)   a.   *I am hungry* → *Give me food*
       b.   *I am hurting* → *Do something about my pain*
       c.   *I am demoralized* → *Cheer me up*
       d.   *I need to pee* → *Please let me out*

This is not to suggest that dogs do not engage in purposive behavior from which, commonly and often systematically, other dogs glean information. Barks, postures, and manner of movement are all quite accurate information-bearing clues for canines, indeed, as are **all** facets of behavior. But here one must distinguish between behavior from which information *can* be *inferred*, and behavior designed *primarily* to *code* information. These two extremes are not discontinuous. Rather, they represent a continuum, synchronically, ontogenetically, and phylogenetically (see Lamendella, in prep.). It is most likely to assume that the evolution of *coded* communicative behavior represents a gradual conventionalization, distillation, symbolization, and abstraction of the more informatively salient element of mere behavior. On this continuum, however, canines are at the less-coded end.

There is one type of informative speech acts that one can nevertheless recognize in canines, a type that may be characterized as *affective–emotive*. This involves fairly well-coded "expressions" that may be translated as:

(6)   *I feel terrific!*
                       I love you!
                       I'm scared!
                       I'm all excited!

There are grounds for believing that these do not represent disguised manipulations, at least not primarily or most frequently. In addition, there is evidence that these are also the only nonmanipulative speech acts with relatively unambiguous *vocal coding* in pongids (Dingwall,

1979), and that they are also the first in the ontogeny of communication in the human child (Lamendella in prep.).

Otherwise, for all I know, a dog in the wild may indeed wish to communicate information of the type:

(7) *There is a wounded water-buffalo on the other side of the hill*

But so far as communicative behavior can be interpreted, he is most likely to code (7) as the manipulative (8):

(8) *Come with me this way!*

The conceptual structure which must underly imperative manipulations in human language is highly sophisticated. To summarize briefly, it involves at the very least the following components, all of which must be at least accounted for (or "have some analogs") in canine manipulative behavior.[20]

1. *States and the time axis.* A $state_i$ prevails at the time of speech, and a desired $state_j$ (non-$state_i$) is "projected" or "intended" for a time following the time of speech. With the time of speech (or "time of communicative behavior") representing the *time-axis* of the manipulation.[21] So far as one can infer from behavior, canines do have some mental representation of *object relations,* which are in turn the direct precoursor of *propositional conceptualization* (Lamendella, in prep.) of *states*. While it is not clear what is the exact manner of the canine neurological coding of states, their behavior suggests awareness of prior and subsequent–desired states.

2. *Intent and motivation.* In humans, manipulating speakers have a notion of their intent, that is, the projected–desired future state as well as their intent to manipulate the hearer in order to achieve the desired state. Dogs' communicative behavior must have some analogs of these features.

In humans, the manipulating speaker must have some *motivation* for trying to manipulate another individual to act, rather than performing the desired action himself. This motivation may involve either *inability* or *unwillingness* to act on one's own. So far as one can tell with canines, perceived inability to achieve the desired goal on their own is the only proper motivation for manipulating another individual to that end.[22]

---

[20] For some linguistic detail, see Gordon and Lakoff (1971).

[21] Givón (1973c). So far as one can tell, the subsequent–desired future state could only mean "directly following." While one would not want to dismiss the possibility that dogs are capable of longer-range *planning,* their communicative *behavior* never pertains to a time other than *directly* following the time of speech.

[22] Dogs seem to be either more charitable or more self-sufficient than humans in this respect, and socially sanctioned motivation of the type quite common in humans, that is, *Do this for me because I'm too lazy/precious* is largely unattested. Although grooming and other affective activities may involve manipulations such as *Do this for me so I can bask in your love*.

3. *The social contract and action probabilities.* In humans, verbal manipulation also involves assessing the likely motivation of one's interlocutor, that is, whether they are *free* to act, *well-disposed* toward acting, *bound* to act by personal, social or physical bonds, etc. All these produce an overall probability for the manipulation—and the attainment of the desired state—to succeed. Much of these considerations involve detailed and often-subtle knowledge of social structure, and of behavioral conventions within it.

The observed behavior of dogs suggests that they do have a clear notion of *obligation* and *authority*. Domestically, they differentiate well between persons of authority ("owner") and those with less authority. Their intuitions about the pecking order are rather canny, and they readily infer the correct hierarchies of human society (*big* > *small, male* > *female, adult* > *child, secure* > *insecure*).[23] In the wild (van Lawick-Goodall and van Lawick, 1971, Ch. 2) the same seems to be true.

4. *Cause and effect.* As is argued in Chapter 8, "cause" is not an observable fact but rather a sophisticated, complex, *inductive* inference based upon *time-sequentiality* and most likely mediated via the concept of *conditionality* ("correlative," *if–then*; see Lamendella, in prep.). In humans, any planning and intentional behavior, of which manipulative speech acts are subpart, must involve an underlying concept of cause-and-effect. Dogs certainly behave, in terms of their action-plans, as if they recognize *some* relation between action and *immediate* consequence. Whether their representation or internal coding of cause-and-effect relations are of the same type as in humans remains open. Lamendella (personal communication) suggests that they have only *correlative* representation (*if–ten*), and that their neurological development does not accommodate the concept of causality as we know it. My own observations of canine behavior, planning, and manipulative communication suggests that the difference is largely a matter of complexity, abstraction and nonimmediacy. Dogs seem to recognize *immediate, perceptually obvious* cause, at least in some instances. In terms of *time*, they seem to understand causal connections only if the cause *directly precedes* the effect. In terms of place, they recognize only *directly adjacent* causes.[24] In terms of perceptual concreteness, dogs seem to recognize only the perceptually most *obvious* causal connections. To sum up, then, the

---

[23] Shaggy-Dog inferred the control-hierarchy of seats in a VW van quite accurately: driver seat > next-to-driver > back, and would always attempt to occupy the available seat highest on the hierarchy. While he would concede the driver seat to an adult, he would not to a child.

[24] A dog tied to a leash will always try to chew the strap at a point *as close to the collar* as possible. If that portion of the leash is made of chain, but the next portion is of chewable leather, the dog will give up without attempting to chew the leather. Similarly, when on a long chain tied to a stake, a dog will attempt to slip his/her collar, but even the most dedicated under-the-fence tunnel expert will not attempt to dig out the visible but slightly remote stake, nor to slip the chain's loop off that stake.

same constraints on here-and-now, you-and-I, this-one-here and that-one-there are apparent in their communicative structure in general (cf. Section 7.4.1), also apply to their representation of causality.

7.4.3. Past, Memory, and Information

So far it seems that dogs have a concept of object-permanence of individual objects, as well as some generic conceptualization of objects. Furthermore, they seem to have some—however rudimentary—consciousness of *states*, and perhaps also of *events* ("changes of states") and *actions* ("changes of states initiated by agents"). Dogs are certainly capable of coding of concrete physical actions such as *sit, bark, eat, lie down, sic-em*, etc. They also seem to have recall, most obviously of objects, places, and individual canines and humans, and such recall could be of long duration. They also seem, to judge from their behavior, to recall specific *experiences*, at least in terms of the *affective* reaction those experiences produced in them.[25] It also seems that dogs are capable of utilizing recalled knowledge in both their communicative and noncommunicative behavior. What is evident is their lack of *reference* to past or memorized events or individuals–objects in their communication. Thus, while past experience, knowledge, and memory may form the presuppositional *background* for canine communication, it is never coded overtly *within* the communication itself. One may thus posit a role for "information" in dog communication, but for the most part that role involves the background for the communicative transaction, rather than the contents of communication itself.

7.4.4. Monopropositional Discourse

Canine speech is monopropositional (or rather monoclausal, since technically speaking imperatives are clauses, although they "involve" propositions). The communicative act itself involves no topic–comment, nor chains of clauses communicated about the same topic. Although clearly communication must take place upon a vast background of presupposed information–knowledge. This contrasts sharply with adult human discourse, which is *multi*propositional, with chains of verbal clauses (propositions) all sharing ("expressed about") the same topic–subject (see discussion in Chapter 2). Furthermore, most commonly the *topic* of clauses in human discourse is the *agent*, with the topic–agent (subject) thus constituting the *continuity element* across long stretches of

---

[25] Either a locale or an individual may trigger in a dog visible apprehension that seems to be connected to a previous unpleasant experience associated with them.

narrative. Edward Keenan (1976a) suggests that the agent–subject in human languages is the most consistently coded element in *sentences*, but there are grounds for suspecting that this generalization could not be true at the level of actual human *discourse*.[26] Thus, if the subject is the topic–agent, then in multipropositional discourse subject deletion—under anaphoric coreference—is a striking feature of human discourse.

7.4.5. Lexical Coding and Deixis

7.4.5.1. TOPIC–COMMENT–OBJECT–GOAL

As far as one can tell, the topic, comment, object, and goal of canine communication are all one and the same. When it pertains to a desired object (*bone, frisbee*), coding is achieved via deictic gestures, that is, *pointing* at the direction of the object. Dogs readily understand the verbal coding of objects—both animate and inanimate—by humans, and react to it the same way they do to pointing. That is, they interpret it as a manipulation, that is, *go get (me) the bone, go fetch (me) the frisbee.*

When the topic–comment–goal of the manipulation is a concrete, perceptually transparent action, (*go, sit, get up, lie down, stay, fetch, sic-em, jump, roll, mount, eat*), dogs readily interpret the human verbal code. But when they themselves are the manipulators (*come with me, let me out, give me food*), they code their communication by deictic gestures again. They may point to the most perceptually salient object figuring in the desired state (*door, food bowl*), or the direction where an invisible object is or a desired activity is to take place. Somewhat inconsistently, they may also "point" at the interlocutor, the desired *agent* of the action. The latter is most likely designed to get *attention*, although it is plausible that the explicit coding of agents may have evolved—both ontogenetically and phylogenetically—from this deictic feature or other actions designed to attract attention (*bark, cry*). Be this as it may, the coding system of dogs is akin to the early child's mode of *enactive coding* (Bruner, 1964).

7.4.5.2. PARTICIPANTS

The imperative structure in adult human language tends to leave both the agent and the benefactive-recipient uncoded. This is so because—much like for the speaker and hearer of declaratives—the agent and recipient of a command are *obvious* from the immediate

---

[26] Keenan's claims must be mitigated by the fact that in multipropositional discourse, which is the backbone of adult-human narrative, the agent tends to be the topic–subject, the topic–subject is *maintained* over a long chain of clauses–propositions, and is thus *predictable* and thus tends to be left uncoded (most commonly) or coded by a short anaphoric pronoun (less commonly).

interactive setting.[27] Given that the agent in human discourse tend to be the topic and thus to be often deleted under anaphora–coreference, one may wish to say that in both human and canine communcation the *agent* is most commonly left uncoded. However, in human communication the identity of the agent—in the largely declarative narrative—is predictable from the verbal *discourse*. While in canine communication the agent is predictable from the communicative *setting*, that is, the identity of the participants in the manipulation. Still, both types manifest the very same universal principle of coding observed in all sentient beings (see Chapter 8), namely that the more surprising, unpredictable element in the communication is the one that is more strongly coded.[28]

7.4.5.3. VERBS

As was suggested in Section 7.4.5.1, dogs can readily code intransitive activity verbs (*sit*), two-argument transitive activities (*catch*) and also, seemingly, three-argument activity verbs (*fetch, bring*). These distinctions are somewhat fuzzy for dogs, however. To begin with, the recipient-dative object of *bring–fetch* is probably inferred for all other manipulations, namely, *do this for me*. In other words, canine manipulation always identifies the speaker as *benefactive*-recipient, equally present, equally obvious, and equally uncoded for all "verbs." Additionally, as we have seen above, much of the coding is inferred from the obvious, immediate situation, where coding either the activity ("verb") or the object most stereotypically associated with it, will elicit the same response. One may tentatively conclude, therefore, that the coding of "verb" is not an independent, distinct feature in canine communication, but rather is part of the complex of coding the topic–comment–goal–object (see Section 7.4.5.1).

7.4.6. Social Structure

It is senseless to talk about a communicative system without reference to the social structure within which it arose and whose specific functions it is designed to perform. Thus, "it is highly probable that cognitive, socio-cultural and communicative evolution occured together in a series of mutually-supportive stages . . . [Lamendella, 1976]." In this section I will discuss canine social structure *in the wild*. As it

---

[27] The communicatively nonsensical *I hereby declare to you that . . .* or *I hereby order you to . . .* are toys linguists sometimes play with en lieu of recognizing the obvious role of the communicative context. In this connection, Dwight Bolinger (personal communication) has remarked: "Reading this chapter makes me realize how artificial a process of 'deletion' is, when all along what has been happening [ontogenetically and phylogenetically—TG] is accretion. . . ."

[28] For an enlightening discussion, see Greenfield and Dent (1978).

7.4. The Communicative System of Canines

turns out, most salient features of their social structure closely resemble that of pongids, so that the discussion below is pertinent to both. What I will try to show, eventually, is that the type of communicative system described above for canines—and largely the same for pongids—is predictable from features of the sociocultural context in which it is called upon to perform tasks.

7.4.6.1. THE SOCIETY OF INTIMATES

Canine packs are largely a close society of blood-related members, with changes of membership occuring mostly by organic means—birth and death. In terms of personal character, social status, probable motivation–intent–goals–needs, as well as the likely sequence of daily activities, each individual member knows all other members intimately and accurately. It is a society that admits strangers into membership only under exceptional circumstances, and where the size of the social unit within which interaction and communication takes place is relatively small, about 10–15 adults per pack (van Lawick-Goodall and van Lawick, 1971, p. 59). It is thus a society with a largely *shared* model of the universe. Commenting on the seeming lack of status quarrels in the pack, van Lawick-Goodall and van Lawick write: "The members of the pack usually know each other well, and it is rarely that a situation arises which induces one or more of the dogs to assert their dominance . . . [1971, p. 92]." They further comment: "The situation may perhaps be compared to a family with sensible parents who understand one another, and well-brought-up teenage children who get along with their elders . . . [1971, p. 92]."

7.4.6.2. LOW SOCIOCULTURAL DIFFERENTIATION

Canine packs have a parallel—male **and** female—hierarchic structure, largely expressed in terms of *dominance* (van Lawick-Goodall and van Lawick, 1971). But, much like pongid society, there is no occupational differentiation per se. Some sex-related functional differentiation is present, notably in terms of suckling the young or caring for them, and such differentiation is stronger in pongids (Goodall, 1965; van Lawick-Goodall, 1968; Sugiyama, 1973). Male-female role differentiation in terms of defense and warfare is also apparent for most primates, but much less so for canines (Michael and Crook, 1973; van Lawick-Goodall and van Lawick, 1971). But, by and large, the same range of daily social activities characterize all members of the social unit. Furthermore, in general, special skills are not confined to certain individuals, but are eventually acquired by all adult members, as a universal product of maturation and experience.

7.4.6.3. SMALL SIZE

Canine packs range between 8-15 adult members (van Lawick-Goodall and van Lawick, 1971). Gorilla bands average 15-20 members (Schaller, 1963, 1965). Orang-utans may live in smaller yet units and are even perhaps solitary (Schaller, 1961). Of pongids, only Chimpanzees seem to have larger—and more open—social units, of 60-90 members, with smaller "feeding groups" moving in and out of the larger "community" (Sugiyama, 1973; Jay, 1965; Goodall, 1965). The small size of the social unit may be determined by both environmental factors (food, predators), and social factors (tensions, sexual or ego-based rivalries). Bands or packs that outgrow the optimal, manageable size, will usually split. The society of intimates is thus, perforce, maintained.

7.4.6.4. LOW GENETIC DIFFERENTIATION

Mating in canines and primates is primarily within the social unit, exogamous mating is uncommon, and the social unit is small and made up largely of blood relatives. Sibling and descendant mating is common and largely unproscribed (van Lawick-Goodall and van Lawick, 1971, report a seeming avoidance of male mating with his mother among wild dogs). The group is thus perforce highly *homogeneous* genetically, and this certainly contributes to the sociocultural homogeneity of the community.

7.4.6.5. LACK OF SOCIAL AND ENVIRONMENTAL CHANGE

While both dogs and primates may migrate considerably over their home range, they by and large inhabit the *same* terrain all their lives, or at least the same type of terrain. Canines may move 10-20 miles within a day, but they are still, largely, within *familiar* home territory. The daily routine seldom varies, the social dominance hierarchies are extremely stable; sociocultural change is minimal.[29] For all intent and purpose, life is as it always used to be, and evolutionary change is sufficiently slow so that it has no impact on the individual's memory or the culture's patterns within the individual's life-time.[30]

7.4.6.6. THE SHARED UNIVERSE OF KNOWLEDGE

The social structure of both canines and pongids is such that, for all intent and purpose, the bulk of background, presupposed knowledge

---

[29] While chimpanzees seem to be the most socially mobile nonhuman primates, this sociocultural stability is still characteristic of their life, see Jay (1965).

[30] Genetic homogeneity must correlate with evolutionary stagnation, insuring relative paucity of mutants that might offer ingenious socioeconomic solutions to both predictable and unpredictable environmental change. A homogeneous sociogenetic structure is indeed incapable of adapting to a rapid, more radical change.

7.4. The Communicative System of Canines

("information") is *shared* by all members of the social unit. This includes knowledge of members' character, social position, skills, and aptitudes. Furthermore, all likely action is relatively *obvious* to all members alike within the social unit, given the unvarying daily routine, low sociocultural differentiation and negligible environmental–cultural change. All this, in addition to the high genetic homogeneity, enables any member of the social group to infer rather accurately most of the emotions, goals, fears, aspirations, anxieties, attractions, perceptual modalities, and cognitive activities of all other members in the largely familiar context. Communicative behavior rises upon this background.

7.4.6.7. COMMUNICATIVE MODE AND SOCIOCULTURAL STRUCTURE

A communicative system never rises in a sociocultural vacuum. Its evolution is intimately connected to and motivated by the interactional properties of the sociocultural universe which gave it rise. Thus it seems to me that under the sociocultural conditions described above for both canines and pongids, their communicative system is nothing but a natural outgrowth. Consider:

1. All background information regarding the terrain, the culture and likely activities is *stable, common knowledge.*
2. All background information concerning one's interlocutors and their likely goals are known to all members
3. All the relevant topics–goals–objects–participants of the communication are within one's immediate perceptual field.

Under such conditions, there is little need for a *declarative,* nor for an *interrogative* speech act, since by and large there is not much new that can be added, with generic knowledge *culturally* shared and specific knowledge *contextually* obvious. The only remaining task for communication, it seems, is the actual *instigation* of action via a manipulative speech act, which may be achieved by deictic or verbal coding of the object–topic–goal of the manipulation in the *presence*—and after gaining the *attention* of—the one being manipulated. The manipulative speech act, of whatever degree of coding specificity, thus serves the triple purpose of:

1. Gaining the attention of the manipulee
2. Indicating that at this moment some action is desired
3. Identifying the more perceptual–inferentially salient object in the environment involved in the desired action.

Everything else is either known or inferred.

7.5. PONGID COMMUNICATION: BRIEF SUMMARY

All available sources suggest that pongid communication *in the wild* is largely of the same type as canine communication discussed above (Jay, 1965; Goodall, 1965; Schaller, 1961, 1963, 1965; Sugiyama, 1973). Lamendella (personal communication) suggests that both canine and pongid communicative behavior is based upon the same (limbic) neurological subsystem (Lamendella, in press, in preparation). As we have already seen above, the social structure of pongids is largely the same as that of canines, at least in terms of the salient features already discussed.

It would probably be wrong to suggest that no significant neurological and cognitive evolution occurred between the canine and pongid stage. Indeed, a survey of recent studies of chimpanzee linguistic capabilities *in captivity* (Dingwall, 1979) strongly suggests that at least these most evolved pongids are capable of propositional—declarative *and* interrogative—speech behavior that is high above the range attainable by canines. An investigation of chimpanzee vocally coded speech acts in the wild (see summary in Dingwall, 1979) also suggests that the same range of *affective-emotive* nonmanipulative speech-acts described earlier for canines, such as threat, aggression, fear, pain, pleasure, separation-anxiety, food recognition, affines-recognition or superior-status-recognition are coded here, though some doubts are cast whether they are not a closed, genetically programmed system. In this connection it is significant that among pongids, chimpanzees are genetically and immunologically closest to humans (Dingwall, 1979), capable of the most complex communicative behavior (Dingwall, 1979), and exhibit the largest social units, the most fluid social structure, the highest rate of social mobility, and the widest range of geographic mobility (Sugiyama, 1973; Jay, 1965). One may suspect that in pongids in general, neurological and cognitive development has outpaced sociocultural development, and that the communicative system *in the wild* remained largely correlated with the functional and adaptive necessities imposed by—and mediated through—the sociocultural environment.

7.6. EXTRAPOLATION NUMBER 2: EARLY CHILD COMMUNICATION

Much of the discussion of the communicative behavior and sociocultural context of canines and pongids, above, may sound disturbingly familiar to anyone familiar with the facts of early child communication, particularly during the first year after birth. This section is a brief comparative survey of some of the facts, as well as an attempt to point out

7.6. Early Child Communication

where legitimate correspondences between language ontogeny and phylogeny may obtain. In the order of presentation, I follow the same general outline as in Section 7.4.

7.6.1. Immediacy

Early child communication is overwhelmingly about here-and-now, you-and-I, and visible object in the immediate perceptual field (Clark and Clark, 1977; Piaget, 1952, 1954; Carter, 1974; Werner and Kaplan, 1963; Bloom, 1973; Sconlon, 1974, 1976; Bates, 1974, 1976).

7.6.2. Illocutionary Force

The first stage of *differentiated crying*, starting about the age of two weeks after birth, exhibits the coding of three internal states: *hunger, pain* and *rage*. One could easily suggest that all three *affective–emotive* speech acts are crypto-declaratives. However, the response elicited from the parent soon embed these crypto-declarative in a *manipulative* function, that of eliciting action from the parent to relieve the undesired state. The inference the neonate must have drawn, that is, that the expressive act can draw the proper response from an interlocutor, seems to be the first act of *interpersonal* communication by the neonate (Lamendella, in prep.).

The *affective* level of information continues to dominate the baby's communication during the first six months, as the parent's emotions, attitudes and dispositions are interpreted via tone of voice, intonation etc. This is essentially a limbic communicative mode (Lamendella, in press, in prep.).

Toward the end of the first year after birth, verbal coding begins to take place, and it seems that the nost common early coded nessages are the following three: *food, general-want, pleasure* (Carter, 1974; Lamendella, in prep.). Of the three, *food* and *general-want* are manipulative, if not initially then eventually, while *pleasure* is again an affective–expressive crypto-declarative.

A more evolved stage is recorded by both Carter (1974) and Reed (1972) and involves *gestural–vocal complexes*. The coded functions seem to be the following (adapted from Carter, 1974 and Lamendella, in prep.):

1. *Request for attention*. A manipulative, although presumably a means to an end, prerequisite to *any* communicative mode
2. *Request for an object*. A manipulative
3. *Object–person dislike*. Initially perhaps an *affective* expression of displeasure with the object, which may eventually code a manipulative, namely, a request for removal

4. *Request for activity.* Most commonly a manipulative involving a request for either moving an object or moving the self
5. *Dislike–rejection.* An affective–expressive act having obvious manipulative undertones (*Don't give it to me, take it away*)
6. *Pleasure–surprise–recognition.* The only clear nonmanipulative of the set, primarily an affective-emotive speech act.

In essence, these speech acts are *primarily* manipulative, and the exception crypto-declaratives are *affective–emotive*. This corresponds very closely to the reported communicative behavior in the wild of both canines and apes. Finally, Bates (1978), Dore (1975), and Bates, Camaioni, and Volterra (1975) trace the early development of *proto-imperatives* to the period prior to nine months after birth, and of *proto-declaratives* to a subsequent period. The human child thus clearly exhibits a coherent developmental stage which recapitulate that of canines and pongids, and where the dominant speech act is manipulative.

7.6.3. Past, Memory, and Information

Much like canines and pongids, early child communication is primarily about the present, although clearly remembered past experience forms a presuppositional background and *immediate* future is implicit in planned, intentional, and manipulative behavior. But even at the next stage of ontogenetic development, the one-word stage, communication is primarily about the present (Bloom, 1973; Antinucci and Miller, 1976; Piaget, 1952, 1954).

7.6.4. Monopropositional Discourse

At the preverbal, manipulative–affective stage, child communication is monopropositional in much the same sense as in canine and pongid communication. There is no topic-*continuity* feature to such discourse, and in that sense no discourse-*coherence* structure over a unit larger than a single clause. This feature gets modified dramatically during the one-word stage, where topic repetition becomes an early prominent feature of multi-clausal discourse (Elinor Keenan, 1974a, 1975b, 1975a, 1975b; Keenan and Schieffelin, 1976). Eventually, sharing multipropositional discourse between the adult and child can be observed (Bates, 1974, 1976; Sconlon, 1974, 1976; Ervin-Tripp, 1970; Keenan and Schieffelin, 1976). Even at the one-word stage the child soon evolves multipropositional discourse, where a number of "comments–assertions" are made in succession about the sane topic (Bloom, 1973). Nevertheless, it is clear that the earlier, largely preverbal discourse mode is monopropositional and roughly of the sane type as the largely nonverbal communication described above for canines and pongids.

7.6.5. Lexical Coding and Deixis

At the preverbal stage (Reed, 1972; Carter, 1974), the coding system of the child is largely as described for canines and pongid, that is, via deictic pointing at the most salient object involved in the desired manipulation. It is again, at this monopropositional stage, the topic–comment–goal–object all rolled into one, as in canine and pongid communication.

As long as the immediate communicative setting remains the primary arena from where communicative topics are drawn, the agent and recipient go largely uncoded, since—much like with canines and pongids—they are obvious from the interactive situation. More complexity of environment and topics eventually results in the emergence of *agent* coding, first in contexts where it is the most *salient*. Thus, for example, Bloom (1973) notes that agent coding is more common first in *stative* or *intransitive* expressions, where there is no patient undergoing a perceptually salient change.

The coding of verbs, even at the stage where about 20% of the recorded utterances are already longer than one word (16 months and 3 weeks, Bloom, 1973) is minimal. In Table 7.1, a count derived from the first 11 pages of the transcripts presented in Bloom (1973, appendix, pp. 150–160) is summarized. Out of 180 tokens ("words"), 18% may be construed as possibly "predicative," and *not a single one* is an unambiguous verb. As to *agent* coding, 5% (9 tokens) could conceivably refer to an agent, but only in *one* instance is the reference unambiguously agent-coding, and all the others may be interpreted as *attention-getters* just as well.[31] The category of OBJECT gets coded at 30.5% of all tokens, and LOCATIVE at 19%. Interjections represent 7.5% of tokens and the "pivot" 20%.[32] There is no coding of the *recipient–benefactive* at all. The verbal interaction was one-on-one, and in all manipulations the child automatically counted herself as the recipient.

In sum, then, even at the early stage of verbal coding, the participants and the verb remain largely unexpressed, and the code goes primarily to the patient–object and location–goal, both of them concrete, perceptually salient features of the environment. Furthermore, while the participants are at the early stage mostly two people—the child and a

---

[31] As suggested in Section 7.6.2, the coded function of attention-getting in imperative–request manipulation could easily become the coding of the agent.

[32] Bloom (1973) considers *iwidi* a semantically empty "pivot." Out of a total of 335 utterances of Allison at 16.3, 78 were longer than one-word, and out of those 65 involved *iwidi* in combination with—usually following—another word.

TABLE 7.1
Lexicalization at Age 16.3

Category	Tokens	Percentage
Object	54	30.5
Locative		
Preposition	22	
There	15	
Total	35	19
Adult		
Mama	7	
Dada	2	
Total	9	5
Predicate		
Negative	6	
Dirty	4	
Gone	5	
More	18	
Total	33	18
Pivot		
-wid-	36	20
Interjection		
oh, uh	13	7.5
Total	180	100

parent, the objects and locations in the immediate environment are from the very start *multiple*. The participants are thus largely predictable, but the objects and locations are not. The child's early coding behavior thus manifests the universal communicative-pragmatic principle of strongest coding going to the element of *least predictability* (Greenfield and Dent, 1978).

7.6.6. Social Structure

While the family setting in which the child is reared during the stage where language development parallels older phylogenetic stages does not, per se, resemble the sociocultural structure of canines and pongids, many of the criterial, salient features are nevertheless present. The child acquires language during his first year primarily among blood-related intimates within the small nuclear family. The small size obviously limits the apparent sociocultural differentiation, although male–female and authority-gradient differences are apparent—and perceived—early, much like in canine and pongid society. The rate of change is eventually fast and the relevant physical and human environmental variety increases rapidly, but so does cognitive and linguistic development.

As to the shared universe of knowledge, one finds here largely the same developmental tendency as in other higher-mammal species exhibiting immature birth and culturally mediated learning. At the very start, cultural *generic* knowledge is not shared, but communication is exclusively about the *immediate* environment, so that *specific* knowledge is largely shared. As the child acquires more universal, generic, shared knowledge, so does the scope of the environment opens up, and more diverse, less-immediate specific information can now be communicated (Greenfield and Smith, 1976).

At the earliest stage, the human neonate is totaly egocentric in terms of knowledge. That is, he/she has not yet differentiated the "self" from the "outside" (Piaget, 1954). Following such differentiation, the young child still tends to assume that information available to him internally is *shared* by others, and early child discourse is characterized by the slow learning of strategies for making the *topic* obvious to those others—when it gradually dawns upon the child that those others are not privy to what is in his mind (Keenan and Schieffelin, 1976; Elinor Keenan, 1974a, 1974b, 1975a, 1975b). The evolution of multipropositional discourse, both ontogenetically and phylogenetically, must then be characterized by three interdependent processes:

1. The *diversification* of the physical and social environment;
2. The rise in *nonshared* specific and generic knowledge stored by individuals;
3. The evolution of communicative devices—namely, discourse—designed to *equalize the universe of knowledge,* and thus create the necessary presuppositional, shared background upon which communication can take place.

7.7. PRESYNTACTIC DISCOURSE AS A PHYLOGENETIC TARGET

In Chapter 5 (but see also Elinor Keenan, 1977, 1979), it was argued that the first discourse type developed by children, as they move from the one-word stage to the two-word stage and onward, is the presyntactic multipropositional discourse that I have termed *the pragmatic mode*.[33] This is already a full-fledged multipropositional mode of discourse, and it is most likely that the ontogenetic evolution from the monoclausal stage to the multipropositional stage goes through a certain number of

---

[33] It is common to label the earliest stages of child communication "pragmatic," since they depend on the *immediate context* of here-and-now, you-and-me, this-and-that visible objects. The "pragmatic mode" is **not** used in that sense, but rather in the sense of *discourse*-pragmatics, to contrast with the syntactic mode.

more-or-less distinct successive stages. It may be argued that, contrary to Lamendella's (in prep.) assertion,[34] at least at the phenomenological–behavioral level the development is *gradual* and follows a nondiscrete continuum. This is so because while the neurological structures and cognitive capacities that evolve in succession are possibly discrete and well-defined, earlier modes of communication are not phased out, but rather persist in the communicative competence of the growing child, so that the considerable *overlap* between stages indeed creates an observable continuum. In this section I will argue that the presyntactic, "pragmatic mode" of discourse must have been not only an ontogenetical intermediate between monopropositional discourse and the syntactic mode, but also a phylogenetic one.

7.7.1. The Pragmatic Mode: A Summary

Let me recapitulate briefly the major salient structural properties of the presyntactic, pragmatic mode of discourse.

1. *Topic–comment word order.* The relevant ordering principle is "topic first, comment follows," with the semantic role functions (subject, agent, patient, etc.) playing no role in controlling word-order.
2. *Concatenation.* In this mode of discourse, there are no tight subordinations (relative clauses, verb complements, subordinate clauses), but complexity is achieved by loose coordination.
3. *Low noun per verb ratio.* Verbal clauses in this mode typically have one argument per verb, so that if anaphora is not counted, the noun:verb ratio in discourse is roughly 1:1.
4. *Lack of grammatical morphology.* No case marking or verb modalities are used. The nonsyntacticized discourse is sufficiently transparent, both semantically and syntactically, so that inflectional morphology seems unnecessary.
5. *Intonation.* The universal principle of pragmatic intonation applies, by which the higher intonation contours are assigned to the focus–assertion (comment), and the lower intonation contour is assigned to the topic–presupposed element(s).
6. *Zero anaphora.* Since pronouns are not used, coreference which

---

[34] "The child at the one-word stage hasn't got the 'beginnings of language,' but a system of communication that is radically different from the adult linguistic system. . . . There is no single feature [the] possession of which qualifies the child or the chimpanzee as a member of the language club. Neither does the child acquire a language system by the gradual accretion of bits and pieces that eventually fall into place as language. . . . The child undergoes a transformation with each successive stage, a transformation during which the environment may be redefined, the needs and capabilities of the child may change, and new types of communication systems may become available . . . [Lamendella, in prep., pp. 168–169, MS]."

makes the identity of an argument obvious merely precipitates deletion of the repeating coreferential argument.

7.7.2. The Sociocultural Context

The pragmatic mode of discourse is used either in the *society of intimates*, where all *generic* information is shared, or in communication about the *immediate context*, where all specific information is shared. These are the two contexts where this mode of communication is used in extant human language, such as in pidgins, child language, and the informal–unplanned register of adults (see Chapter 5). The union of these two disjunctive conditions is precisely the sociocultural situation that was defined above for early man's immediate ancestors.

Thus, phylogenetically, one must envision a gradual, protracted process of opening up the behavioral and communicative context:

1. Expanded geographic *area* of obtaining food, probably related— at least in part—to the shift towards hunting
2. A correlated expansion of the *variety* of the physical environment
3. The beginning of specialization of *sociocultural modes* of making a living, including hunting, tool-making, etc.
4. A correlative increase in sociocultural *role differentiation*
5. A move—for whatever motivation—toward *exogamous mating* and the institution of various blood-relation mating taboos
6. A correlated exponential rise in the *size* and *variety* of the relevant social unit, and an increased contact—both competitive and cooperative—with other hominid bands
7. A correlated increase in the *variety* of sociocultural experience
8. A correlated increase in the *genetic* variability of the population
9. A correlated slow dissolution of the society of intimates, and a move towards the urban, currently attested *society of strangers*

The last stage (9) is obviously a *relative* matter, and can be observed even now as traditional societies are dissolved under the impact of the urban civilization. But urban civilizations of considerable size must be postulated in certain areas (Meso-America, Mesopotamia, Egypt, India, and China) as far back as perhaps 9000 B.C. The current variant merely represents the apex of a development which began long ago.

In the development of both the sociocultural context and the communicative system of human children, one may observe the same mutually dependent opening up, with an increase in the variety, complexity, and unpredictability of the physical and sociocultural experience, correlated with the rise of a communicative mode capable of handling interaction in the social universe of strangers.

7.7.3. Coordination as the Early Mode of Language Complexity

Coordination (rather than subordination) seems to be the earliest mode of increasing the size and complexity of discourse in the ontogenetic evolution of language (Elinor Keenan, 1977, 1979). This mode survives in the *informal* register in all extant languages, at least at the level of text frequency (Kroll, 1977). It also survives in note-taking under stress (Janda, 1976), in spite of the fact that the written register is normally at the apex of the syntacticized language. Furthermore, there are some languages extant to this day—all in preindustrial, illiterate societies with relatively small, homogeneous social units—where one could demonstrate that subordination does not really exist, and that the complexity of discourse–narrative is still achieved via "chaining" or coordination, albeit with an evolved discourse-function morphology (Thurman, 1978).

More related to phylogenetic evolution is the observation that chimpanzees, when taught human language via ASL (Gardner and Gardner, 1969, 1974), colored magnetic chips (Premak, 1977) or computer console (Rumbaugh and Gill, 1977), find it quite easy to handle coordination, but almost impossible to handle subordination. All the evidence thus points out to the probability that the development of subordination out of coordination must have also been a phylogenetic process, correlated with the increase in both cognitive capacity and sociocultural complexity. Thus the fact that diachronically, in extant human language, subordination *always* develops out of earlier loose coordination, may be another link in the chain of evidence and legitimate inference.

7.7.4. Multipropositional Discourse and the Rise of "Topic"

The pragmatic mode of discourse is already complex and multi-propositional. In it, a certain *coherence structure* is evident, with overall hierarchic characteristics. The story or narrative has a global theme or topic to it. Subparts have intermediate themes. Paragraphs have their own topics (for details see Longacre, 1977; Hinds, 1979; Chafe, 1979; among others). Roughly at the paragraph level and downward, the notion of "sentential topic" begins to assume relevance and structural reality. Roughly, it is one of the argument—most frequently a *human agent*—that serves as the "leitmotif" or "continuity marker" for a chain of assertions that are in some sense "made about the same topic" (see Chapter 2). In this connection, I would like to quote Lamendella (in

7.7. Presyntactic Discourse as a Phylogenetic Target

prep.) about the development of *coherence networks and propositional networks,* ontogenetically and implicitly also phylogenetically:

> Most mammals appear to possess Neuro-Functional-Systems capable of constructing conceptual categories that function at the *object level.* Some infra-human primates further give all appearance of being able to internally represent the equivalent of *activity* and *relation* concepts.[35] However, it is the human infant who gets better and better in organizing *high level propositional schemata.* . . . The domain where this superiority [of the human child over the developing mouse or chimp—TG] is most noticeable begins to be manifested at about the *end of the first year* based in part on knowledge of *temporal relations.* The ability to internally represent and organize *complex series of temporal orderings of event and state propositions* is one of the specifically human things that is denied other species. . . . The child begins to put propositional schemata into *recall networks* and, at a new level of *propositional learning,* acquiring knowledge of *how* things happen. . . . Such learning is based on an internal representation of relations *between propositions* rather than only between concepts. These new relations, what we will call *coherence relations,* are not defined in terms of concrete sensory properties as are spatial and temporal relations. They are *conceptual derivatives* . . . [Lamendella, in prep., pp 142–143, MS; emphasis added].

Our multipropositional discourse is thus the communicative vehicle carrying those "complex series of temporal orderings of event and state propositions." The leitmotif *topic* at the sentential-paragraph level, is part of the coherence structure that manifests itself hierarchically up to the higher level of narrative theme. Just as much as the child develops such coherence structure ontogenetically, so must have the species phylogenetically.[36]

7.7.5. The Rise of Topic-Comment Word Order

Once coherence, theme, and topic are established, the rise of the universal pragmatic order positing known–shared–previously-established element first, and the asserted–surprise–new information following is just about a foregone conclusion. To begin with, the *context* within which "shared information" is construed shifts radically between the stage of monopropositional and that of multipropositional communication. As we have seen above, at the earlier stage, context is primarily of

---

[35] That is, in essence, a *propositional* representation of states and events. As I have suggested above, canines too "give the appearance" of being capable of similar propositional representation, although Lamendella (personal communication) questions the validity of viewing this as "the same" capacity as in human adults.

[36] The inability of canines to evolve discourse, beyond the monoclausal speech act, must be correlated to their limited ability to represent temporal-chain relations between events–states, above and beyond the most *immediate,* perceptually obvious (here-and-now) direct precedence and direct consequence. On the ontological relation between temporality, conditionality and causality, see Chapter 8.

two kinds: (*a*) generic shared knowledge, globally available to all adult members of the speech community and (*b*) *specific* shared knowledge available equally well to all interlocutors from the immediate speech situation. As multipropositional discourse arises, a different sense of context emerges, that is, the *previous context*. Within such a schema, *automatically*, shared, presupposed, "more topical" information must appear *earlier* than newer information, given the time-sequentiality constraints of speech delivery. To this day, the most common mode in all human language of dealing with an obvious, previously mentioned topic argument, is by zero anaphora. This is done when the no possible confusion of topic-identity is suspected, most commonly in equi-topic chains (see cross-language studies in Li and Thomson, 1979; Hinds, 1979; Bolinger, 1978; as well as discussion in Chapter 2 of this volume). The presupposed–topical argument is mentioned only when possible confusion may arise, that is, several available prior coreferents or a long gap between prior and subsequent mention (see Keenan and Schieffelin, 1976, 1977; Givón, 1977a; Keenan and Duranti, 1979; as well as Chapter 2 of this volume). In that context, the most common strategy is to stop the flow of delivery, reestablish or remention the topic, then go with the next assertion. The reestablished topic thus appears, most commonly, as a *left-dislocated* element, that is, the first element, *followed* by the relevant assertion. Hence the universal topic–comment word-order.

7.7.6. The Rise of Pragmatic Stress

At the early single-word stage (Bloom, 1973), as well as at the corresponding early phylogenetic stage of monopropositional discourse, most of the message coded is the *assertion,* and the topic is not yet coded. The agent may already be the topic, but as we have seen above, both ontogenetically and phylogenetically, the agent at this stage tends to go *uncoded.* In essence, the same underlying coding principle is obvious here as in pragmatic stress (intonation), namely that the least predictable information receives the more prominent perceptual coding (Greenfield and Smith, 1976; Greenfield and Dent, 1978). With the evolution of multipropositional discourse, the topical–presupposed element is *added* to the overtly expressed linguistic structure, and since it is *not* the information foreground, it automatically receives less-prominent stress.

7.7.7. The Rise of Agent Coding

As we saw above, in both children and most likely early hominids in monopropositional discourse, the agent—obvious from the interactional context—is left uncoded. In multipropositional discourse, however, agent coding takes place, although since it is most commonly also the topic, the tendency to leave it unexpressed persists. But this is now predicted from the *discourse* context rather than from the interactive context. The rise of agent coding must have been correlated to at least the following gradual developments:

1. The introduction of *nonpresent* (both in place and time) *third persons* as topics of the communication, not only as objects–goals but also as agents. They thus cannot be inferred from the immediate interactive context.
2. The correlated rise of the *declarative* mode, *about* third-person actors
3. The rise of *nonimmediate* time and place as the domain *about which* communication is made
4. Eventually also the rise of the *interrogative* speech act, as a further refinement of action-oriented manipulatives

The ontogenetic equivalent to this developmental stage must be somewhere around the two-word stage, where one finds rudimentary sentences of the type of (9) below, with only agent and object–goal verbally coded.[27]

(9) *daddy chair*

The illocutionary force of such sentences at a certain stage could be either manipulative or declarative:[38]

(10)   a.   *Daddy, you sit on the chair!*   (IMPER)
           b.   *Daddy, put me on the chair!*   (IMPER)
           c.   *Daddy, put the chair here!*   (IMPER)
                But also:
           d.   *Daddy is sitting on the chair.*   (DECL)

Furthermore, it is plausible that the development of agent-coding, both ontogenetically and phylogenetically, is cotemporal with the development of the discourse topic. It is often assumed that the emergent agent–patient ordering apparent at this early stage (Bloom, 1973) must be motivated by the perceptual prominence of agent over patient. But it could equally well reflect the emerging topic–comment ordering and the identification of agent with topic. Bloom (1973) observed that the agent tends to be overtly coded first in stative–intransitive expressions, that is,

---

[37] John Lamendella (personal communication) points out that in children even at this early stage the "action–verb" may be gesturally coded. But clearly, the coding of verbs surely lags behind the coding of agents and patients–goals.

[38] See Bloom (1973).

those where there is no patient undergoing a perceptually prominent change of location or state. If anything, this may suggest that the patient is perceptually more prominent—at least at this stage of construing the universe—than the agent.

7.7.8. The Rise of Verb Coding

Verbs are a much more abstract entity than concrete nouns, they are perceptually less obvious, and as we have already seen, they receive lexical coding later than nouns in the ontogenesis of human language. There is no reason to assume that this was not also the case phylogenetically. Much like example (10), one may then suggest a stage in the evolution of human language where the agent and the patient–goal were coded, by deictic pointing if present on the scene or verbally if not, (and perhaps by a combination of gesture-and-sound),[39] but the verb was left uncoded, to be *inferred*. Suppose that a member of the community wished to inform others of the event of *A lion killed a gazelle,* which took place away from the communicative scene. At this stage this would be rendered, roughly, as:

(11)   *lion!* . . . [pointing at the direction of the event]
         gazelle! . . . [pointing in the same direction]
         [gesture]

In a universe that is well-shared by all members of the community, and where possible actions by agents upon patients are highly *stereotypical*, it is hard to conceive of many other interactions between an agent-lion and a patient-gazelle except for those related to hunting, chasing, killing, or devouring. Thus, the important sociocultural basis for the stage in which verbs are *not* coded is that the universe of action has not yet opened up, it has not *diversified* beyond the largely shared, *generic* knowledge of who is likely to do what to whom under most conditions.

As the universe of discourse expanded, as communication began to report events–actions that did *not* take place here and now, and as the diversification of possible actions—particularly by *humans*—progressed to the point where it was less and less easy to infer the verb from the coded agent and patient via generic knowledge concerning stereotypical behavior, verb coding became a communicative necessity. Since it is most likely that the perceptually-more-obvious verbs of *motion* and other *physical* activity were the first to be coded (and in fact also the first to be "conceptualized"), the *gestural* origin of verb coding is quite a viable

---

[39] Bloom (1973) suggests that at the one-word stage in the ontogeny of language, verbs may be coded *gesturally*. Dingwall (1979), following Dore (1975), Carter (1974), suggests that gestural coding precedes vocal coding in child language development, and (following Hewes, 1973a, 1973b) also that the same must have been true phylogenetically.

suggestion, since these are precisely the kind of verbs that are amenable to gestural coding.[40] Finally, the diversification of the universe of possible action, the gradual destereotypization of human behavior and conceptualization of less and less concrete verbs, must have again led to a gradual shift toward full verbal coding of verbs. At this stage then, one would expect the verb to be added to the already coded AGENT-PATIENT clause, so that one would now expect clauses-propositions of the general type AGENT-PATIENT-VERB, as in:

(11)   *lion! . . . gazelle! . . . kill! . . .*

as well as the less concrete:

(12)   a.   *lion! . . . gazelle! . . . look! . . .*
           b.   *lion! . . . gazelle! . . . want! . . .*

7.7.9. The Identification of Agent with Topic

Human language as we know it tends to make the human-agent the most likely topic-theme of discourse, the participant about whom the story is told, whose actions and attitude are depicted. Perforce, this makes the human agent also the most frequent topic-subject argument of clauses-sentences (propositions) (Keenan, 1976a; Givón, 1976a; as well as Chapter 2 of this volume). At an evolutionary level where discourse is already multipropositional and where coherence and topic have emerged, the clausal order of AGENT-PATIENT-VERB is also, at least in terms of discourse frequency, also most likely to be TOPIC-PATIENT-VERB.

7.8. A SHORT SUMMARY OF THE EVOLUTIONARY SCENARIO

The evolutionary scenario spanning the gap between pongid and early-hominid communication and currently attested presyntactic discourse may be now summarized as follows:

1. *Physical environment.* Increasing range and diversity
2. *Sociocultural structure.* Increasing diversity, specialization and complexity, decreasing stereotypical-predictable behavior
3. *Experiential universe.* Increased diversity, complexity, and unpredictability
4. *Communicative contents.* A shift from the immediate time,

[40] See preceding footnote 39.

locale, and present participants toward communicating about third-persons remote in both time and place
5. *Illocutionary force.* A shift from manipulatives to declaratives
6. *Discourse type.* A shift from monopropositional to multipropositional discourse, and the correlative emergence of *coherence* at the level of "narrative," and of the notions "theme" and "topic"
7. *Communicative context.* A shift from relying only on generic-shared knowledge and specific-contextual information, toward assigning an increasing role to discourse context, that is, what transpired *verbally* in the preceding portion of the communication
8. *Word-order and coding:*
   (a) OBJECT/GOAL
   (b) AGENT/TOPIC–OBJECT/GOAL
   (c) AGENT/TOPIC–OBJECT/GOAL–VERB

7.9. SYNTACTICIZATION AS A PHYLOGENETIC PROCESS

The discussion above takes us from the monopropositional, prediscourse stage of pongid and early hominid communication to the stage of the *pragmatic mode* of multipropositional discourse. As shown in Chapter 5, the pragmatic mode is a feature of extant human language as we know it, of early child communication, of pidgins and "foreign-talk," and of the informal, unplanned register of all human languages. The move from monopropositional discourse to the pragmatic mode was obviously a major evolutionary jump in terms of the cognitive and memory-processing capacity of the human organism. The topic–comment, presupposition–assertion structure of information processing in the pragmatic mode is very much characteristic of current human language.

In chapter 5 I also suggested that the *syntactic mode* of human language arises out of the pragmatic mode via the process of syntacticization, evident in both diachronic change and ontogenetic development of language. In this section I will briefly outline the arguments for considering the syntactic mode also the last *phylogenetic* stage in the evolution of human language.

7.9.1. From Pragmatic to Syntactic Discourse

Given the summary of the major features of the pragmatic mode of discourse, Section 7.7.1, the following is a summary of the changes associated with syntacticization:

1. *Word order.* The pragmatic order of topic–comment gram-

maticalizes into the semantic order of subject-predicate, that is, word order defined upon the semantic role of arguments (agent, patient, subject).
2. *Mode of complexity.* Loose coordination grammaticalizes into tight subordination under unified intonation contours, thus giving rise to relative clauses, verb complements and other subordinate clauses.
3. *Noun:verb ratio.* Via various processes of VP condensation, more complex, multiargument verbs are created.
4. *Grammatical morphology.* The various processes of condensation involved in the rise of complex, subordinate structures also give rise to inflectional morphology, marking nominal case-function, deixis and pluralization, and verbal tense–aspect–modality and clitic pronouns.
5. *Anaphora.* There is a shift from zero pronominalization toward gender–number–person marked pronouns.
6. *Mode of processing.* There is a shift from analytic processing to routinized, automatic processing.
7. *Speed of delivery.* There is an increased speed of delivery.
8. *Social context.* There is a shift from communication among *intimates* or about the *immediate* context, to communication among *strangers* or about remote topics.
9. *Shared background knowledge.* There is a shift toward communication under the assumption of a relatively low degree of shared-background knowledge.

7.9.2. Arguments

7.9.2.1. THE SOCIOCULTURAL CONTINUUM

In terms of the sociocultural environment and shared knowledge, we have seen that the evolution from the pongid-like stage of monopropositional communication toward the pragmatic mode involves the gradual *opening up* of the society of intimates, an increase in the variety and unpredictability of experience, and an increase in the amount of not-universally-shared information. The sociocultural conditions associated with the use of the syntactic mode as a *synchronic* register, as well as the sociocultural change associated with the ontogenetic rise of the syntactic mode, all extrapolate onto the same curve of gradual change, from the society of intimates toward the society of strangers.

7.9.2.2. LINGUISTIC, COGNITIVE, AND NEUROLOGICAL COMPLEXITY

A coordinate mode is a less complex system of multipropositional messages than a subordinate, hierarchized mode (Lamendella, in prep.), and this must be true cognitively as well as neurologically. If the cognitive, neurological, and communicative development of *homo sapiens* is to be viewed in terms of increasing the complexity of information processing that the organism is capable of handling, the syntactic mode clearly places at the top of the complexity continuum. Similarly, multiargument verbs are cognitively more complex than single-argument verbs, and the syntactic mode is noted for a higher noun verb ratio, as the result of the development of multiargument verbs.

7.9.2.3. SYNTACTICIZATION AND
PREINDUSTRIAL SOCIETIES

In Chapters 2 and 3 I noted that there are some syntacticized constructions that tend to be found mostly in literate, more complex societies. One of those is the use of *indefinite subjects* without existential verbs. In English, Hebrew, Spanish, Japanese, or French, among others, both the condensed variant as in (13a) and the tripropositional variant as in (13b) can be found:

(13)   a.   *A man who had no clothes on was standing there*

         b.   *There was a man, he had no clothes on, he was standing there*

Most traditional, rural, nonliterate, preindustrial societies use languages which shun the condensed, syntacticized (13a) in favor of the loose, uncondensed (13b). In the same vein, English and Hebrew allow the introduction of referential–indefinite arguments into discourse in negative clauses (see Chapter 1), while most languages spoken in preliterate, small societies do not, and would prefer the loose, coordinate (14b) over the condensed, syntacticized (14a):

(14)   a.   *She didn't read a book she was supposed to read*

         b.   *There was a book, and she was supposed to read it, but she didn't*

Furthermore, as serious, unbiased (i.e., non-Eurocentric) typological accounts of diverse languages become more available, it slowly becomes clear that a certain type of languages—those which have only coordination ("clause chaining") but no subordination (Longacre, 1979; Thurman, 1978)—are found only in preliterate "societies of intimates."

7.9.2.4. WRITING SYSTEMS

Written language is the most syntacticized register in any language (see Chapter 5). It is also the register assuming the *least* amount of shared information between the interlocutors, most commonly used in communication *between strangers*. It is also the last register added to human language in history. Most particularly, it is a register which evolved spontaneously *only* in societies which have grown beyond a certain threshold of size and sociocultural complexity. It is the direct product of the *information explosion,* and one may characterize societies which developed this register spontaneously as "societies of strangers," where culturally relevant knowledge has become too massive and complex to be stored in the mind of each individual member equally, where it is *not shared by* all members of the large community. On the evolutionary continuum just discussed, the written register of human language is at the apex of the phylogenetic continuum, and so it the society which produced it. This clearly enhances the plausibility of viewing the process of syntacticization as the last step in the evolution of human language.

7.10. VESTIGIAL SURVIVAL OF EARLY LINGUISTIC MODES

As was suggested in Chapter 5, the pragmatic mode of language is not lost when the child acquires the syntactic mode. Rather, a whole range of intermediate mixes of both modes is retained by the adult, who is thus multiregistered along a continuum between these two extremes, capable of switching appropriately given the right communicative context. Even in the use of writing, it has been shown (Janda, 1976) that the literate adult may—appropriately—revert to a register closely approximating our pragmatic mode.

The same may also be said about the earlier mode of monopropositional communication. Under situations of extreme stress, this is precisely the communicative mode adults revert to, successfully, appropriately. The stress may be precipitated by foreign language learning (Lamendella, 1977b), or by brain damage and language disorders,[41] but also by urgent real-world situations. Thus consider the following:

(15)   Utterance   Context
   a. *Help!*   drowning, rape, mugging,
   b. *Fire!*   fire
   c. *Water!*   dying of thirst, dehydration shock
   d. *Scalpel! . . .*   surgery
       Forceps! . . .
   e. *My leg! . . .*   injury

[41] John Lamendella (personal communication).

In characterizing these speech acts and their context, one finds a striking similarity to the stage of monopropositional discourse described above:

1. They are one-word utterances.
2. They are manipulative rather than declarative.
3. The agent and recipient are not coded, and are obvious from the interactive context.
4. The coded element is topic–object–goal all rolled into one.
5. It must be monopropositional, or else time will run out.
6. The range of contents communicated does not exceed the immediate communicative setting of here-and-now, you-and-I and visible objects.

Just as in the vestigial survival of phylogenetically older structures in the anatomy and physiology of organisms,[42] older stages of language evolution can and do survive. Furthermore, they do not always survive as dead relics, but sometimes also as *functional* components in the rich range of communicative modes that can be manipulated to advantage by adult humans.

7.11. CONCLUSION: THE SOV MYSTERY REVISITED

The reason why SOV seems to have been the earliest attested word-order type in human language may be now given as follows:

1. Prior to the evolutionary stage of the 'pragmatic mode', the evolution of word-order in human language was:
    (a) OBJECT/GOAL
    (b) AGENT–OBJECT/GOAL
    (c) AGENT–OBJECT–VERB
2. In the evolution of the pragmatic mode of discourse, the agent was reinterpreted as topic–agent, and word-order then became:
    (d) TOPIC/AGENT–OBJECT–VERB
3. In the evolution of the syntactic mode, the topic–agent was syntacticized into subject, and word-order then became:
    (e) SUBJECT–OBJECT–VERB

Why then do human languages seem to be drifting away from SOV? The answer seems to be, tentatively, as follows: SOV did not rise as a *pragmatic* word order in the context of multi-propositional discourse of

---

[42] Lamendella (1976) observes that vestigial organs often switch their function at some ontogenetic stage in the descendants as compared to their original function in the matching phylogenetic stage. Furthermore, their vestigial survival is more likely if they retain *some* function, rather than becoming dead relics.

7.11. Conclusion: The SOV Mystery Revisited

the type currently evident in human language. Rather, it reflects the AGENT–OBJECT/GOAL lexicalization of an earlier stage or the AGENT–OBJECT–VERB of a rather early stage in the rise of multipropositional discourse. Whatever evidence we have about the factors motivating the drift from SOV to VSO and SVO (Hyman, 1975; Vennemann, 1973a; Stockwell, 1977; Givón, 1975e, 1977a) suggests that the factors are *discourse-pragmatic* in nature, involving various topicalization and focusing movement rules. The AGENT–OBJECT–VERB may have been the most suitable word-order at the stage of monopropositional discourse, but somehow it seems that either SVO or V-first are more compatible with topic-oriented, multipropositional discourse. Such discourse involves recurrent (topical) agents as well as patients. When zero anaphora or verb-agreement is used in the context of a recurrent argument, the only remaining stable element in the verbal clause is the verb itself. If this is done at the evolutionary, sociocultural stage when syntacticization is likely, that is, under sociocultural conditions where people will tend to *routinize* or "automate" their speech-processing strategies, then a preponderance of V-first clauses at the text-frequency level will become the input for the adult's and child's syntacticization, and V-first will then be interpreted as a "grammatical" word-order.

The SOV mystery is thus, I believe, a relic of the way in which phylogenetic evolution has fashioned our functional–communicative modalities, human language. Since some of the intermediate stages seem to recapitulate themselves in the acquisition of language by children, one may indeed assert that in language and cognition—much like in biology and neurology—ontogeny may recapitulate phylogeny.

8
LANGUAGE AND ONTOLOGY
on construing a universe

8.1. INTRODUCTION[1]

> *The world is all that is the case. . . .*
> *The limits of my language means the limits of my world.*
> —Ludwig Wittgenstein (1918, pp. 5, 115, respectively)

It is a tribute to the conceptual poverty of any scientific discipline that a practitioner feels bound to apologize every time he takes an inferential leap and comes up with an idea whose factual and deductive foundations are less than 100% secure. In the preceding chapters, particularly at times when I felt I was about to make novel, unprecedented points, I found myself trying to placate the wrathful deities of science for real and imaginary infractions. The force of habit—particularly **bad** habits—is, alas, strong. I would therefore like to open this final chapter of my book by exorcising bad habits, and I cannot imagine a better way of doing so than offering the following observation as a *mantra*, to be chanted daily by an aspiring scientist:

(1) *While observed facts and facts deduced from facts are the flesh and bone of scientific inquiry, its heart and soul is creative speculation about the facts.*

---

[1] I am indebted to Martin Tweedale, Tora Kay Bikson, Haj Ross, Derek Bickerton, Pete Becker, Dwight Bolinger, and Joe Goguen for many helpful comments on earlier versions of this chapter as well as for much encouragement.

What I refer to as "creative speculation" or "inferential leap" must be akin to Peirce's *abduction* (Peirce, 1955; Anttila, 1977), and in this connection I wish to cite Anttila (1977):

(2)   "Abduction is always a gamble, whereas deduction, with little risk and low return, never introduces anything new . . . [p. 14]."

A logician honest with his tools would be the first to acknowledge the limits of deduction, as did Wittgenstein in his *Tractatus*, observing that a deductive system is by itself a flawed instrument for gaining knowledge, since all its propositions are perforce reducible to either contradictions or tautologies.

In a recent lecture I attended, the speaker[2] offered as part of his conclusions the observation that "the structure of the linguistic description of events *reflects* the structure of the events themselves." The observation followed in the wake of a discussion of Wittgenstein's *Philosophical Investigations* and in particular of the epistemological theme "meaning as use." As Wittgenstein points out there, being able to identify a "hammer" by its physical attributes, and thus being able to successfully identify each and every referential hammer in the world, does not guarantee our knowledge of the meaning of "hammer," that is, as an instrument used for driving in nails. But even in this context of discussing the nonreferential nature of meaning, the speaker's observation about "language reflecting events" gave pause to no one. The presupposition invoked in the use of "reflect"—namely, that somehow events exist independently of our cognitive coding of them—was successfully executed, with no murmur of protest from the audience.

Wittgenstein's exhortations are to this day taken by cognitive scientists to apply only to those "special cases" where an "element" of the meaning has a conventionalized, less-referential contents. But this was hardly the intended force of Wittgenstein's original discussion, which meant to illustrate a fundamental feature of semiotics, namely, that no sooner is a concept formed and coded—however concrete it may be—the concept or "cognitive representation" assumes a life of its own. It is *that* reference-independent existence which is the core of meaning in language. As in objects, so it is with events, only with a vengeance.

Suppose you were my guest in pre-Columbian Southern Colorado, and suppose we were both walking in the hills and saw a man in the distance, climbing a low hill, then sitting on a pile of rocks, raising his arms, face uplifted, and maintaining that position. Suppose someone else were present and asked us: "What is that man doing?," and supposed we disagreed then, and you said: "He is mourning his dead mother," while I said: "He is praying to the great spirit." Suppose it would have turned

---

[2] Robert van Valin (1978), "Remarks on meaning, language and culture," lecture given at the Department of Anthropology, University of California, Los Angeles, February 27, 1978.

8.1. Introduction

out that I was right and you were wrong, but being sensitive to the sitting man and his grief–prayer, we refrained from asking *him*. Suppose now the third person who queried us shakes his head and observes: "You two are not really in disagreement about *the event itself,* but only about the *interpretation* of the event in the cultural context. But so far as *I* can see, what happened—at the very least—was that (*a*) a man walked up the hill; (*b*) he sat down on a pile of rocks; (*c*) he raised his arms and uplifted his face, and (*d*) he is still holding that position. It seems to me," our observer would conclude, "that sitting in such a position on top of a hill must constitute a necessary part of the meaning of 'praying' for one of you and 'mourning' for the other."

Our observer has thus expressed a rough equivalent of the normal linguists' misinterpretation of Wittgenstein's "meaning as use," by allowing that while *some* components of meaning may be totally nonreferential, a large irreducible portion remains strictly referential, that is, grounded in the solid rock of observable facts. However, in the case of both concrete objects ("hammer") and concrete events ("man sitting on top of the hill") we could now proceed to spring upon our confident observer the discussion at the end of Chapter 3. That discussion is compatible with solid facts concerning human perception, namely that we do not perceive "a hammer," nor "a man sitting," but rather we *construe* those from an input universe that is per se—in principle— random.[3] The fact that the universe *as given to us* is apparently ordered must be the result of our cognition–perception having calibrated itself to conceive–perceive the universe as nonrandom. Thus the seeming irreducible, observable, "objective" element in the meaning of both objects and events is by itself an elaborate *construct,* rather than an independent "fact" that can be "reflected" in a linguistic or cognitive mirror. Wittgenstein's "hammer" is thus the rule rather than the exception.

This chapter examines evidence from human language concerning the way the human organism construes its universe. It is a preliminary investigation, focusing primarily on some of the fundamental parameters of our cognitive map of the universe of individuals (nouns) and actions– events (verbs). Much of the factual foundation on which I will attempt to construct my ontological conclusions is neither new nor original, but the juxtapositions are, as well as the various suggestions as to what it may all mean. By "mean" I must again resort to the pragmaticist's[4] sense,

---

[3] Kant was perhaps both right and wrong in assuming that the world *am sich* was in principle unknowable. If the world *am sich* is indeed random, and if cognition–perception involves *calibration* of the organism so that the world appears to it as ordered, then while one might suspect that the world *am sich* is random, there is no way of actually *knowing* this, since our very mode of cognition *precludes* randomness.

[4] Peirce is reputed to have coined the term "pragmaticist" as a desperate gambit against being forever coopted by the ethical "Pragmatists" (James and Dewey), observing that "if I make it ugly enough, perhaps they will refrain from stealing it . . . [T. K. Bikson, personal communication]."

namely, "fit within a *larger* system or context;" or, following I. Rabi, "relate to something more profound."

8.2. SPACE, TIME, AND BEING

There is a wide range of facts from human languages which suggest that the semantic features by which we classify the noun universe are hierarchically arranged in a fashion that yields an *implicational scale*. Here I will concern myself only with the very top of that scale, that is, with the *most generic* features of "concrete," "temporal," and "abstract." Furthermore, it is easy to show that the three are translatable into, respectively, *exist in space, exist in time,* and *exist*. The progression along that scale toward the most generic pole is that of successive *abstraction*, and the implicational relations between the three are as follows:[5]

(3)   *exist in space* > *exist in time* > *exist*

What the implicational hierarchy means is that what exists in space must perforce also exist in time, but not vice versa. What exists in time must also perforce exist, but not vice versa. A *chair* is an example of *exist in space*. An "action," "event," or "period of time" have no spatial existence but only temporal. Finally, the most abstract notions in our nominal vocabulary, such as *idea, love, freedom,* etc., have neither spatial nor temporal existence.

When entities are related to each other via an implicational hierarchy, it is appropriate to ascribe to them the set-theoretical relation of *inclusion*. Thus, the three classificatory features in (3) may be also represented as:

(4)

In terms of *criterial properties* defining the membership in classes that relate via inclusion as in (4), one may say that temporal has all the properties of abstract but in addition it also has some properties (here *existence in time*) which abstract does not have. Similarly, concrete has

---

[5] The implicational sign ">" here stands for the unidirectional conditional in logic, namely, *if . . ., then. . . .*

8.2. Space, Time, and Being

all the properties of temporal (here *exist in time*) but in addition it also has other properties (*exist in space*) which temporal does not have.

There are several types of facts about language which suggest that such an inclusion relation indeed exists. First, there is the phenomenon of "selectional restrictions," which is a fancy jargon for "the kind of *predications–qualities* that can be true of nominal entities." There are a number of "nontemporal," "nonspatial" predicates that have to do with identity, similarity, or the lack of those which may qualify all nominal entities. Thus, for example:

(5) a. *This chair/event/idea is the same as the one we discussed a while back*
 b. *This chair/event/idea is different*
 c. *This chair/event/idea is similar*

Furthermore, syntactic constructions which deal with only *identification* or *existence* can be used with all three types of nouns. Thus:

(6) a. *There's a man/event/idea that is important here* (EXISTENTIAL)
 b. *It's this man/event/idea that is important here* (CLEFT)

Finally, all three classes of entities can be the object of *knowledge*, *thinking about* or *talking about*:

(7) a. *We talked about this man/event/idea*
 b. *Think about this man/event/idea*

There are a number of temporal predicates specific to temporal nouns, so that they can predicate neither concrete nor abstract nouns. These are, for example, *happen, occur, take place*. But there is another group of predicates which can be said of both concrete and temporal nouns, but not of abstract nouns—unless the latter undergo a *figurative shift* and are thus to be interpreted *temporally* or *spacially*. Thus consider:

(8) a. *The field begins here and ends there*
 b. *The concert began at 8:00 and ended at 10:00*
 c. **My idea of freedom begins here and ends there*
 d. **The concept of relativity began at 8:00 and ended at 10:00*

A word normally used to render an abstract entity may of course undergo a figurative shift and become temporally interpreted, as in:

(9) *Chaos begins at 8:00, when they close the bars*

However, it is the *state* of chaos that is treated as temporal here, not the *concept*. A figurative shift may also render a normally abstract-concept word spatial, as in:

(10)   *Chaos begins at the gate and ends at the back fence*

But again, *begin* and *end* here delimit the *area* in which chaos may reign, not the *concept* of chaos.

Finally, there is a whole range of predicates, such as *be behind the barn, break–bend–get lost, appear on the scene,* etc. that can only be true of concrete nouns but not of temporal or abstract ones. In addition, numerous verbs (*break, bend, touch*) in their original sense[6] take only concrete objects.

The second set of facts concerning the hierarchic, implicational relation of our concepts of space, time, and being involve diachronic change, most specifically the process of *semantic bleaching* via which spatial concept develop into temporal concepts but never vice versa, and temporal ones into expression of existence–identity but never vice versa. This is first obvious with the history of verbs *to be* in any language group. What one finds is that they usually enter the *be* paradigm as concrete, *be in space* verbs such as *'sit', 'stand', 'stay', 'lie', 'sleep'.* Thus the "younger" Spanish copula *estar* (rel. to *stay, stand*) is still spatial **and** temporal, while the older copula *ser* is already atemporal, and is used for expression of timeless properties (*be tall, be a man*) or identity (*be this one*). But *ser* is also etymologically of a *locative* origin, as is the Germanic *be*. In Bantu, the oldest copula *ni* often survives only in *clefting* constructions or their reflexes,[7] while the younger copula *-li* may be still found, at least in some languages, with time-span or locative meanings. The process of semantic bleaching in diachronic change is not confined to these three hierarchic features only, but to any portion of the system that has a hierarchic structure in terms of *degree of generality* of the features. It is the *most generic* semantic features that survive longest, and in fact the morphemes carrying them become grammatical–inflectional morphemes. Thus, for example, the relatively abstract word for 'new' in Bantu (-**pya*) is derived from 'young' and further back from 'child' (-**bi*), with the bleaching process first eliminating the most specific feature [human], then the next-to-most-specific feature [animate].

A similar process of *bleaching toward the less concrete* may be seen in the history of space-deictic expressions (*this, that*), which always give rise to time–discourse deictic expressions (*the*), but never vice versa. In fact, the most common source of definite articles in language is by bleaching the distal spatial deictic *that*.

---

[6] The process of *metaphoric extension* quite often yields nonconcrete senses of such verbs, as in *We broke their spirit, They broke the world record, Freedom is fragile,* etc. But the original senses were concrete.

[7] See Givón (1974b).

A similar process can be observed in the history of indefinite articles, where they invariably enter the paradigm as the more concrete ("referential") numeral *one*, then slowly evolve, via a number of small steps, toward the more abstract ("nonreferential") indefinite marker as in English, German, or French.[8]

Finally, Traugott (1974) has presented massive evidence showing that in general our temporal expressions develop diachronically from spatial expressions, in the areas of tense marking, adverbs of time and prepositions expressing time. To summarize, the implicational hierarchy of space, time and being is, indeed, well supported by data from natural languages.

8.3. TAO AND THE UNCONSTRUED UNIVERSE

Suppose, given the randomness of the precognized, undifferentiated universe, one were then to begin the cognitive–perceptual task of construing the universe, that is, bringing order out of chaos.[9] There are two preliminaries which one must dispense with before one can proceed, both expressible in terms of *existential axioms*. The first is a familiar Cartesian preliminary, rechristened here as the AXIOM OF SELF-EXISTENCE:

(11)   *If an individual is to construe–cognize a universe, that individual must perforce exist*

The second axiom may be labeled the AXIOM OF UNIVERSE EXISTENCE:

(12)   *If an individual is to construe a universe, then that universe must perforce exist*

These two existential axioms are the presuppositional foundation of inquiry, perception, and cognition; they are, in principle, *not* deducible from any other knowledge, being *preconditions* to knowledge.[10]

While axiom (12) postulates the existence of the universe as a whole,

---

[8] The first stage of this development can be currently observed in Israeli Hebrew, Turkish, Mandarin, Sherpa, Swahili, all Creoles, and probably numerous other languages. For some discussion see Givón (1975b), Bickerton (1975a).

[9] Here the various metaphors used by the mystics may or may not be accidental, but the Biblical metaphor of chaos (Gen. 1:2) as well as the initial step towards order via a *binary* distinction (Gen. 1:1) are certainly suggestive. In this chapter I elected to follow mostly Taoist metaphors.

[10] Another axiom exists *tacitly* in the tradition of Western epistemology, one which may be labeled "the *separateness* axiom" or, alternatively, "the axiom of impossibility of *direct* knowledge." While axioms (11) and (12) establish the existence of a universe and of the subject–cognizer, they do not disallow the possibility—acknowledged by all mystics since time immemorial—that the cognizer may be in some "fundamental *unity*" with the universe and therefore have some *"direct"* access" to knowledge about the universe. For the moment, the discussion here will proceed under the tacit acknowledgment of the separateness axiom.

it says nothing about the existence of individuals within that universe, aside from the subject-cognizer itself established in axiom (11). Can other individuals be construed, perceived, or cognized at this point? Let us approach such a possible task with the criteria available to us thus far. The subject-cognizer could presumably try to construe other putative individuals by the property of *similarity* which they may share with one another. That is, being members of the same set ("universe"), they must have at least one criterial property in common, namely, their *membership* in that universe. But a difficulty soon arises: So far as we know, at this point all potential individuals are *equally* members of the set "universe," so that the criterion of membership nets us nothing tangible by which to construe them *apart* from each other, that is, as individuals. Their membership or existence in the universe—even if true—leaves them on equal footing, we cannot tell them apart.

Having presupposed the existence of the universe and even suspecting that individual entities may exist within it, we have no *means* of construing anything within that universe. We are relegated to dealing with it at the precognized, preperceived, preconstrued level, where it must have all the Biblical characteristics of randomness, or the undifferentiated "oneness" of Lao Tse's universe of *Tao*. What such a universe lacks, then, is some kind of *criterial property* by which individual entities may be differentiated.

8.4. AN UNORDERED BINARY PROPERTY: AN ABORTED ATTEMPT AT INDIVIDUATION

Suppose we introduce into our hitherto undifferentiated universe any of the numerous binary distinctions–properties by which we normally differentiate individuals in our current, cognized universe. Say, *black–white, long–short, light–heavy, loud–quiet, good–bad,* etc. This single binary property will now segregate the universe for us into two subsets, one with entities having the property, the other with those which do not have it. But in this momentary success is harbored defeat, since within each subset we are still left with unindividuated members who cannot be told apart. Suppose then we introduce more and more unordered, binary distinctions and thus reduce our sets to smaller and smaller memberships, but suppose then—horror of horrors—that our universe is *infinite*, that is, has an infinite number of members within it? This supposition of infinity is not devil's advocacy but is quite real. This is so because the undifferentiated universe *has no members*, it only has the *potentiality* of having individuated members, a potentiality only realized via cognition. The more binary, unordered distinctions we introduce, the more members the universe will have, ad infinitum. We are thus, on grounds of principle, in a bind. Our first attempt at constructing a universe, via the formally most primitive tool of an unordered binary distinction, has not yielded the desired results.

8.5. THE FIRST ORDERED RELATION: TIME

Suppose we try an alternative approach, introducing instead the first dimension into the undifferentiated universe; an *ordered relation* called TIME. Formally, this dimension will yield an ordered set via the property of PRECEDENCE, whereby all individuals in the universe will be ordered *uniquely*, so that they can directly precede only one other individual and be directly preceded only by one. The ordering relation of *precedence* has the following formal characteristics:

(13) Transitivity: *If a precedes b and b precedes c, then a precedes c*

(14) Nonreflexivity: *a cannot precede itself*

(15) Nonreciprocity: *If a precedes b, b cannot precede a*

(16) Uniqueness: *If a directly precedes b and b directly precedes c, then there could be no other individual such that it both precedes c and is preceded by a*

By introducing an *ordered* binary relation ("precedence"), we have in fact succeeded in affecting individuation within our universe, that is, we have assigned each individual—ad infinitum—a unique position within that unidimensional universe. This is a feat we could not achieve by using the property of *being–existence–set–membership,* nor by any unordered binary property. One may suggest then that the first cognitive step in construing a universe depends on the introduction of an *ordering relation*.

Suppose we tried instead to introduce first an *unordered* relation, such as "proximity?" In other words, is the *ordering* a necessary feature, or only the *relation*? It will become rapidly apparent that proximity—and thus all other unordered relations—will fail the task of affecting individuation. This is so because even in a unidimensional universe, both *a* and *c* are equally proximant to *b*. Furthermore, *b* itself must be given a unique position before "proximity to *b*" may be used to individuate either *a* or *c*, and an unordered relation can furnish no basis for achieving this.

Finally, why call our first ordered dimension "time" rather than "extension?" Certainly, *precedence* in our four-dimensional universe could be either temporal or spatial. While this is certainly true, and while there are grounds for believing that in the ontogenetic development of the human child, the more concrete *spatial* dimensions are recognized first and the more abstract "time" is extracted from them later on via "semantic bleaching" or "generalization," I believe there are nevertheless legitimate reasons for assuming that the *first* dimension of construing a universe is temporal rather than spatial. The argument runs roughly as follows: While it is possible to define the experiential uniqueness of entities by reference to time but *without* reference to space [as in (17)], it is *impossible* to define space-uniqueness of entities without reference to time [see (27), (28)]. In other words, in our four-dimensional world, time and space are not interchangeable, they are somehow *of a different kind*. But the same kind of conclusion could have been drawn from the discussion of time, space, and being in Section 8.2. That is, while temporal entities exist outside of space, spatial entities exist in *both* time and space. In other words, while time may exist without space, space does not exist without time. All this makes it reasonably clear that the first dimension—if it were to exist by itself—must have been time.

8.6. AN ONTOLOGY OF EXPERIENCE IN A UNIVERSE OF TIME

The first dimension, time, turns out to be the basis for one of our prime *experiential* criteria for "individual entity." This criterion may be given as follows:

(17) THE TIME-STABILITY CRITERION FOR ENTITIES: *An entity x is identical to itself if it is identical **only** to itself but not to any other entity (y) at time a and also at time b which directly follows time a.*

There is nothing that is logically–deductively necessary about criterion (17), but nevertheless it is one of the most fundamental experiential criteria we use for identifying the self, other humans and the entities in the phenomenological universe at large. Furthermore, there are a number of subcomponents to criterion (17) which are *relative* to the particular entity construed and the context–situation serving as the background for construing it. For example, the *number of points in time* that must elapse before an entity may be judged "stable" and thus "identical to itself" may vary enormously from one context to another.

A major body of language-derived evidence in support of our first criterion of entity identify–stability is found in the facts of lexical classes in human languages. In general, one finds *no* languages without two major classes: *nouns* and *verbs*. Furthermore, while all languages possess abstract nouns (*idea, concept,* etc.), the majority of abstract nouns in

8.6. An Ontology of Experience in a Universe of Time 321

all languages are *derived* from verbs (or adjectives). Thus the noun universe of languages, at its embryonic core, codes "more concrete" entities, that is, those which exist in space and time. The primary modality of the noun universe is *spatial deixis,* nouns are characterized by space-indicating demonstratives, most commonly hinging the noun vis-à-vis the spatial position of the speaker or hearer.

On the other side of the lexical continuum we find *verbs*, which most commonly map actions or events. That is, they most commonly map entities that are "less concrete" than nouns, that have most typically only *existence in time*. In fact, the most common linguistic modality associated with verbs involves *time deixis*, that is, tense–aspects.

The most interesting lexical class, however, is one which is not universally attested, that of *adjectives*. This is a class that is peculiar in a number of ways:

1. Although some languages do not have the adjective class, and concepts corresponding to our adjectives are found in either the noun or verb lexicon, when a language does have a class of adjectives, its properties are highly comparable cross-language. Chiefly, adjectives have a reduced or aborted tense–aspect morphology, as compared to verbs. They usually require the "support" of a copula in order to express past and future tenses, and in a number of other morphological ways they stand between nouns and verbs.

2. Dixon (1972a) has noted that the most likely qualities to be lexicalized as adjectives are the more *stable, permanent* qualities, such as *size, length, width, gender, color, texture*, etc. Thus, if a language has only a few adjectives, those will be the *time-stable* properties, while less-durable qualities such as *hot–cold, broken, angry, happy, sad, undressed*, etc. will be expressed as verbs.[11]

3. Some of the concepts that are lexicalized as "adjective" in one language may be expressed as nouns in another language, and those are invariably concepts of *extreme* time stability, such as *male, female, youth, adult, old,* etc.

4. We thus have two *swing-categories* in the lexicon of potential adjectives: The most time-stable concepts may lexicalize as *nouns*, while the less time-stable concept may lexicalize as *verbs*.

What we are faced with is then a *continuum of time stability*: The *most time-stable* percepts, the ones that change slowly over time, the ones that are likely to be identical to themselves (in terms of properties), are lexicalized as nouns. The *least time-stable* percepts, events, and actions, which involve *rapid change* in the universe, are lexicalized as verbs, which by and large characterize *changes* from one steady state to

---

[11] Bemba is such a language, and in fact in most Bantu languages "original" adjectives is a small class, historically an off-shoot of nouns, expressing mostly time-stable qualities.

another.[12] While percepts of *intermediate time-stability*, that is, those which depict states of varying degree of intermediate duration, lexicalize as adjectives. Among the latter, the more time-stable ("permanent") qualities have a higher chance of lexicalizing as nouns, while the less time-stable ("temporary") qualities tend more to lexicalize as verbs.

One of the most striking facts about languages is that, by and large, the universe of nouns is roughly coextensive with the universe of *entities*. Verbs or adjectives in order to "become entities" must undergo nominalization, that is, become lexical nouns (*long* → *length*, *act* → *action*). Since the class "noun" codes our most time-stable concepts, it thus seems that indeed our criterion (17) is not only a *plausible* experiential criterion for the individuation of entities in our cognized universe, but it is also a major *attested* criterion, if our language is to serve as evidence.

There is another type of evidence that indicates the time-stability continuum of nouns–adjectives–verbs. It involves, in one specific case, the use of the two copulas in Spanish. The copula *estar* is used to render 'be in place' or 'be temporarily', and cannot be used with nouns, but only with *temporary-location* and *temporary adjectives*. Thus:[13]

(18)   a.   *Está en la casa*   (LOCATION, TEMPORARY)
                 'He's in the house'

         b.   *Está enfermo*   (TEMPORARY ADJECTIVE)
                 'He is sick (right now)'

         c.   **Está un hombre*   (*INHERENT NOUN IDENTITY)
                 ('He is a man')

         d.   **Está muy guapo*   (*PERMANENT ADJECTIVE)
                 ('He is handsome')

On the other hand, the copula *ser* is used with *nouns* as well as with permanent-quality adjectives. Thus:

(19)   a.   **Es en la casa*   (*LOCATION, TEMPORARY)

         b.   *Es enfermo*   (PERMANENT ADJECTIVE)
                 'He's an invalid'

         c.   *Es un hombre*   (INHERENT NOUN IDENTITY)
                 'He's a man'

         d.   *Es muy guapo*   (PERMANENT ADJECTIVE)
                 'He's very handsome'

---

[12] The preceding and following steady state—vis-à-vis the action—are extremely important in the semantic characterization of verbs (Givón, 1973c). By "percepts" one must mean "perceptual *judgment*," since obviously we do not deal here with unprocessed, atomic units of perception à la the empiricist, and chances are that even the most "primitive" percepts involve judgment (Anttila, 1977, p. 15).

[13] The description here is a bit simplified, and for a more complete description see Bolinger (1971).

8.6. An Ontology of Experience in a Universe of Time

When the locative concept involves place of origin, which is totally unchangeable, only *ser* can be used:

(20)   a.   *Es de España*
                   'He is from Spain'
          b.   *Está de España

In clefting, which is the most identity-oriented copular expression, only *ser* can be used. Thus:

(21)   a.   *Es mi amigo que vino*
                   'It's my friend who came'
          b.   **Está mi amigo que vino*

Finally, a conflict ensues when the prediction involves the PERMANENT LOCATION of entities which normally don't move too rapidly, such as *house* or *village*. Here, while "the grammar" says to use *estar*, speakers do their level best to use *ser*, if possible via clefting:

(22)   a.   ?*Mi casa está en Ignacio*
                 ?'My house is temporarily in Ignacio'[14]

          b.   *Mi casa, . . . es en Ignacio*
                 'My house, . . . It's in Ignacio'

          c.   ?*Es en Ignacio donde está mi casa*
                 ?'It's in Ignácio that my house is'

          d.   ?*Nuestra ciudad está al otro lado de las montañas*
                 ?'Our town is on the other side of the mountains'

          e.   *Nuestra ciudad, . . . es al otro lado de las montañas*
                 'Our city, . . . it's on the other side of the mountains, . . .'

          f.   ?*Es al otro lado de las montañas donde está nuestra ciudad*
                 ?'It's on the other side of the móuntains that our city is'

Sentences (22b, e) are an elegant escape, since *es* is left incompleted and could be interpreted as an aborted cleft, that is, involving a *permanent* state of affairs. Sentences (22 a, d) remain pragmatically bizarre, somehow imparting temporal instability to the location of a house or a town. While (22c, f) are problematic because the cleft escape hatch is subverted by the use of *estar*, which again imparts temporality. The whole force of the Spanish data, however, reaffirms the lexical continuum of nouns–adjectives–verbs as a continuum of temporal stability. What is temporally most stable has the highest chance of being lexicalized as a noun in a human language, and thus granted the experiential status of entity.

[14] This is acceptable referring to a mobile home, but much less so referring to a constructed, well-founded immovable house.

8.7. THE SECOND, THIRD, AND FOURTH DIMENSIONS: SPACE

The first ordering relation, resulting in the construction–cognition of time, makes the individuation of entities possible. However, those entities are perforce only points on the time scale. Thus, if two concrete entities could exist at the very same point in time, the cognizer armed only with the tools of the first ordered relation would be, in principle, incapable of cognizing–construing or individuating such entities as different from each other. By introducing further dimensions ("parameters," "degrees of freedom") one can next construe a universe of more concrete entities. Thus a universe of two dimensions allots each entity two degrees of freedom, so that it may vary along a *time axis* as well as along one spacial line. With the introduction of another dimension we may have entities that exist in time as well as in a euclidean geometric plane, and thus have three degrees of freedom. With the introduction of the next dimension we have entities with four degrees of freedom, existing in time as well as in three-dimensional space.

8.8. SPATIAL PERCEPTION, PERCEPTUAL JUDGMENT, AND CALIBRATION

In Section 8.6, I suggested that percepts or *instances of perceptual judgment* receive cognitive–lexical coding in human cognition–language as nouns, adjectives, or verbs according to the criterion of *temporal stability* ("change"). I further suggested (with a bibliographic reference to Anttila, 1977) that percepts by themselves are not atomic units of fact, but involve perceptual judgment. That is, they do not depict experience *per se* but rather *construed* experience. One could continue to push back this problem further and further until one ultimately arrives at the most rudimentary, basic reflection of it, namely the precalibration of our perceptual–cognitive apparatus to a range where the phenomenological word is *nonrandom*, and where binary distinctions can be made so that one pole of the binary feature is *more frequent*, more prevalent in its appearance to us and thus becomes the *background* or *absence* of the binary property, while the other pole is *less frequent*, thus perceptually more *salient*, standing out on the background, that is, it is the *foreground* pole that becomes the *presence* of the feature.

The relevance of this formulation can be illustrated by probing into the ontology of our spatial experience. One of the most reliable criteria by which we judge that entity A begins at point A_1 and ends at point A_n, then empty space ("absence of entities") follows, and then entity B

8.9. The Paradox of Order and Chaos

begins with point B_1, etc., is by judgment of *perceptual density*. Perceptual density by itself must be *time-based*, and may be thus formulated as:

(23) *Perceptual density is the frequency of encounters of our perceptual apparatus with "atomic percepts"*

Thus, as our perceptual apparatus scans space over time, contiguous areas of rapidly recurring perceptual stimulation will be judged to be contiguous zones within the *same entity*. While areas with relatively low perceptual density will be judged to be *empty space* between different entities. This may be represented diagrammatically as:

(24)
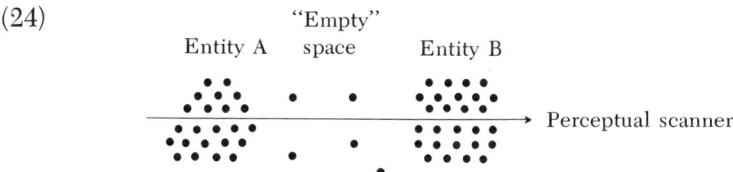

Now, it takes only a simple argument to show that—at the borderline of dense entities and "empty" space—the judgment as to what perceptual density will be still considered empty space and what higher density will be considered *high enough* to be included inside the physical boundary of a dense entity is, *in principle, not* a logically necessary judgement. Rather, it is a matter of *degree*, it involves a *density continuum,* and thus depends on the *fineness of calibration* of the perceptual scanner. We thus live in a universe with entities of certain relative size (vis-à-vis each other) and certain relative density (within entities as well as within the universe) precisely because our constructive tools—perception–cognition—calibrated themselves at that level.

The unfolding story of the discovery of atomic and more and more—smaller and smaller—subatomic particles is a nice, concrete metaphor of the relationship between the universe and our calibrated perception. Our natural tools were calibrated to a scale where bodies below a certain size cannot be construed. Our scientific tools can be viewed as ways of artificially achieving finer resolution of our perceptive–constructive tools. Thus, in principle, we are bound to discover smaller and smaller subparticles as long as we continue to calibrate our perceptive tools finer and finer.[15]

8.9. THE PARADOX OF ORDER AND CHAOS

There are two parallel paradoxes that suggest themselves at this point. The first is a paradox of Taoist cosmology, the second presumably

---

[15] This is not to suggest that our tools perceive the subparticles themselves, but rather they perceive some consequences of the behavior of those subparticles, from which we go on and *abduce* their existence.

of mathematics. The normal Taoist term for the unconstrued, undifferentiated universe is *Tao*, the unnameable, unthinkable, indivisible "one." The principle of cognitive–perceptual *differentiation,* underlying the world of forms, perceptual judgements and individuals, where distinctions are perceived, individuals cognized and an entire universe is construed, is the principle of *Yin and Yang*. This is the Taoist stand-in for diversity, criterial properties, relations, qualities and thus the prerequisite for individuation. The *Yin and Yang* principle is the cosmological prerequisite for judgements of similarity and identity. Now, given this formulation, one finds a baffling sutra in the *Tao Teh Ching,* one which goes like this:[16]

(25)   *From Tao one is born,*
         From one, two,
         From two, three,
         From three, all.
                                        (Sutra 42)

Since Tao is normally refered to in the Tao Teh Ching as "one," why then the redundant transition from Tao to one? However, strictly speaking, Tao is not really "one," since in the preconstrued universe the scale of *one, two, three,* etc. does not yet exist. Further, Tao is only "one" by resorting to a post hoc process of elimination, that is, it is neither "two" nor "three" nor "many." It is indeed "all there is," but the sense in which "all" can be equated with "one" violates Lao Tse's first exhortation concerning the unnamable, unspeakable, uncognizable nature of Tao. The term "one" for Tao is thus used metaphorically and imprecisely, to contrast with "diversity," and Tao is thus "one" only because of the cognitive trap of human language which resorts to labeling the unnamable in order to deal with it. If this is understood, then the transition from Tao to "one" becomes coherent: "One" is the first dimension, the first ordering relation, the first degree of freedom, TIME. The transition from Tao to "one" is thus the transition from the predimensional into the one-dimensional universe. It is the real quantum jump—as Lao Tse correctly asserts—from the unconstruable universe of *white light*[17] into the construable–perceivable–cognizable universe. From there on, the enrichment of the universe depends on adding more dimensions, eventually many more binary and n-ary distinctions, a process of construction extendable ad infinitum.

The mathematical paradox also involves a linguistic trap, or rather a linguistic insufficiency. Set theorists normally assume that an *ordered set,* that is, one in which membership is arbitrated by an *ordered rela-*

---

[16] This particular rendition, like other quotations from the Tao Teh Ching in this book, is my own.
[17] "White light" is a common Buddhist metaphor.

tion, is a more complex notion than an *unordered set* (or unordered relation–property). This assumption obviously has some intuitive merit, since while both the ordered and unordered set involve *set membership* and thus a *criterial property* which determines such membership, it is only the *ordered* set that involves an ordering relation–principle. Now, the axiom of existence of the universe (12) suggests that a precondition for construing a universe must be the assumption that a universe exists. If there existed at that stage any individual members of the set "universe," there would have existed no way of knowing them or their existence, since at the preconstrued universe of Tao, the potential members of the set universe could share only one pristine property—that of membership in that set, that is, of existing in the universe. The Tao universe of preconstrued chaos is therefore an *unordered-set* universe, since "membership" is per se not an ordering relation. Now, consider the following extrapolation:

1. A uni-dimensional universe is one in which each individual has *one* degree of freedom. The behavior of such individual is thus highly regimented and predictable.
2. A two-dimensional universe allows individuals within it *two* degrees of freedom. That is, their freedom is increased relative to the uni-dimensional universe.
3. In a three-dimensional universe the freedom of individuals is again increased by one degree.
4. Therefore, a *more complex* order is an order in which the freedom ("unpredictability") of individuals is larger than in a less complex universe.
5. Thus, if the number of dimensions–properties–distinctions in a universe reaches infinity, the degree of freedom of individuals in that universe must also reach infinity. In other words, they are then *capable*[18] of *complete unpredictability*, which is another way of saying that the universe has arrived at total *chaos* or *randomness* once again.

Our paradox can therefore be formulated as:[19]

(26)   *The infinitely ordered universe is a randomly ordered one*, or *Chaos is merely the most complex ("infinitely complex") form of order*

Now, is the maximally ordered universe with its newly arrived chaos also the universe of Tao? Obviously not, since in the universe of Tao

---

[18] It is not necessary that *each* individual in such a universe has infinite freedom–unpredictability, but only that *some* individual *could*.

[19] For a similar conclusion supported mathematically regarding order and complexity in music, see Gougen (1975).

there were *no* dimensions and thus *no* degrees of freedom. But obviously also *yes*, since individuals within both universes are equally unpredictable. One reading of total unpredictability is also *total inscrutability* or total opacity vis-à-vis our perceptual–cognitive tools. Here again language seems to fail us, since the universe of Tao was neither **un**ordered nor was it **maximally**-ordered, it was **pre**ordered, that is, the notion of ordering was irrelevant to it. Individuals within such a universe are not **non**existant but rather **pre**existant, simply had the potential of existence, a potential not yet realized. Only via construction–cognition–perception did the universe in fact step out of its potentiality and into real existence. The set-theoretician may thus be right about the more primitive nature of unordered sets, but the term unordered is inaplicable to the preconstrued, preordered universe of Tao. It is the total, principled *incompatibility* of our perception–cognition with the state of preexistence, preorder, predistinction, and preindividuation of Tao, which created the illusion of a paradox.

8.10. UPPER BOUNDS AND OPTIMALITY

In Sections 8.4 and 8.5 we saw that there are good reasons why individuation of phenomena in a potentially infinite universe cannot be affected without recourse to an *ordered* relation. Even in a less-than-infinite universe, a great many binary relations will be necessary in order to affect individuation of entities, while *one* ordered relation can affect the individuation of an infinite number of entities. Thus the first ordered relation, that of PRECEDENCE, is not only at the very base of mathematics but also at the foundation of our experience of the universe.

However, another question must be raised, and it is a question of fact rather than principle: How come in the construction of the universe, sentient beings used four ordered relations—our four spatiotemporal dimensions—and then quit and proceeded to increase the complexity of the construed universe largely via *binary, unordered* relations–properties? I see no discernible *logical* grounds why this should be so, but nevertheless it is a striking *fact*. These facts may illustrate an "upper bounds" phenomenon: Perhaps four linear coordinates are "enough" for a basic mapping diagram of our universe. Perhaps at the present level of calibration of our constructive apparatus, four ordered dimensions could take care of the phenomenological multiplicity and diversity, so that from there onward we resort to adding less powerful constructive tools, that is, binary or n-ary *unordered* distinctions. Perhaps, finally, a certain principle of *parsimony* is at work here, so that a four-dimensional spatiotemporal grid is all we really need, with the help of a number of less powerful unordered properties, to place the limited diversity of our experiential universe on a perceptual–cognitive map. As I shall argue in

Section 8.12.3, the size and complexity of our experiential universe is not an objective function of the environment, but rather an *interactive* function of the behavior of organisms within their environment.

8.11. THE ONTOLOGY OF EXPERIENCE IN A SPATIOTEMPORAL UNIVERSE

In Section 8.6, I discussed our first experiential criterion for individual identity, that of *time-stability*. Having complicated our universe by three more spatial dimensions, we are now in the position to discuss space-related experiential criteria. Consider first the following:

(27) SPACE EXCLUSIVITY OF ENTITIES AT A FIXED TIME. *An individual a is identical to itself and nonidentical to any other individual b if at the time when a occupies a certain unique position in space (as defined by our second, third and fourth dimensions), b cannot occupy the same space.*

Criterion (27) is attractive and intuitively characteristic of our experiential judgment of concrete bodies. It is not, however, unproblematic. To begin with, our concepts of *enclosure, containment, being dissolved in liquid, pregnancy, crowd, mass,* and *whole–part* seem to violate this criterion. On the face of it, further, our system of language-coded dexis, by which entities are said to be "at the same point" as other— anchoring—entities (speaker, hearer), suggest that criterion (27), while partially revealing of our experiential judgment, is by itself insufficient, being too strong.

Let us consider (28):

(28) THE SPACE-UNIQUENESS CRITERION FOR ENTITIES AT FIXED TIME. *An individual a is identical to itself if at a unique point in time it can only be at one uniquely defined coordinate-point in space, but not at any other point.*

It is easy to see that criteria (27) and (28) supplement each other. Criterion (27) defines in a rough way our experiential judgment of entities being *different* from each other, by observing that *in general* they would tend to occupy mutually exclusive space. Furthermore, the linguistically based objections to (27) are of a peculiar nature: They involve, first, pairs of entities (*mother–embryo, water–salt, room–furniture, bottle–contents*) which can *temporarily* occupy the same space and thus violate criterion (27), but which can also be brought to occupy *different* spaces and thus at least at *some* time abide by (27). Thus, if (27) is modified to read . . . *at least at some point in time* . . . rather than . . . *at the time* . . . , it then becomes more reoperable. This leaves behind the cardinal case, however, that of *whole–part* relations and thus, perforce, of *type–*

token relation as well. What one must do here is acknowledge an *inclusion hierarchy* in which the space-exclusivity of individual entities is defined vis-à-vis entities *at the same metalevel,* that is, at the same type–token level. Thus, parts of the whole will be indeed space-exclusive of each other, but not of the whole. Tokens of the same type will be space-exclusive of each other but not of their type. And members of a crowd will be space-exclusive of other members of the same crowd but not of the crowd itself. With this universal proviso, the difficulty seen in criterion (27) dissolves. It then is the criterion for "occupying a different physical space," while (28) remains the experiential criterion of "not occupying more than one space at the same time."

It is easy to see that criterion (28) is also the one which proscribes *infinitely fast motion,* since only by this means can an individual occupy more than one unique space at the same time. Thus, while our universe is largely construed so that we can be at the same place at two different times, we cannot be at two different places at the same *time.* Our four dimensions are thus *not* on equal footing in our experiential-judgment. Rather, the use we make of them in construing our universe is *skewed,* with [time] occupying a certain privileged position that [space] could never occupy. Furthermore, our experience of temporal entities need make no reference to [space], but our experience of spatial entities cannot exist without reference to [time]. Thus, in our first experiential criterion (17), time-stability was shown to be a necessary feature for the individuation of concrete as well as temporal entities. While our criteria (27) and (28), both pertinent to concrete entities, must make reference to both [space] and [time].

8.12. SOME EVOLUTIONARY CORRELATES OF THE TIME–SPACE UNIVERSE

Since in some sense I am not making here only logically necessary ontological claims about the universe as it *must be,* but also about the factual universe as it *probably is,* it would be of interest to investigate whether there is some support to the progression Tao > Time > Space in the evolution of sentient beings.

8.12.1. Purely Temporal Experience

The most primitive *sentient*[20] beings were probably akin to bacteria, though perforce without the parasitic adaptation, since there were no

---

[20] While this is not immediately obvious, I would like to count as "sentient" only organisms which (a) metabolize on their own; and (b) replicate on their own or sexually. This excludes viruses, which may in any case be *escapees* out of the nuclei of higher organisms, and thus do not represent an independent evolutionary stage in their own right.

8.12. Some Evolutionary Correlates of the Time–Space Universe

higher organisms existing at that stage to rely upon. In terms of their size, such organisms are so small that even the most rudimentary experience of the consequences of space, namely the *up–down* differentiation due to gravity, was not experienced by them within the lifetime of a single organism.[21] Such organisms live *in solution,* suspended, with their motion largely reflecting the random bombardment by the solvent molecules, due to the latter's heat-induced motion. Their feeding (absorbing chemicals out of the solution) is done in all directions, and there is no indication that they react in a purposive manner to either light or sound. One may claim that the selective absorbtion of chemicals through their membrane constitutes an olfactory–savory behavior–perception, but that may be in doubt, and I suspect that it merely constitutes a *biochemical* prerequisite for the eventual development of olfactory–savory experience.

It is, of course, impossible, on grounds of principle, to rule out the possibility that bacteria do have some perceptual distinctions which go undetected, but at the present state of our knowledge, behavioral manifestations of having such perceptual distinctions is not available. However, there is one absolutely incontrovertible piece of behavior which bacteria (and other monocellular organisms) do indeed exhibit: Regularly, on the clock (given steady temperature and unvaried concentration of chemicals in their medium), at precisely timed intervals, bacteria *split.* In other words, while they may possess no coherent perceptual modality of space, light, sound, taste, etc., they certainly seem to possess some—however rudimentary—*time consciousness.* Their clock may indeed be chemically based, but it is certainly effective. And while they may not have perceptual modes to construe the universe outside themselves in any *other* way, they certainly construe the dimension of time rather successfully, again to judge from their behavior. They thus constitute a certain type of evidence that our scenario for construing a universe may have also been reflected in the evolutionary scenario via which sentient beings arose.

8.12.2. Unidimensional Space

I cannot bring to mind an organism reflecting precisely the next-complex stage of construction, that is, with time and one spatial dimension. But the closest that comes to mind is the *amoeba.* What was said above concerning the manner of splitting of bacteria is also true of amoebas. In addition, however, their relative weight is sufficiently large

---

[21] The question of what constitutes "the same" organism with bacteria is a bit muddled, since they replicate via splitting–cloning and one may thus claim that the previous whole still lives in the subsequent parts. However, given that we have decided to apply our criterion of space-exclusivity (27) only at the *same* meta-level of type-token, the problem is not serious. Bacteria may also gravitate rather slowly, within hours or days, towards the bottom of the solution. However, within the lifetime of an individual bacterium (seconds), such slow change has no experiential consequences.

so that they sink downward in solution, and thus may be found "crawling" on upward-facing surfaces. In that sense, they may have some—however weak—differentiation of a single, up–down spatial dimension. However, their totally amorphic physique strongly suggests that in terms of behavioral consequences and evolutionary adaptation, they are still primarily adapted to a uni-dimensional universe. Now, while they may not *construe* a four-dimensional universe, they certainly possess a number of binary sensory distinctions, such as light–dark and touch–empty. Thus it seems that the introduction of further dimensions—beyond time—into the constructive aparatus of sentient beings may not directly proceed after the introduction of TIME. Perhaps the principle of parsimony is here at work (see Section 8.10), so that given the narrow scope of their experiential universe, one (or two) dimension suffices, and the rest is handled by the less powerful binary distinctions.

Next I would like to contrast the amoeba and other free-floating organisms with those larger ones who maintain a fixed position over time. Let us first consider trees. They maintain a fixed position, but their behavior certainly suggests consciousness—at whatever level—of the *down–up* spacial mode. Their roots grow downward, their shoots grow upward, and they certainly change over time, however slowly. Thus, any serious discussion of their perceptual–cognitive apparatus—which, if existing, is most likely to reside separately in individual cells—must take account of their lifetime, slow rate of change and the calibration of their perceptual–cognitive apparatus to such an extended time scale. Certainly, it would be foolish to rule out cognitive–perceptual processes in trees just because their sense of time is much slower than ours, and thus relevant internal change is much more protracted. Certainly, their behavior bears evidence that they are conscious of the up–down spatial dimension, that they are conscious of light and dark, of temperature, relative humidity and, at least for some species, also of touch. However, their stationary position and the way they derive their livelihood via the single up–down spatial dimension makes it unnecessary for them to deal with the other spatial dimensions at the level of perception–cognition, and their symmetry is obviously neutral with respect to the other spatial dimensions, being uniformly *round*.

Nonvertebrate stationary ("relatively stationary") organisms such as *sea anemones* exhibit the same indifference as trees to the need for more than one spatial dimension in their construed universe. Their distinct up–down differentiation contrasts sharply with their round, undifferentiated form vis-à-vis the rest of space. Since they are stationary and stuck to a ground that is relatively time-stable, both their food and their perceptual input comes from the water above, and that is indeed where both their orifice and their perceptual equipment is located.

8.12.3. Motion and Three Dimensional Space

The real quantum jump toward behaving in and construing three-dimensional space seems to have occured when organisms—at whatever evolutionary point[22]—developed a mode of livelihood by which they began to *move under their own volition* in search of food. All of a sudden their universe changed drastically:

1. The density of perceptual input is much higher on the side which "faces" the direction of motion, that is, faces the hitherto unexplored universe. Conversely, the density of perceptual experience is much lower on the side facing the already explored universe, where percepts emanate from old, familiar entities.[23]
2. The density of potential food sources is likewise higher in the direction of motion, where *new* food sources exist. On the other hand, the older environment was left relatively depleted of nutrients.

It is far from accident that organisms which move in search of their food develop another dimension in their body symmetry, that of *front–back*. Furthermore, both their perceptual apparatus and their food-gathering tools gravitate toward the newly established front, where a more dense bombardment of experience and food is to be expected. The reverse process is also well documented: Fish species which became stationary again on the ocean's floor rapidly lose their front–back differentiation, they become round, their eyes "migrate" to the top-center, and thus they perceptually, cognitively, and behaviorally readapt to a universe with only one spatial dimension, up–down.

The ontological implication to be drawn from this discussion are rather far reaching: The evolution of the consciousness–construction of the second and third spatial dimensions beyond the up–down dichotomy was not prodded by environmental change per se. Rather, it was the product of a compound, *interactive* change—in terms of time-density of perceptual experience—precipitated by the organism's embarking upon *self-propelled motion*. Thus the introduction of the third and fourth dimensions into the construed universe of the evolving sentient beings, and thus the construction of the time–space universe as we know it, became an evolutionary necessity because of the accelerated change—that is, increased perceptual bombardment per time—caused by voluntary motion. Our phenomenological universe thus became *en-*

---

[22] This move must have taken place somewhere between the stage of *coelenterates* (hydra, sea anemone) and mollusks or worms.

[23] Once again, the distinction here is *not* logically necessary but rather a matter of experiential calibration, where repeating "similar" percepts from "the same" source become *background* experience, old information.

larged, in terms of the time-density of perceptual experience, as a result of voluntary motion. The introduction of the second and third spatial dimensions into our cognitive schema may be viewed as an adaptation to that change. This reinforces the suggestion made in Section 8.10 concerning the reasons for the upper-bounds of *four* on our dimensional system of construing our universe. Evolutionarily, it seems, dimensions were added when motivated by an increase in the potential for differentiable entities, as *judged* by the increase in the time-density ("frequency") of perceptual experience.

The evolution of consciousness is thus not blind or indifferent, nor is it a passive product of environmental change per se. Rather, it must have been motivated by *interaction* between the environment and an *active* organism, an organism which exerted its *purpose*, a *creative* organism,[24] an organism which began to *move under its own volition*, an organism which began to behave like an *agent*.

8.13. ACTION, AGENTS, INTENT, AND CAUSALITY

In the preceding section we have arrived, via the investigation of the ontology of time–space experience, at the second major topic to be investigated here, namely the cluster of semantic and experiential properties which define our concepts of *action, volition, causality,* and *agent*. In brief,[25] the universe of *actions* or *events*—as concepts—is mapped in language via the sublexicon of *verbs*. As we have seen above, some verbs denote *states* rather than event. Those two differ from each other by the element of *change over time*. *States* involve no change over time, and as seen above they may last shorter or longer stretches of time. But so long as they are coded in language as states, they are construed to involve no change across time. *Events,* on the other hand, involve change across time. Thus, (29a) depicts a state, while (29b) depicts an event:

(29) a. State: *The house sat on the hill*
 b. Event: *The house slid down the hill*

The linguistic coding of events always imparts to them an initial and final state. Thus, in (29b) the house is depicted[26] as being at a higher position on the hill prior to the *time axis*[27] of *slide,* and then during the

---

[24] For discussion of the creative, interactive nature of biological evolution, see Koestler (1967, Ch. 11) and Lamendella (1976, in prep.).

[25] For more details see Chafe (1970), Langacker (1975), and Talmy (1976), among others.

[26] Most commonly verbs tend to code ("assert") the final state resulting from the event, while the intial state is left to be inferred or presupposed.

[27] See discussion in Givón (1973c).

8.13. Action, Agents, Intent, and Causality

event of *sliding* it arrived at a subsequent state of being at a position somewhat lower than its initial position (perhaps even all the way to the bottom of the hill), and that was the *terminal* state. Verbs depicting events may or may not explicitly characterize a terminal state, and (29b) above did not. But, in contrast, (30a, b) do:

(30)   a. *The orange **fell** off the tree*
               (i) Initial state: *On the tree*
               (ii) Final state: *Off the tree*
      b. *The orange **fell** to the ground*
               (i) Initial state: *Above the ground*
               (ii) Final state: *On the ground*

Next, events may be *volitional–intended,* that is, "caused" events, or they can be *nonvolitional–unintended* and thus, so far as the cognitive map reflected in language is concerned, without an explicitly mentioned cause. Thus, for example, the events depicted in (29b), (30a), and (30b) were all nonvolitional events. On the other hand, typical volitional–caused events are:

(31)   a. *John **ran** down the hill*
         b. *Mary **walked about** restlessly*
         c. *John **broke** the window in his rage*
         d. *Mary **put** the box into the cupboard*

Volitional events are called *actions* and the verbs mapping them in language are called *active verbs*. Just as any other event, they depict a *change in the state of the universe* from a state$_i$ prior to a time axis to a state$_j$ sometime after the time axis. The change could involve the state of the subject itself, as in (31a, b), or the state of various objects, as in (31 c, d). But in addition to depicting the change in the state of the universe via the event, actions also assign *responsibility* for the event, by singling out the subject as being the *agent–causer*. In other words, they make a statement about the *intentional behavior* of—primarily—human agents. Many verbs in language may be used ambiguously with respect to this assignment of causal responsibility. They may either characterize the *cause* without imparting *intent* and responsibility, as in:

(32) *John **broke** the window by tripping on the toy poodle and falling*

Or they may characterize actions in which the agent *intended* to cause the result, as in:

(33)   *John **broke** the window on purpose*

The event described in (32) is, strictly speaking, not an action, since John did not do anything active, he simply tripped and *fell*. On the other hand, the event depicted in (31c) is problematic. The adverbial *in his rage* clearly implies that the subject was *acting*, that is, using his own volition.[28] But it may well be that John actually intended to do something else, that is, achieve a different *result* (*Smash the vase on the floor*) and then accidentally wound up breaking the window.

Many and perhaps most languages seem to mark in various ways the distinction between *intended* and *unintended* causation, and the relevant notion which separates the two seems to be that of *control*.[29] That is, the agent is assigned responsibility to a particular *causal chain* of events if the agent *had control* over his actions. The notions of *volition–intent* and *control* are hierarchically related. Every instance of controlled-causation also involves intent, but some *intents* may involve no controlled-causation, as in:

(34)   *John wanted very much to leave the room, but he was bound and gagged and tied to the bed.*

Controlled action is thus akin to *intentional behavior*, not simply intent.

8.14. EXPERIENTIAL CRITERIA FOR AGENTS

In the cognitive map of caused events as represented in human language, only agents can be the subjects of verbs–predicates which depict such events. The class of agents in language is almost exclusively human, with rare allowances for cars, computers, winds and fires, occasionally water, and—as a *swing category*—higher vertebrates. Furthermore, there seem to be two criteria involved in the decision as to who is agent and who is not, and those two are hierarchically arranged. They are best reflected in the classification of verbs. In general, most verbs which depict *causal actions* are confined to humans, and to humans capable of intentional behavior and having control of their behavior. Predicates[30] of this type are, for example:

(35)   a.   *He left the room*
       b.   *He danced the jig on top of the wine cask*
       c.   *He fired all his employees*
       d.   *She completed the assignment*

---

[28] For the moment I will disregard the ethical problem of responsibility for one's actions under diminished capacity, such as in rage.

[29] For many details see Shibatani (1973), Kachru (1976), and Givón (1975d).

[30] Since quite often the causative ("intent–control") properties of a proposition are not determined by the verb alone but by some combination of the verb with various objects and adverbs, the term "predicate" is a bit more precise here than "verb."

8.14. Experiential Criteria for Agents

Neither a 4-month-old baby nor a bound adult could be the subjects of these predicates, nor a machine, nor the wind or fire, though a dog could perhaps be the subject of (35a).

There is, however, another class of verbs which selects almost exactly the same class of subjects, namely, *adult humans*, with fuzzy-edge exceptions occasionally. That is the class of verbs of *cognition, emotion,* and *intent*. Representative examples of these verbs are:

(36) a. Cognition: *Know, think, believe, understand, guess, suspect, etc.*

b. Emotion: *Fear, hope, be sad, be angry, be happy, etc.*

c. Intent: *Want, intend, plan, refuse, etc.*

I will call the common denominator of all these verbs *consciousness*. It seems that an implicational relation holds between the two language-based criteria for agents, and that *intentional-action* implies *consciousness* but not vice versa. In other words, intentional action is a subcategory of consciousness.

In addition to being subjects, conscious entities—usually depicted by us as obligatorily human—may also appear in highly specific *object* positions in sentences, and those positions are restricted to a *conscious* participant just as rigidly as the position of agent-subject and conscious-subject. Typical examples are:

(37) a. *John told **Bill** that . . .*
b. *It pleases **me** that you did that*
c. *Mary talked **to John***
d. *She ordered **him** to leave*
e. *They fired **him***
f. *She gave **him** a flower*

To summarize, the relation between the two experiential criteria for *agents* may be given in the implicational hierarchy:

(38) *actor under **own power** > **conscious** participant*

and 'own power' may be translated into 'own intent/volition', so that:[31]

(39) *purposeful agent > conscious participant*

---

[31] As we shall see below, "own power" in more concrete physical terms is evolutionarily prior. Ultimately, we can have a paralyzed executive *with authority* instructing an underling to press the doomsday button, and the behavior of such an executive is coded linguistically as that of an agent *in control*. Our notion of control has already evolved beyond the merely physical and has *social* parameters as well.

8.15. THE ONTOLOGY OF CAUSATION AND AGENCY

In this section I will attempt to suggest how our notions of conditionality, causality, agent, intent, and power are derived, via a succession of inferential steps, from the experience of our first ordered dimension, *time*. The inferences involved are never purely deductive, they are probably instances of Peirce's *abduction*, and as far as I can see they always involve some *inductive* component. They are thus typical inferences which sentient beings are likely to make in the process of enlarging their cognitive map of a universe and thus, perforce, of enlarging their universe itself. The most common nondeductive step seen in those inferences is normally labeled "fallacy" by logicians, that is, the step of inferring from a *unidirectional* conditional a *biconditional* ("two way implication") relation. I will attempt to show that far from being a fallacy, such behavior may represent a coherent *heuristic strategy*.

8.15.1. From Time-Sequence to Conditionality

Consider two events sequenced in time, a and b, where b (or rather its *type*[32]) always occurs following a. Other events, such as c or d may also follow a, so that logically one could not claim the conditional implication:

(40) $$a > b$$

However, since b occurs only if a occurs first, one is indeed justified in drawing the opposite conditional implication:

(41) $$b > a$$

However, notice that the leap from b *follows* a to b *implies* a is not, per se, a deductive leap. Rather, it is an *experiential*, intuitive, abductive conclusion based on *frequency* of occurence. That is, while it is not inductively air-tight, it nevertheless involves *inductive intuition*, that is, the generalization from repeated individual *tokens* of the a, b sequence of event to a *rule* of necessary behavior a, b.

Furthermore, the development of the implicational conditional (41) is also justified by this inductive intuition. Thus, at the time when a occurred, the experiencer is not justified in predicting that b will automatically occur. But the minute b has occured one could safely conclude that a must have also occured. Thus, there is always a point in time when a is *true* or *certain* but b is not true, that is, as yet *uncertain*. But on the other hand, there is never a point in time in which b is certain but a is

---

[32] The notion of "conditionality" requires *generalization*, that is, the repetition of more than one token per type and their recognition or tokens of the same type.

8.15. The Ontology of Causation and Agency

not. When one translate the one-way implicational conditional in (41) into set-theoretic terms, one obtains an *inclusion* relation as in:

(42)

Therefore, if *a* is predicted from *b* but not vice versa, then *b* must be a subpart or member of the set *a*, while *a* is a super-set ("genus") of *b*.

One of the most striking results of this formulation is the relation between *certain–uncertain* and *past–future*. Notice that when *b* is still in the *future* and only *a* is the case, *b* is yet uncertain. But on the other hand, when *b* has already occured and thus *a* is part of the *past* of *b*, *a* is certain. This corresponds precisely to the observed modal structure of natural languages,[33] where [past] is the main mode of *certainty–truth* while [future] is the major mode of *uncertainty*. Thus, our experiential ontology is indeed reflected in the facts of natural language.

At this point it is also possible to explain the seemingly universal human propensity for making what logicians in their blindness for the role of *induction* in human inference have chosen to label "fallacious inferences" from the unidirectional conditional *if . . . then. . . .* In deductive logic, given the conditional (43a) as a premise together with the premise that the first term (p) is true, one may legitimately derive the truth of the second term (q) via *modus ponens*. furthermore, (43b) must be also true via *modus tolens*. But both (43c) and (43d) are considered false inferences from (43a) or (43b).

(43) a. $p > q$
b. $\sim q > \sim p$
c. $q > p$
d. $\sim p > \sim q$

The implication in (43a) can be represented by the inclusion diagram in (44) below, where p is a subset of q. However, in situations where the subset almost fills the superset, so that 90% and over of the instances that are q turn out to also be p, human beings—by making an *inductive* inference—have only 10% chance of being wrong by inferring the "fallacious" (43c) from (43a). Similarly, since very few instances can be not p but still q, the deductively fallacious (43d) may also have some plausible inductive foundation. In other words, people make inductive inferences that are not 100% deductively tight because in the flawed universe in which they live, 90% correct decisions is a rather high score.

---

[33] See extensive discussion in Givón (1973b) and Jackendoff (1971). The most striking example of this is found in Creole languages, where the [future] mode also codes all other [uncertainty] modalities, see Bickerton (1975a). But all natural languages show some reflection of this modal structure.

(44)

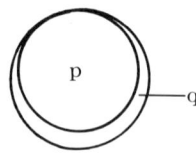

8.15.2. From Conditionality to Causality

As we have seen above, the notion of conditionality is *not* deductively derived from the notion of time-sequence. Rather, it is experientially derived, via inductive intuition. Similarly, the notion of "cause" is not logically deducible from a conditional relation between two events. Neither is it, strictly speaking, intuitively induced from conditionality either. In fact, the move from conditionality to causality represents a *quality leap* in cognitive representation, from the world of mere facts and certainty or uncertainty about them, to the world of *explanation*. The leap may be described as follows:

(45) a. Condition: *If b occurred, a must have earlier occurred*
      b. Precondition: *Therefore the occurrence of a is a necessary precondition for the occurrence of b*
      c. Causation: *Therefore a is the cause of b*

Such an interpretative–explanatory leap from the world of facts to the world of explanation is truly astounding. To begin with, in natural language the necessary relation between causality and time-sequence is well established,[34] so that causes always precedes effects, but could never follow them. Roughly, what is experientially abduced here is the notion of *dependency* versus *independent existence*. Thus our experiential abduction may be described informally as follows:

(46) *If b can never appear without a appearing first, then while a seems to be independent of the occurrence of b, b is always dependent on the occurrence of a. (This observation is strengthened if one never observes any other event x that also occurs always before b.*[35]*) Therefore a must be the cause of b.*

Such a formulation must be tempered by the notion of *causal chains*. That is, while *a* is abduced to be the cause of *b*, another event which always precedes *a*, say *y*, may be abduced to be the prior cause of *a*, and thus the ultimate cause of *b*. In that case, *a* is only the *mediating* cause of *b*. And indeed, natural languages seem to, rather systematically, assign different cognitive coding to *direct* causation versus *mediated–indirect* causation.[36] This is logically speaking a true observation, though its

---

[34] See Vendler (1967), Givón (1975d), and Talmy (1976).
[35] Thus eliminating a conflict of causal explanations.
[36] See Shibatani (1973), Givón (1975d), and Kachru (1976).

impact on the human cognitive experience of causation is apparently negligible.[37] This is so first because of the finite nature of human experience. Thus humans always face, ultimately, some events for which no prior antecedent has been observed. Those are *precisely* the situations where the question of causal relation between two events—one without any apparent antecedence and the other always following it—does arise.

8.15.3. From Cause to Agent

Vendler (1967) observed that, logically speaking, causative expressions in language really involve a relation between two propositions, one the cause-event, the other the result-event. Indeed, there are expressions in natural language which are patterned after such a logical structure, such as:

(47)   a. **Because John left, Mary stayed**

        b. *John's leaving* **caused–induced** *Mary to stay*

While structures such as (47a) occur in most or all natural languages, structures such as (47b)—that is, compacted into a *single* proposition with one causative *verb*, are relatively rare. Rather, what one finds more consistently in natural languages is that if a causal chain is expressed by a single proposition, with a single lexical verb, that is, *viewed as a single event*, then rather than placing the entire *event-cause* as the subject of the causative verb, natural languages prefer to pick up a single *nominal argument* of the cause-event and make it the subject of the causative verb.[38] That subject is then interpreted as the *agent* of the causal chain, the one who had *control*, the one who *acted volitionally*, the one *responsible* for causing a change in the state of the universe. In this section I will investigate the ontology of the inferential leap which takes us from judgments about cause-events to judgments about cause-agents, that is, reinterpretations of (47b) as:

(48)   **John made Mary stay**

As seen in Sections 8.13 and 8.14, the two experiential criteria for agents as expressed in the cognitive map of language are (a) *consciousness* and (b) *action under own volition*. Furthermore, as seen in Section 8.12.3, the cardinal, essential type of volitional action as apparent from the evolution of agents is (c) *motion under own volition*. More complex actions must be therefore extensions of and elaborations on motion.

Let us now consider the two events a and b discussed in Section 8.15.2, where a was judged–abduced to be the *cause* of b, due to an observed, recurring time-sequentiality of a before b. Suppose now that

---

[37] Once again, a problem that is enormous for the logician tends to be down-scaled in the actual context of human language.
[38] See discussion in Givón (1975d).

event *a* involves a conscious human participant, and in fact depicts the *action* of that participant. That is, the human participant in *a* is not there as an inert body (*patient, location, instrument*), but rather as the *agent*. Now, in attempting to *explain* why *b* occured, we have arrived at an obvious *external* explanation, that is, the recurring prior occurrence of *a*. On the other hand, we observed no external cause ("recurring prior event") to explain the occurrence of *a*. If we nevertheless seek an explanation (as organisms at this stage of experiential/cognitive development apparently do) to the occurrence of *a*, where shall we find it? We certainly observed no coherent *external* explanation, that is, another event. However, we did observe something else—the agent involved in the action depicted in *a* is *conscious*; and furthermore, it is *capable of volitional action*. That is, it is capable of moving, of changing the state of the universe *of its own accord*, without any external prod. Our internal experience as agents must convince us of the absolute validity of *internal, own motivation* as an explanation–cause for action. Our observation of other agents—that is, the fact that they seem to consistently initiate action on their own and without external prodding—reinforces the internal observation. Being—at this stage of the evolutionary scenario—an organism seeking causal explanations, we have no recourse but to posit the following *teleological imperative:*

(49) *Where no external cause can be observed, and a change in the state of the universe nevertheless occurs, then an **internal** cause must be at work. That is, at least some participant in the change must be an **agent**, capable of volitional action.*

We will therefore conclude that since no visible *external* cause was forthcoming by which to explain event *a*, and since an *agent* was involved in event *a*, therefore the explanation–cause must reside in the *internal* motivation of that agent, that is, the fact that he *acted on purpose*.

The assignment of internal–intentional causation via principle (49) must reflect a common-sensical awareness of *Occam's Razor:*

(50) *One need not assign an invisible, unobservable—and thus experientially unverifiable—explanation to an event for which a visible explanation already exists*

On the other hand, (49) per se is more concerned with the converse principle of explanation, namely, Leibnitz's *principium rationis sufficientis*.[39] Leibnitz's and Occam's principles are the twin edges of inquiry, one exhorts to explain, the other not to over-explain. It is rea-

---

[39] I am indebted to Martin Tweedale and Tora Kay Bikson for discussing with me these two principles. While Tweedale contends (along with the more current modern interpretation) that Occam's Razor is only a *parsimony* principle, Bikson suggests that the inclusion of "more than necessary" in a reasonable formulation of Occam's Razor must presuppose the *necessity* for explanation, that is, Leibnitz's *Principium*.

sonably clear that both must have been involved in the ontology of our concepts of condition, cause, and agent.

Our abductive inference of cause, agent, and intent is thus a natural manifestation of our teleological approach to the universe, and that teleological approach motivates the inference of conditionality from time-sequence, the further inference of causality from conditionality, and the final coup de grâce—the inference of internal cause, that is, *intention*—from the behavior of agents (including ourselves) in cases when no external motivation–explanation can be assigned.

There is much linguistic support for the suggestion that *motion under own volition* must be the prime experiential criterion in our construing *agents* and *intent*. Such support comes from observing the class of entities which can be added to the class [human] as provisional, honorary or semi-agents. Animals, which can *move of their own power*, behave like agents for the purpose of some language mappings (*run, jump, howl*). That is, they are clearly considered capable of acting under their own *intent*, although Cartesian arrogance quite often induces us to interpret their actions as the product of *instinct*. Furthermore, we certainly allow them the benefit of the second manifestation of consciousness, namely, *emotion;* that is, they can be the subjects of 'fear', 'love', 'be angry', 'be happy' etc. However, we seem to hedge about the third manifestation of consciousness, *cognition*, and thus we balk at making them the subject of *think, believe, know, understand, suspect,* etc.

A second, more recent, class of semi-agents is that of machines, cars, computers, robots, etc. Here it seems that we only abide by the criterion of *motion under their own power*, that is, internal motivation for motion, although we keep reverting to inferred intent, as any car owner may attest.

Finally, an ancient class of semi-agents are *fire, running water, wind, lightning, thunder, the sun, the moon,* and *the stars*. Here again it is clear that our major experiential criterion was involved, namely motion that cannot be explained by external causes, and therefore is inferred to arise from internal motivation. In fact, one may view the intellectual and religious evolution of *Homo sapiens* as a progressive *ruling out* of classes of entities as potential agents, that is, capable of intentional behavior. The major criterion involved in the judgment of capability of intent was clearly motion under own power–intent. Thus inorganic objects were ruled out first, except for the persistent water and fire. Trees were ruled out via the inference of the wind as cause of their motion, while the wind itself remained a semi-agent to this day. The concept of animates as agents remains endemic in most extant cultures, Cartesian arrogance and Skinnerian reductionism notwithstanding.[40] Finally, our

---

[40] Skinner seems to have been more consistent and in a way more humble or less anthropochauvinistic, attempting to do away with volition and free choice not only in animals but also in humans.

invoking the Deity in close conjunction with our interpretation of water, fire, lightning, thunder, the wind, the sun, the moon, and the stars is a curious explanatory venture, a symbolic assignment of a resident agent, a typical abductive inference driven by the teleological imerative.

8.15.4. The Ontology of Power

In Section 8.15.1 we observed that in terms of set inclusion or token-type relations, the *cause-event,* that is, the *preceding* one, occupies the position of *super-set* or *genus,* while the result-event ("following") is the member, subset or subspecies of the cause. Now, if causes are precipitated by agents, and agents have the *power to act* or the power to affect change (due to their ability to act–move upon *own* intent), then agents–causes *have the power over* patients–results. A superset could only be larger but never smaller than its subsets–members, thus the entities which have more power also turn out to have a larger size. This is a rather fortunate accident, since our major experiential criterion for power is indeed size. In fact, one might argue that our notion of *rule* is also thickly involved in this schema. This is so because the superset is the *type* of the subsets–members, and thus it is the *rule,* the *generalization* by which all member—*qua* members—must *abide.* Thus size, generality, and power go hand in hand.

8.16. THE ONTOLOGICAL UNITY OF INTERPERSONAL BEHAVIOR

In the preceding sections of this chapter we have investigated, albeit tentatively, the feasibility of considering language and cognition as map of our universe, indeed in a fundamental way our *very* universe itself. The cognitive map we discussed involved no communication per se. That is, it pertained only to the aspects of language which point out to our system of cognitive representation, memory and retrieval. In the course of the investigation, however, we have exceeded the bounds of the cognizing organism almost without notice. This happened when, while investigating the ontological connection between events ("changes in the universe") and causation ("explanation"), we wound up having to develop the notions of *action, intent,* and *agent.* Having done so, we thus established a connection between the behavior of organisms and the changing states of their universe, that is, the environment. In fact, we wound up discussing biological and cognitive evolution as a process of *interaction* between a purposeful organism and its (presumably purposeless) environment.

8.16.1. Action, Behavior, Environment, and Communication

The concept of action itself, as we have already construed, is already by itself an *interactive* notion, involving the relation between the organism and its environment. As we have seen, events may be neutral to the behavior of organisms, and may thus depict initial and final states of the universe where no sentient beings or agents were involved *as such.* On the other hands, actions are changes in the state of the universe where the *intentional behavior* of agents was involved. In other words, the cause-agent perceived the preceding state of the universe, then through intentional behavior caused it to *change* into a different subsequent state. The agent has thus *acted upon* the environment, his purpose was exerted not only internally,[41] but toward entities *outside* the bounds of the organism. Such behavior should rightly be considered as the first step toward *interaction,* although it is admittedly a unidirectional interaction.

An action performed by an agent is intentional, but the intention does not apply equally to all states of the universe depicted in the action. Thus intent is *irrelevant* to the initial state, since that state is already extant, it is *a given fact* pertaining to the time *prior* to the time-axis of the action. On the other hand, the agent's intent is most relevant to the *subsequent* or intended state, the one that follows the time-axis, the one that is *new fact.* In behavior vis-à-vis the environment we thus already perceive the fundamental distinction between *old fact* and *new fact.* And while old facts ("past") are *certain* ("unchallenged"), intended–new facts are tentative, *uncertain, challengeable.* Furthermore, while certain facts may be construed by *both* agents and nonagents alike (i.e., organisms which are passive may already construe the universe), the concept of new states, uncertainty and *intended universe* are only relevant to agents, that is, to organisms capable of intended action.

In Section 8.12.3 I suggested that there was a cogent, necessary reason why the sensory apparatus of organisms migrated to the front—that is, the side *facing* the direction of motion—and that reason was the *perceptual density* of experiential input bombarding that side, as com-

---

[41] It is intriguing to speculate that perhaps for the more primitive organism, action upon itself merely represents an embryonic stage of *inter*action, and that perhaps at that stage the separation between the self and the environment—that is, our existential axioms (11) and (12) as *separate* axioms—has not yet been affected. It is reasonably clear that in the ontologic development of human cognition, this primitive state is indeed prior (Piaget, 1954; Lamendella, in prep.).

pared with the back—the side facing *away from* the direction of motion. In other words, the *new environment* in motion provided a larger information input. But strictly speaking, in pure physical terms, this could not possibly be true, given an assumed random distribution of sense-data in the universe. Therefore, we must be dealing here with an *experiential,* construed truth once again. And at the bottom of such truth lies the most fundamental fact of perception:

(51)   *A recurring experience eventually loses its perceptual saliency, while a new, surprising experience has a higher perceptual saliency.*

Thus the sense-data confronting the organism in its new ("moved-toward") environment as it moves onward are *judged* to be more frequent only because they have a higher perceptual saliency.

The frequency-based principle (51) is the basic foreground–background, figure–ground principle underlying perception and cognition. In the guise of presupposition–assertion or old–new information it is also the principle underlying communication. In psychological terms, this principle is not a primitive, but rather rests on more rudimentary *judgments.* In order to categorize a sense-input as "repeating," one must first have a *taxonomy* of sensory input, that is, a distinction between repeating tokens of the *same type* as against novel tokens of a *different type.* Thus, at the bottom of criterion (51) lies *perceptual judgment* and the ability to tell "same" from "different" (Anttila, 1977, p. 15).

Next consider the implications of our evolutionary suggestions in Section 8.12. Sensory input into stationary organisms must be *random* as far as the four directions are concerned (excluding the up–down dimension). This is evident from their round symmetry as well as from the circular distribution of their sensory apparatus. Therefore, the distinction between recurring versus surprising experiences in the sensory input of such organisms must be totally dependent on the presumably random bombardment by their environment.[42] Therefore, in a fundamental way the dichotomy between old versus new states of the environment does not yet exist in the same evolved way as it must exist for organisms which move under their own power–volition, although some more rudimentary reflection of the same principle must be at work for perceiving *any* "atomic" sense data on any background.

The quantum jump in the organismic concept of *old* versus *new information* is thus not due to communicative behavior, but rather to the rise of agents and motion under intent. This is so because intentional, nonrandom motion introduces an inbuilt bias between *new* expe-

---

[42] In a universe predating the rise of agents, the occasional skewing of perceptual bombardment due to the effect of nonrandom behavior of intent-given agents presumably does not yet intrude.

riences—those which are encountered in the new environment *toward which* the individual moves—and *old*, familiar, perceptually less-salient experiences, those encountered repeatedly in the old environment *from which* the individual is moving. Thus the information-theory potential for communication is already present in the unidirectional interaction between the moving volitional agent and its environment. In fact, volitional motion has opened the gate for the emergence of our construction of new versus old information.[43] The evolution of agents and volitional motion thus derandomized the universe of cognitive mapping, and must have been a necessary precursor in the evolution of communication.

8.16.2. From Behavior to Communication

The evolution from unidirectional behavior (vis-à-vis the environment) to bidirectional behavior or *social interaction* must have required—and must have been motivated by[44]—parallel evolution of social structure. The most likely evolutionary precursor for this must have been the *sexual* mode of replication. Organisms prior to the emergence of this mode as the prime[45] mode of replication required no other members of the same species for food gathering, metabolism, or procreation. They replicated by division or cloning. Division and cloning imply maximal *genetic uniformity* of the population and thus behavioral and informational homogeneity. On the other hand, sexual replication must be viewed as the origin of intraspecies genetic diversification. And as I suggested in Chapter 7, genetic diversification in higher mammals must have gone hand in hand with the emergence of language and unpredictable behavior. One may thus suggest that a similar development occured in the shift from asexual to sexual replication.

Whether sexual or otherwise in origin, the evolution of social interaction and interpersonal communication must have gone hand in hand. As previously suggested, both are characteristic of organisms which act intentionally. Obviously, the cognitive–constructive map involved in trying to "make sense" or "explain" the behavior of another

---

[43] The foreground–background element in rudimentary perception could not have caused this, since it pertains to the most elementary sense-data, rather than to cognitive representation of states of the universe. Although perhaps these two modes are fundamentally one and the same, differing only in the scale of calibration.

[44] See Lamendella's (1976) remarks concerning the interdependence of sociocultural and cognitive evolution, as well as Chapter 7.

[45] Many lower organisms exhibit a dual cycle of reproduction, involving both an asexual (splitting) and sexual (splitting plus merging) modes. Their life-cycle is thus divided into a *haploid* (half nucleus) stage and a *diploid* (full nucleus) stage. In higher organisms, the haploid stage has become incorporated into the body of the organism and has a rather short duration. The main body is diploid, while the premerged ovum and sperm are haploid.

agent must be much more complex than the cognitive map used to construe the more random nonagentive environment. If the behavior of other members of the species[46] were to be relied upon or predicted for the purpose of *common action* ("interaction"), some *inferential schemata* must be developed by which one individual could judge the meaning, intent or purpose of other individuals by observing their overt behavior. *Behavior* thus becomes the clue to *information*. And the rise of a specialized, coded, conventionalized system of communication is nothing but the progressive *refinement* of those *inferential schemata*, so that eventually some facets of behavior becomes specialized, they become more *informatively loaded,* and thus language is off the launching pad and sailing into orbit.

8.16.3. On the Unity of Communicative Modes

I would like to open this section by reiterating the fundamental new–old information dichotomy which underlies communication, and by reminding the reader that old and new information are never on a par with regard to frequency. Rather, old information is in principle of *higher frequency*, more predictable, representing the *bulk* of past experience, the *background*. While new information is a *rarity, surprise,* and thus gains its perceptual–cognitive saliency. Next I would like to allude to Wittgenstein's discussion at the end of his *Tractatus*, concerning the low utility of deductive systems as a mode of learning. Wittgenstein pointed out there that ultimately nothing new can be derived via a purely deductive system, since it is capable of expressing only *tautologies*, that is, totally predictable, old information, or *contradictions*, that is, information that is at *extreme variance* with existing knowledge, so much so that it cannot be integrated with it.

Our communication system as reflected by language exists somewhere in the intervening space between tautology and contradiction. The background of old information is in some sense redundant, yet not redundant enough to be judged tautological. The asserted new information is indeed novel and surprising, but not so surprising as to create a *total* break with existing knowledge. Indeed, our communication system seems to fail most often when the presuppositional and assertional poles are pulled too close to Wittgenstein's extremes. That is, when the information is so predictable so that the hearer loses *interest*; or alternatively, when the information is so unexpected and at such variance with our existing knowledge that the hearer experiences *confusion* and *frustra-*

---

[46] I here tacitly assume that communication and systematic social interaction between individuals of species of radically different evolutionary stages was not a major factor in the evolution of social behavior and communication.

8.16. The Ontological Unity of Interpersonal Behavior 349

tion. Successful communication in human language thus involves the maintenance of *coherence*, and that implies a compromise, a happy medium between old and new information.

One can next observe that in the structure of sentences as well as in the structure of discourse, the informational division between presupposed (old) and asserted (new) information is the backbone of the communicative structure. Since earlier chapters of this book dealt with this aspect of language in great detail, I shall forego further elaboration here.

An interesting reflection of the old–new information dichotomy may be seen in Bernstein's (1959) distinction between *restrictive* and *elaborate* code in language use. Without admitting Bernstein's inferences of social structure,[47] the phenomenon itself is real enough. Restrictive code is basically a *cliché* mode, where set phrases are used in the most automatic, conventionalized fashion, where most of the moves in the exchange are pre-set and predictable, and thus in *some* sense[48] the new-information or "surprise" element in the communication is very low. The elaborate code is the opposite. What is striking about the use of these modes in interaction is that the restrictive code is most commonly used *among strangers* at the *opening stage* of interaction, when the presupposed background is relatively low. On that meager background, the presumably low informative contents of the restrictive code is perforce *salient*. Further, in that context the restrictive code also communicates some *tangential* information, such as *I'm OK, you're OK, I mean well, I'd like to do business, I am familiar with the prevailing communicative code (I speak your dialect), we have enough shared background to transact successfully*, etc. But another context where the restrictive code is used is among familiars, intimately, where so much background is shared that there is relatively little new information to transact. But this is again a slightly misleading depiction, since tangential information is again transacted here, namely, *I still love you, we're still friends, I still like being around, we still understand each other, we still share the same code*, etc. The restrictive code may be thus viewed as the "idle" portion of the information process, the one that *keeps the engine warm*, the one that *keeps the channels open* by constant monitoring and fine-tuning of the code between the full-throttle, information-laden instances of use of the *elaborate* code.

Next, consider successful story-telling, that is, fiction. The best written, most successful fiction involves the subtle blending of familiar

---

[47] As far as my experience goes, both lower and upper socioeconomic classes possess a rich *range* of codes along this register continuum.
[48] New information contents of a communication must be judged relative to the background. It may well be that the seemingly "objective" low information contents of the restrictive code is an artifact of its being construed on a different presuppositional background, one with relatively little shared information.

("connecting") and unfamiliar ("surprising") information. The first element repeatedly *anchors* the story to the reader's experience and provides for *integration,* while the second provides for *suspense,* for interest, and for keeping the reader on his mental toes.

Nonverbal creative modes are just as dependent on the vary same balance. Thus in most traditional music, a delicate balance is woven between the sense of *tradition, continuity* and adherence to the predictable tenets of the *style,* and *innovation,* surprise, creatively, inventiveness, and elaboration. The musician could "fail to communicate" in two ways,[49] either by slavishly following the traditional mode without adding any spice to it, or by breaking with the tradition too rudely. The successful traditional musician thus walks the tight rope between Wittgenstein's tautology and contradiction. One of the major difficulties in experiencing modern music and modern art involves their tendency to overload the dice toward the unexpected and away from the familiar.

The same bipolar balance can be observed in interpersonal relationships, with the two poles being *security–love* versus *freedom–independence.* The first is the *familiar* mode, but by itself it tends to breed boredom. The second is the *surprise* mode, but by itself it tends to breed insecurity. It is in interpersonal relationships that the foreground–background principle (51) tends to play havoc with the individual, often leading to depersonalization of familiar others and the pursuit of novelty-of-experience for novelty's sake. A successful construction of the familiar intimate thus requires *resistance* to the normal experiential judgment via which organisms since time immemorial have construed their external universe. Here one must resist the type–token imputation that "this instance is *merely* a token of the very same behavior type." Rather, one must remind oneself constantly that familiar intimates—and indeed all sentient beings—are fundamentally capable of unpredictable tokens of behavior *at any time,* since they are endowed with free will, and are capable of intentional behavior. Our most common pattern of interpersonal behavior, it seems, carries the experiential judgment which raised us from the primeval swamp too far. It is based on misinterpretation of the unpredictability potential of conscious agents. It certainly flies in the very face of our experiential judgment of ourselves.

Ultimately, one must confront the fundamental trap alluded to by the mystics since time immemorial, the trap inherent in the construing mode itself as a mode of perceiving and cognizing distinctions and of disregarding fundamental unities. The springs which power this trap are to be found in the two fundamental *existential axioms* (11) and (12)

---

[49] The most common comment you hear from Flamenco audiences when the performer lacks inventiveness is *Eso no dice nada!* 'This says nothing!'. And in *Ol' Time Country Fiddlin'* contests you lose points either for breaking with the tradition too flagrantly, or for sticking to it too slavishly and being uninventive.

BIBLIOGRAPHY

Adler, M. (1967). *The Difference of Man and the Difference it Makes*. New York: World Publications Co. (ppbk).
Akiba, K. (1978). Topics in Japanese Historical Syntax. Ph.D. dissertation, Los Angeles: University of California.
Anderson, S. (1970). A little light on the role of deep structure in semantic interpretation. NSF Report #26, Harvard Computational Laboratory. Cambridge, MA.
Anderson, S. (1976). On the notion of 'subject' in ergative languages. In C. Li (Ed.), *Subject and Topic*. New York: Academic Press.
Andrews, A. (1976). The VP complement analysis in Modern Icelandic. Manuscript. Camberra: Australian National University.
Antinucci, F. and Miller, R. (1976). How children talk about what happened. *Journal of Child Language*, 3:167–189.
Antilla, R. (1977). Analogy, State-of-the-Art Report #10. The Hague: Mouton
Ard, W. (1975). Raising and Word-Order in Diachronic Syntax. Ph.D. dissertation. Los Angeles: University of California.
Ashton, E. O. (1944). *Swahili Grammar*. London: Longman's.
Bach, E. (1970). Is Amharic an SOV language? *Journal of Ethiopian Studies* 8(1).
Bartsch, R. and Vennemann, T. (1972). *Semantic Structure*. Frankfurt: Athenäum.
Bates, E. (1974). Language in Context: Studies in the Acquisition of Pragmatics. Ph.D. dissertation. Chicago: University of Chicago.
Bates, E. (1976). *Language and Context: The Acquisition of Pragmatics*. New York: Academic Press.
Bates, E. (1978). The emergence of symbols: Ontogeny and phylogeny. Manuscript. Boulder: University of Colorado.
Bates, E. Camaioni, L., and Volterra, V. (1975). The acquisition of performatives prior to speech. *Merrill-Palmers Quarterly*, **21**(3).
Bell, S. (1974). Some notes on Cebuano and Relational Grammar. Unpublished manuscript.
Benett, T. (1977). An extended view of written and spoken personal narrative. In E. Keenan and T. Bennett (Eds.), *Discourse across Time and Space, Southern California Occasional Papers in Linguistics* **5**. Los Angeles: University of Southern California.

Bernstein, B. (1959). A public language: Some sociological implications of a linguistic form. *British Journal of Sociology* 11:271-276.
Bickerton, D. (1975a) Creolization, linguistic universals, natural semantax and the brain. Manuscript. Honolulu: University of Hawaii.
Bickerton, D. (1975b). Reference and natural semantax. Manuscript. Honolulu: University of Hawaii.
Bickerton, D. (1975c). Creoles and natural semantax. Manuscript. Honolulu: University of Hawaii.
Bickerton, D. (1977). Creoles and language universals. Manuscript. Honolulu: University of Hawaii.
Bickerton, D. and T. Givón (1976). Pidginization and syntactic change: From SOV and VSO to SVO. Papers from the *Parasession on Diachronic Syntax*. Chicago: Chicago Linguistic Society.
Bickerton, D. and C. Odo (1976) Change and Variation in Hawaiian English, Vol. I, NSF Report. Honolulu: University of Hawaii, Social Science and Linguistics Institute.
Bickerton, D. and C. Odo (1977). Change and Variation in Hawaiian English, Vol. II, NSF Report. Honolulu: University of Hawaii, Social Science and Linguistics Institute.
Bierwisch, M. (1967). Some semantic universals of German adjectives. *Foundations of Language* 3(1).
Blatty, W. (1971). *The Exorcist*. New York: Bantam. (ppbk).
Bloom, L. (1973). *One Word at a Time: The Use of Single-Word Utterances Before Syntax*. The Hague: Mouton.
Bloomfield, L. (1924). Review of Saussure's Course Linguistique General. *The Modern Language Journal* 8.
Bokamba, E. G. (1971). Specificity and definiteness in Dzamba. *Studies in African Linguistics* 2(3).
Bokamba, E. G. (1976). Question Formation in Some Bantu Languages, Ph.D. dissertation. Bloomington: Indiana University.
Bolinger, D. (1952[1965]). Linear modification. In D. Bolinger (Ed.) (1965), *Forms of English*. Cambridge: Harvard University Press.
Bolinger, D. (1954). Meaningful word order in Spanish. *Boletín de Filología, Universidad de Chile, Tomo* 8.
Bolinger, D. (1958). A theory of pitch-accent in English. *Word* 14:109-149.
Bolinger, D. (1971). *Ser* and *estar*. Manuscript. Palo Alto.
Bolinger, D. (1972). Accent is predictable (if you are a mind reader). *Language* 48:633-644.
Bolinger, D. (1975). Yes—no questions are *not* alternate questions. In H. Hiż (Ed.), *Questions*, pp. 87-105. Dordrecht: Reidel Publishing Co.
Bolinger, D. (1977a). Another glance at main clause phenomena. *Language* 53.
Bolinger, D. (1977b). Intonation across languages. In J. Greenberg, C. Ferguson, and E. Moravcsik (Eds.), *Universals of Human Language*. Stanford: Stanford University Press.
Bolinger, D. (1977c). Accent that determines stress.
Bolinger, D. (1979). Pronouns in discourse. In T. Givón (Ed.), *Syntax and Semantics, Vol. 12, Discourse and Syntax*. New York: Academic Press.
Boucher, J. and Osgood, C. (1969). The Pollyanna hypothesis, *Journal of Verbal Learning and Verbal Behavior* 8:1-8.
Brown, H. D. (1971). Children's comprehension of relative English sentences. *Child Development* 42:1923-1926.
Bruner, S. J. (1974). The course of cognitive growth. *American Psychologist* 19:1-15.
Bucellati, G. (1970). A Structural Grammar of Babylonian. Manuscript. Los Angeles: University of California.

Canale, M. (1976). Implicational hierarchies of word-order relationships. Paper read at the 2nd International Congress on Historical Linguistics, Tucson, January 1976.
Carter, A. (1974). Communication in the Sensory-Motor Period. Ph.D. dissertation. Berkeley: University of California.
Chafe, W. (1970). *Meaning and the Structure of Language.* Chicago: University of Chicago Press.
Chafe, W. (1976). Givenness, contrastiveness, definiteness, subjects, topics and point of view. In C. Li (Ed.), *Subject and Topic.* New York: Academic Press.
Chafe, W. (1979) The flow of thought and the flow of language. In T. Givón (Ed.), *Syntax and Semantics, Vol. 12, Discourse and Syntax.* New York: Academic Press.
Chomsky, N. (1957). *Syntactic Structures.* The Hague: Mouton.
Chomsky, N. (1964). Current issues in linguistic theory. J. Fodor and J. Katz (Eds.), *The Structure of Language.* Englewood Cliffs, NJ: Prentice-Hall.
Chomsky, N. (1965). *Aspects of the Theory of Syntax.* Cambridge: MIT Press.
Chomsky, N. (1968). *Language and Mind.* New York: Harcourt, Brace and World.
Chomsky, N. (1973a). *For Reasons of State.* New York: Pantheon (ppbk).
Chomsky, N. (1973b). Conditions of transformations. In S. Anderson and P. Kiparsky (Eds.), *A Festschrift for Morris Halle.* New York: Holt, Rinehart, and Winston.
Chomsky, N. (1975). Reflections on Language. New York: Pantheon.
Chomsky, N. and Halle, M. (1968). *The Sound Pattern of English.* New York: Harper and Row.
Christie, A. (1939). *Sad Cypress.* New York: Dell.
Chung, S. (1975). Dative and grammatical relations in Indonesian. Manuscript. San Diego: University of California.
Chung, S. (1976a). Case Marking and Grammatical Relations in Polynesian. Ph.D. dissertation. Cambridge, MA: Harvard University.
Chung, S. (1976b). On the subject of two passives in Indonesian. In C. Li (Ed.), *Subject and Topic.* New York: Academic Press.
Chung, S. (1977). On the gradual nature of syntactic change. In C. Li (Ed.), *Mechanisms of Syntactic change.* Austin: University of Texas Press.
Clark, E. (1971). What's in a word? In T. Moore (Ed.), *Cognitive Development and the Acquisition of Language.* New York: Academic Press.
Clark, H. (1969) Linguistic processes in deductive reasoning. *Psychological Review* 76(4):387-404.
Clark, H. (1971a). The primitive nature of children's relational concepts. In J. Hayes (Ed.), *Cognition and the Development of Language.* New York: Wiley and Son.
Clark, H. (1971b). The chronometric study of meaning components. In *Colloques Internationaux du CNRS, #206, Problémes Actuelles en Psycholinguistique,* pp. 489-505, Paris: CNRS.
Clark, H. (1974). Semantics and comprehension. In T. Sebeok (Ed.), *Current Trends in Linguistics, Vol. 12, Linguistics and Adjacent Arts and Sciences,* pp. 1291-1428. The Hague: Mouton.
Clark, H. and E. Clark (1977). *Psychology and Language.* New York: Harcourt, Brace, and Jovanovich.
Cole, P. (1976). The grammatical role of the causee in universal grammar. Manuscript. Urbana: University of Illinois.
Cole, P. (Ed.) (1978). *Syntax and Semantics, Vol. 9, Pragmatics.* New York: Academic Press.
Comrie, B. (1975a). The formation of relative clauses. Manuscript. Conference on Universals in Human Thought: Some African Evidence. Cambridge, England.
Comrie, B. (1975b). The anti-ergative: Finland's answer to Basque. *Papers from the 11th Regional Meeting.* Chicago: Chicago Linguistic Society.

Comrie, B. (1976). The syntax of causative constructions: Cross-language similarities and divergences. In M. Shibatani (Ed.), *Syntax and Semantics, Vol. 6, The Grammar of Causative Constructions*. New York: Academic Press.
Comrie, B. (1977). Ergativity. In W. P. Lehmann (Ed.), *Syntactic Typology: Studies in the Phenomenology of Language*. Austin: University of Texas Press.
Comrie, B. (1978). Aspect and voice: Some reflections. Manuscript. Cambridge: Cambridge University.
Cook, V. J. (in press). Studies in the comprehension of relative clauses. *Language and Speech*.
Creider, C. (1975). Thematization and word-order. Manuscript. LSA Winter meeting.
Creider, C. (1976). The semantics of adjectives in Kipsigis. Manuscript. London, Ont.: University of Western Ontario.
Creider, C. (1979). The explanation of transformations. In T. Givón (Ed.), *Syntax and Semantics, Vol. 12, Discourse and Syntax*. New York: Academic Press.
D'Aquili, E. G. (1972). The bio-psychological determinants of culture. *McCaleb Modules in Anthropology* **13**:1–29.
DeBeer, G. R. (1951). *Embryos and Ancestors*. Oxford: The Clarendon Press.
Dingwall, W. O. (1979). The evolution of human communication systems. In H. Whitaker and H. A. Whitaker (Eds.), *Studies in Neuro-Linguistics, Vol. 4*. New York: Academic Press.
Dixon, R. (1972a). Where have all the adjectives gone? Manuscript. Canberra: Australian National University.
Dixon, R. (1972b). *The Dyirbal Language of North Queensland*. Cambridge: Cambridge University Press.
Dore, J. (1976). Speech acts and language universals. *Journal of Child Language* **2**:21–40.
Duranti, A. and Keenan, E. (1979). Left dislocation in spoken Italian. In T. Givón (Ed.), *Syntax and Semantics, Vol. 12, Discourse and Syntax*. New York: Academic Press.
Elimelech, B. (1973). Conjunction reduction and splitting verbs in Yoruba. Los Angeles: University of California.
Emonds, J. (1970). Root and Structure Preserving Transformations. Ph.D. dissertation. Cambridge, MA: MIT.
Epée, R. (1975). The case for a focus position in Dwala. In R. Herbert (Eds.), *Proceedings of the Sixth African Linguistics Conference, Working Papers in Linguistics* **20**. Columbus: Ohio State University.
Ervin-Tripp, S. (1970). Discourse agreement: How children answer questions. In J. Hayes (Ed.), *Cognition and the Development of Language*, New York: Wiley and Son.
Fillmore, C. (1963). The position of embedding transformations in a grammar. *Word* **19**.
Foley, W. (1976). Comparative Syntax in Austronesian. Ph.D. dissertation. Berkeley: University of California.
Fulas, H. (1974). A pseudo-object construction in Amharic. *Proc. IV Congresso Internazionale di Studi Etiopici*. Rome: Academia Nazionale dei Lincei.
García, E. (1975a). *Other than* ambiguity. Manuscript. H. Lehmann College, CUNY.
García, E. (1975b). *On the Role of Theory in Linguistic Analysis: The Spanish Pronoun System*. Amsterdam: North Holland.
García, E. (1979). Discourse without syntax. In T. Givón (Ed.), *Syntax and Semantics, Vol. 12, Discourse and Syntax*. New York: Academic Press.
Gardner, R. A. and Gardner, B. T. (1969). Teaching sign language to a chimpanzee. *Science* **165**:664–672.
Gardner, R. A. and Gardner, B. T. (1974). Comparing the early utterances of child and chimpanzee. *Minnesota Symposium on Child Psychology* **8**:3–23.

Bibliography

Gary, J. and E. Keenan (1975). On collapsing grammatical relations in universal grammar. In P. Cole and J. Morgan (Eds.), *Syntax and Semantics, Vol. 8, Grammatical Relations*. New York: Academic Press.

Gary, N. (1974). A discourse analysis of certain root transformations in English. Manuscript. Los Angeles: University of California.

Geertz, C. (1962). The growth of culture and the evolution of mind. In J. Scher (Eds.), *Theories of Mind*. New York: Free Press of Glencoe.

Givón, T. (1969). Studies in ChiBemba and Bantu Grammar. Ph.D. dissertation. Los Angeles: University of California.

Givón, T. (1970a). Notes on the semantic structure of English adjectives. *Language* **46**.

Givón, T. (1970b). The resolution of gender conflicts in Bantu conjunction: When syntax and semantics clash. *Papers from the 6th Regional Meeting*. Chicago: Chicago Linguistic Society.

Givón, T. (1970c). On ordered rules and the modified base of ChiBemba verbs. *African Studies* **20**(1).

Givón, T. (1971). Historical syntax and synchronic morphology: An archaeologist's field trip. *Papers from the 7th Regional Meeting*. Chicago: Chicago Linguistic Society.

Givón, T. (1972a). Studies in ChiBemba and Bantu Grammar (revised and expanded). *Studies in African Linguistics, Supplement* **3**.

Givón, T. (1972b). Pronoun attraction and subject postposing. The Chicago Which Hunt: Papers from the Relative Cause Festival. Chicago: Chicago Linguistic Society.

Givón, T. (1973a). Complex NPs, word order, and resumptive pronouns in Hebrew. *Papers from the Comparative Syntax Festival*. Chicago: Chicago Linguistic Society.

Givón, T. (1973b). Opacity and references in language: An inquiry into the role of modalities. In J. Kimball (Ed.), *Syntax and Semantics, Vol. 2*. New York: Academic Press.

Givón, T. (1974a). Toward a discourse definition of syntax. Manuscript. Los Angeles: University of California. (Revised as chapter 2 of this book.)

Givón, T. (1974b). Syntactic change in Lake Bantu: A rejoinder. *Studies in African Linguistics* **5**(1).

Givón, T. (1974c). Verb complements and relative clauses: A diachronic case study in Biblical Hebrew. *Afroasiatic Linguistics* **1**(4).

Givón, T. (1975a). On the role of perceptual clues in Hebrew relativization. *Afroasiatic Linguistics* **2**(8).

Givón, T. (1975b). The development of the numeral 'one' as an indefinite marker in Israeli Hebrew. Manuscript. Los Angeles: University of California.

Givón, T. (1975c). Focus and the scope of assertion: Some Bantu evidence. *Studies in African Linguistics* **6**(2).

Givón, T. (1975d). Cause and control: On the semantics of interpersonal manipulation. In J. Kimball (Ed.), *Syntax and Semantics, Vol. 4*, New York: Academic Press.

Givón, T. (1975e). Serial verbs and syntactic change: Niger-Congo. In C. Li (Ed.), *Word Order and Word Order Change*. Austin: University of Texas Press.

Givón, T. (1975f). Promotion, accessibility, and case marking: Towards understanding grammars. *Working Papers in Language Universals* **19**. Stanford University. (Revised as Chapter 4 of this book.)

Givón, T. (1975g). Prolegomena to any (sane) Creology. In E. Polomé, B. Heine, I. Hancock, and M. Goodman (Eds.), *Readings in Pidgins and Creoles*.

Givón, T. (1976a). Topic, pronoun and grammatical agreement. In C. Li (Ed.), *Subject and Topic*. New York: Academic Press.

Givón, T. (1976b). On the VS word-order in Israeli Hebrew: Pragmatics and typological change. In P. Cole (Ed.), *Studies in Modern Hebrew Syntax and Semantics*. Amsterdam: North Holland.

Givón, T. (1976c). Some constraints on Bantu causativization. In M. Shibatani (Ed.), *Syntax and Semantics, Vol. 6, The Grammar of Causative Constructions*. New York: Academic Press.

Givón, T. (1976d). On the SOV reconstruction of So. Nilotic: Internal evidence from Toposa. In L. Hyman and L. Jacobson (Eds.), *Papers in African Linguistics in Honor of Wm. E. Welmers, Studies in African Linguistics, Supplement* **6**.

Givón, T. (1977a). The drift from VSO to SVO in Biblical Hebrew: The pragmatics of tense-aspect. In C. Li (Ed.), *Mechanisms of Syntactic Change*. Austin: University of Texas Press.

Givón, T. (1977b). Definiteness and referentiality. In J. Greenberg, C. Ferguson, and E. Moravcsik (Eds.), *Universals of Human Language*. Stanford: Stanford University Press.

Givón, T. (1977c). On the SOV origin of the suffixal agreement conjugation in Indo-European and Semitic. In A. Juilland (Ed.), *Linguistic Studies Offered to Joseph Greenberg on the Occasion of his 60th Birthday*. Saratoga: Anma Libri.

Givón, T. (Ed., 1979). *Syntax and Semantics Vol. 12, Discourse and Syntax*. New York: Academic Press.

Givón, T. and Kimenyi, A. (1974). Truth, belief and doubt in KinyaRwanda. In W. Leben (Ed.), *Papers from the 5th Conference on African Linguistics, Studies in African Linguistics, Supplement* **5**

Gleitman, L. and H. Gleitman (1970). *Phrase and Paraphrase*. New York.

Goguen, J. (1975). Complexity of hierarchically organized systems and the structure of musical experience. *Computer Science Department Quarterly* 3(4). Los Angeles: University of California.

Goodall, J. (1965). Chimpanzees of the Gombe Stream reserve. In E. deVore (Ed.), *Primate Behavior*. New York: Holt, Rinehart, and Winston.

Gorbet, L. (1974). Relativization and Complementation in Diegeño: Noun Phrases as Nouns. Ph.D. dissertation. San Diego: University of California.

Gordon, D. and Lakoff, G. (1971). Conversational postulates. *Papers from the 7th Regional Meeting*. Chicago: Chicago Linguistic Society.

Green, G. (1976). Main clause phenomena in subordinate clauses. *Language* **52**.

Greenberg, J. (1966). Some universals of grammar with particular reference to the order of meaningful elements. In J. Greenberg (Ed.), *Universals of Language*. Cambridge: MIT Press.

Greenberg, J. (1974). The relation of frequency to semantic feature in a case language (Russian). *Working Papers in Language Universals* **16**. Stanford: Stanford University.

Greenfield, P. M. and Dent, C. H. (1978). A developmental study of the communication of meaning: The role of uncertainty and information. In P. French (Ed.), *The Development of Meaning: Pedolinguistics Series*. Japan: Bunka Hyoron Press.

Greenfield, P. M. and Smith, J. H. (1976). *The Structure of Communication in Early Language Developments*. New York: Academic Press.

Grey, Z. (1926). *Nevada*. New York: Bantam (ppbk).

Gruber, J. (1967a). *Functions of the Lexicon in Formal Descriptive Grammars*. Santa Monica: Systems Development Corporation.

Gruber, J. (1967b). Topicalization in child language. *Foundations of Language* **3**.

Haeckel, E. (1874). Die Gastraea-Theorie die Phylogenetische Klassifikazion des Thierreisches und die Homologie der Keimblätter. *Jenaische Zeitschrift für Natur-Wissenschaft* **9**.

Haile, G. (1970). The suffix pronoun in Amharic. In C.-W. Kim and H. Stahlke (Eds.), *Papers in African Linguistics*. Admonton: Linguistic Research Inc.

Hale, K. (in preparation). A sketch of Walbiri syntax. In T. Shopen *et al.* (Eds.), *Syntactic Typology and Linguistic Field Work*.

Harris, Z. (1957). Cooccurrence and transformation in linguistic structure. *Language* 33(3).
Hatch, E. (1971). The young child's comprehension of relative clauses. Technical Note #2-71-16. Los Alamitos: South-West Regional Laboratories.
Hawkins, J. (1977). Word-order change in relation to the logical status of linguistic universals. Manuscript. Los Angeles: University of Southern California.
Hawkins, J. and Keenan, E. (1974). On the psychological validity of the accessibility hierarchy. Manuscript. (LSA Summer Meeting).
Hawkinson, A. and Hyman, L. (1974). Natural topic hierarchies in Shona. *Studies in African Linguistics* 5(2).
Haycox, E. (1975). *The Adventurers*. New York: Signet (ppbk).
Heine, B. (1975). The study of word-order in African languages. In R. Herbert (Ed.), *Proceedings of the 6th Conference on African Linguistics, Working Papers in Linguistics* 20. Columbus: Ohio State University.
Heny, F. (1972). Bantu lexical structure and semantic universals. *Studies in African Linguistics* 3(2).
Herzberger, H. (1971). Setting Russell Free. Paper presented to the Philosophy Colloquium. London, Ont.: University of Western Ontario.
Hetzron, R. (1970). Toward an Amharic case grammar. *Studies in African Linguistics* 1(3).
Hetzron, R. (1971). Presentative function and presentative movement. *Proceedings of the 2nd Conference on African Linguistics*, Studies in African Linguistics, Supplement 2.
Hewes, G. W. (1973a). Pongid capacity for language acquisition: An evaluation of recent studies, In K. W. Montagna and E. Menzel (Eds.), *Symposia of the IV International Congress of Primatology*. S. Karger.
Hewes, G. W. (1973b). Primate communication and the gestural origin of language. *Current Anthropology* 14.
Hinds, J. (1978). Anaphora in Japanese discourse. In J. Hinds (Ed.), *Anaphora in Discourse*. D. Reidel Publishers.
Hinds, J. (1979). Properties of discourse structure. In T. Givón (Ed.), *Syntax and Semantics, Vol. 12, Discourse and Syntax*. New York: Academic Press.
Hooper, J. and Thompson, S. (1973). On the application of root transformations. *Linguistic Inquiry* 4.
Hoosain, R. (1973). The processing of Negation. JVLVB, 12:618–626.
Hoosain, R. and Osgood, C. (1975). Response time for Yang (positive) and Yin (negative) words. Manuscript. Urbana: University of Illinois.
Hopper, P. (1979). Foregrounding and aspect in discourse. In T. Givón (Ed.), *Syntax and Semantics, Vol. 12, Discourse and Syntax*. New York: Academic Press.
Hudson, G. (1972). The unity of focusing transformations: An argument for linearization rules and the prohibition of extrinsic rule ordering. Manuscript. Los Angeles: University of California.
Hudson, G. (1974). The role of SPC's in natural generative phonology. *Papers from the Parassession Volume on Natural Phonology*. Chicago: Chicago Linguistic Society.
Hyman, L. (1971). Consecutivization in Fe'fe'. *Journal of African Languages* 10.
Hyman, L. (1973). How do natural rules become unnatural? Manuscript. LSA Winter Meeting.
Hyman, L. (1975). The change from SOV to SVO: Evidence from Niger-Congo. In C. Li (Ed.), *Word Order and Word Order Change*. Austin: University of Texas Press.
Jackendoff, R. (1971). Modal structure in semantic representation. *Linguistic Inquiry* 2(4).
Janda, R. (1976). The language of note-taking as a simplified register. Manuscript. Stanford: Stanford University.

Jay, P. (1965). Field studies. In A. M. Schrier, H. F. Harlow, and F. Stollnitz (Eds.), *Behavior of Non-human Primates*. New York: Academic Press.

Johnson, D. (1974). *Relational Constraints on Grammars*. Yorktown Heights, NY: IBM T. J. Watson Research Center.

Justus, C. (1976a). Topicalization and relativization in Hittite. In C. Li (Ed.), *Subject and Topic*. New York: Academic Press.

Justus, C. (1976b). Syntactic change: Evidence for restructuring among co-existant variants. Manuscript. Berkeley: University of California.

Kachru, Y. (1976). On the semantics of causative constructions in Hindi. In M. Shibatani (Ed.), *Syntax and Semantics, Vol. 6, The Grammar of Causative Constructions*. New York: Academic Press.

Karttunen, L. (1974). Presupposition and linguistic context. *Theoretical Linguistics* 1(2).

Katz, J. and Postal, P. (1964). *An Integrated Theory of Linguistic Description*. Cambridge: MIT Press.

Kay, P. and Sankoff, G. (1974). A language universals approach to Pidgins and Creoles. In D. Decamp and I. Hancock (Eds.), *Pidgins and Creoles: Current Trends and Prospects*. Washington, D.C.: Georgetown University Press.

Keenan, Edward (1971). Two kinds of presupposition in natural language. In C. Fillmore and T. Langendoen (Eds.), *Studies in Linguistic Semantics*. New York: Holt, Rinehart, and Winston.

Keenan, Edward (1972a). Logic and language. *Dædalus*. New York: New York Academy of Science.

Keenan, Edward (1972b). Relative clause formation in Malagasy. *The Chicago Which Hunt, Papers from the Relative Clause Festival*. Chicago: Chicago Linguistic Society.

Keenan, Edward (1975). Some universals of passive in relational grammar. *Papers from the 11th Regional meeting*. Chicago: Chicago Linguistic Society.

Keenan, Edward (1976a). Toward a universal definition of subject. In C. Li (Ed.), *Subject and Topic*. New York: Academic Press.

Keenan, Edward (1976b). The remarkable subject in Malagasy. In C. Li (Ed.), *Subject and Topic*. New York: Academic Press.

Keenan, Edward (1977). The syntax of subject-final languages. In W. P. Lehmann (Ed.), *Syntactic Typology: Studies in the Phenomenology of Language*. Austin: University of Texas Press.

Keenan, Edward and Comrie, B. (1972). Noun phrase accessibility and universal grammar. Manuscript. LSA Winter Meeting.

Keenan, Edward and Comrie, B. (1977). Noun phrase accessibility and universal grammar. *Linguistic Inquiry* 7.

Keenan, Elinor (1974a). Conversational competence in children. *Journal of Child Language* 1(2).

Keenan, Elinor (1974b). Again and again: The pragmatics of imitation in child language. Manuscript. Los Angeles: University of Southern California.

Keenan, Elinor (1975a). Making it last: Uses of repetition in children's discourse. *Proceedings of the First Annual Meeting of the Berkeley Linguistic Society*, Berkeley: Berkeley Linguistic Society.

Keenan, Elinor (1975b). Evolving discourse: The next step. Manuscript. Los Angeles: University of Southern California.

Keenan, Elinor (1977). Why look at planned and unplanned discourse? In Elinor Keenan and T. Bennett (Eds.), *Discourse across Time and Space*, Southern California Occasional Papers in Linguistics 5. Los Angeles: University of Southern California.

Keenan, Elinor (1979). Planned and unplanned discourse. In T. Givón (Ed.), *Syntax and Semantics, Vol. 12, Discourse and Syntax*. New York: Academic Press.

Keenan, Elinor and Bennett, T. (1977). *Discourse across Time and Space, Southern California Occasional Papers in Linguistics*, **5**. Los Angeles: University of Southern California.
Keenan, Elinor and Schieffelin, B. (1976). Topic as a discourse notion: A study of topic in conversations of children and adults. In C. Li (Ed.), *Subject and Topic*. New York: Academic Press.
Keenan, Elinor and Schieffelin, B. (1977). Foregrounding referents: A consideration of left-dislocation in discourse. Manuscript, Los Angeles: University of Southern California.
Kimenyi, A. (1976). A Relational Grammar of KinyaRwanda. Ph.D. dissertation. Los Angeles: University of California.
Kirsner, R. (1973). Natural focus and agentive interpretation: On the semantics of the Dutch expletive *er*. *Stanford Occasional Papers in Linguistics* 3:101–114. Stanford: Stanford University.
Kirsner, R. (1976). On the subjectless pseudo-passive in standard Dutch and the problem of background agent. In C. Li (Ed.), *Subject and Topic*. New York: Academic Press.
Klima, E. and Beluggi, U. (1973). Syntactic regularities in the speech of children. In C. Ferguson and D. Slobin (Eds.), *Studies in Child Language Development*. New York: Holt, Rinehart, and Winston.
Koestler, A. (1967). *The Ghost in the Machine*. New York: McMillan.
Kroll, B. (1977). Ways communicators encode propositions in spoken and written English: A look at subordination and coordination. In E. Keenan and Bennett, T. (Eds.), *Discourse across Time and Space, Southern California Occasional Papers in Linguistics* **5**. New York: Academic Press.
Kunene, E. (1975). Zulu pronouns and the structure of discourse. *Studies in African Linguistics* 6(2).
Kuno, S. (1972). Functional sentence perspective. *Linguistic Inquiry* **3**.
Kuno, S. (1976a). Subject, theme and the speaker's empathy: A re-examination of relativization phenomena. In C. Li (Ed.), *Subject and Topic*. New York: Academic Press.
Lakoff, G. (1971). On generative semantics. In D. Steinberg and L. Jakobovitz (Eds.), *Semantics*. Cambridge: Cambridge University Press.
Lamendella, J. (1976). Relations between the ontogeny and phylogeny of language: A neo-recapitulationist view. In S. R. Harnad, H. D. Stelkis, and J. Lancaster (Eds.), *The Origins and Evolution of Language and Speech*. New York: New York Academy of Science.
Lamendella, J. (1977a). Neuro-functional foundations of symbolic communication. Manuscript. Wurg-Wartenstein Symposia 24. New York.
Lamendella, J. (1977b). General principles of neuro-functional organization and their manifestation in primary and non-primary language acquisition. *Language Learning* **27**.
Lamendella, J. (1978). The limbic system in human communication. In H. Whitaker and H. A. Whitaker (Eds.), *Studies in Neurolinguistics, Vol. 3*. New York: Academic Press.
Lamendella, J. (in preparation). *The Early Growth of Language and Cognition: A Neuro-Psychological Approach*.
L'Amour, L. (1965). *Under the Sweetwater Rim*. New York: Bantam (ppbk).
Langacker, R. (1975). Functional stratigraphy. *Papers from the Parassession on Functionalism*. Chicago: Chicago Linguistic Society.
Langdon, M. (1977). Syntactic change and SOV structure: The Yuman case. In C. Li (Ed.), *Mechanisms of Syntactic Change*. Austin: University of Texas Press.
Legum, S. (1975). Strategies in the acquisition of relative clauses. Technical Note #2-75-10, South-West Regional Laboratories, Los Alamitos.
Lehmann, W. P. (1973). *A structural principle of language and its implications. Language* **49**.

Li, C. (Ed.) (1975). *Word Order and Word Order Change.* Austin: University of Texas Press.
Li, C. (Ed.) (1976). *Subject and Topic,* New York: Academic Press.
Li, C. (Ed.) (1977). *Mechanisms of Syntactic Change,* Austin: University of Texas Press.
Li, C. and Thompson, S. (1973a). Historical Change in word-order: A case study in Chinese and its implications. Manuscript, Los Angeles: University of California, Los Angeles.
Li, C. and Thompson, S. (1973b). Serial verb constructions in Mandarin Chinese: Subordination or coordination. *Parasession Volume,* Chicago Linguistic Society #9, University of Chicago.
Li, C. and Thompson, S. (1973c). Co-verbs in Mandarin Chinese: Verbs or prepositions. Manuscript, Los Angeles: University of California, Los Angeles.
Li, C. and Thompson, S. (1975). The semantic function of word-order: A case study in Mandarin. In C. Li (Ed.), *Word Order and Word Order Change.* Austin: University of Texas.
Li, C. and Thompson, S. (1976). Subject and topic: A new typology for language. In C. Li (Ed.), *Subject and Topic.* New York: Academic Press.
Li, C. and Thompson, S. (1979). Pronouns and zero-anaphora in Chinese discourse. In T. Givón (Ed.), *Syntax and Semantics, Vol. 12, Discourse and Syntax.* New York: Academic Press.
Lightfoot, D. (1975). Diachronic syntax: Extraposition and deep-structure reanalysis. In E. Kaiser and J. Hankamer (Eds.), *Proceedings of the 5th N.E. Linguistic Society.* Cambridge: Harvard University Press.
Lightfoot, D. (1976a). Syntactic change and the autonomy thesis. Paper read at the Symposium on Syntactic Change, University of California, Santa Barbara, May, 1976.
Lightfoot, D. (1976b). The base component as a locus of syntactic change. In W. Christie (Ed.), *Proceedings of the 2nd International Conference on Historical Linguistics.* Amsterdam: North Holland.
Limber, J. (1973). The genesis of complex sentences. In T. Moore (Ed.) *Cognitive Development and the Acquisition of Language.* New York: Academic Press.
Linde, C. (1974). The Linguistic Encoding of Spatial Information. Ph.D. dissertation. New York: Columbia University.
Linde, C. and Labov, W. (1975). Spatial networks as a site for the study of language and thought. *Language* **50.**
Lindenfeld, J. (1973). *Yaqui Syntax.* Berkeley: University of California Press.
Longacre, R. (1979). The paragraph as a grammatical unit. In T. Givón (Ed.), *Syntax and Semantics, Vol. 12, Discourse and Syntax.* New York: Academic Press.
Lord, C. (1973). Serial verbs in transition. *Studies in African Linguistics* 4(3).
McCawley, J. (1970). English as a VSO language. *Language* **46.**
Madugu, I. G. (1978). The Nupe verb and syntactic change. Manuscript. Ibadan: University of Ibadan.
Mardirussian, G. (1975). Noun incorporation in universal grammar. *Papers from the 11th Regional Meeting.* Chicago: Chicago Linguistic Society.
Mardirussian, G. (1978). The drift from VO to OV in Armenian. Manuscript. Los Angeles: University of California.
Michael, R. P. and Crook, J. H. (Eds.) (1973). *Comparative Ecology and Behavior of Primates.* New York: Academic Press.
Morolong, M. and Hyman, L. (1977). Animacy, objects and clitics in SeSotho. *Studies in African Linguistics* 8(2).
Mould, M. (1975). The syntax and semantics of the prefix-initial vowel in Luganda. In E. Voeltz (Ed.), *Proceedings of the 3rd Conference on African Linguistics.* Bloomington. Indiana University Press.
Munro, P. (1974). Topics in Mojave Syntax. Ph.D. dissertation. San Diego: University of California.

Noback, C. R. and Montagna, W. (Eds.) (1970). *The Primate Brain*. New York: Appleton.
Noback, C. R. and Moscowitz, M. (1963). The primate nervous system: Functional and structural aspects in phylogeny. In J. Beuttner-Janusch (Ed.), *Evolutionary and Genetic Biology of Primates, Vol. 1*. New York: Academic Press.
Ohala, J. (1974). Phonetic explanation in Phonology. *Papers from the Parasession on Natural Phonology*. Chicago: Chicago Linguistic Society.
Orwell, G. (1945). *Animal Farm*. New York: Penguin Classics (ppbk).
Osgood, C. and Richards, M. M. (1973). From Yang to Yin to *and* or *but*. *Language* 49(2).
Otero, C. P. (1974). Grammar's definition vs. speakers' judgment: From the psychology to the sociology of language. Manuscript. Los Angeles: University of California.
Otero, C. P. (1975). Agramaticality in performance. Manuscript. Los Angeles: University of California.
Peirce, Ch. S. (1955). *Philosophical Writings*. J. Buchler (Ed.) New York: Dover.
Perlmutter, D. and Postal, P. (1974). Relational Grammar. LSA Summer lecture notes.
Peters, S. (Ed.) (1972). *The Goals of Linguistic Theory*. Englewood Cliffs, NJ: Prentice-Hall.
Piaget, J. (1952). *The Origins of Intelligence in Children*. New York: International Universities Press.
Piaget, J. (1954). *The Construction of Reality*. New York: Ballantine.
Premack, D. (1977). *Intelligence in Ape and Man*. Hillsdale, NJ: L. Erlbaum and Assoc.
Price, T. (1966). *The Elements of Nyanja*. Blantyre: The Synod Bookshop, Church of Central Africa (Presbyterian).
Ross, J. R. (1967). Constraints on Variables in Syntax. Ph.D. dissertation. Cambridge, MA: MIT.
Ross, J. R. (1969). Adjectives as noun phrases. In D. Reibel and S. Schane (Eds.), *Modern Studies in English*. Englewood-Cliffs, NJ: Prentice-Hall.
Ross, J. R. (1970). Gapping and the order of constitutents. In M. Bierwisch and K. E. Heidolph (Eds.), *Progress in Linguistics*. The Hague: Mouton.
Ross, J. R. and G. Lakoff (1967). Stative adjectives and verbs. NSF Report #17, Harvard Computational Laboratory, Cambridge, MA: Harvard University.
Rumbaugh, D. M. and Gill, T. (1977). Language and language-type communication: Studies with a chimpanzee. In M. Lewis and L. Rosenblum (Eds.), *Interaction, Conversation and the Development of Language*. New York: John Wiley and Son.
Russell, R. (1977). Thematization and relativization in Arabic. Paper read at the University of Hawaii, Honolulu, Linguistics Colloquium, March 3, 1977.
Rybarkiewicz, W. (1975). Word Order in Old English Prose. M.A. thesis. University of Lodz (Poland).
Sacks, H., Schegloff, E. and Jefferson, G. (1974). A simplest systematics for the organization of turn-taking for conversation. *Language* 50.
Sadock, J. and Zwicky, A. (in preparation). Major sentence types. In T. Shopen, *et al*. (Eds.), *Syntactic Typology and Linguistic Field Work*.
Sanders, J. and Thai, J. (1972). Immediate dominance and identity deletion. *Foundations of Language* 8:161–198.
Sankoff, G. (1976). Grammaticalization process in New-Guinea Tok-Pisin. Manuscript. Montreal: Université de Montreal.
Sankoff, G. and P. Brown (1976). The origins of syntax in discourse. *Language* 52.
Saussure, F. de (1915[1959]). *Course in General Linguistics*. Edited by Ch. Bally and A. Sechehaye, translated by W. Baskin, New York: Philosophical Library.
Schachter, P. (1967). Transformational grammar and contrastive analysis. In H. Allen and R. Campbell (Eds.), *Teaching English as a Second Language*. New York: McGraw-Hill.

Schachter, P. (1973). Focus and relativization. *Language* **49**.
Schachter, P. (1976). The subject in Philippine languages: Topic, actor, actor-topic or none of the above? In C. Li (Ed.), *Subject and Topic*. New York: Academic Press.
Schachter, P. (1977). Reference-related and role-related properties of subjects. In P. Cole and J. Morgan (Eds.), *Syntax and Semantics, Vol. 8, Grammatical Relations*. New York: Academic Press.
Schaller, G. B. (1961). The Ourang-Utan in Sarawak. *Zoologica* **46**.
Schaller, G. B. (1963). *The Mountain Gorilla: Ecology and Behavior*. Chicago: University of Chicago Press.
Schaller, G. B. (1965). The behavior of the mountain gorilla. In I. deVore (Ed.), *Primate Behavior: Field Studies of Monkeys and Apes*. New York: Holt, Rinehart, and Winston.
Schegloff, E. (1973). Recycle turn beginning: A precise repair mechanism in conversation's turn-taking organization. LSA Summer lecture notes.
Schegloff, E. (1979). Some aspects of same-turn repair. In T. Givón (Ed.), *Syntax and Semantics, Vol. 12, Discourse and Syntax*. New York: Academic Press.
Schegloff, E., Jefferson, G., and Sacks, H. (1976). The preference for self-correction in the organization of repair in conversation. *Language* **52**.
Schmerling, S. (1971). Presupposition and the notion of normal stress. *Papers from the 7th Regional Meeting*. Chicago: Chicago Linguistic Society.
Schmerling, S. (1974). A re-examination of 'normal stress'. *Language* **50**(1).
Sconlon, R. (1974). One Child's Language from One to Two: The Origins of Structure. Ph.D. dissertation. Honolulu: University of Hawaii.
Sconlon, R. (1976). *Conversations With a One-Year Old Child*. Honolulu: University of Hawaii Press.
Sheldon, A. (1974). The role of parallel function in the acquisition of relative clauses in English. Journal of Verbal Learning and Verbal Behavior. JVLVB, **13**:272–281.
Shibatani, M. (1973). The semantics of Japanese causativization. *Foundations of Language* **9**(3).
Shibatani, M. (Ed. 1976). *Syntax and Semantics, Vol. 6, The Grammar of Causative Constructions*. New York: Academic Press.
Shimanoff, S. and Brunak, J. (1977). Repairs in planned and unplanned discourse. In E. Keenan and T. Bennett (Eds.), *Discourse across Time and Space, Southern California Occasional Papers in Linguistics* **5**. Los Angeles: University of Southern California.
Shir, N. (1979). The discourse function of dative shifting. In T. Givón (Ed.), *Syntax and Semantics, Vol. 12, Discourse and Syntax*. New York: Academic Press.
Silva-Corvalán, C. (1977). A Discourse Study of Some Aspects of Word-Order in the Spanish Spoken by Mexican-Americans in West Los Angeles. M.A. thesis. Los Angeles: University of California.
Slobin, D. (1977). Language change in childhood and history. In J. MacNamara (Ed.), *Language Learning and Thought*. New York: Academic Press.
Slobin, D. and T. Bever (1978)
Stahlke, H. (1970). Serial verbs. *Studies in African Linguistics* **1**(1).
Stockwell, R. P. (1977). Motivation for exbraceration in Old English. In C. Li (Ed.), *Mechanisms of Syntactic Charge*. Austin: University of Texas.
Sugiyama, Y. (1973). Social structure of wild chimpanzees: A review of field studies. In R. P. Michael and J. H. Crook (Eds.), *Comparative Ecology and Behavior of Primates*. New York: Academic Press.
Takizala, A. (1972). Focus and relativization: The case of Kihung'an. *Studies in African Linguistics* **3**(2).
Talmy, L. (1976). Semantic causative types. In M. Shibatani (Ed.), *Syntax and Semantics, Vol. 6, The Grammar of Causative Constructions*. New York: Academic Press.

Thompson, S. (1973). Resultative verb compounds in Mandarin Chinese: A case for lexical rules. *Language* **49**(2).
Thurman, R. (1978). Clause Chains in Chuave. M.A. thesis. Los Angeles: University of California.
Timberlake, A. (1975). Hierarchies in the genitive of negation. Manuscript. Los Angeles: University of California.
Traugott, E. (1974). Spatial expressions of tense and temporal sequencing: A contribution to the study of semantic fields. Manuscript. Stanford: Stanford University.
Traugott, E. (1977). Pidginization, creolization and language change. In A. Valdman (Ed.), *Pidgin and Creole Linguistics*. Bloomington: Indiana University Press.
Trithart, L. (1976). Relational Grammar and ChiChewa Subjectivization Rules. M.A. thesis. Los Angeles: University of California.
Trout, K. (1974). *Venus on the Half Shell*. New York: Dell (ppbk).
Valli, A., Hernandez, N., Achard-Boule, M. and Beretti, M. (1972). *Compterendu d'une experience réalisée dans une classe de 6e-2, dont le but était d'étudier les mechanismes de la production des relatives chez l'enfant,* Institute de Didactique, Document # 13. Paris: Groupe Linguistique et Pedagogique.
van Lawick-Goodall, J. (1968). A preliminary report on expressive movements and communication in the Gombe Stream chimpanzees. In P. C. Jay (Ed.), *Primate Studies in Adaptability and Variability,* New York: Holt, Rinehart, and Winston.
van Lawick-Goodall, J. and van Lawick, H. (1971). *Innocent Killers*. Boston: Houghton and Mifflin.
van Valin, R. (1978). Remarks on meaning, language and culture. Talk given at the Anthropology Department, University of California, Los Angeles, February 1978.
Vendler, Z. (1963). The Transformational Grammar of English Adjectives, TDAP #52. Philadelphia: University of Pennsylvania.
Vendler, Z. (1967). *Linguistics in Philosophy*. Ithaca, New York: Cornell University Press.
Vennemann, T. (1973a). Topic, subject and word-order: From SXV to SVX via TVX. In J. Anderson (Ed.), *Proceedings of the 1st International Conference on Historical Linguistics.* Cambridge: Cambridge University Press.
Vennemann, T. (1973b). Explanations in Linguistics. In J. Kimball (Ed.), *Syntax and Semantics, Vol. 2,* New York: Academic Press.
Wald, B. (1973). Variation in the Tense Markers of Mombasa Swahili. Ph.D. dissertation. New York: Columbia University.
Wells, H. G. (1975). *Star Begotten*. New York: Manor, ppbk.
Werner, H. and Kaplan, B. (1963). *Symbol Formation*. New York: Wiley and Son.
Williams, M. (1977). Word order in Tuscarora. In M. Foster (Ed.), *Papers in Linguistics from the 1972 Conference on Iroquoian Research*. Ottawa: National Museum of Man.
Wittgenstein, L. (1918 [1960]). *Tractatus Logico-Philosophicus*. Translated by D. F. Pears. and B. F. McGuinness. New York: The Humanities Press.

INDEX

A

Abduction, new knowledge and (Anttila), 312, 350
Abstractness, concreteness and temporality versus, 314–317
Accessibility hierarchy (Keenan and Comrie), 143–144, 152
Accusative and nonaccusative differentiation, data-shift and, 164–166
Accusative objects in negative and affirmative sentences, 95–97
Accusative-only constraints
  agent-deletion and, 206
  direct-object-only constraint and, 205
  passive and, 205
  passivization and, 196
  Philippine verb-coding typology and, 206
  topic-shift and, 206
Acquisition of language, 86–87, 89–90
Action, agents, intent, and causality, 334–336, 346–347
Adequacy, Chomsky's three levels of, 7–8
Adjectives
  concreteness of, 321
  derivation of, 265–266
  history of morphology and (Bantu), 266–267
  inherent (Bantu), 264–265
  peculiarities of, 321
  problematic nature of, 13–14

Adverbs
  ambiguity of, in periphrastic causatives, 117–119
  scope of negation and, 105–111
Affective–emotive speech acts
  canine, 281–282
  child, 291
Agency and causation, ontology of, 338–344
Agent
  in canine communication, 280, 285–286
  cause and, 341–344
  coding
    in child language, 293–294
    rise of, 300–301
  identification with topic, 303
Agent-causer, 335–336
Agent-deletion
  passivization, accusative-only constraint and, 206
  typology
    object constraints and, 195
    passive morphology and, 193
    passivization and, 191–193
  Ute, 192
Agents
  consciousness versus intention, 337
  experiential criteria for, 336–337
  intent, causality, action and, 334–336, 346–347
  semi-, classes of, 343–344
Ambiguities, restrictions on, 116

367

Index

Ambiguity, "other than", negation and, 111–112
Anaphoric pronoun strategy
  in Bemba (Bantu), 170
  case-recoverability and, 179
  impossibility of, in Bikol, 156
  relativization and, 151, 156
  in Rwanda (Bantu), 177
Anaphoric pronouns, 17–18
  accusative, and dative-shift rule, 162–163, 170–177
  markedness and, 65–66
Antonyms, affective loading of, 133–134
Apes, great, *see* Pongids
Arguments, nominal 37
Assertion-focus stress, 117–119

B

Background, presuppositional, *see* Presuppositional background
Background–foreground principle, 324, 346–347
  interpersonal relationships and, 350
Behavior and communication, 347–348
Being, space, and time, implicational hierarchy of, 314–317
Binary property, individuation and, 318–319

C

Calibration, perceptual judgment and, 325
Canine communication, 277–290
  accessibility of, 278–280
  immediacy of, 278–280
  objects in, 279–280
  participants in, 280
  place in, 279
  time in, 278–279
Canine social structure, 286–289
Case, pragmatic function and, 143–206
Case confusion, passivization and, 197
Case function, coding of, morphologically mixed, 245–246
Case markers, serial verbs and, 220–221
Case-marking, typological explanation of, 203–204
Case realignment, affirmative and negative, in Russian, 126–128
Case-recoverability
  in Bikol, 156

problem, 145–146, 156
pronoun attraction principle and, 249
in Rwanda (Bantu), 171
strategies, promotional rules and, 205
WH-prepositional pronouns and, 179
Categorial and noncategorial levels, 28
Categorial and noncategorial rules, 31–41
Causality
  agents, action, intent and, 334–336, 346–347
  concept of, canine versus human, 283
  conditionality and, 340–341
Causation and agency, ontology of, 338–344
Causatives, periphrastic, ambiguity of adverbs in, 117–119
Cause and agent, 341–344
Causes, external versus internal, 342
Change
  diachronic
    effect of, on language, 13
    synchronic states versus, 43
  elaborative
    in Bemba (Bantu), 122
    in Ethiopian languages, 123–124
    in Swahili, 122–123
    tense-aspect systems and, 121–124
  social and environmental
    canine, 288
    child, 294–295
Chaos and order, two paradoxes of, 325–328
Child communication, 290–295
  affective–emotive speech acts and, 291–292
  illocutionary force and, 291–292
  immediacy and, 291
Child development, diachrony and, 231–232
Child language
  acquisition of, 86–87, 89–90, 227–228
  versus adult, 226–228
Choices, communicative, 32–33
Cleft constructions
  diachrony versus synchrony and, 246–249
  distributional restrictions and, 68
  syntactic complexity (distance) and, 78
  syntacticization and, 217–218
CNCP, *see* Constraint, complex NP
Coding
  agent, 293, 300–302
  canine, deixis and, 284–286
  morphologically mixed, of case function, 245–246

Index 369

object, 293–294
verb, 293–294
rise of, 302–303
Coherence structure, 298–299
Communication
  behavior and, 347–348
  evolution of social interaction and, 347–348
  grammar and, 31–33
  presuppositionality and, 349
  syntacticization and (summary), 268–269
  syntax and, 87–90
Communicative modes
  pragmatic versus syntactic, 222–223
  sociocultural structure and, 289
  unity of, 348–351
Communicative situation
  canine, 289
  of children, 227–228
  Creole, 226
  Pidgin, 225–226
  planned-formal speech and, 230–231
  pongid, 290
  unplanned-informal speech and, 229–230
Comparatives, negative and affirmative, 137–138
Competence (Chomsky), criticized, 236–237
Competence versus performance, 23–43
  agentless passives and, 31–32
  definiteness of subjects and, 26–28
  elevation to theoretical significance, 23–26
  negative clauses and, 97–102
  referential–indefinite objects and, 28–30
Complements, sentential, in Biblical-Hebrew, 218–219
Completeness, privileged status and, 46–48
Complexity, dative-shift, diachronic source and, 183–185
Concreteness
  of nouns, verbs, and adjectives, 321
  temporality and abstractness versus, 314–317
Conditionality
  causality and, 340–341
  time-sequence and, 338–339
Conjunction versus subordination in verb phrase, 213–215
Conscious entities in object positions, 337
Consciousness
  evolution of, 333
  as map of universe, 351

versus physics as methodology, 352
universe as one with, 350–351
Conservatism, syntactic, 83–86, 89
Constraint, complex NP, 17–18
Constraints, *see* specific constraints
Context versus function of negation, 103–105
Contradiction and tautology, 348–349
Contrastive stress, scope of negation and, 105–106
Coordination
  complexity of, 298, 305–306
  subordination and, 261–262, 298
    complexity, 305–306
Copulas, Spanish, contrasted, 322–323
Crazy syntax (CRAZ), 235–269
  adjectives and, 264–267
  cleft constructions and, 246–249
  lexical patterns, frozen, and, 264–267
  morphology and, 238–246
  object pronouns, frozen, and, 239–245
  object relativization and, 249–251
  objects and, 253–261
  phonology and, 237–238
  pronoun attraction and, 249–251
  relativization (Swahili) and, 252–253
  summary, 268–269
  syntactic constraints, frozen, and, 261–264
  verb phrase syntax and, 253–261
  WH-questions and, 246–249
Creole versus Pidgin, 223–226
Critical properties
  inclusion relation and, 314–315
  set membership and, 327

D

Database
  curtailment of, 2–3
  gutting of, 22–23, 25
  limiting of, 31
Dative-shift
  in Bantu, 166–178
  in Bemba (Bantu), 167–171
  case-marking typology and, 180–181
  complexity and diachronic source, 183–185
  differentiation of accusatives and nonaccusatives, 164–166
  in Indonesian, 164–166
  nonobligatory, 178–180
  object-cases, various, and, 202

Dative-shift (Cont.)
  obligatory, 164–168
    instrumentals and, 201–202
    passivization and (Rwanda), 199–200
    relativization and, 159–184, 204
  in Rwanda (Bantu), 174–178
  in Swahili (Bantu), 171–173
  topicality and, 204–206
  topicality explanation and, 181–183
  verb-coding and, 164–168
Dative shift rule
  case-marking and, 180
  defined, 160–164
  semantic differences and, 163–164
  topicality of objects and, 161
Declarative speech acts, 280–281
  sociocultural structure and, 289
Deductive systems, low utility in learning (Wittgenstein), 348, 352
Definiteness
  accusative direct objects and, 52–53
  dative-benefactive objects and, 52–54
  locative objects and, 53–54
  markedness and, 51–52, 65–66
  of objects, affirmative and negative, 125–126
Deixis
  canine, 285–286
  child, 293–294
Density
  of perceptual input
    development of organisms and, 333
    motion and, 333
  perceptual judgment of, 324–325
Dependency, privileged status and, 46
Development of organisms, density of perceptual input and, 333
Diachronic change
  effect of, on language, 13
  expressive-elaborative and simplificatory, 121
  inclusion relation and, 316–317
  perception and, 134–135
  semantic bleaching and, 316–317
  syntacticization and, 208–222, 231–233
  word-order and, 124–126
Diachronic source, complexity and, 183–185
Diachrony
  adjectives and, 265–266
  child development and, 231–232
  synchrony versus, 235–267

Dimensions
  calibration and, 328–329
  space as second, third, and fourth, 324
  time as first, 319–323
  upper bounds of, 328–329
Direct object, promotion to, *see* Dative-shift
Direct-only constraints, 195–198
Discourse
  condensation of inflectional morphology and, 12–13
  context and discourse function of negation, 103–105
  evolution of, 271–309
  presupposition, *see* Presuppositionality
  sharing in child language, 86–87
Distribution
  freedom of, 46, 48
  in negative speech acts, 93–103, 139
  statistical, markedness and, 51–54
Distributional restrictions
  markedness and, 67–74, 88
  negatives and, 115–121
  presuppositionality and, 67–74, 88

E

Economy, privileged status and, 46–47
Embedded clauses
  distributional restrictions and, 68
  presuppositionality and, 53
  syntactic distance and, 77
Embedded constructions, syntactic complexity and, 75
Embedded sentences, completeness argument and, 48
Embedding of negatives, restrictions on, 119–120
Empiricism
  criticism of, 23–43
  irresponsibility of, 41
  versus rationalism, 22–23, 43–44
Entities
  coextensive with nouns, 322
  time-stability criterion for, 320
Environment, interaction between organism and, 344–347
Equi-case strategy
  in Bemba (Bantu), 169, 171
  relativization and, 151
Ergatives, 64–65
  dative-shift and, 179–180
  in Sherpa, 179

Index 371

Events
  intended versus unintended, 335–336
  language as, 312
  versus states, 334–335
Evolution
  of consciousness, 333–334
  of discourse, 271–309
    dismissal of (Chomsky), 271–272
    irrelevance of (Chomsky), 4
    phylogeny and ontogeny, correspondence, 271–275
    to presyntactic discourse, 303–304
Existence
  copulas, two Spanish, and, 323
  implicational hierarchy of, 314–317
  of self and universe, axioms of, 317
Existential-presentative constructions, 26–27
  distributional restrictions and, 73–74
  presuppositionality, markedness and, 66–67
  universal characteristics of, 72–73
Experiments, controlled, 23–26
  linguistic, 24–26
  scientific, 23–24
Explanation
  formalism as, 3–22
    Emonds' constraints and, 18–19
    innateness as (Chomsky), 21–22
    morphology as, 12–13
    nomenclature as, 14–15
    relational grammar as, 19–21
    rule ordering as, 11–12
    second lexicon as, 12–13
    taxonomy as, 13–14
Explanatory adequacy (Chomsky), 7–8
External and internal negation, 112–115

F

Family structure, 294–295
Fiction as new and old information, 350
Figure-ground principle, 346–347
Figure versus ground, 132–140
First dimension, time as, 319–323
Focus, *see also* Scope of negation
  dative-shift rule and, 161
Focusing, syntactic complexity (distance) and, 78–79
Formal properties of variants, presuppositionality and, 49
Formalism as explanation, 3–22

Freedom, degrees of, 324, 327–328
Frozen syntactic constraints, 261–264
Function, pragmatic, and semantic case, 143–206
Functional explanations, topicality and, 204–205

G

Gap strategy
  semantic redundancy and (Sherpa), 184
  in Sherpa, 180
  relativization and, 148–149, 156
  weakness of, 156
Generative grammar, shortcomings of, 2–3
Genitive constructions, complex, rise of, 216–217
Grammar
  as automatic processing strategy, 233
  communication and, 31–33
  as competence or performance, 26–31
  versus lexicon, 47–48
  versus speaker, 26–28
Grammaticality as abstract entity, 26

I

I-rule, *see* Interpretation rule
Illocutionary force
  in canine communication, 280–284
  in child communication, 291–292
  of two-word sentences, 301–302
Imperatives, 280
  in canines, 280–284
  conceptual structure underlying, 282–284
  distributional restrictions and, 68–69
  markedness and, 54–56
  presuppositionality and, 54–56
  syntactic complexity (distance) and, 80
Implicative verbs, 93–94
Inclusion relation
  critical properties and, 314–315
  diachronic change and, 316–317
  predications-qualities and, 314
Indefinite subjects
  distributional restrictions and, 72–74
  without existential verbs, 306
  markedness and, 66–67
Individuation
  binary property and, 318–319

Individuation (Cont.)
  precedence and, 319
  proximity and, 319
  space exclusivity of entities and, 329–330
  space-uniqueness of entities and, 329–330
  unordered relation and, 319
Inflectional morphology, condensation of discourse into, 12–13
Informal speech
  formal versus, 228–231
  structure of, 229
Information
  in canine communication, 284, 288–289
  in child communication, 292
  new and old, see also Presuppositionality
    fiction as, 349–350
    frequency and, 348
    interpersonal behavior and, 350
    music as, 350
    restrictive and elaborate codes and, 349
    tautology versus contradiction and, 350
  tangential, 349
Innateness as explanation (Chomsky), 21–22
Instrumental objects, passivization of, 201
Intent
  agents, action, causality and, 334–336, 346–347
Intention
  versus consciousness in agents, 337
  new information and, 346–347
  new states and, 345–346
  presuppositionality and, 346–347
Internal and external negation, 112–115
Interpersonal behavior, ontological unity of, 344–351
Interpretation rule, 10
Interrogatives, 280, see also Questions
  sociocultural structure and, 289
  syntactic complexity (distance) and, 80
Intimates, society of
  canine, 287
  child, 294–295
Intonation
  in negatives and positives, 117–118
  relative clauses and, 247

K

Knowledge, shared
  canine, 288–289
  child, 295

L

Language
  events as, 312
  explanatory parameters of, 3–4
  as map of universe, 313
  objects as, 312
  ontology and, 311–352
Learning, culturally mediated, 274–275
Learning capacity, innate, 22
Left-dislocation, see Topic-shift constructions
Lexical classes, stability and, 320–321
Lexical passives, as agent-reason, 62–63
Lexical patterns, frozen, 264–267
Lexicalization,
  summary of, 266
  time-stability and, 14
Lexicon
  grammar versus, 47–48
  handling of, by Chomsky, 10
  morphology versus, 47–48
  second, as explanation, 12–13
Linguistic methodology, 1–44
Linguistic Theory, Goals of (conference), 10
Linguistic universals, 269
Locative objects, passivization and (Rwanda), 201
Logic versus pragmatics in negation, 108

M

Manipulative speech acts
  child, 291–292
  markedness and, 54–56
  one-word, 308
  presuppositionality and, 54–56
  purposes of, 289
  sociocultural structure and, 289
Map of universe, language as, 313
Marked structure, argument for, 47
Markedness, 67–83, 87–89, see also Presuppositionality
  definiteness and, 51–52, 70–74
  distributional restrictions and, 67–74, 88
  embedded clauses and, 68, 77
  grammatical morphology and, 74–75
  imperatives and, 68–69, 80
  interrogatives and, 80
  of negatives, consequences of, 115–131, 139
  negatives and, 80
  nondeclarative speech acts and, 54–56

Index 373

passive sentences and, 57–65
presuppositional clauses and, 77–80
privileged status and, 47–48
questions and, 68–69
strictly presuppositional constructions and, 68
syntactic complexity and, 74–83, 88–89
syntactic distance (complexity) and, 74–83, 88–89
topicality and, 56–57, 70–74, 81–83
Meaning, referential versus nonreferential, 313
Membership in a set, 318
  power, rules, and, 344
Memory
  canine, 284
  child, 292
Modals, English
  diachrony and, 129
  sense extension of, 128–130, 141–142
Model(s)
  formal, 41–42
    abuse of, 6–8
    use of, 6
  power of, debate about, 10
Modes, coexisting, pragmatic and syntactic, 227
Monopropositional discourse
  canine versus human, 284–285
  in child communication, 292–293
  survival of, 307–308
Morphemes, grammatical versus lexical, 47–48
Morphological innovation, semantic conservatism and, 85
Morphology
  grammatical ("inflectional"), 220–222
    condensation of discourse into syntax and, 12–13
  lexicon versus, 47–48
  passive, agent-deletion typology and, 193
  and syntax, inconsistencies between, 238–246
Motion
  density of perceptual input and, 333
  three dimensional space and, 333–334
Motivation, canine versus human, 282
Multipropositional discourse
  evolution of, 295
  presuppositionality and, 66
  topic, rise of, and, 298–299
  word-order and, 309
Music as new and old information, 350

N

Negation
  complexity of, reasons for, 131
  context and function of, 103–105
  external and internal, 112–115
  in language versus logic, 91–92, 138–139
  markedness and, 121
  ontological basis of, 132–140
  processing time for, 130–131
  psychological complexity of, 130–131
  scope of, and adverbs, 105–111
  as speech act, 139
  summary of facts about, 114–115
  with verb *fail*, 247
Negative comparatives, affirmative and, 137–138
Negative events, ontology of, 134–138
Negative polarity items, markedness and, 120–121
Negative properties, ontology of, 132–134
Negative sentences, referential–indefinite objects and, 28–30
Negatives
  versus affirmatives, presuppositionality and, 92–115, 139
  distributional restrictions and, 115–121
  oddity of, 135–137
  referential-indefinites, restrictions on, 93–103
  syntactic complexity (distance) and, 80
Nomenclature as explanation, 14–15
Nominalization strategy, relativization and, 149–150
Nondeclarative speech acts
  markedness and, 54–56
  presuppositionality and, 54–56
Nonreduction strategy
  inapplicability in Bikol, 156
  relativization and, 147–148
Norm and counternorm, 135–138
Normative versus counternormative action, negation and, 106–108
Nouns
  coextensive with entities, 322
  concreteness of, 321
  referential indefinite, "one" with, 39–41
NP constraint
  complex, 17–18
  violations of, 33–37
  coordinate (Ross), 262
NP-negation pattern, markedness of, 113

O

Object cases, various, dative-shift and, 202
Object constraints, accusative-only versus direct-only, 195–198
Object pronouns, frozen, 239–245
Object relativization, pronoun attraction principle and, 249–251
Objects
  concrete
    canines and, 279–280
    language as, 312
  conscious entities as, 337
  definite, syntactic complexity (distance) and, 81–82
  instrumental, passivization of, 201
  mixed typologies and, 253–261
    definite versus indefinite, 257–259
    direct versus indirect, 253–254
    nominalized versus free, 254–256
    referential versus generic, 256–257
  pronominal, syntactic complexity (distance) and, 81
  referential–indefinite, under negation, 28–30
  topicalization of, 163
  various, definiteness and, 51–54
One (numeral), with referential indefinite nouns, 39–41
Ontogeny, *see* Evolution
Ontology
  language and, 311–352
  negation and, 132–140
Operators versus operands, 15
Order and chaos, two paradoxes of, 325–328
Ordered relation, time as first, 319–323
Ordered universe, perception–cognition and, 313
Organism and environment, interaction between, 344–347
"Other than" ambiguity, negation and, 111–112

P

Parallel syntactic behavior ($\overline{\text{X}}$ convention), 15–17
Parameters of language, explanatory, 3–4
Participants in canine communication, 280, 285–286
Passive, defining, 185–186
Passive sentences
  agent recoverability of, 59–64
  definiteness ratio of, 58, 59, 63
  distributional restrictions and, 69–71
  frequency of, 58–59
  markedness and, 57–65
  nature of, summary, 20–21
  presuppositionality and, 57–65
  text distribution and, 59–60
  topicality of agent and, 57
Passives
  agentless and agented, 30–31
  syntactic complexity (distance) and, 82–83
  topicality and, 206
Passivization
  accusative-only constraint and, 196, 205
  agent-deletion and, 30
    typology, 191–193
  case-confusion and, 197
  dative and (Rwanda), 199–200
  direct (Bantu–Bemba), 199
  direct object, promotion to, and, 185–205
  instrumental objects and, 201
  locative objects and, 201
  Philippine typology, 186–187
  recoverability problem in, 194–195
  reflexive-passive typology and, 193–194
  relativization and, 205
  topic-shift typology and, 187–191
  topicality and, 204–206
  topicalization and, 211–212
  typological conditions for, summary, 205
  typology of, 186–194
    agent-deletion, 191–193
    Philippine, 186–187
    reflexive-passive, 193–194
    topic-shift, 187–191
Past
  canine concept of, 284
  in child communication, 292
Perception, spatial, and perceptual judgment, 324–325
Perception–cognition, ordered universe and, 313
Perceptual judgment
  calibration and, 325
  of density, 324–325
Periphrastic causatives, ambiguity of adverbs in, 117–119
Philippine verb-coding typology
  accusative-only constraint and, 206
  passivization and, 186–187
Phonological irregularity, reregularization of, 13

Phonology, synchronic, crazy, 237–238
Phylogeny, see Evolution
Pidgin versus Creole, 223–226
Place, canine, 279
Polarities, 348–351
Polemics, necessity of, 1–2
Pongids
  communication of, summary of, 290
  society of, 287–288
Power, ontology of, 344
Pragmatic function, semantic case and, 143–206
Pragmatic mode
  child language and, 226–228
  informal versus formal speech, 228–231
  Pidgin, 223–226
  sociocultural context of, 297
  structural properties of, 296–297
  survival of, 307–308
  versus syntactic mode, 222–223
Pragmatic stress, rise of, 300, see also Intonation
Precedence
  formal characteristics of, 319
  individuation and, 319
Predications-qualities, inclusion relation and, 314
Prepositional case, passivization via, 199
Presuppositional background, 19, 48–90
  canine, 284, 288–289
  related to assertion, 50
Presuppositional clauses, syntactic distance (complexity) and, 77–80
Presuppositionality, 48–90, see also Markedness
  assumptions and, 50
  communication and, 349
  definiteness and, 51–54
  distributional restrictions and, 67–74, 88
  embedded clauses and, 53
  formal properties of variants and, 49
  intention and, 346–347
  negatives versus affirmatives and, 92–115, 139
  nondeclarative speech acts and, 54–56
  passive sentences and, 57–65
  pragmatic nature of, 50
  scale of, 76–77
  syntactic constructions and, 50–67, 87–88
  topic recoverability and, 56–67
  topicality and, 56–57
  WH-questions and clefts and, 248

Presyntactic discourse
  evolution to, 303–304
  phylogeny and, 295–303
Privileged status, arguments for, 45–48
Probabilities, canine versus human, 283
Promotion
  to direct object, passivization and, 185–205
  to subject, relativization and, 152–159
  summary, 206
Pronominal objects, syntactic complexity (distance) and, 81
Pronominalization in negative and affirmative sentences, 94–95
Pronoun attraction principle
  object relativization and, 249–251
  object topicalization (fronting) and, 250–251
Pronouns
  anaphoric, see Anaphoric pronouns
  clitic versus independent, 239–245
  frozen object, 239–245
  preverbal versus postverbal, 240–244
  resumptive, choice of, 33–37, see also Anaphoric pronouns
Properties
  critical, inclusion relation and, 314–315
  negative, ontology of, 132–134
Proximity, individuation and, 319
Pseudocleft constructions
  distributional restrictions and, 68
  syntactic complexity (distance) and, 78
Pseudoexplanations in linguistics, 9–22
Psycholinguistic explanations, relativization and, 157–159
Psychological complexity
  negation and, 130–131
  object versus subject relativization (Comrie), 158–159

Q

Questions, see also Interrogatives; WH-questions
  distributional restrictions and, 68–69
  markedness and, 54–56
  presuppositionality and, 54–56

R

Randomness versus order, universe as, 327
Rationalism versus empiricism, 22–23, 43–44

Recipient in canine communication, 280, 285–286
Recoverability
  agent
    from general knowledge, 60–64
    in passive sentences, 59–64
    problem, passivization and, 194–195
  strategy
    accusative-only constraint and, 196
    NP-coding, 201
    verb-coding (Rwanda), 201
  topic
    markedness and, 56–57
    presuppositionality and, 56–57
Reference, meaning and, 312–313
Referential–indefinites
  diachronic change and, 100–101
  nouns, 27
  objects under negation, 28–30
  restrictions on, 93–103
    in negatives, 120
  subjects, 26–28
Referentiality
  negation and, in Bemba (Bantu), 98–99
  of subjects and objects under negation, 113
  unstressed numeral one and, in Hebrew, 99–100
Reflexive-passive typology, 193–194
Registers, coexisting, 227–230, 232
Relational grammar as explanation, 19–21
Relative clauses
  distributional restrictions and, 68
  syntactic complexity (distance) and, 77–78
  topic sentences versus, 212–213
Relative pronoun strategy, relativization and, 151
Relativization, 146–185
  accusatives versus instruments and, 184
  anaphoric pronoun strategy of, 151, 156
  dative-shift and, 159–184, 205
  equi-case strategy of, 151
  gap strategy of, 148–149, 156
  nominalization strategy of, 149–150
  nonreduction strategy of, 147–148
  object, constraint on, 180
  passivization and, 205
  promotion
    to direct object and, 159–184
    to subject and, 152–159
  pronoun attraction and, 249–252
  psycholinguistic explanations and, 157–159

relative pronoun strategy of, 151
restrictions on
  data-shift, 144
  obligatory passivation, 144
  promotion to direct object, 144
strategies of, 146–152
subject versus object, in Indonesian, 165–166
topicality and, 206
typological conditions for, summary, 205
verb-coding strategy of, 151–152, 154–156
word-order strategy of, 149
Rule ordering as explanation, 11–12

S

Scope
  of assertion, tense-aspect system and (Bemba), 109–111
  of negation
    adverbs and, 105–111
    restrictions and (Bemba–Bantu), 110–111
  restrictions on, 116
Self-existence, axiom of, 317
Semantic bleaching, diachronic change and, 316–317
Semantic differences, dative-shift rule and, 163–164
Semantic elaboration, 85–86
Semi-agents, classes of, 343–344
Sentential complements in Biblical-Hebrew, 218–219
Sets
  membership in, 318, 326–327
  ordered versus unordered, 326–327
Social interaction, evolution of communication and, 347–348
Social structure
  canine, 286–289
  child, 294–295
Social unit, size of
  canine, 288
  pongid, 288
Society
  of intimates
    canine, 287
    child, 294–295
  of strangers, 297, 307
    written communication and, 231
Sociocultural conditions, change in, 305

Index

Sociocultural differentiation
  canine, 287
  child, 294–295
Sociocultural structure, communicative mode and, 289
SOV syntax
  drift from, 276–277, 308–309
  reasons for, 308
  survival of, 275–276
Space
  consciousness, see Time and space consciousness
  exclusivity of entities, individuation and, 329–330
  time, being, and, implicational hierarchy of, 314–317
Space-uniqueness of entities, individuation and, 329–330
Spatial perception, perceptual judgment and, 324–325
Stability, see Time-stability
States versus events, 334–335
Statistical property of texts, syntax and, 49–50
Strangers
  society of, 297, 307
  written communication and, 231
Structuralist dogma, 2–3
  major characteristics of, 2
Subject(s)
  definiteness of, 26–28
  indefinite
    distributional restrictions and, 72–74
    without existential verbs, 306
  markedness and, 66–67
  postposing
    pronoun attraction principle and, 249–250
    rule, 247–250
  preverbal, 37–38
  promotion to, relativization and, 152–159
  referentiality in negative constructions and, 102–103
  versus topic, 209–211
Subordination
  versus conjunction in verb phrase, 213–215
  coordination and, 261–262, 298
  diachronic development of, 298
Surprise, 74, 88, 133, 348
  versus familiarity in interpersonal relationships, 350
Synchronic variations, overlapping, 236
Syntactic complexity (distance), 77–83

assertional and presuppositional, 75
embedded constructions and, 75, 77
grammatical morphology and, 74–75
grammaticalization and, 75–76
negatives and, 121–130
presuppositional clauses and, 77–80
Syntactic conservatism, see Conservatism, syntactic
Syntactic constraints, frozen, 261–264
Syntactic mode
  Creole, 224–226
  evolution of, 304–307
  formal versus informal speech, 228–231
  versus pragmatic mode, 222–223
Syntactic variants, 51–52
Syntacticization, 207–233
  causativization and, 215–216
  changes associated with, 304–305
  child language to adult, 226–228
  cleft and WH-question constructions and, 217–218
  communicative factors and (summary), 268–269
  from conjunction to subordination in verb phrase, 213–215
  diachronic process of, 208–222, 231–233
  genitive constructions, complex and, 216–217
  grammatical ("inflectional") morphology and, 220–222
  from object-topic to passive, 211–212
  phylogeny of, 304–307
  from topic sentence to relative clause, 212–213
Syntax
  communication and, summary, 87–90
  crazy, 235–267
  versus discourse, summary, 207–208, 233
  discourse presuppositions and, 50–67, 87–88
  morphology and, inconsistencies between, 238–246
  rise of, 207–233
  statistical property of texts and, 49–50

T

T-rule, see transformation rule
Tangential information, 349
Tao, 351
  paradox of, 325–328
  unconstrued universe and, 317–318
Tautology and contradiction, 348–349
  music and, 350

Taxonomy as explanation, 13–14
Temporal experience, primitive sentient beings and, 330–331
Temporality, concreteness and abstractness versus, 314–317
Tense-aspect-modality markers, auxiliary verbs and, 221–222
Tense-aspect system, scope of assertion and (Bemba-Bantu), 109–111
Theory
　construction of, 3
　trivialization of, 25–26
Three dimensional space, motion and, 333–334
Time
　canine, 278–279
　as first ordered relation, 319–323
　sequence and conditionality, 338–339
　space, being and, implicational hierarchy of, 314–317
Time and space consciousness
　of amoebas, 331–332
　of bacteria, 330–331
　of nonvertebrate stationary organisms, 332
　of trees, 332
Time-axis, canine versus human, 282
Time-stability
　as criterion for entities, 320
　lexical classes and, 320–321
　lexicalization and, 14
Topic
　identification with agent, 303
　orientation and multipropositional discourse, 309
　rise of, 298–299
　versus subject, 209–211
Topic–comment–goal–object, identity of
　canine, 285
　child, 293
Topic–comment word-order, rise of, 299–300
Topic sentences versus relative clauses, 212–213
Topic-shift constructions, 38–39
　markedness and, 65–66
　syntactic complexity (distance) and, 82
Topic-shift passivization, accusative-only constraint and, 206
Topic-shift typology
　Bantu, 188–189
　Bhasa Indonesian, 187–188
　ChiChewa (Bantu), 190–191
　Hebrew, 190
　passivization and, 187–191
　Spanish, 190
Topic-shifting, distributional restrictions and, 71–72
Topical constructions, syntactic complexity (distance) and, 81–83
Topicality
　dative-shift and, 204–206
　explanation, dative-shift and, 181–183
　functional explanations in terms of, 204–205
　markedness and, 56–57
　of object arguments, 159, 163
　of objects, dative-shift rule and, 161
　passivization and, 204–206
　presuppositionality and, 56–57
　relativization and, 157, 206
　subject and object
　　in Bikol, 154–155
　　in English, 152–154
　word-order change and, 84
Topicalization
　of objects, 163
　passivization and, 211–212
　word-order and, 309
Transformation rule, 9–10
Transformational-generative grammar
　criticism of, 233
　crypto-structuralist nature of, 1–44
Transformational relation (Harris, Chomsky), 45
Transformations
　stylistic, restrictions on (Emonds), 18–19
　syntactic, 9–10
Two-word sentences, illocutionary force of, 301–302
Typological conditions, promotion and, 156–157, 181, 203–204
　summary, 205–206
Typological explanation of case-marking, 203–204
Typological predictability, stronger and weaker conditions, 156–157
Typology of passives, *see* Passivization, typology of

U

Unconstrued universe, Tao and, 317–318
Unity and diversity, 350–351
　of universe, 326
Universals, linguistic, 42, 269

Index

Universe
  axiom of existence of, 317
    mathematical paradox and, 327
  consciousness and, as one, 350–351
  construction of, language and, 311–352
  structures of cognition and, 352
  unconstrued, Tao and, 317–318
Unordered relation, individuation and, 319

V

Variants
  of basic sentence type, 45, 49
  formal properties of, presuppositionality and, 49
  syntactic, 51–52
Verb-coding
  in Bantu, 166–168
  in Bemba (Bantu), 167–171
  canine, 286
  dative-shift and, 164–168, 180–181
  in Indonesian, 164–166
  object-cases, various, and, 202
  passivization via, 199
  as recoverability strategy (Rwanda), 201
  rise of, 302–303
  in Rwanda (Bantu), 174–178
  strategy
    in Bikol, 154–155
      relativization and, 151–152, 154–156
  in Swahili (Bantu), 171–173
Verb complements, 213–214
  infinitive word-order change and, 84
  scope of negation and, 105–107
Verb compounds, 214–215
Verb phrases
  conjunction versus subordination in, 213–215
  mixed typologies of, in syntax, 253–261
Verbs
  auxiliary, change to tense-aspect-modality markers, 221–222

  complex, rise of, 215–216
  concreteness of, 321
  implicative
    definiteness of objects and, 93–94
    in negative and positive sentences, 93–94
    referentiality of objects and, 93–94
  modal auxiliary, English, 128–130, 141–142
  serial, change to case markers, 220–221
Volition, see Intent
Volitional motion, development of organisms and, 333, 345–346

W

WH-particles and dative-shift, 166
WH-prepositional pronouns, case-recoverability and, 179
WH-questions
  dative-shift rule and, 161
  diachrony versus synchrony and, 246–249
  distributional restrictions and, 68
  syntactic complexity (distance) and, 78–79
  syntacticization and, 217–218
Word-order, underlying, 42–43
Word-order change, syntactic conservatism and, 83–85
Word-order conservatism, affirmative versus negative, 124–126
Word-order strategy
  dative-shift and, in Indonesian, 165
  relativization and, 149
Writing systems, syntacticization of, 306–307
Written register of speech, 230–231

X

$\overline{\text{X}}$ convention, 15–17